HRe

D0594143

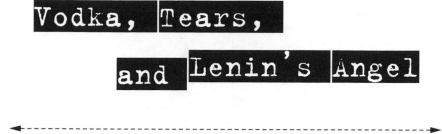

Vodka, Tears, and Lenin's Angel

A Journalist on the Road in the
Former Soviet Union

Jennifer Gould

ALFRED A. KNOPF CANADA

Published by Alfred A. Knopf Canada

Copyright © 1997 by Jennifer Gould

All rights reserved under International and Pan-American Copyright
Conventions. Published in 1997 by Alfred A. Knopf Canada, Toronto.
Distributed by Random House of Canada Limited, Toronto.

Canadian Cataloguing in Publication Data

Gould Jennifer
        Vodka, tears, and Lenin's angel

ISBN 0-394-28155-1

1. Former Soviet republics - Description and travel.
2. Former Soviet republics - Social conditions.
3. Gould, Jennifer - Journeys - Former Soviet republics.
4. Journalists - Canada - Biography. I. Title.

DK29.G68 1997   947.086   C96-932136-8

This book is dedicated to my parents,
Marilyn and Michael, and to
my grandfather, C. Lewis Gould

CONTENTS

←---→

Nor sole was I born, but entire genesis:
For to the fathers that begat me, this
Body is residence. Corpuscular,
They dwell in my veins, they eavesdrop at my ear,
They circle, as with Torahs, round my skull,
In exit and in entrance all day pull
The latches of my heart, descend, and rise—
And there look generations through my eyes.

— A.M. KLEIN, "A Psalm Touching Genealogy"

We need a moral philosophy which can speak significantly of Freud and Marx, and out of which aesthetic and political views can be generated. We need a moral philosophy in which the concept of love, so rarely mentioned now by philosophers, can once again be made central.

— IRIS MURDOCH, *The Sovereignty of the Good*

What we need is a return to Marxism, early Marx of course.... We've got to get rid of our vile, stupid, rapacious bourgeois civilisation, capitalism must go ... but we must hold on to our morals, we must civilise and spiritualise politics.

— IRIS MURDOCH, *Jackson's Dilemma*

NOTE TO THE READER

Much of the first part of this book grew from *Moscow Times* reporting. Chapter 14 stemmed from *Toronto Star* and *Saturday Night* assignments, reprinted with permission. Chapter 16 is based on "Sexpionage," an article that first appeared in *ELLE* magazine in October 1994; Chapter 19 is based on the March 1995 *Playboy* Interview: both are reprinted with permission. All Chechnya and election chapters stem from *Village Voice* assignments. The final chapter is also based on *Daily Express* reporting.

Some names and details related to certain characters have been changed to protect the innocent—and to respect people's privacy.

Russian words commonly used in English are not italicized, while less familiar ones are italicized the first time they appear. Some Russian words have also been anglicized, such as the plural of babushka, which is written as babushkas, instead of the grammatically correct babushki. Unless otherwise specified, all dollar figures are in U.S. dollars.

<--->

CHAPTER 1

Getting There

Paris, Warsaw, Moscow, and the Man with the
Accent—You Gotta Have Faith

Be favorable to bold beginnings.

— VIRGIL, *Georgics*

T anks and Gorby. Red meets red, white, and blue. Yeltsin stand-
ing on a tank during the attempted August 1991 coup. Mikhail
Gorbachev resigning that Christmas Eve. Cities burning from the
civil war in Georgia that follows the union's collapse. The gesture,
Yeltsin on the tank. The moment, Gorbachev resigning. The image,
Tbilisi on fire. This is what draws me to Russia.

I am working as a correspondent for the *Philadelphia Inquirer*
during the 1991 attempted putsch against Gorbachev, the last
leader of the Soviet Union. I love my job. But I'm in suburban Philadelphia. I want to go overseas while I'm still young, instead of waiting for a newspaper to send me. By December, presidents of three
Soviet republics dissolve the empire with pen strokes. The collapse
of the Communist empire, the post-Cold War close of our century,
has begun.

Just about everyone warns me not to go. (There's no food and
no apartments—you'll be lucky to share a room with somebody's
grandmother.) Western news reports are filled with babushkas,
Russian grandmothers, in bread lines. I don't doubt the reports,
but I know they can't be the whole story. Some sort of middle class
has to be emerging, and the privileged will, as usual, be doing just
fine. If they can survive, I figure, so can I.

A publication agrees to sponsor my hard-to-get visa. Some newspaper editors say they'll take freelance. But by the day of my going-away party at home in Toronto, the visa still hasn't arrived. I have already bought the first half of my plane ticket, to Paris.

"So when will you be in Moscow?" asks a family friend at my going-away party. I tell him what has happened.

"I think I know someone who can help," he says, and gives me a telephone number in Eastern Europe. I call.

"No problem," says the Man with the Accent. "My company will invite you to Moscow. Just show up at the Russian consulate in Paris. The visa will be waiting."

I go. It isn't.

I phone back the Man with the Accent.

"I'm so sorry, Ms. Gould," he says. "Could you fly to Warsaw? The consulate there knows me. The paperwork will be so fast, you can fly to Warsaw for lunch and be in Moscow for dinner."

I don't know this man. But my options are limited: Fly to an Eastern European capital to meet a stranger—whose promise, for which I have crossed an ocean, has already fallen through—or return home in defeat without even getting to Russia, where I may at least have the chance to fail honorably.

I buy a plane ticket to Warsaw, significantly depleting my financial reserves. The plane is practically empty, save for a few shabby suits and dour faces. At the small Warsaw airport, I buy a day visa and ask an elderly woman if I can leave my two suitcases behind the counter where she works. (There is nowhere else to put them.) Lugging my new laptop and camera—and hoping my suitcases will be there when I return—I change some money and take a bus into town.

It's a ride back through time; tough to tell where the 1940s end and the 1990s begin. Warsaw is a stream of gray concrete filled with unsmiling men and women—pasty skin, bland overcoats, and wool hats. I never see the sun that day. A prelude to Moscow winter.

Past the oppressively ugly low-rise concrete buildings, I arrive at the Grand Marriott Hotel. It emerges suddenly, revealing itself majestically, spewing moneyed comfort and Western luxury in the midst of this unbearably grim, dull gray pall that smothers the city like an all-enveloping, relentless fog of hopelessness—impenetrable, filled with an unbearably sad sense of loss, nostalgia, shattered empire. That loss, that swelling sadness, is the essence, what's left, of postwar, post-Communist Eastern Europe. And that's what makes the unreality of luxury, like the Marriott, so assuring and reassuring—to rich and poor alike.

Gloved, gracious doormen let me into the hotel. When the doors open, they shut out the cold, leaving Warsaw behind. I'm back in the West. Not Paris, or Toronto, but not Warsaw either. I am looking for my wild card, my Joker, my ticket to the adventures I hope to encounter, the experiences I hope to accumulate, in Russia.

A tall, dark-haired man waits for me in the lobby. He is slightly heavyset; prosperously chubby, you might say, shielded by thick aviator glasses that hide milk-green, questioning, Talmudic eyes, which may share something unexpectedly in common with my own. He smells of cologne, wears a monogrammed shirt with cuff links, and embodies all that is old—even though he is much younger than I imagined. I recognize him because of the red-print silk scarf that he told me he'd wear. The scarf hangs insolently from his dark navy cashmere overcoat. The choice of color is deliberately, belligerently defiant: a bright splash of red in a dark sea of gray.

"Ms. Gould?" he asks. "Welcome."

Another man takes my bulky down-filled coat, made for walking to college classes during Canadian winters. (The coat is the color of Warsaw, of a Moscow winter: dreary gray, the hidden warmth of mauve within.) Perfect for Russia, I think, but a definite eyesore next to navy cashmere.

I hand my visa application, passport, and two photos to the assistant. "Why don't we have some lunch while we wait?" says the Man with the Accent, inviting me to what turns out to be the best lunch in town.

I'm so nervous I can barely eat. Will I make the plane? Will I really be in Moscow by evening?

"Why don't you stay in Warsaw for a few days, relax, and explore the city?"

"Thanks," I say, "but the sooner I get to Moscow, the better."

"If you permit me to ask, why on earth do you *want* to go there?"

"I'm a journalist," I say.

But I'm also a woman. And a young one at that. I don't think he believes me, or takes me seriously.

I'm suddenly reminded of a sixties radical I met in L.A.

"As a woman, you go through the first part of your life not being taken seriously because you're too young," she said. "And then, all of a sudden, you're too old."

If this is the moment when I'm young, I want to get as much out of it as I can.

Over the years, the Man with the Accent and I become friends, and laugh over our first encounter. "I thought you'd last a few months, maybe a year," he says. So did I. Sure, I wanted the Moscow Experience. At the very least, for six months. At the most, a year. How am I to know, over buffet lunch at the Marriott, how Moscow sneaks up on you, right into your blood? Once bitten, it's hard to leave.

After lunch, we wait for the assistant in the hotel's casino, whose nicotine levels would narcotize Jesse Helms and the entire executive staff of R. J. Reynolds. Hard-drinking, pot-bellied middle-aged men dot the room, some accompanied by unnaturally blonde women of various ages, whose one common trait appears to be a morbid fascination with the caked-on makeup stylings of the young Ursula Andress.

The atmosphere: grown-up, chronic compulsion mixed with boredom. It is my introduction to the sickness of gambling that has spread faster than Big Macs through post-Communist Eastern Europe and the Former Soviet Union (FSU). Festering snakepits capitalizing on greed mixed with some tainted notion of glamor, decadent excess; a way for the lonely and bored, rich and poor to pass some time.

The Man with the Accent gambles, and loses. I will soon get used to watching people—executives, *mafiya* (organized criminals), diplomats—spend vast amounts: thousands of dollars at bad restaurants and nightclubs or in a few seconds at roulette.

He describes his business, but I get the feeling there's more I'll never know, as with many people I soon meet. He shows me pictures of himself in special rooms inside the Kremlin. "I'll put you on the list next time I arrange a tour for visiting business associates," he says. "I spend quite a lot of time in Moscow. If you ever need my help, or if you just want someone to talk to, please don't hesitate to call."

I thank him and hail a cab back to the airport. Visa in hand, I retrieve my suitcases, which are, mercifully, still there. I buy some chocolate—afraid there may really be no food in Moscow—write some postcards, forget to mail them, and pile into a plane with a small, sorry-looking set of Soviet-style suits.

A Russian family I do not know is supposed to meet me at the airport. They are almost my only contacts in this foreign, frozen land.

Before I left Philadelphia, professor and documentary film director Irene Shur insisted I could not move to Moscow without knowing anyone. Through the Jewish network (the international conspiracy thrives!) she introduced me to some refuseniks. They knew a thirty-year-old American I'll call Faith, who was also moving to Moscow. Faith wrote and asked if I wanted to be her roommate. Now her Russian friends will meet me at the airport.

It is February 1992. Yeltsin's team of radical reformers, led by the young economic "guru" Yegor Gaidar, have just instituted economic shock therapy. Inflation has wiped out the savings of millions of Russians overnight. Others, through the privilege of Communist Party elitism, are on their way to becoming so nauseatingly wealthy it could cause California Republicans to turn Red.

Night has fallen somewhere below the clouds. I look out into darkness, speckled with light—a fair assessment of my current knowledge of Russia—as the plane descends. We land in an icy chill.

HARLOT MEETS MOSCOW; ALICE MEETS HARLOT

Arriving at Sheremetyevo International Airport, I feel like Alice falling down the rabbit hole. There is no doubt I've landed in some sort of Wonderland, a grim, dirty, bustling kaleidoscope without order or logic but bursting with life—and character. Finally. The buildup to history is over. Creation, after seventy years of Communist undoing, is about to begin again. This is the Moment. This is the Story. You can feel the excitement. Nobody, Communists or capitalists—apathists, atheists, deists, opportunists, adventurers, anarchists, or extremists—knows anything, except for a handful of apparatchiks and henchmen who change faster than New York club music—and are robbing their country's resources in an appallingly crude manner and on a mind-numbingly, massively large scale. It really is the dawn of a New World Order, even if it is not what George Bush promised. Everyone, though, agrees on this: Moscow is the perfect place, the right moment, for beginnings.

My Russia is just that: an empty journal waiting to be filled. Even the airport is a mystery. Although I studied some Russian history and Marxist political theory at college, the last time I read anything even semicurrent was that summer in Ibiza, loyally devouring Norman Mailer's *Harlot's Ghost*. I grew up admiring Mailer. Soon our paths will almost meet, in Lee Harvey Oswald's adopted city of Minsk, where we'll both interview the alleged assassin's friends and lovers within days of each other.

Mailer's description of Sheremetyevo intrigued me. His was an entrée to the Communist superpower. Mine is an entrée to an empire's collapse. But the foundation is still strong enough to instill fear. Is my hours-old visa okay?

The boys in khaki look so serious, forbidding. Years later, they will seem like what they are: adolescent boys and girls in uniform, who do smile—if you smile first.

The hazy airport pulses with people and smoke. Slowly I wade through the primordial soup mix of emerging capitalism. So much moving and shouting. The blend of European and Asian faces makes a lasting impression. Perhaps this really is where East meets West.

It's one thing to read about Russia's ethnic diversity, its 128 or more nationalities, depending on whose figures you believe. It's another thing to see it. I had no idea Russia would be filled with so many different-looking people, that you could still see traces of Mongol blood in so many blue-eyed, white Russian faces.

At the airport, there are people, it seems, from all fifteen ex-Soviet republics. Men slump, smoking cigarettes. Women in colorful kerchiefs clutch children and shopping bags, stuffed with belongings, that clutter the grimy floors. They seem to live in these filthy, smoke-plagued corridors, which are never clean despite the joyless efforts of blue-clad women endlessly dragging their dirty mops across the floor. Some of these families are fleeing ethnic wars that are exploding across the old empire. Others were visiting relatives before inflation hit. Now they are penniless. The cost of transportation has skyrocketed: They can't afford to go home.

This group will soon expand to include Somali, Iraqi, and other Third World refugees who bribe their way into Russia, but can't bribe their way out to the West. Some are escaping war and dictatorship. All want to make a better life for their families. But for now, that better way of life seems to be limited to eating Russian-donated plates of rice and beans at the airport restaurant.

As Communism collapses, ethnic war erupts, borders change, and more people migrate. Many of them become prisoners in the airport no-man's-land.

As the influx of asylum seekers grows, so do the queues of Russians leaving. Some depart for good, others for mass tours to Turkey or shopping sprees to Paris. In a year or two the airport will swell with well-minked women and Benetton babies, trench-coated bank directors and mobsters off to see their families who live in London because there are too many murders and kidnappings in Moscow.

For now, the airport is filled mainly with the poor and with hustlers hawking cheap goods from Ankara and Beijing out of rainbow-colored shopping bags.

Am I in the right country? It seems more like a Third World train station than the transportation hub of a former superpower.

I write my customs declaration on cheap newsprint. Most of the forms are in Russian or German. The date on the declaration is "198_."

Emerging from a chaos of lines, I am engulfed in an overwhelming crush of people, of thick coats and grim faces, that ubiquitous color gray, the dust of neglect and poverty.

An anxious-looking middle-aged woman with gold teeth holds a sign with my name scrawled in English letters. She is with two men in *shapkas*, hats of wild, matted fox.

"Welcome to Russia," whispers Irina. "Please," she adds in shaky English, "don't talk until we get in the car. There are too many bandits here."

We rush past the painful, primitive cries of preying men: "Taxi? Khow much?" Now it is three to ten dollars. Later mafiya enforcers will ensure that sixty is minimum. We climb into an ancient Lada and drive down darkened streets, snow piled high on the sides of the roads. The car breaks down on Leninsky Prospekt.

Mikhail, in his forties, pulls over, gets out in the subzero weather, and fixes the car. Most Russians are self-taught mechanics who drive old cars they are forever repairing at the sides of potholed roads, where often you see bloodied accident victims like castoffs from a David Lynch film, waiting for ambulances that never come.

Now, the only foreign cars are Volvos with the special yellow license plates of foreigners. Soon, you can buy any luxury car you want—new or stolen. There will be more Mercedes in Moscow than in any other European city.

After asking about her friends in Philadelphia, Irina turns around and says, "Tell me, why do you *want* to live in Moscow? Don't you know how dangerous, how absolutely *miserable*, how *hopeless* it is here?"

"Canada is a beautiful country," I say. "But so is Russia. Besides, nothing much *happens* in Canada." I try to explain that I'm here for the news, the adventure, the opportunity.

"But everyone we know is just trying to save up enough money to leave," she says.

I tell her about my late maternal grandmother, born in a shtetl near Odessa: "She remembered the Revolution, people dancing in the streets. She was twelve when she escaped with her mother and nine siblings. My great-grandfather was waiting for them in Canada."

My grandmother's adventure included traveling hidden in a hay wagon, soldiers poking the hay with guns; living in a shack by the sea for six months, waiting for the man who had their passports to get out of jail. The boys chopped wood and the older girls stole into town to sell sea salt. A Russian peasant hid my great-aunt when soldiers searched the train for the "Jewess." Finally, in one nerve-wracking night, my great-grandmother smuggled all ten of her children across a river and out of Russia on a cable ferry, big enough for only the ferrier and one passenger at a time, not knowing for sure each time the boat returned for another child what had really happened on the far bank, in the dark.

One of my grandmother's sisters, who was twenty when they left, still spoke Russian in Canada and loved Russian poetry. (My grandmother hated Russian so much she wouldn't speak it, opting for Yiddish and English instead.) Like my grandmother, my late great-aunt remembered a politically active village: Jewish self-defense, boys with guns who kept the Cossacks from attacking their shtetl. She also remembered a secret cellar where young people, Bundists, discussed socialism and Zionism. She knew young Russian-Canadians who returned to Russia to help build Communism under Stalin, and one rare man who made it back again, his illusions shattered by the gulags.

My late grandfather's stories were similar. Cossacks who burned down his home three times, an "aunt" adopted into his family after hers was murdered. Mounted Cossacks racing into a village to a synagogue to slaughter a class of twelve-year-old boys studying for their bar mitzvahs, my grandfather spared only because he stayed home that Saturday with a bad cold.

I remember telling my grandmother about my best friend, off to Russia on a college trip. My grandmother laughed so hard tears came to her eyes. Sipping tea with a sugar cube between her teeth, the Russian way, maker of the best beet borscht and gefilte fish in the world, she said, "My only nightmares were about going back to Russia. I can't believe anyone would go there of their own free will." I often wonder what she'd think of my journey.

Irina shakes me out of my reverie. We have arrived at the apartment complex of unfriendly, alienating high-rises where Faith lives.

"Don't say a word!" Irina says. "If the neighbors know you're a foreigner, they'll rob you."

We are in a tough, industrial section of Moscow, at the far end of a subway line, where factory smoke pollutes the neighborhood and everyone walks mean-looking dogs. (Moscow rule: The smaller the apartment, the bigger the dog; a perestroika-era status symbol.)

In the better areas, where these same high-rises are filled with academics and books, the neighborhoods are more friendly. There, the babushkas sit outside in the courtyard, even on the coldest days, communally watching children in the playground, yelling at parents for not dressing their children warmly enough, gray hair tucked under bright wool hats, primly but keenly watching who goes home with whom, on the lookout for *khooligani*, hoodlums.

Here, though, is war. It will only get worse. As crime becomes more organized, hoodlums charge residents—those who can't afford a ten- or sixteen-year-old Lada—for the "right" to park in their own buildings' outdoor lots, now overrun with mafiya Mercedes and rocket launchers and plagued by frequent gunfire.

FAITH

We struggle to maneuver the car into the snow-blocked driveway. The run-down buildings are mysterious in the dark. We walk silently through crisp, moonlit snow to Faith's unnumbered building. I feel as if I'm entering a Kafka novel. People, out strolling or on their way home, stare at the procession.

We walk up several flights of concrete stairs in darkness. As in many Russian apartment buildings, the lights and elevators don't work. Eyes peer from behind doors opened only an inch or two.

I am uneasy, especially after Irina's warnings. It's my first experience with the Russian paranoia that is based in Soviet-era reality, when any neighbor could be an informer, when spouses reported on each other, children denounced their parents; surveillance was a fact of life. Fear—of the unknown, of government, of your neighbors, let alone death—is still part of today's Russian mentality. (One American friend's Russian neighbor reportedly demanded ten dollars a month—as compensation for having to live beside a foreigner.)

A perky, dark-haired American woman opens the door. She immediately puts me at ease. Faith lives in a small but comfortable flat, typically crammed with dark green sofa beds, cheap Russian-manufactured carpets on the floor and walls, old china and crystal jammed into wooden cabinets, and a wall calendar displaying three pastel-painted kittens. Like most Soviet-era flats, this one comes with orange polka-dot teacups and awful wallpaper —all bought at the same centrally planned state stores in Moscow or Makhachkala, Siberia or Samarkand. An entire family used to live in these two rooms.

I thought I'd spend the winter in freezing apartments, weighed down by layers of clothing, near-paralyzed by cold, but Faith's apartment is stifling hot. "We have to keep windows open even on the coldest days," Faith says.

Faith makes up the sofa bed in the living room for me, pulling a cotton cover over a scratchy woolen blanket, the Russian version of a comforter. "I'm sure you're exhausted," she says. "I remember the first time I came here. It's overwhelming."

We talk more the next morning, over California earth tea and oatmeal and raisins with Canadian maple syrup. "All my friends here are Russian," Faith says. "You're the first foreigner I've talked to."

Faith came here for the romance. Most Muscovites live without much in the way of material goods. It is not by choice. Such deprivation, under Communism, was considered repression. But for some Americans, giving up ties to materialism can actually be liberating. "I came here for the first time when I was a travel agent," Faith says. "I fell in love with the country and knew I'd have to come back. I'm here to live like a Russian."

Faith gave up her job to teach English at an all-Russian school. She will not save money from her ruble salary, though she won't spend much either. Nor will she advance her career. Instead, perhaps, she hopes to add spice to her life against a background of struggle set in an exotic locale.

Other foreigners come to escape a past that—for some businessmen, housewives, and professionals—even includes jail. Still more come to save money, now more difficult, or to find jobs they could not get in their recession-plagued countries. Others are sent here: diplomats, journalists, and executives, who receive "hardship pay" and perks like cooks, drivers, dachas, and regular "outs" to Europe and home.

Faith came to Moscow prepared: duffel bags stuffed with food —dried fruits and nuts, salamis and cheeses—and with the tools of food—cookie trays, thermometers, and cake mixes. "I love to cook," she says, staying in to make chicken soup for some women who live nearby.

When Faith wrote to me, she advised me what to bring: tampons, mainly, along with stockings, shampoo, peanut butter, chocolates, candies, and cosmetics to give as gifts. My mother, thankfully, slipped in some cans of tuna and packages of dried soup. None of this is available. Later, when it is, most Russians can't afford it.

Faith lives—and shops—like a Russian. The only stores we see are kiosks, which sell chocolate and liquor, and the neighborhood *Frukti i Ovoschi*, fruit and vegetable store. It's practically empty, save for miserable-looking pickled or preserved objects in glass jars that remind me of high school biology class.

EXPLORING MOSCOW

Faith takes me exploring. We begin with Moscow's crowded but efficient metro system, with its stench of sweat, urine, and alcohol. Thousands of men and women, as in Warsaw, with not much to smile about. Cavernous escalators descend to a throbbing underworld crammed with people loaded with goods they've bought or hope to sell or trade. Most Russians carry plastic bags sold by babushkas on the street for small change; you never know what bargain you may find on the streets, from lightbulbs and sweaters to toilet seats, oranges, and toothpaste.

The metros are also museums, filled with impressive statues, monuments, and frescoes glorifying the 1917 Revolution with quasi-religious zeal. An old woman sits in a booth at the bottom of the escalators; a post left over from Communist days. Her job, I'm told, is to monitor the escalator and to stop it in case of emergency.

On the metro, I see all sorts of faces, a compilation of humanity, like the airport. I see Asian, Mongol, and White Russian faces; an old man with red, glazed eyes in a not-too-warm lumberjacket and no gloves, dead drunk, with a rusty saw in an open bag at his feet. I see an old woman with a puffy face and heavy dark circles under her eyes, holding the chubby hands of two small, round grandchildren with old faces; more men so drunk they can barely stand; baby-faced soldiers; old men reading newspapers; a student with an English-language romance novel; graffiti. A young woman pushes a babushka out of the way. More men and women sleep with their mouths open. It's so packed no one can fall; we're pressed too tightly together.

Faith helps me decipher this sprawling netherworld. But just as I learn one metro stop, the name reverts to its pre-1917 status. (Everything "Marx" goes, though "Lenin" stays.) Sometimes maps inside the subway cars have old names whited out and new names scratched on. But not always—even more than a year later. I wonder if those responsible are inefficient bureaucrats, secret anarchists, or closet Marxists. Just try asking an old Muscovite how to get to a newly named street.

Faith takes me to the Intourist Hotel, an inhospitably plain building near Red Square, on Tverskaya Street. Tverskaya is Moscow's Fifth Avenue, its Champs-Elysées. When I arrive, the street is drab and uninspiring. Later, while there are no designer shrines of gold, Tverskaya does boast an eclectic capital collection of colors, shops, and advertising: Mexican food; Moscow's first decent beauty salon; an Indian restaurant; the first McDonald's; old Russian state stores where you can buy antique silver and crystal; some of the best small grocery stores; Pushkin Square; Pizza Hut; vendors selling boiled sausage, ice cream, and concert tickets; a little-known wax museum; and the Dannon yogurt store—big news when it opens.

Intourist was one of the main hotels before the Western luxury hotels sprang up. It's also the name of the state agency that organized all foreign travel under Communism. The Intourist is still the essence of a Soviet hotel. Doormen—un-uniformed, ungloved — insolently question every *deyavushka*, young woman, who enters, insinuating that she's a prostitute who hasn't paid the doorman his cut.

"Deyavushka, where do you think you're going? Are you a guest? Show us your pass." The stone-faced guards are then delighted to throw the woman—terrified, humiliated, outraged—out.

At the start of the Yeltsin years, some of my Russian friends are so intimidated that they don't believe they are allowed in such hotels. Western women, of course, don't take this. One cool look, a frosty "Good morning," and the guards usually back off.

The lobby is filled with men, old and young, lounging aimlessly; cheap leather jackets, chewed-up cigarettes. Only the women work: mounds of Soviet-dyed white-blonde, orange, or purple bouffant hair, à la Dusty Springfield, behind reception desks and small stands selling cheap postcards and *matrioshkas*, the colorful wooden Russian dolls that come stacked one inside the other. We buy some postcards for dollars, the same cards I later see underground for kopecks. They are decades old, but never mind. Soon the underground offerings will expand from cheap souvenirs and newspapers to pornography, outstanding jazz bands, pirated editions of English best-sellers, and videos. New glass-encased stores will sell French perfume, Italian shoes, leather jackets, CDs, and fast food.

I use the international telephone—twenty-five dollars a minute —to call my parents. "I never make long-distance calls from the apartment," Faith says. "I don't want anyone to know I'm a foreigner." Since the telephone bills go to the landlords, they often freak at foreigners' monthly phone bills, which can be more than they earn in a year.

While I think the Intourist is slightly sleazy, it does not seem sinister. How am I to know about the fleet of corrupt cab drivers who wait outside, preying on young women; that I will come back here for an investigative piece on child prostitution; that the hotel lounge is nicknamed *gadyushnik*, the snakepit, and populated by clueless foreigners on cheap group tours, some looking for old prostitutes, some just having coffee; that it is the meeting ground for young and old prostitutes, pimps, and gangsters.

Back in the cold, we walk to Red Square. "Take notes the first time you see it," says one friend. "You'll get so used to it you'll never look at it the same way again." She couldn't be more wrong. I never lose my amazement, appreciation, and wonder at Red Square—the ancient citadel, or Kremlin, and beside it, St. Basil's Cathedral. It's magical. St. Basil's is magnificent, with its incredible, inspiring primal colors—reds, greens, yellows, whites, and blues—its geometric swirls and patterns. It is one of those rare places that gets more beautiful and awe-inspiring each time I see it. I also love the wedding-cake tower, the kitsch red stars that glow at night, the bells, the brides in white who still lay flowers on the Tomb of the Unknown Soldier, in the Alexandrov Garden adjacent to the Kremlin; the snow-capped towers of the Lenin Museum, the crunches and clicks of heels on snow-soaked pavement, the never-ending flow of people that reminds me of a medieval king's courtyard; even the old men who take cheap souvenir photos with ancient Polaroids.

St. Basil's, though, is my favorite.

St. Basil's is beautiful on a late summer evening as the sun sets, past 11 P.M. But there is nothing like St. Basil's in the twilight of an early winter evening, or well past midnight, with the snow softly falling white on cobblestone. You can hear people's footsteps, the snot-nosed kids, the exhausted housewives, young lovers, entrepreneurs, artists, and khooligani. Amidst all the bustle will be some people standing still, even just for a moment, to drink up the sight surrounding them. I never fail to stop and reflect, to devour this vision for all it's worth.

It is one of those rare places that gives energy without taking anything in return. Even the surliest taxi driver, who inevitably asks if life is better here or in Canada, never fails to say, gesturing proudly if we are by the Kremlin, "But you don't have *this* in Canada!"

Sometimes, for reasons unknown, police block off Red Square. Public squares are supposed to be for the public. In Russia, even this basic right can be irrationally denied. But this is a country still ruled by privilege and status, or at least the appearance of privilege. Then all I have to do is show a press pass and I'm allowed through to enjoy a walk alone through the square. Whether it's early morning or past midnight, whether I'm alone or with friends, Red Square never loses its aura of absolute greatness. When I see it, I get the feeling I can do anything.

Ivan the Terrible, who commissioned St. Basil the Blessed, understood the feelings it inspires only too well. He built the cathedral to commemorate the conquest of Kazan, then paid for it with blood-stained funds from the vanquished. (Ivan marched from Moscow to capture Kazan from a Tatar khan in 1552. The Tatars—Turkic descendants of the Mongol Golden Horde—never forgot.) Church construction began in 1555 and was completed in 1560. Its creation sparkled an incredible tale, which, true or not, seems to capture some essence of Russia.

Ivan loved St. Basil's so much, legend has it, that he ordered the architect's eyes gouged out. That way, he reasoned, St. Basil's would remain forever unrivaled. That's Russia—tsarist, Communist, or post-Soviet—Eternal Russia.

The soul of this country is so deep, the beauty it can create so powerful, perhaps unique in the world. But there is always that other dark, brooding, violent, and greedy side that is never far from the surface. It is the story of the Russian bear who stumbles onto a giant apple tree. The bear wants only the one apple that is out of his reach. With brute force he shakes the tree, destroying it, and the apples, for nothing.

It is this greed and rage that murdered the architects and builders of the Revolution and the children of Stalin, that dooms soldiers to murder and die in Chechnya, that drives the price of some contract killings down to twenty dollars, that nurtures the popularity of crypto-fascist and neo-fascist politicians. And it is the soul that guarantees Russia's survival, despite the greed. No one can forget that it was Russia that in a series of titanic battles stopped Hitler—no matter how many of her own people died in the struggle or betrayed Russia's ideals before, during, and after the war.

From St. Basil's, Faith and I walk across Red Square to the Lenin Museum, now called the State Historical Museum. The Germans did something similar, after reunification, when their former memorial to the victims of fascism and militarism was renamed as a memorial to the victims of war and tyranny. Nazi wives now come to lay wreaths for their Nazi husbands, and now everyone—victims and perpetrators alike—blur into an indistinct mass of "victims," all equally to be mourned and none, least of all the guilty, to be condemned.

I can't help but think that something horrifying will come out of the Russian desire to sweep away the last seventy years. Lenin is part of a proud and powerful Russian legacy. In the rush to forget, topple, obliterate, hide, Russia may be on her way to repeating the mistakes of her past—and others.

The museum is still a tribute to Lenin. Although there are no English explanations, we breathe in pictures, photographs, mounds of earth, and other artifacts impaled, classified, and captured like the relics of saints. I move through pictures of Lenin's childhood. He grew up in a modest, book-filled home on the Volga, which I will later visit, where his parents placed a strong emphasis on education. I see him as a young revolutionary; his books, pamphlets in many languages. I see the paintings of him replicated in offices of factory directors, academics, and politicians in all of Russia long after the collapse of Communism. The top floor displays tributes from the old empire: Central Asian paintings of Lenin in sand, macaroni, feathers, mosaics, like offerings to a god.

Soon Yeltsin will cut the museum's funding. The red-brown coalition—old Communists, ultra-nationalists, and neo-fascists— are already rallying outside. This is the place for racist speeches and anti-Semitic propaganda, a place to vent anger about the loss of empire and national pride, to collectively long for a return to the old days—and to plot the downfall of the new. It's chilling to see the mix of people: old and poor, young toughs with imperial flags and swastikas, professors in berets.

At the same time, the Lenin Museum ironically metamorphoses from Guardian of Sacred Communism to a capitalist office building. The floors meant to honor freedom in the equality and fraternity of socialism now display a car exhibit and modeling agency, which is run by Sergei Mavrodi, head of the notorious MMM firm, until it collapses in scandal with its pyramid scheme and untold multitudes of poor Russians lose their savings. The scandal culminates in Mavrodi, then a member of parliament, being dramatically arrested by masked men. (He is eventually charged with fraud and tax evasion, after parliament expels him, ending his parliamentary immunity.)

After seventy years of Lenin worship, the museum's capitalist phase, like Mavrodi's, turns out to be brief. In 1994, the museum is taken over by the Moscow parliament, which used it before 1917.

Faith and I stop by Lenin's Tomb, well guarded by two impeccably dressed young soldiers. (A friend claims she once seduced one of the guards.) A popular, and romantic time to come is during the midnight changing of the guards.

I drop off my camera with a woman in an almost hidden booth, and stand in a long line, which moves fast. An old woman in front of me weeps for Stalin. I see the plaque for John Reed, the American journalist and revolutionary, who is also buried in Red Square. Lenin wrote the introduction to Reed's classic book, *Ten Days That Shook the World*.

I soon find myself face-to-face with Lenin. He is lying down, all waxy, polished, pointed, and, possibly, at peace. The encounter is brief. "Don't lean on the glass—and keep moving!" a soldier shouts. (Soon a Texan will seriously offer to *buy* Lenin. I wonder how much longer he'll rest here.)

From Red Square, Faith and I walk into the adjoining Manezh Square. Manezh is a public place, with parades, concerts, and political demonstrations, which are held almost every Sunday, by the red-browns, the first year or so after Communism's collapse. Later it will become a monstrous construction site, like the rest of Moscow.

Mayor Yuri Luzhkov is turning the square into a giant four-story shopping mall with underground parking and an archaeological museum. It's expected to be complete by the fall of 1997, in time for Moscow's eight-hundred-and-fiftieth birthday.

I have this vision of the mall filled with the most expensive stores—some with the worst taste—in the Western world. I fear it will become a symbol for all that is wrong with Russia, a site attractive to terrorists, as in the surrealist movie *Brazil*. Archaeologists complain that Luzhkov's rush to create the future is needlessly destructive of the past, as he bulldozes heedlessly through artifact-rich historical sites.

We walk across the street to the Hotel Rossiya, built by Brezhnev in the 1950s. It was supposed to be the biggest hotel in the world, a tribute to Communism. It is horribly ugly. The hotel is free for Russian deputies. Many Russians complain that such perks, including free air transportation, telephone calls, and—most important—parliamentary immunity are the main reason most people go into public service. "In America," one Russian friend will soon tell me, "only the rich can afford to enter politics. In Russia, poor people enter politics to become rich."

The Man with the Accent lives and works here, when he's in town, in a well-furnished suite with a majestic view of Red Square. Other rooms are small and dismal, with the narrow cots, orange bedcovers, dim lights, and cockroaches of Soviet hotels across the empire.

The Rossiya is a maze of entrances as confusing as the Intourist. Although there are many doors, most are locked or chained: Entering is a challenge. Here, too, the doormen ask our "purpose" before letting us in.

We splurge on three-dollar Baskin-Robbins ice cream cones, excited to find something familiar. The same ice cream is sold cheaper, in rubles, on the Old Arbat, a pedestrian shopping area filled with antiques, souvenirs, and soon Italian cafés and McDonald's.

We discover a *beriozka*, one of the only hard-currency stores in Soviet times, at the hotel. Because these stores' Soviet-era quality, service, and selection are far from exceptional, their use is dwindling as the hard-currency grocery market expands. I buy what I can from a limited selection: British mango tea, bottled German white asparagus, and Scandinavian lemon soda. I soon learn how to decipher Norwegian cooking instructions and how to distinguish Finnish dishwashing soap from laundry detergent. With time, selection increases. There will be American stores with peanut butter and Pop-Tarts.

Even the Hotel Rossiya will expand: high-priced jewelry, fur, and Manhattan Express, a New York steakhouse and club with great food (if not music). Gun-toting bodyguards wait outside in luxury cars.

Faith and I also visit state stores, at subsidized prices, near the flat. There are no lines, but there's hardly any food either. I will soon discover Russian bread stores, with delicious and filling black breads and walnut loaves. We are also delighted by the fresh oranges and bananas sold outside the metros. "You could never find this in Moscow before!" exclaims Faith. I pass on Russian milk, with the sign of the cow that is duplicated in New York's Brighton Beach, but discover some Russian stores with fresh salmon and caviar.

Gradually, I stumble across the new hard-currency stores, which mushroom and amaze old-time foreigners. Their ever-expanding selection soon makes the beriozkas obsolete. "We used to have to import smoked salmon by train from Helsinki," one journalist says. "When the first hard-currency store opened, Russians would stand outside, watching the privileged foreign and domestic set walk out with overstuffed plastic bags. There were always special stores for the elite under Communism, but they were hidden; you needed special passes to get in." Conspicuous consumption, not privilege, is what's new.

Westerners feared the disparity would cause riots, but many Russians are just pleased that the stores exist. Now I'm warned not to carry bags with hard-currency logos, which are targets for criminals. Although more goods are available when I arrive, I have to visit many stores to find what I need: the Italian store for pasta and olives, say, or the German store for cheese. Because I can afford to shop at hard-currency stores, I don't have to stand in lines. Most Russians do. Still, the act of consumption, so taken for granted in the West, becomes a time-consuming challenge in Russia.

I also discover the city's *rynoki*, or markets. I adore the historic, multileveled central market, which Mayor Luzhkov will later close for "health reasons." He will also shut down an outdoor pool for "health reasons," and then rebuild the Napoleonic-era

Cathedral of Christ the Savior, destroyed by Stalin in 1931. (The pool was supposed to have been a Palace of Soviets—a monument to Communism.)

Starting in 1995, twenty-five hundred men labor twenty-four hours a day, in twelve-hour shifts, to ensure that the church—symbolizing Moscow's powerful new trinity—the Russian Orthodox Church, city government, and post-Communist entrepreneurs—will be ready for 1997. Luzhkov is even offering free glasses of *kvas*, the traditional Russian drink of fermented yeast, and mead, a fermented mix of honeyed water, to help boost worker morale.

It's not just that the city government has sunk so much money into the church, or that the banks have bathed it in gold while millions starve—the city is in desperate need of soup kitchens and homeless shelters.* It is also monstrously ugly.

I go to the market, beside the circus, to practice my Russian and bargain with the sellers: Central Asians with spicy carrots and pickled garlic; Russians with fresh honey, white, salty cheese, and *smetana*, sort of like sour cream. People bring their own plastic bags and glass jars to fill up. My favorites are wild sweet strawberries in summer, saffron, caviar, and, always, fresh flowers: tulips and roses, birds-of-paradise, tiger lilies, orchids, and daisies. With time, I discover the markets' underground life. My favorite, Cheryomushky, is also the place in town to buy opium and AK-47s.

Faith is still afraid that people will know I'm a foreigner. I hesitate to wear my cowboy boots because they look "foreign." Boots fast get destroyed on Moscow streets anyway. One of the first things I search for are shoe repair stores, hidden in tiny stalls by metro stations, with their bizarre pictures of a black high-heeled boot.

---

* Stolichny Bank has donated 110 pounds of gold to fund the project—not to mention a 32.5-ounce gold medallion for the Russian Orthodox Church's patriarch, Alexei II, and another 1,607 troy ounces, worth about $615,000, to help cover the cathedral's domes and interior. The patriarchate has subsequently transferred its bank accounts to Stolichny, which is run by Mikhail Smolenski, who is Jewish. At the same time, an April 1996 World Bank report states that 30 percent of all Russians live below the poverty line, which is officially estimated to be $35 a month.

I dress for warmth, trekking by metro in old jeans over long underwear, turtlenecks, layers of sweaters, and my bulky coat. There's no such thing as winter, Russians say, only warm clothes.

By the winter of 1996, I will have long ago traded that coat for Italian sheepskin, which I buy at a kiosk. (It was probably stolen.) By then I feel like a slob next to Russian women dripping in fur and the latest designer outfits. Now even my friend's cleaning lady wears a white fox over polyester. "It was so cheap," Tanya says. "Only nine hundred dollars." No matter that that was all she earned in 1994, that she buys only the cheapest, worm-eaten apples. "Everyone must have a fur in Moscow these days," she says.

Now, amidst Escada and French fur, I often see pensioners shell-shocked by glitz. "Look," a man says to his wife in amazement. "Ten million rubles [two thousand dollars] for a coat—can you believe it?"

It is the Weimar Republic all over again: resentment feeding on national humiliation and the loss of an empire. A shaky democracy transposed upon a people with absolutely no history, no experience, however remote, of such a system. Longing for Lost Glory Days of Empire turns *Cabaret* into a hit once again. I reread Christopher Isherwood's novel, *Goodbye to Berlin*, on which the musical is based, and feel eerily at home. His description of Berlin in the early 1930s is striking in its resemblance to 1990s Moscow.

As I stand in line on Tverskaya Street to buy French cosmetics at ridiculously cheap prices (they rise with time, once consumers are hooked), the woman in front takes twenty minutes. She is paying thousands of rubles for lipstick, in neatly tattered stacks of five- and ten-ruble notes. Inflation will be twenty-five to thirty percent a month by the end of 1992. I am reminded of my Grade Twelve history teacher, Mr. McCartney, telling of Germans carrying wheelbarrows full of money to buy bread during the Weimar days. Then, as now, the West did nothing until it was too late.

Faith and I had planned to move into a larger apartment. But by the end of my first week, Faith tells me she doesn't want to move. "I'm happy here. I'm close to the school and my friends—and it's only fifty dollars a month," she says. "But don't worry, Irina and I will help you find an apartment."

I am eternally grateful to Faith for her hospitality. I don't mind at all. I know I need to be—at least a little—closer to the center.

Not wanting to be a burden, I plan to move out as soon as possible: in the next few days.

Another Canadian freelancer has arrived in Moscow. We have friends in common, and agree to meet at McDonald's, the only place we both know.

I carry a Berlitz travel book with me wherever I go. We walk the streets and feast on what we bring from home: my peanut butter and Sandy's "power bars," which taste like cardboard and freeze as soon as we try to eat them as we wander, lost, around the city, and through Novodevichy Cemetery, amidst the graves of Gogol and Shostakovich, Krushchev and Stalin's wife, Nadezhda Alliluyeva, in a cold, sunless February chill. But this is Moscow. I don't mind at all.

←--→

CHAPTER 2

The Apartment

Moving Right In—Imperialism Revisited,
Raves, Tea, Ivy League Gangsters, and the
Moscow Times

> I wake to sleep, and take my waking slow.
> I feel my fate in what I cannot fear.
> I learn by going where I have to go.
> We think by feeling. What is there to know?
> I hear my being dance from ear to ear.
> I wake to sleep, and take my waking slow....
>
> — THEODORE ROETHKE, "The Waking"

Irina finds me a flat. It's in southeast Moscow, an even worse part of town. Moscow is one of the world's greenest cities. But there are no parks here, just bad air that confines the soul and makes your lungs sick.

The apartment complex looks like Faith's. Tall blue-and-white buildings provided free for Russians—the wait can be decades—if you have the right *propiska*, residence permit, which regulates where you live. For the average comrade, free shelter is a tiny communal flat crammed with strangers, functional space that zaps individualism and creativity.* Sociologists predict that violence will increase with post-Soviet joblessness. People aren't meant to stay in closet-sized flats all day.

---

* Some of these buildings are called *khrushchyoby*. It's a word play on *trushchoby*, which means slums, because they were built during the time of Soviet premier Nikita Khruschev. The communal flats are like shoe boxes with low ceilings and thin walls.

We walk up concrete stairs in darkness. The flat is worse than dismal: one not-too-clean room, with a bare lightbulb hanging miserably from the ceiling. "It's seventy-five dollars a month. A bargain!" says the kerchiefed landlady, Galina, in English.

After asking why I've moved to Moscow, Galina asks me the second most popular question: "Where is your husband?"

"I don't have one," I respond.

"But what happens if you fall down the stairs and break your leg?" she asks. "Who would know? Who would take care of you?"

I'd never thought about it in quite this way before.

"I have a daughter around your age," Galina says. "She's now studying with some Orthodox Jews who want to take her to Israel. The last rabbi at the school was from Israel, but he left without paying his long-distance phone bill. Do you think I should let her go?"

"There are many different ways to be Jewish. You don't have to go to Israel," I tell her. I hate the apartment, but I have nowhere else to go. I'm about to take it when fate intervenes.

At a press conference later that day at the Canadian embassy, I meet a guardian angel who gives me some great advice and even sneaks my friend Sandy and me invaluable phone directories. (There are no public phone books in Russia.) The press conference is about Red Cross aid to small Russian towns, where even basics like aspirin and bandages are lacking. Canadians accompany the aid to keep it off the black market. This leads to my first investigative article in Russia, about chaotic distribution of humanitarian aid: how some ends up in Moscow kiosks, some is too defective to use, while aid that does arrive often goes astray, like condoms winding up in a children's hospital.

Leaving the press conference, I do what some Russians do for transportation: stand in the street, stick my arm out, and wave my fingers. A car stops and I'm on my way to the *Toronto Star* office to file my first article. I can't pronounce the street name properly, so I write it out.

The *Star*'s bureau chief, Stephen Handelman, is out of town. His impeccably well-mannered British assistant, the debonair Toby Latta, an Oxford graduate in his mid-twenties, speaks flawless Russian. I tell Toby where my apartment is.

"That's absolutely the worst part of Moscow," he informs me calmly. "You cannot live there."

"Unfortunately, I have no choice. I need a flat immediately," I explain.

"I'll talk to a bureaucrat I know," Toby says. "He just lost his job. He, his wife, and teenage son want to move in with their daughter and her husband so they can rent out their flat."

Although Russians wait decades for apartments, plenty are available, if you have money or connections. Many Muscovites, desperate for hard currency, rent their flats and move in with relatives, or to modest dachas that are often meant for summer use only.

I meet the bureaucrat, Alexei, the next day, at the subway stop Prospekt Vernadskogo. He is tall, middle-aged, in a long gray overcoat and navy blue ski cap with pom-pom. Alexei speaks no English. We carry phrase books and practice sentences like "Good afternoon" (*Dobry dyen*).

Alexei works out of his old office, even though it's part of a ministry that no longer exists. He has a passion for shiny tracksuits and tennis, like Yeltsin, and loves to cross-country ski. "There are excellent trails near the apartment," he says.

We take a crowded bus five stops to the apartment. It's not in the center, but it is near the *Toronto Star*, and not far from the Stalinist wedding-cake-tiered Moscow State University. The building looks like Faith's, but the people have better jobs. And it's safer.

The apartment is in one of six identical buildings. Like most Russian buildings, it's hard to find the numbers, and difficult to drive into the complex after a heavy snowfall. The entrance door has a code, but if I forget, I soon discover that every building with a code has the secret number cryptically written above the entrance. The paradox is typical Moscow. In any case, the door is rarely locked. If all else fails, the glass at the entrance has been kicked in, allowing for quick and easy access.

The buildings remind me of a classic film, *The Irony of Fate*, by the Georgian director Eldar Ryazanov. A bunch of bachelors get drunk in Moscow on New Year's Eve. One of them is off to St. Petersburg for business. In a drunken stupor, the wrong man gets on the plane. He arrives in St. Petersburg still drunk and asks a cabby to take him to his Moscow address. He ends up in an identical apartment on a street just like his own.

This flat radiates good vibes. Alexei's family moves out, and I move in, within two days. I'm paying $150 a month. Soon the oil companies will raise their prices and rents will skyrocket: up to $3,000 and higher a month for a flat.

My new home is a large one-bedroom flat: living room, with green sofa bed, couch, rugs, two tables, bookcase, and old black-and-white television that sometimes works.

When I arrive, the floor rugs and one of the tables are missing. "Typically Russian!" says Toby, who has a word with Alexei. The objects reappear. My bedroom has a standard ugly rug-on-the-wall and, to my delight, a piano. Galina, landlady of the seventy-five-dollar flat, sends over her husband, an engineer, to tune it. He also plays some original compositions.

There's even a balcony that looks onto a snow-covered field and pond. Children skate there in winter and float on rafts, in muck-colored water, in summer. As in most Russian flats, the balcony doubles as storage space. (Sometimes these balconies collapse.) In summer, there is just enough room to wedge between the junk and write in the sun. Traffic-congested Moscow is relatively far away. The air is considered good here in the Ramenky region.

Even the wallpaper, pink and lime green in one room, faded mauve in another, isn't as bad as it could be. Russian flats are so notorious for their wallpaper that one editor commissioned an article on the topic. "The writer," she said, "apparently found a government bureau that dictated patterns for all wallpaper manufactured in the FSU. Even wallpaper was political because some colors were associated with national independence movements within the Soviet republics."

The apartment, built in the 1960s, is still considered new. That means the water and phone lines work and it's roach-and-rodent-free: not to be taken for granted, I learn from later apartments.

It's peaceful here, despite the graffiti and the dog-fouled elevators which don't always work. Sometimes, when the hall lights don't work, I run up the stairs in the pitch dark at 3 A.M. clutching my keys and, if I remember, Russian-bought mace. It's only when my parents come to visit, and I see the look on my mother's face, that I realize how far I am from North America.

IVY LEAGUE GANGSTERS

I begin to meet other young women who also arrive without jobs, looking for work in whatever field strikes them, from journalism to multinationals and humanitarian organizations. Our lives are different from those who come to learn the Russian language and culture, who live like poor Russians, without fresh fruit but with lots of excellent, cheap theater. We're also different from the privileged young foreign set: *biznesmeni* who come to make—and spend—money. As fast, and as much, as they can. Young Ivy League Gangsters, YILGs, is what a visiting American colleague calls them.

Some YILGs—doctors, lawyers, accountants—make their money legitimately. Others work as advisers to Russian ministers and gleefully explain (off the record) how they spun their minister's latest press conference.

Still others are into the murky, and dangerous, world of "import-export"—including smuggling art, Communist Party kitsch, medals, and statues. They scour the old empire snagging Lenin statues, fading portraits on village walls; bribing the village idiot with vodka to blurt out which old woman owns what icon. Some buy factories, producing kitsch like matrioshka dolls. One YILG brags about getting a Lenin statue out of a large town. He sounds like an engineering student who stole the college mascot. They also smuggle arms, drugs, oil, and other natural resources. Most are Ivy League graduates who were bored in London's "City" and on New York's Wall Street. They now drive BMWs or Jeeps— they even rent Russian MiG fighter planes—and indulge in strings of, well, intellectually nonstimulating serial relationships with women whose tastes are more expensive than their pocketbooks. Among themselves, the women call the men sponsors. What they want is no longer a passport, just an expensive dinner, an apartment, even a clothing allowance—for the new Gianni Versace store and, for the younger set, French Kookai suits and Freelance boots from Galeries Lafayette in GUM, an acronym for the one-hundred-year-old State Department Store by Red Square, which used to house nothing but the sorriest of Russian goods.

These businessmen—I never meet any businesswomen—make me think about imperialists of the last century, in India, maybe. I meet them on story assignments. A thirty-something business-man, one of Moscow's first Western success stories, interviews me as much as I interview him. "If you're looking for a job, I'm starting a business newsletter," he says. I don't take it, but at least I know that, whatever happens, I won't starve.

"I know someone perfect for your story," he says with a smile, and gives me the name of "Frank."

Frank and I meet at the Oktyabrskaya Hotel, which used to be the elite hotel for Communist Party bosses. I have to pass through a special guard and gate to get in. Frank, twenty-six, is tall, polite, handsome in a standard, uneventual sort of way. (Too-close cropped brown hair, square jaw; prep blazers, and Moscow turtle-necks.) There is something unsettling about his eyes.

"How do you like the hotel?" he asks, with a firm handshake.

"I've been here for about a year," he adds over thick coffee in the hotel café, which is filled with yellowed Communists who look as though they've been here since Lenin died.

"This hotel is ruled by privilege, not money," he later explains. "Once you're in, rooms and food are cheap."

Before Moscow, Frank worked as a ski instructor at a European resort owned by a family friend. "Now I'm a biznesman, in real estate," he says. "I can't be in your article. My Russian partners wouldn't like it. But I'll give you names of other people to call."

"What are you doing now?" he asks.

"I've got to write. I'm on deadline."

"Why don't you come out for dinner?"

I thank him, but beg off.

"There'll be a group of us, including some diplomats," he says. "I can promise you'll meet some interesting people."

We drive in a chauffeured Mercedes with an "ex" KGB driver. Dinner is in a charming restaurant; fountains and incredible Geor-gian dishes in clay pots. Frank and his friends are in the business of renting apartments, renovating and subletting them. (While Russians can now own businesses, no one can own land in Moscow, just long-term leases.)

As the years of my stay go by, I watch Frank transform. He moves from blazer to black turtleneck, black jeans, black metal stud belt, and crew cut. I don't even recognize him when he approaches me at a trendy Italian restaurant one night. He is with a group of tough-looking Russian men, also in turtlenecks. We make plans to go for dinner. Frank picks me up. Late.

"I'm sorry," he says. "I had to do some vodka shots with my Russian partners. We were celebrating a new contract." By now, his projects have moved from small apartments to large supermarkets. As the stakes increase, so do the risks.

"I was in a car chase with gunmen shooting at me," he says with a grin. "I had to drive into an embassy for protection." He's also bought "equipment" for a special organized crime unit of the Moscow police to help "protect" him from mobsters who want to take over one of his apartments. After some prodding, he says the "equipment" is laser guns. He takes Russians on exorbitant, splendacious trips to the United States, to enroll in an "academy" where you learn how to dodge pursuers while driving, at a cost of tens of thousands of dollars.

"I'm going to be in Russia for a long time," he says. As Frank approaches his thirties, one of his big projects seems to be to find a wife. "She'll have to be Russian," he says matter-of-factly. "No Western woman would put up with me. She has to be the type who can smile with the kings—and the scum. I'll move her and my children to London. Russia will not be safe for them."

Frank is part spy novel, part F. Scott Fitzgerald (expat), and part Great Gatsby (excess). Some YILGs have their own money to invest. Some make money. Others merely lust after it. Wealth is the aphrodisiac they share, the kiss (empty, broken, illicit, evasive?) that draws them here.

Beyond the amoral limitlessness of it all is a straight, simple, focused, unembarrassed—even proud—lack of pretense. These men have one goal: to make money and more money and more money and then some. They don't even try to hide behind a noble, altruistic cause because they believe their cause, their raison d'être, is the most noble one of all.

Some YILGs live in hotels. Others, like "Milo," whom I meet through mutual friends back home, have their own apartments. Milo's, in a run-down building, is huge. It is also completely *remonted*, an anglicized version of the Russian word *remont*, which means to renovate.

I call Milo my first week in Moscow. He invites me for dinner—our first and last—that Saturday evening.

"Where do you live? I'll pick you up."

I tell him.

"That's way out. Do you think you could take the subway into the center? I'll meet you in front of the horse [statue] on Tverskaya Street."

I emerge from the underground in total darkness. A head pops out of a car and calls my name. Thin brown hair, leather jacket, blue jeans; tall, decent build, pleasant features.

"So, are you married?" he asks, almost as soon as I get in the car.

Over the telephone, Milo suggested we go out for dinner. Instead, he takes me to his apartment. Opening the triple-locked steel door reveals a New York flat, complete with wall-to-wall carpeting. Milo gives me a tour, then opens his cupboards to show me crates of imported food: I've never seen a stockpile like this before, but they turn out to be fairly common in expat apartments.

We have champagne, caviar, and cabbage-roll leftovers made by Milo's housekeeper. "I just love this city," he says. "But most people can't handle it. I know one guy who arrived at the airport, freaked out, and flew home."

He looks at me, then adds, "You'll either leave in a few weeks or stay for a while."

Milo switches on CNN, a luxury, and turns to me. "I don't understand how freelancing works. How much money will you make?"

I tell him the standard rates for newspaper articles. Milo pulls out a calculator. The annual figure he reckons I'll earn, based on my (rather modest) estimates, makes him laugh out loud.

"Don't take it personally, but I don't like reporters," he says. "All they do is report about what people like me do."

These young men (boys, in fact) have maids, cooks, and masseurs who come to their homes. "When I wake up, my housekeeper makes sure there's fresh cut grapefruit on the table," one of Frank's friends tells me. For parties, they rent clubs, bands, and security with guns. They soon hire twenty-four-hour bodyguards, the Russian version of valets. When one young man's apartment is robbed—the thieves steal everything from the VCR to his underwear—he moves into Moscow's most expensive hotel. Others are there before him.

Frank and Milo live lives they may not have had the imagination to dream of. Even those who grow up with privilege can't indulge like this in the West. The excess makes me uncomfortable. It just doesn't seem right. Especially here.

I don't date these men, but I become friends with some. We go for dinners, at the Hotel Savoy, the Atrium, Arlechino, restaurants filled with post-Communist just-out-of-the-closet gangsters and food trucked fresh from Italy. Maybe they are relieved to *talk*, to have someone interested in their stories instead of their credit card balances.

I call one man the Great Gatsby. Tall, blond, with decent blue eyes that aren't vacant and don't frighten. The Great Gatsby, twenty-six, is quiet and reserved. Polite, charming even, with a face that knows how to fade, how to blend into the woodwork when he doesn't want to be noticed. We meet at a dinner party. (YILGs often eat in large clusters, as if they don't like being alone, or getting into conversations that may make them think.)

At that dinner, I notice only a quiet silhouette sitting beside someone who talks more. When the silhouette calls, he says it's business. Our lunch is rather formal. I am surprised when, afterwards, he kisses me on the cheek instead of shaking my hand, and asks me out for dinner. A strange sort of friendship begins.

He invites me to the Bolshoi, then calls from out of town to cancel. His young KGB chauffeur stops by with flowers and—his trademark—a note written on the back of a photograph.

He takes me to a Middle Eastern restaurant in the middle of nowhere, the only one in Moscow. We eat first-rate food in a place that's empty save for a few tables of well-clad, whispering men. "It's a hangout for arms dealers," he says proudly.

The Great Gatsby hangs with his old college roommates. They live and work together. "Our neighbors think we're CIA," jokes "Clive," twenty-six, who introduces me to the lady who cooks for them. Clive got his start selling chunks of the Berlin Wall to rich American businessmen. Rumor has it he smuggled gas across the Persian Gulf during the war.

The Great Gatsby proudly shows me his office. He recently commissioned a famous but impoverished artist, formerly specializing in busts of Lenin, to do one of him; another artist painted a fresco of the Great Gatsby and his gang on the wall behind his desk.

Once he disappears for more than six months.

"Sorry I haven't called," he says.

"But where have you been?"

"Some people were looking for me. It was better if I disappeared for a while."

Apparently, a gang in St. Petersburg tried to cut in on the Great Gatsby's territory. "They learned I wasn't going anywhere," he says. "They now realize they have to live with me, just as I have to live with them."

Before he disappears, we have one dinner that disturbs me. By making his own fortune—even if it means circumventing the law—the Great Gatsby says he is helping Russia (instead of contributing to the state's general descent into anarchy).

"Part of the money I make goes to hiring more people," he says, using the standard claim to justify exploitation around the world. By his logic, he's doing more for the new "democracy" than any humanitarian organization. Enlightened capitalism, he might call it.

He calls me a Communist.

This obsession with power, combined with a bizarre, impassioned attempt to justify exploitation, grafted onto a fragile, embryonic democracy where there are no effective constraints on individual conduct. The mix is frightening.

"Klaus" is another YILG, a twenty-something German biznesman I meet while interviewing his boss my second week in Moscow.

"You must meet Klaus," the man says after our interview, over warming cups of tea. A quick phone call, and a young executive soon enters. He is, like so many YILGs, tall, blond; short-clipped hair, Armani glasses, starched shirt, impeccable designer suit.

Klaus wears shiny, well-polished black shoes in the midst of winter, unlike my black boots, scuffed from sand and covered with snow and salt stains. His heels actually click when he walks. I think the noise pleases him.

"Can I offer you a lift into town?" Klaus says in sharply accented staccato English.

A chauffeured Mercedes is waiting.

"If you have time, we could stop for coffee," he adds. "I'll take you to the best-kept secret in town."

We go to the Metropol, a historic hotel recently restored to its pre-Revolutionary splendor. The Metropol is one of my favorite places, home to everyone from Lee Harvey Oswald to presidents. In 1992, it's famous for its gourmet restaurant and Sunday brunch in a grand room complete with a live jazz band.

"I can show you the 'other' side, the mafiya side of Moscow life," promises Klaus over cappuccino. He is referring to the ex-Soviet organized crime groups who work with government officials. "The mafiya even wants a cut of my humanitarian project," he adds. Soon there won't be one executive I know who hasn't been approached by the mafiya. By 1996, Control Risks Group Limited, a British-based political and security risk analysis and consultancy firm, estimates that 80 percent of all foreign businesses have been victims of extortion.

"If you want to see one of the bosses, there's a restaurant I can take you to," Klaus offers.

Since Moscow has only a handful of decent restaurants, most of which close at 10 P.M., you have to reserve in advance. Inside this one, men take my coat. (Despite the freezing weather, my companion wears no coat. That, too, is a sign of status. It means he's used to being chauffeured about town.) Up by elevator, down a passage, is the restaurant itself, Italian, which contains well-dressed Russians and expats who do not resemble anyone on the streets.

Once seated, I spot Milo dining with some older Western businessmen.

"What are you doing here?" he asks, approaching our table. "This is the best restaurant in the city."

Admittedly, I am a tad underdressed, a gray grunge queen hidden under layers of thick wool sweaters and a long, green, corduroy dirndl skirt. I thought Moscow would be drab. Perhaps it was, but it is fast becoming one of the most sophisticated, and garish, cities I know. While service is painfully far from Western standards, Moscow's elite is so international that Paris and New York often seem provincial by comparison.

The restaurant owner comes over to schmooze, to send for wine, to sit down for drinks. Klaus has promised a show. Not the gaudy, barely dressed dancers that plague most Soviet-era restaurants, but a real live mafiya show.

Organized crime always existed under Communism.[*] By 1992, mafiya—who backed both the leaders of the attempted coup against Gorbachev, and then the reformers, led by Yeltsin—are openly solidifying their government ties. They are beginning to gain visible power, but they are not yet dominating the news.

It is still a time of optimism, when people seem to believe in democracy. The old Communist order has not yet completely broken down. The media still feature the democratic "firsts" of Russia: the first privatized factory, stock exchange, millionaires' club, the March toward the Market. There has not yet been time for the firsts to fail, for "entrepreneurs" worshipfully described in *Newsweek* cover stories and the *New York Times* to be jailed or to become fugitives. Reporters write about Russia's "fledgling," "shaky" democracy, which implies that the system has a chance to take root, instead of the later catchphrase, "experiment" with democracy, as if the experiment had already failed.

A procession of mobsters soon enters. It begins with a fur-swathed woman tottering against gravity in white spikes. She zigzags into the room, clutching long-stemmed red roses to her breast; black hair swings down her back, hot pink mouth pouts seductively. She is surrounded by men with hands on guns that bulge beneath shiny, double-breasted suits. They are followed by a short, fat man in pinstripes, stringy threads of black hair side-swept across a shiny, near-bald head.

Behind him are toughs packing cellulars and more guns, giggling miniskirted women, serious and sour-faced miniskirted women. The entourage oozes into a back room, closed off by curtains.

---

* In fact, it always existed in Russia. Mafiya dons were called *vory v zakone*, thieves in law: outlaws who helped run the underground shadow economy—and lived by their own strict codes of honor. Such men had lived outside government control for centuries, since their beginnings as highwaymen and Cossack robbers. However, while proud to live outside the rule of law, the vory v zakone also, at times, worked for the state: helping to enforce collectivization in the 1920s and 1930s, similar to the way American organized crime groups busted unions; keeping order and terrorizing political prisoners in exchange for better treatment in the gulags; and then controlling the black market—from blue jeans to computers—in the 1970s and 1980s.

Through the curtains, I see the silhouette of the young woman holding roses. She is singing in honor of a birthday celebration that lasts until dawn.

When YILGs date, it's often Russian women looking for sponsors. Ed, well aware of this, is one example.

Ed, a young, cigar-smoking Ivy League graduate, says he came to Russia to make a million dollars. While here, Ed, from the Midwest, is dating a series of women.

"I never had success with women back home," he says, clad in a red crushed-velvet smoking jacket and black leather pants. Ed also wears black Ray-Bans indoors, rarely takes off his bushy fox hat, and tells jokes about calling the wrong girl to say she left her bra at his flat. He carries pictures of one of them, topless, on a beach.

"American women are so aggressive," he says. "But so many of these women come from nothing. I can help them, and they're so grateful. They've had such hard lives, they don't *want* to work. They want to stay home, have babies, and wear nice clothes. What's wrong with that?"

GOING FOR TEA

The foreign community, around ninety thousand people in a city of nine million officially, but up to eleven million unofficially, is still considered small. I spend my first two weeks phoning North American papers looking for work. Most bureau chiefs try to help. They know what it's like to move here, and that it's even worse without a job.

After one meeting with the bureau chief of a large American paper, we go down from the bureau to his flat, filled with books and Western comfort. "So, your husband got transferred here, I gather," he says, adding to the chorus of Russians, and foreigners, who can't imagine a woman coming here, with nothing, alone.

We discuss a potential job, where I could organize graphics, gathering facts for other reporters' stories, with the promise that I could also write my own. Other local hires move into staff positions from such beginnings. I couldn't expect a better offer. But after a year at the *Inquirer*, I want to work on my own stories instead of spending even part of my time gathering information for other reporters.

While the recession may be hurting friends back home, no capable foreigner can fail to find a job—survival to dream level—in Moscow. For some, the city is a Klondike-style boomtown. Hiring a Westerner locally in Moscow can save companies big bucks. The discrepancy among the salaries of expats, equally qualified local hires, and Russians is outrageous. Shipping over newly hired expats is expensive. There are the costly relocation fees, plus all the hardship perks. Hiring expats locally can alleviate much of the expense, since the expats are already here, and in a weaker bargaining position. Hiring Russians is even cheaper—regardless of their qualifications. Companies justify the inequality by saying that cheap labor is what induced them to invest here, that they couldn't afford to be here without it.

When I phone one American paper, a French woman answers. "The bureau chief is out of town," she says. I tell her my story: young journalist, new in town, looking for work. She phones back the next day.

"I'm just calling to tell you I delivered your message," says Maguy. "I'm sorry I couldn't talk longer, but I was in the middle of a Russian lesson. Would you like to come over for tea?"

My friendship with Maguy begins over tea in a tree-shaded, roomy old flat by a dilapidated tennis court and school yard, near Baumenskaya Metro. A young woman with long blonde hair opens the door. She sports a smart tweed skirt, bought for rubles, she tells me, with Parisian élan. Born of American and Italian parents and raised in Paris, Maguy is fluent in many languages. She is working on her Ph.D. for a prestigious university, and moved here just a few weeks ago.

I soon meet other young journalists, students, musicians, diplomats, artists, and academics from New York and Alaska, Montreal, Paris, Guinea, and elsewhere, who have come to Moscow for reasons similar to mine. It is comforting, and inspiring, to move to a place so foreign and to feel so at home.

Under Communism, most entertaining occurred in homes: small, drunken dinner parties at Russian flats; opulent, catered affairs at diplomats', journalists', and executives' flats with Grecian columns, and, in some cases, mazes of rooms; some dinner parties on the town, in Moscow's first cooperative restaurants.

By 1992, there are a few places to go but not many: no nouveau riche, one-hundred-dollar-entrance-fee clubs. Still, there's the Irish bar, where expats mingle with Russians, including those looking for passport husbands. The bar is attached to one of Moscow's first hard-currency stores. It's so packed that people sit on the floor in the hall outside, near the fruit and vegetable section.

Russians harbor an odd love of exclusivity and secrecy. Elite Communist stores, offices, and sprawling mansions on Leninsky Prospekt were hidden from the public by closed curtains, high gates, and no signs. Some of Moscow's best restaurants and clubs are still in unmarked buildings. Knock on an unadorned door and someone may let you in. If lost, you can always spot the place by the Jeep Cherokees and Mercedes outside.

At Russian restaurants, most of the menu is often unavailable. At Eastern European or Georgian restaurants, the bill is a surprise: hard currency (expensive) one day; rubles the next. Or you pay for food in rubles, alcohol in dollars.

When I arrive, there is not much to do at night. But the pace picks up fast. I feel like I'm witnessing an evolutionary explosion in the development of Moscow nightlife. Some clubs begin in obscure places, like an ex-Communist house of artists, off the Old Arbat. Under Communism, Party-approved artists enjoyed privileges unavailable to the proletariat. It's invigorating to see such houses of elitism transformed by post-Communist youth, artists, and hipsters, entrepreneurs in suspenders, women with style— but no sponsors—before the nouveaux launch their assault. No mobster molls, no greed in tweed. Even some foreigners.

A few "floaters" begin, temporary spaces rented by trendy, enterprising young Russians, often from St. Petersburg. T-shirts are sometimes sold, along with ten- or fifteen-dollar entrance fees. There is lots of space in ex-Soviet clubs of the cultural elite or suburban warehouses.

People seem to trust each other. If Russia is going to succeed as a democracy, *this* is how it will happen. If I think of a Communist Party boss who now owns the state factory he used to direct, using democracy to retain Communist privilege, and I think of young Russians committing Soviet sacrilege, invading elite Communist space and—using capitalist, entrepreneurial initiative—converting it into public space (it sounds almost Communist, except for the steep entrance fee), it's easy, for me, at least, to see which example carries the essence, the spirit, of democracy.

Then comes the first big all-night rave, a Western trend where young people dance to music with a monotonous techno beat. The rave is organized by twenty-five-year-old Alexei Hass and a group of St. Petersburg artists. (Moscow-St. Petersburg rivalry is fierce: The Petersburg crowd think they are more European and avant-garde.)

It seems so international, so sophisticated, Russian and yet non-Russian. Fifteen hundred people—Russians, Europeans, North and South Americans, Middle Easterners, Cubans, Africans, and Asians—desperate for nightlife shell out fifteen dollars each, an enormous amount.

The rave is in the surreal old Cosmos Pavilion of Soviet Achievement, at VDNKh, a sort of kitsch version of the Smithsonian. We are celebrating the thirty-first anniversary of the first cosmonaut, Yuri Gagarin's, historic blast into space. Gagarin's face beams down at the crowd, flecked with green ribbons of laser. It is so cold—even though it's mid-April—that partygoers dance to an acid-house beat in parkas. A sputnik is outside, spaceships and floating astronauts inside. Photos of Gagarin and lights are everywhere.

"We're just dancing and having a good time," yells a young Syrian journalist as he jumps off a platform to chat, leaving his companion oblivious to all but the beat. I find relief from the cold dance area in the VIP bar, which serves overhyped, California trendy, legally high-energy drinks. I pass in favor of some sickly sweet Russian champansky being swigged on the dance floor. There are drugs, too, for those who so desire. The cheapest and most easily accessible are chemical drugs manufactured in factories from Moscow to Central Asian capitals, and LSD. Easy access to coke takes a bit more time.

"Welcome to Moscow. It's either too cold or too hot, like a Yeltsin decree," says Vova, a twenty-three-year-old Muscovite wearing a Western striped shirt, tweed jacket, and duffel coat.

"The Western-style party—and price—is still new for Moscow," says Vova, who has never been to a Western disco. "I kind of like it. Tomorrow you'll go out and everything will be the same. But tonight everyone has forgotten. They've gone crazy."

But for many young Russians, the rave is a sign of significant change. When not co-opted by the market as another means of social control, music can be revolutionary, a way to liberate and unify people, to promote and encourage ideas and ideals of freedom that would send Stalin spinning. I think of this at the rave, and later, when American rock music blares from Russian taxi cabs.

"The juxtaposition of foreigners, Russians, journalists, artists, and intellectuals is like pre-Revolutionary Russia," says Bruce Singleton, a thirty-year-old real estate broker from Dallas. One friend even falls in love at the rave.

We dance, our group forming one of many circles, until it's light outside. We are so hot that when we stumble out for taxis under a light snowfall, the cold morning air refreshes instead of chills. There are no fights. No one checks you for guns, as they later do. No chauffeurs wait for gangsters and *zolotaya molodezh*, golden youth, outside.

Soon the raves become regimented, or at least regularized. The concept becomes just another thing to do that, consequently, is not; at least, not all the time. By then, the choice for dining and nightlife, from the crassest to the most charming of clubs, is unlimited. There are punk clubs with skinheads; gambling, wrestling, and naked women in cages. There is Chance, a hip gay club, and 011—started by some expats from Belgrade who named the spot after their beleaguered city's area code. In these clubs, sex and money, the two verbotens of the Communist empire, are intricately linked.

DOMESTICITY—à LA RUSSE

Unlike the Ivy League gangsters, I live a comfortable, modest existence. The one anomaly is a housekeeper, who becomes my surrogate mom. Maguy's housekeeper, Lyuba, gets her sister, Katya, to work for me. I want someone to come once every other week, mainly to wash my clothes. (There is no washing machine here, nor street-corner Laundromats.)

Katya, with short salt-and-pepper hair and an old but serviceable blue parka, looks at my humble apartment and clucks. She speaks only Russian, but I get the basics. "The flat is so *big*," she says. "I've never seen such a flat for one person. I'll have to come three times a week."

The salary Katya wants is so low that I agree. She also supports two single, near-middle-aged daughters. Soon Katya calls me her third daughter. As my Russian language skills increase, so do our conversations.

Katya is in her sixties. She is practical and resourceful, fixing what needs to be fixed (a broken plug, a shattered iron) with skilled, creative resourcefulness that stems from years of Soviet depriva-tion. (She even finds a Western-standard dry cleaner when they're not yet supposed to exist in Russia.)

I only shock her once, when I drape an old Communist flag I bought over a wooden chair for decoration. It's as if a devout Catholic has caught me using a crucifix as an ashtray.

"I don't understand all these changes," she says. "I cried when Stalin died. Why is Communism, good for so long, now so bad?"

Katya laughs at all the tea I drink and washes plastic garbage bags instead of throwing them out. She refuses to throw anything away.

After settling in, I also begin Russian lessons. I am about to hire Maguy's teacher when I meet a young Russian I'll call Anya.

Anya, twenty-two, is fluent in French and English. She trans-lated for a colleague visiting Moscow last year. I call Anya to pass on a gift, and invite her for tea. She arrives with carnations. I end up with a new Russian teacher and friend. We start off with gram-mar and end up talking, in Russian, reading newspapers and old fairy tales. (They're a great way to learn a language and an entirely new perspective. At first, I learn more about Russian princes than comrades or gangsters. I also learn that being "too skinny' used to be associated with ugliness.) Anya's family invites me for dinner, an endless feast with fried fish, champagne, and vodka. They live in a beautiful apartment in the city center, but Anya must share her tiny room with her grandmother.

Exploring, Maguy and I scour Russian stores. In 1992, any for-eigner can be considered rich. Maguy buys a smart red wool coat, which makes her look like a Russian Madeline. Europeans flock to Slava Zaitsev, one of the top Russian designers, to buy custom-made tuxedos at cut-rate prices. (When I interview him in the spring of 1993, Zaitsev reflects Russian times with his new line of white zoot suits: an updated American gangster look.)

While the number of hard-currency stores may be growing, many goods are still unavailable. A colleague I know imports her shampoo and cosmetics. I discover it's impossible to find Chopin sheet music. Musicians near the conservatory say finding non-Russian (or Soviet) classics is almost impossible. "We photocopy what we need," one musician says.

When expats leave Moscow, they offer to take each other's mail and buy whatever is needed. One friend, Euan, brings back the *Nocturnes* for me.

I test the postal system. Some letters I write arrive respectably. One, to my Great Aunt Violet in New Jersey, arrives ripped and taped back together. Others arrive more than a year late.

Maguy and I dine at cheap Russian restaurants in the oddest places, like the basement of a pre-Revolutionary medical building. Russian fare is champagne, caviar, blinis, sturgeon (probably irradiated), and mushrooms in cream. (Picking mushrooms is a national, occasionally fatal, hobby.) There are Georgian restaurants, the grand but run-down Peking Hotel, and the only Indian restaurant, the Delhi, with its scantily clad dancers, sword swallowers, and fire eaters. Intimidating men in combat fatigues guard the entrance. They work for one of Moscow's first security firms, which capitalizes on newly unemployed (or moonlighting) KGB lifers and the fearsome Interior Ministry OMON troops.

Like many restaurants, the Delhi has two sections: ruble (cheap, for Russians) and dollar (expensive, for foreigners). As far as I can tell, there's not much difference between the two sections, except, of course, for price. In January 1994, Yeltsin issues a decree prohibiting foreign currency from circulating in Moscow. But this is the new Russia, where laws seem to apply only when convenient. Storekeepers too lazy to convert still charge in dollars or Deutsch marks, not rubles. Foreign currency exchanges sprout up in portable buses and inside hard-currency stores. Many shopkeepers continue to accept payment in dollars, though, when faced with no alternative.

When I first arrive, Moscow is safe. Under Communism, foreigners could walk anywhere anytime—streets were deserted at 3 A.M.—secure that the KGB would ensure their safety *because* they were foreigners. In 1992, that's still mainly true.

One colleague tells of a Western journalist stumbling home one drunken evening. "He had just walked another journalist to her door and was about to collapse, from too much vodka, when two Russians appeared from nowhere," the colleague says.

" 'We know you've just walked S home. Now we'll help get you home,' the two men say, and then walk the journalist to his flat—without asking where it is."

The story intrigues me. Moscow police I interview say there is still a post-Communist unit in charge of surveilling foreigners, although it's smaller than it used to be.

"Of course we're still followed and foreigners' phones are still tapped," a Western diplomat says, "although there may not be as many people listening." It's also tough to know who's listening: the Russian government, the mafiya, KGB-ers, in private biznes or not, or even the American government.

FRIENDS AND NEIGHBORS

"Don't talk to anyone in the building," Alexei said, echoing Irina and Faith as he handed me the keys to my apartment. "In an emergency, call me."

The first time I lock myself out, at night, I walk around the corner to the "sports" store, the only shop in the neighborhood, which, when it's open (sometimes it's closed, inexplicably, for weeks), sells cheap skis. The store is closed, but the area is lit. An ancient pay phone is nearby. Luckily, it works. (They often don't. The government is also short of the small coins—so cheap they're practically free—needed to operate them.) I call Alexei in a panic.

"Alexei is at the hospital with our daughter," his wife says. "I'll tell him to come over as soon as he calls." To my surprise, Alexei rushes over, concerned about my safety instead of complaining about the inconvenience.

The second time, I knock on my neighbor's door. Like many Russian women, Natasha, a pensioner in her fifties, looks older. With short gray hair, faded blue eyes, a handsome face, and sensible shoes, she spends days in lines, buying goods in state stores.

By now, I know the words *klyuch*, for key, and *dver*, for door. Natasha phones the superintendent. (I didn't know one existed. Nearby workers service buildings in the area.) A man soon arrives and saws off the lock—a source of entertainment for my neighbors. One babushka shyly offers me a chair while the sawing continues.

I think Natasha has taken it upon herself to be my guardian, of sorts. By now I am prepared for the perennial question: "But where is your husband?"

One night, Faith and I have dinner with friends of the Philadelphia refuseniks. Bella is a social scientist, Paul an engineer. They live in a tiny two-room flat, with two daughters, Sveta, fourteen, and Natasha, eight, and Bella's mother. After dinner, Sveta plays piano and sings with her mother while Natasha dances. Paul escorts me home by metro. I say it's not necessary. He insists, like most Russian men, even though it will take him an hour each way.

I take Sveta and Natasha to McDonald's, their favorite lunch spot. In early 1992, there is only one, in Pushkin Square. Twenty-seven thousand Russians applied to work there; six hundred and thirty were hired. Standing in line takes forty-five minutes. Street kids are beginning to charge to stand in line for new Russians. Old women sell chocolate. The girls have only been here once. They order everything, from burgers to fries, shakes, apple pies, and ice cream. Natasha looks green.

McDonald's is fast becoming incorporated into Moscow culture. One Canadian friend, an executive at a big firm, is taken here on a date. "I wore blue jeans and a sweater. He was in a three-piece suit," she says. (As of 1996, the two busiest McDonald's in the world are both in Moscow.)

I attend Sveta's graduation from her Jewish day school, which is relatively new for Moscow. "We're moving to California, where my uncle lives," she says not long after. "I don't want to go." A dozen of her classmates have already emigrated this year, to Israel or the United States.

"I love Russia, but I'm thankful my grandparents left. I think you'll feel the same," I say.

There are so many more opportunities now that many émigrés are returning. But I can't shake the feeling that something terrible will happen. In Russia, it always does.

Young reformers, later characterized by Alexander Rutskoi, Russia's vice president and Yeltsin's future arch-enemy, as "little boys in pink shorts," are trying to wipe out seventy years of

Communist thinking and build "democracy." They are helped by Western economists like Jeffrey Sachs and Anders Aslund. The program is spearheaded by Prime Minister Yegor Gaidar, the thirty-six-year-old, pudgy-cheeked grandson of a famous Russian children's writer and Bolshevik hero, Arkady Gaidar, and the son of a Soviet Navy rear admiral—and *Pravda* foreign correspondent.

Yegor Gaidar, a former *Pravda* columnist who wrote about economic reform before being introduced to Yeltsin's government, says he's on a suicide mission. He doesn't think he'll last three months; he just hopes he can institute some fundamental change before he is kicked out of office. Wiping out people's savings, axing state subsidies, and shutting down unproductive enterprises lead to low marks at the polls. The pace of change is intoxicating. The West is in ecstasy. "We won the Cold War!" the statesmen cry. Then they relax.

No matter how impractical, the West—and Russia—glow with euphoric optimism: This is the Beginning of Democracy/End of the Cold War era. But now hot war has already begun to ripple across the old empire. Soon it will spread to Russia itself.

And yet, the statesmen cry with authority, Russia is no longer a Threat. The West, awash in pictures of bread lines, interprets democratic convulsions as growing pains. An average monthly pension can't buy butter and sausage for a week: Basic food prices shoot up as much as 500 percent when state controls are lifted in January 1992. Invisible unemployment soon jumps to 3 million and higher, as factories try to become more efficient. Workers are forced on extended holidays and onto part-time salaries. Millions more don't receive salaries in a savage effort to stave off unemployment. By 1996, the government owes $28 billion in unpaid wages to industry, construction, transportation, and agricultural workers—who haven't been paid for up to nine months—and billions more to teachers, miners, and the military.

Grandparents—desperate on pensions so low they sell their medals for butter—who believed in Communism so strongly they refused to sign papers that would have allowed their children to begin new lives in America decades ago, are lost. Cossacks move to Moscow, while fascists—members of anti-Semitic groups like Pamyat—launch training camps for young brownshirts in the countryside. Spies, their expense accounts slashed, come in from abroad. Industrial and political espionage, nuclear sales, and drug running keep them busy and overloaded with cash they are delighted to kill for, even though the ideology they once hid behind is now dead.

Crude capitalism, created in crime, emerges in embryonic forms that replicate faster than the *Invasion of the Body Snatchers*'s pernicious pods, those Cold War propaganda symbols of the Red Menace. Imported goods and independent kiosks multiply across Moscow like mutant swamp algae.

Soon thousands of people will cram around the area outside Detsky Mir, an enormous children's department store by the infamous gray Lubyanka, the old KGB headquarters, and the juxtaposed ritz of the Savoy Hotel and its sign excluding "non-guests." You have to fight your way through the capitalist chaos: scores of street vendors display their entire stock of merchandise draped over their outstretched arms, in bags, or at their feet—sweaters, lightbulbs, toilet seats, mismatched nuts and bolts, ancient-looking toothpaste tubes. The impromptu capitalist insurgency is eventually disbanded by police.

The Russians call it *dikiy kapitalism*: wild, primitive capitalism. The first capitalists were Communist criminals, even if their business would have been legal in the West. The second phase of post-Soviet capitalism centers on looting the state, racketeering and profiting from Communism's collapse—smuggling goods through the old empire's porous borders. Business executives say that bribing corrupt officials—and paying protection money—is just another expense no one writes off, since cheating, or ignoring, Russia's new taxman is now a national hobby.

Gleefully, maliciously, cynically, helplessly filled with despair and frustration, Russians have transformed the word for privatization, *privatizatsiya*, into *prikhvatisatsiya*, which means grabbing. Privatization becomes a way for managers of state-run industries to become private owners of the same industries. Some economists say that this is natural, that America's first captains of industry also began as robber barons.

Russia's new rich, terrified of bombings and kidnappings and sheltered by armed guards in bulletproof homes and cars, will soon send their wives to London and their sons to Oxford. New-rich aspirations for their daughters will end in marriage to children of biznes associates. This is how, some economists say, the new rich will legitimize themselves and the new market. Still others say the new rich are building their castles outside Russia and the inevitable outcome will be a return to iron rule—or anarchy.

But in these early days, the glory days, of post-Soviet euphoria, nobody mentions fascism, anarchy, or totalitarian rule, the kind of Pinochet-style government soon talked about by entities as diverse as anti-Semitic, ultra-nationalist KGB generals and Jewish intellectuals who'd be the first to go under any such regime.

Comparing Russia and the Weimar Republic is taboo. Democracy is the natural outcome, the logical outcome of the Communist collapse. The Reds have been saved by the God of Money and (for the haves) Financial Freedom and Liberty, in the minds of the Bush-Clinton suits.

America is so easy to fool, Russian politicians chuckle. All Yeltsin has to do is appear to have shattered the dreaded KGB by slicing it up, and shifting and renaming its parts, which will grow back spontaneously. Between drinks, Yeltsin waves the red, white, and blue flag of the Russian Federation and makes himself, and his team, occasionally available to Uncle Sam's advisers. The West seems to buy it all.

My knowledge of this is limited when I arrive. In my three weeks of Russian lessons before moving here, I learned that Russian textbooks call Lenin "Uncle Lenin," that Russians drink kvas at kiosks —and everyone uses the same glass. I knew friends who traded ski jackets and old jeans for cartons of caviar.

By the time I arrive, kvas has been replaced by Pepsi and Coca-Cola. Russians stopped wanting your old clothes when merchants began traveling to Beijing for ten-dollar ski jackets.

GETTING ORIENTED WITH THE *MOSCOW TIMES*

I continue to explore. Strangers scold if I sit on concrete while waiting for the bus. ("You'll catch a cold!") A babushka puts her gloves on a mittenless child and scowls at the mother.

I drop by the English-language weekly *Moscow Times*. Called from Toronto, editors told me they hire only Russian speakers. I'm assigned one piece, then three.

The *MT* is about to go biweekly, then daily. The Independent Press, under the brilliant, sharp eye of Derk Sauer—a teenage Dutch Communist turned magazine editor-in-chief, and now publishing magnate—launched the *Moscow Times*. Sauer's empire will soon include Russia's *Cosmopolitan, Good Housekeeping, Playboy, Harper's Bazaar*, and more.

Editor Michael Hetzer says that the publisher wants to meet me. We enter his office, which is filled with eclectic Russian art. A small, trim man with round glasses sits relaxed and confident behind a desk. I realize I brushed by him once when he was making photocopies in a long, narrow hall where some Russian drivers lounge, smoking foul-smelling cigarettes. I rushed by, asking where the editor was, thinking Derk—who looks so young and is dressed so casually—was a copy boy.

Today Derk is just as casual, speaking English with a somewhat harsh accent. We talk about some story ideas. Skipping the small talk, Derk then mentions a salary figure. "What?" says Michael, who has already said they're not hiring. "Are you offering her a job?"

The week I begin, the paper moves from a dilapidated building in Kitai Gorod, or China Town, the main downtown area of old Communist Party buildings, to the marble-floored Radisson-Slavjanskaya Hotel (the Slav) by the Kievsky Metro.

Soon my new driver, Valery, picks me up each morning in his run-down orange Jhiguli. We travel bumpy roads alongside the Moscow River, and I get happy just watching old men cast their lines in the smelly river water, hoping for oil-coated slime fish. As the car pulls up to the hotel, to be met by a red-caped, fur-hatted doorman, I can't believe my luck. I glide across marble floors listening to the Slav's white-haired Gershwin- and Chopin-playing pianists. My days of riding the metro, trekking for hours knee-deep in snow, are history. I now have a full-time newspaper job, complete with up-to-date office, computer, translator, driver, photographer, library, and any other backup I could ever want.

It's an exciting time to be at the paper. The *MT* is *the* English paper for expats, diplomats, journalists, business executives, and Russian officials. There's a real sense of growth, of covering Moscow as a city where we live in such a historic time, instead of reporting from a foreign capital for an export readership.

I am excited to be able to witness, report, write, to cover "the Story." The *MT* is filled with young journalists from North America, Europe, and Russia. It's sort of like college all over again. There is even a competitive spirit with the *Moscow Guardian*. Soon another English daily, the *Moscow Tribune*, starts up. *MT* "graduates" can now be found everywhere from the *Wall Street Journal* and *Newsweek* to the *Sunday Times*.

At first the staff is so small that everyone participates in editorial meetings. Sometimes a group of us will cover the red-brown demonstrations, which occur almost every Sunday: old people with red flags who look archaic until they are joined by unemployed young hoods in black boots who reek of vodka.

I cover the first Communist Party Congress since the Party was banned by Yeltsin in 1991, and meet Vladimir Zhirinovsky. (He is described as a clown: an unknown lawyer from Kazakhstan who came in third—behind Yeltsin, who received 57 percent of the vote, and Nikolai Ryzhkov, the former Soviet prime minister sacked by Gorbachev—in the June 1991 presidential elections.

The outlawed Communists[*] are afraid the police may break up the meeting, so they ask journalists to be at the Hotel Moskva at 6 A.M. (The hotel, by Red Square, has two odd-shaped wings. Legend has it that the architect drew two different designs and Stalin, by mistake, approved both. Terrified of displeasing him, the architect incorporated both into his plan.) Hours later, the foreigners are instructed to follow Communist Party buses to a secret meeting place outside Moscow.

But the procession is stopped by police. In 1992, journalists are still required to give the Foreign Ministry notice when planning trips outside Moscow.

---

* Yeltsin formerly disbanded the Communist Party of the Soviet Union and nationalized their property in November 1991. In 1993, the constitutional court partially rescinds Yeltsin's actions. By then, "successor groups" are firmly established, party members have "re-registered," and local branches resume their activities. This is easier to do than in Eastern Europe because there is no Communist witch-hunt following the collapse of the Soviet Union, or anything that resembles post-World War II Germany's de-Nazification process: In post-Communist Russia, many of the top Communist brass remain in positions of power.

We are in a restricted zone, police say. The convoy breaks up. Lines of cars with foreign plates go from village to village, searching for the congress. Zhirinovsky, decked in army green and out with a bullhorn, is also lost. I'm terrified I've screwed up until I realize that so has almost every other foreign correspondent. Our procession finally reaches the congress. The local government has turned off the electricity. A generator from a car battery gives some light. The nightly news shows a comedy of cars lost in the country trying to get to a congress that barely happens.

Back at the Slav, some colleagues and I dine at one of Moscow's first salad bars (which soon triples in price). Russians didn't grow lettuce until McDonald's showed them how. The Slav also has some of Moscow's first designer stores, a steak house, and a health club (where I swim). Soon, there will also be an international press club, squeezed into a spot originally meant for a tacky type of disco, and a twenty-four-hour restaurant, which looks like an outdoor patio transplanted indoors. The only "democratic" aspect is its nonexclusivity. Fugitive from justice? Dealer in murky biznes? All are welcome. The only requirement is money, or anything of material value, including, for many woman, their Selves. (One of the hotel gym's evening staff sports unusual health club attire: thigh-high gold lamé boots.)

The Slav's main floor lounge is always packed with loud Americans just this close to clinching that fifty-million-dollar deal. Sometimes I see politicians, including the late Richard Nixon, Gary Hart, former U.S. Secretary of State Alexander Haig, alleged arms dealers, even President Clinton. I see scammers, con men, and other fugitives, including billionaire oil-dealing tax evaders, a sports-team owner once arrested on a team tour to America for not paying child support, and a radio personality facing U.S. fraud charges.

For a time, it is also home to American-based groups such as the Center for Democracy, which is supposed to be nongovernmental, unbiased, giving support to *all* who favor democracy. A press release boasts it helped keep Yeltsin's team in communication with the world during the 1991 attempted coup. Silly me, I thought it was the CIA.

The first time I interview KGB Colonel Oleg Kalugin at the Slav, he can't help but laugh. That's before he writes his book, hawks his spycatching computer game and plunges into the high-paying world of the international lecture circuit.

"I see so many familiar faces here," he says, referring to the Arabic-, French-, and English-speaking doormen and other "invisible" hotel workers who may still keep tabs on Western firms, news agencies, and international organizations with offices here. The French still bug and rifle through hotel rooms. Why would the Russians have stopped? The hotel is a dance between Americans, here to make money and "help," "spin," "control," "monitor," Russia's "democratic progress" and Russians, here to "work with," "learn from," "keep an eye on," their "former" enemy-turned-democratic-mentor.

Newspapers and televisions overflow with the "firsts" of capitalism. I decide, instead, to focus on the market economy's underbelly: those who have fallen through the cracks—democracy's disenfranchised. Freedoms gained also include the new "right" to be homeless, hungry, sick, unemployed—and no longer the moral or practical responsibility of the Benevolent State.

I focus on children, the homeless, and refugees, as well as women jailed for economic crimes that no longer exist and men in jail for "crimes" like homosexuality. I visit convicted killers on death row who are uncertain of their status in democracy. I examine Russia's (nonexistent) rehabilitation system and visit AIDS patients, some of whom say they unknowingly, or unwillingly, took unapproved and experimental drugs due to a lack of government regulation. (Some say they were told they could only stay at the hospital if they cooperated in the experimental programs.) I call it social welfare reporting.

CHAPTER 3

Pioneer Capitalist Women in Prison, Street Kids in Train Stations, Psych Wards and Labor Camps

"Don't your boys often run away?"

"Hardly ever," said Brink... "Where shall they run to? Here it is bad. At home it is worse. The majority of them know that."

"But isn't there a natural instinct for freedom?"

"Yes, you are right. But the boys soon lose it. The system helps them to lose it...." Brink sighed deeply: "Sometimes I almost despair," he added. "It seems as if there were a kind of badness, a disease, infecting the world today."

— CHRISTOPHER ISHERWOOD, *Goodbye to Berlin*

Dzherzinsky, March 1992: The male guard at the all-women's prison keeps my documents, then buzzes me in. The gloomy corridor, coated in cracking pale gray paint, opens to a frosty courtyard. Hundreds of women in blue prison uniforms crunch through snow. Three link arms and sing, thick legs in brown scratchy tights, scarves wrapped tight around their heads. The melody is haunting and defiant, like a centuries-old Russian version of the blues.

I walk up the crumbling stairs of an old building. A portrait of the still ubiquitous Lenin surveys the cold, stark room. A stern-looking woman, with bright orange hair drawn back into a nasty little bun, greets me. Her heavy frame bulges out of a tight, rough khaki shirt and belted jacket, revealing too many pouches and folds of potato-fed skin. It is her feet, though, that throw me. Thick ankles, tree-stump legs totter on shiny, high-heeled black boots, so incongruous for a prison setting, for a woman so otherwise devoid of femininity.

"This should keep you busy," she says, tossing me a thick file of dossiers, which include black-and-white mug shots of babushkas. They are some of the Colony of Ordinary Regime No. 5's eight hundred inmates.

One picture is of Alevtina Gulyolova, a thick-faced fifty-one-year-old grandmother who, in 1986, was caught selling ten pairs of Yugoslavian underwear, among other goods. Her profit, which she says was to help send her daughters to Communist "Pioneer" summer camp, was sixty rubles, then worth about ninety-seven dollars. For that and similar deals, she was convicted of speculation —buying and selling goods for profit—and sentenced to seven and a half years in jail.

The prison woman leads me back outside, to a small, one-story building. Inside is a Potemkin* showroom, prisoner-drawn friezes on pristine, peeling walls. The room crawls with painted vines, desperate for escape, a lonely plant or two, and the sound of chirping birds. It is here, in the "relaxation" room of the psychiatric building, that I meet Gulyolova and others, stuck in a time warp. Trapped like characters in a Milan Kundera novel, they are serving time for crimes that no longer exist.

The prisoners sit at a bare wooden table. Their hair, pulled tightly back, frames red, raw faces as freshly scrubbed as the barren floor.

"They don't think about us," says Gulyolova, a substantial woman with a proud, lined face, jet black hair, dyed, maybe, and bright pink lips that smack of rebellion. "Nobody cares that we're still sitting here."

Since Gulyolova, an ambulance dispatcher, was put behind bars, Yeltsin has issued a decree legalizing most private trade. Streets are flooded with Russians doing what Gulyolova did. Only now the

---

* Prince Potemkin constructed fake villages to cover up widespread poverty during Catherine the Great's visit to Ukraine and the Crimea in 1787. Since then, Potemkin villages have come to mean any type of elaborate facade to cover up or divert attention from embarrassingly shabby places.

primitive peddlers are praised, while Gulyolova, a pioneering per-estroika-era entrepreneur, a capitalist visionary, is still in prison.

"I've heard about the changes outside through letters from my daughters," says Gulyolova. But if democracy and Coca-Cola really have come to Russia, why is Gulyolova—along with 27,000 Russians like her—still in jail?

"The common people are in jail for commerce that is done on every street corner," cries Gulyolova. About twenty women in Prison No. 5 are in the same position. Knowing that their crimes are now legal—and that they will no longer recognize the world outside—makes incarceration even more painful.

"It's very upsetting for them to watch television and read letters," says Deputy Prison Director Lydia Pustavoit. "They understand what's going on. Personally, I think that if you give people freedom, you should make steps toward it here too. I feel sorry for them, but there's nothing we can do. We listen and send their petitions. That's all."

At the time of my reporting, Yeltsin has appointed a commission to "investigate." Some staunch old Communists say the prisoners should serve out their sentences. Others, like Alexander Yakovlev, a legal specialist at the Institute of Law and Government, say prisoners jailed for crimes that are now legal should be freed immediately. "Keeping them in jail is a direct violation of law," he says.

Other stories are similar to Gulyolova's. In 1990, Tamara Tyatenkova, fifty-one, was sentenced to six years in jail for selling three pairs of boots she bought at a state store. "A woman I sold to betrayed me," she says. Tyatenkova's sentence, for speculation, was recently reduced to three years.

She still can't believe she's in jail for a crime that is now legal. "I was sent a letter saying everybody is selling openly—and the police are even guarding and protecting them," she says, amazed.

The police confiscated Tyatenkova's apartment and possessions, as they do with most convicts. "They treat us the same as killers," Tyatenkova complains. "Isn't there a difference between killing a person and selling boots?"

Although this was Tyatenkova's first clash with police, Gulyolova, her prison file notes, had been warned by police a year before her arrest.

"I went to sell goods at the market. But I didn't give any money to the police, so they arrested me," says Gulyolova, her voice rising, three gold teeth shining.

Only one of the women I interview seems to be in for a more sophisticated level of biznes. Irina Gulyaeva, forty-two, is serving nine and a half years for violating speculation and hard-currency laws. Gulyaeva, a stocky blonde prone to nervous shaking, has red-rimmed, tear-stained, and swollen, faded blue eyes. Her mug shot, of a thinner, younger face, looks like a different woman. Gulyaeva used to be an Aeroflot stewardess, an elite job that gave her access to foreign travel and Westerners.

A KGB investigation led to charges that Gulyaeva was buying hard currency from other stewardesses and buying and selling cars and other goods for a total profit of 89,312 rubles, earned between 1977 and 1985.

In the fall of 1991, Gulyaeva was allowed to visit her sister in Moscow. It was part of a national experiment to give prisoners in six prison colonies a twelve-day "vacation" each year.

"It was hard to see everything so new," Gulyaeva says. "I was so confused. So many years weren't free." Now, she says, living in prison is "just a big gap. Maybe something like fog."

Pustavoit, the deputy prison director, says she supported Gulyaeva's petition for release, but the prison has yet to get a response from an October 1991 appeal. "Of course I feel uneasy in front of them," Pustavoit says. "We speak with lawyers and deputies to speed up the legislation, but we personally can't set people free. I don't know why they just don't make new laws."

For women like Gulyaeva and Gulyolova, getting screwed by the system doesn't change, even when ideology does. Capitalist mentality under a Communist system landed them in jail; ingrained Communist thinking in a newborn pseudo-democracy keeps them there. But the women have made one vow: No system will crush them.

"A lot of families have been broken here," Gulyolova says, pink lips shining. "But I will fight for complete rehabilitation until the end of my life."

On the long drive back to Moscow, I think about others who have fallen through the cracks. Mainly, I think about children. I think about the newsboys—dirty faces, tattered clothes—I see every day, trying to sell papers by the metro near the Slav. They remind me of the smudge-cheeked boys in checkered caps from old black-and-white prewar films. I think about the kids who run up to cars, rubbing dirty windshields with filthy rags, selling atlases or sodas, washing cars, and filling tanks with siphoned gas, and the other kids permanently lined up at McDonald's. Some of them are runaways, caught in a vicious cycle of abuse, in their homes, orphanages, and mafiya "families."

This new generation of Russian children has already lost its youth to the grasping hands of Money. In 1992, whatever little help the state offers is losing its value through inflation. Young people in school often quit, without telling their parents, attracted by the promises of capitalism. Teenage army recruits are often killed in vicious hazing rites, or die from starvation.

Children were once the pride of the empire. Under the stern gaze of Felix Dzherzhinsky—founder of the Soviet Secret Service, first known as the Cheka, which became the KGB—the orphan became the ideal symbol of the international socialist revolution: the child of the state. Schools were set up to care for Children of the Revolution. But by 1992, after the end of the Second Revolution, children have fallen through whatever social net used to exist.

More than one hundred thousand children from across the old empire now live on Moscow streets, says Yekaterina Lakhova, who advises Yeltsin on children.

There are no social services to help these children. Social work wasn't even a recognized profession in the FSU until 1991. By the spring of 1992, when I begin this reporting, there are still no social workers on the streets or inside the broken homes and abusive orphanages.

Children are even worse off later. With adults unable to live on their salaries and threatening to strike, the state is too preoccupied to help the powerless children whose voices are unheard—for the time being.

Life in the new Russia is so uncertain that women are having fewer children. Teenage suicide is up. So are alcohol-related deaths. Life expectancy has fallen by close to five years since 1991: down to fifty-eight years for men and seventy-two years for females in 1996, according to Russian government statistics obtained by the World Bank. (In the United States, for comparison, life expectancy is seventy-two years for men and seventy-nine years for women.) The death rate has surpassed the birth rate for the first time since World War II. The number of runaways is soaring. Violence in schools has jumped as radically as attendance has declined. If fascism is an excrescence rooted in poverty, humiliation, anger, and defeat, these children are a perfect breeding ground.

TSARS OF THE TRACKS: MISHA'S GANG; SERGEI, KING OF THE VIDEOS

Kazansky Train Station
Late evening, April 1992. Long after thousands of commuters have shuffled home, a new kind of customer emerges: the dispossessed. Fifteen-year-olds, soldiers, homeless, drunks, and runaways play the slot machines at the far end of the train station.

Some of the runaways are as young as four years old, though they never seem to be around when you look for them. Suddenly, I see two children, like ghosts, maybe four, six years old. One tiny, scrawny creature is clad in a filthy white shift. His hair is shorn to the skull, face and body covered with scabs and bumps: abuse, poor hygiene, malnutrition? They see me coming and run, fading into crevices, masters of an underground network, too fast for my seemingly ancient legs.

It is after midnight. I am with Kolya, my Arabic-speaking translator and colleague, who is also an editor, columnist, biznesman, and art specialist.

We hang out in so many different stations, meeting homeless families and runaways, that I'm beginning to know the personality of each place. Paveletsky, for example, is for families. Kazansky is the worst. (By 1996, the station has undergone an astounding transformation, extensive renovations courtesy of Mayor Luzhkov. The other train stations are next in line.)

We move to the food stand. There's a line for alcohol: old men and bearded young homeless men. Teenage gang members with their leader, a lean girl with thick black eyeliner, stand around one table. (There is nowhere to sit.)

I offer to buy some meat patties for Misha, twelve, whom we've just met. Kolya insists on paying. "These are my people," he says, far from his usual cynicism.

Misha is filthy. Blond, matted hair sticks to his head. His blue eyes are swift. He is a natural charmer, a scammer, a survivor. After some encouragement, he induces some friends to come out of hiding.

Tableau #1:

An old drunk sits near us, silently, on an overturned crate. Suddenly, the pack of boys, led by Misha, moves in. Three, four, then six boys, no older than twelve. At first, they circle edgily, wearily. Then they close in. The boys taunt the man, mocking him for the bottle he depends on. Without warning, the taunts turn to light kicks. Nervous laughter seeps in. Kolya and I intervene. The boys stop giggling, fearless, maybe, only in situations they can control. The old man remains as expressionless as ever. Silently, he slips away.

Street children live in these stations, in railway sleeper cars, nearby abandoned buildings, and shabby flats run by drug-dealing pimps. Under Communism, police arrested wanderers without residence permits and placed them in jails or shelters. Now they are mainly left on their own. And their numbers are growing.

Some days, Kolya and I target three main train stations, Leningradsky, Yaroslavsky, and Kazansky, which we visit during the early mornings and at night. (The kids often sleep in the day.) From the stations, I track the life cycle of these children. Too often, it's a vicious circle.

Thousands of Russians pass through these commuting stations, which give them the impression of a powerful, throbbing city.

We walk up one station's stairs, by rows of kiosks, through the dimly lit interior, down more stairs by the child ice-cream sellers.

"Come back later," whispers one young seller, motioning toward a group of men in their twenties who joke with some corrupt cops, in for a cut, nearby. The men, clad in mean leather jackets, eye us suspiciously. They are the children's keepers.

We continue our journey. Out on the streets, by cars unloading passengers with heavy cartons, back upstairs, onto the tracks, by the big old clock; another station and back again.

We chat with a ten-year-old newspaper boy selling *Argumenti i Fakti*, a Communist-era newspaper which has seen its circulation plummet from twenty-five million to four million in the past few years. It's a beautiful spring day, still cold enough for a wool jacket, but now warm enough to leave it unbuttoned. I finally see the sun.

Tableau #2:

> *Suddenly, an old man, face unshaven, gray hair limp, suit jacket threadbare, approaches. He carries a single long-stemmed red carnation, which he graciously hands me with a royal Shakespearean flourish, almost a bow.*
>
> *"Please," he says. "I don't want you to think that all Russians are like this."*
>
> *His hand extends symbolically, to the beer and the news-boys, the brown leather jackets and biznesmeni, commuters, old ladies, thugs, and drunks. Dostoyevsky as interpreted by Fellini.*

Not long after, I meet Sergei Glinia, fifteen: an angel's face with a scabby head crawling with lice. Round cigarette burns mark his body.

I find Sergei shortly after dawn. He is sitting at a small wooden table, smoking, red-eyed from lack of sleep and selling five-ruble tokens for the station's video machines to drunks and night prowlers. It's like a scene from Pinocchio's underworld. This is his job, between midnight and 7 A.M.

"I live here with my friends, my *family*," says Sergei.

By day, Sergei is outside, selling ice cream and beer. Most of the money he earns—about 1,000 rubles a day—goes to a mafiya gang. The 100 rubles he's allowed to keep goes quickly: 35 rubles to sleep in a filthy train compartment with about 25 other children and 30 adults; 30 rubles for a breakfast of coffee and kasha. "The rest," he says, "is for clothes, cigarettes, and more food. I've been living this way for five years."

Once, when Kolya can't make it, I take another translator with me. "Galya," twenty-four, who speaks fluent English and French, educated at a top language institute, doesn't believe we'll find any homeless.

"We don't have homeless people," she says, her usually good-natured voice rising in a frosty, condescending huff. "I've seen the television footage of homeless people in New York. We don't have anything like that here."

The new underclass—which includes the runaways and begging women who kneel in classical poses for hours at a time—has not yet captured the media's attention. One old woman, whose eyes don't leave the ground, waits patiently outside a new McDonald's on the Old Arbat. As two young men with short hair and European-cut suits and trench coats walk out, they toss her ruble notes without looking, like royals with gold coins. They don't even see her cross herself dramatically and bless them like the mother of God. Soon a middle-aged woman walks by, a member of the now radically underprivileged intelligentsia. She presses crumpled notes into the old woman's hand and then she, too, looks away.

The old people, who sacrificed so much, expected—if they survived the wars and purges—to be taken care of by the state. The children expect less. In post-Soviet Russia, there are even more ways for children to fall through the cracks. The pattern often goes as follows.

THE INTERNAT

When children are orphaned, or when parents are unfit or don't want their offspring, the children are sent to orphanages, called *internats*. Some are for children with special needs.

But Russia's social service network is so overstrained that healthy children are often shuffled into special orphanages with genuinely ill children. It's so bad that Westerners who want to adopt Russian babies often go to the special internats. Russian law doesn't permit foreigners to adopt healthy children, so they find in the special internats these misplaced children whom Western doctors can diagnose as healthy.

For children who remain, their lives in the internats are often filled with brutal beatings from teachers and older children. The next step for children in the orphanages is often the special-treatment psychiatric facilities—whether the children need them or not.

At the *MT*, I write about healthy orphans who are abused in special-needs internats and sent to psychiatric institutions, where they can be drugged and tied to their beds for months as a form of punishment, just as political prisoners—"ideological enemies" of Communism—were once confined.

Pasha, a tough-talking fourteen-year-old with James Dean good looks, is one such child. I meet him at Internat No. 98, for children with "mild disabilities," although the children I meet don't seem to have any disabilities at all.

Internat No. 98 is a large, rambling building in a residential area on Novospassky Pereulok. Some of its lime green-, pink-, and acid-yellow-colored walls are filled with bright paintings. It even has a small pet room with caged rats, rabbits, and a fox. But the paint is cracked, the water cold, and some of the children have eyes that cry of neglect. Police say they regularly receive reports charging teachers with abusing children and stealing everything from international humanitarian aid to furniture and rugs—even butter and kitchen supplies.

Pasha's life is like a post-perestroika nightmare by way of Charles Dickens. With eerie matter-of-factness, he describes beatings, trips to psychiatric hospitals, and mysterious injections that leave him in vegetable-like states for days.

Sitting on his stark cot covered with a worn burgundy blanket, Pasha, in a small, steady voice, tells stories of random violence. He explains how teachers used to beat him for being late. "I spent a full summer in a psychiatric hospital," he says, "and I still don't know why."

Pasha's friend, Slava, stares into space as he describes a beating by classmates that put him in the hospital. "The teachers knew, but they were too afraid to do anything," he says. An eleven-year-old girl describes in a monotone how older teens killed her adopted cats and threw them out the window.

Ten out of twelve orphans I interview have each spent between four months and two years in psychiatric hospitals. Some say they were sent there after they were accused of crimes like stealing. One orphan says he was sent to a hospital for four months after he told the director of his internat that he saw a teacher stealing food. During my investigation, I meet dozens of teachers, social workers, orphans, government officials, and police who have documented such cases.

"As soon as you break a rule they send you there," says Pasha.

"These are the kids [the orphanage] administration wasn't happy with," says Valery Semyonov, head of the Defense of the Rights of Children, a nonprofit Moscow group that works out of city hall.

"Children lose all rights once they enter the internats," says Semyonov, a shy, slight twenty-three-year-old who was also abused in an orphanage when he was a child. "Younger children are often abused—physically, psychologically, and sexually—by older children as well as teachers.

"When they try to protest something, they are sent to the psychiatric hospitals," he adds. The number of children in the psychiatric hospitals also increases in summer, when the orphanages close down. If the Pioneer camps, where children are supposed to be sent, are full, "troublesome" children are often sent to psychiatric hospitals instead.

In an interview in her office, Svetlana Tasich, director of Internat No. 98, denies such claims.

"Of course the children say they don't belong in the hospitals. It's because they're ashamed that they're there," says Tasich, an imposing, dark-haired woman.

"It's impossible for healthy children to be sent to psychiatric hospitals because the teacher's decision to send a child must be approved by myself and a doctor," she adds.

"But how can the doctors know you're good if they [the teachers] say you're bad?" asks Slava, fourteen. "You're diagnosed as strange because you're so nervous. Then you get to the hospital and they just give you pills."

The consequences of such treatment are lifelong. Some children commit suicide. Others run away. Still more perpetuate the violence they grew up in—both within and outside the orphanage system. One dissident teacher says that some older students become "personal bodyguards" for teachers, replicating the mafiya system outside.

I visit the orphanage a few times, once with Alexei, a recent alumnus who says he was beaten on the head by a teacher and shows me the scars to prove it. Alexei, seventeen, is now looking for a job. He also wants to help reform the internat system. My next challenge will be to get into one of the psychiatric hospitals.

* * *

Vitaly Ilynin, the grandfatherly, white-haired director of Psychiatric Hospital No. 15, with its 240-bed teenage unit, finally agrees to an interview. I am surprised by how forthcoming he is.

"All of the children are here because they need to be," he says, adding, however, that not all are seriously ill.

The orphans are treated for disorders ranging from epilepsy and schizophrenia to stress and suicide attempts. Yet Ilynin, a typical Russian functionary who works with a portrait of Karl Marx over his desk and a Polaroid of Boris Yeltsin on his bookcase, admits that some children are sent here for "other reasons."

"Some children are sent here because they're too hot-tempered and get into too many fights," he says.

Instead of receiving counseling, these children are given tranquilizers and antidepressants like chlorpromazine, an antipsychotic medication.

In the ward's recreation room, fifteen boys in blue hospital uniforms line wooden benches. They blankly stare at flickering images on a television screen, filtered through a drug-induced stupor. It's as if they're in a deep collective trance, a state of perpetual slow motion. One gets up, walks toward me and then past me in aimless, eerie silence. The director brusquely guides him back to one of the benches.

One thirteen-year-old orphan, who spent two four-month periods in a psychiatric hospital, says he was told that the hospital visits would cure his "disease," although he was not told what the disease was.

"When you want to play, they just inject you with something to make you sleep," he says. "You can't run away, because you're naked. You're like an imbecile, totally drugged."

Children at the hospital say they are terrified of some of the staff as well as older children, who torment and abuse them.

And despite hospital promises, children here are rarely "cured." Once an orphan is sent to Internat No. 98 and stigmatized as "special," it is difficult to escape the confines and the diagnosis. In 1992, about 20,000 orphans live in the Moscow area, including 1,800 diagnosed with "mild" disabilities. Semyonov believes that at least 65 percent of these children belong in mainstream schools.

Yet Tasich, the orphanage director, says that only a handful of her 170 students are mainstreamed each year.

The rest are drilled to believe they will never fit into society. At best, they are groomed for working-class jobs: Rarely are they encouraged to continue their education.

"They always think we're not intelligent," says Alexei, the recent graduate of Internat No. 98.

Some of the internat's teachers, though, do want to see change.

One night, crammed into a room in a tiny apartment so crowded there is no place to move, I meet a group of such teachers. An old woman with long gray hair and no teeth brings me a cup of warm tea.

"Most teachers consider assignments at the special internats to be demotions," says one teacher, who withholds her name for fear of losing her job.

"Anyone who tries to reform the system is either fired or moved to another school," adds another teacher.

I leave impressed with their concern, but frustrated with their helplessness. The babushka thrusts a macramé owl that she made into my hands as I leave.

At the time of my reporting, authorities are investigating complaints by some elected Moscow city officials that some teachers at Internat No. 98 are "cruel and neglectful" to children, keeping them in unsanitary conditions and stealing from them. I learn this from the assistant to the local prosecutor. Among the accusations: physical, sexual, and mental abuse; sending healthy children to psychiatric hospitals; pouring cold water on children; and depriving them of meals.

"This system brings children up with physical violence," says one dissident teacher. "The administration uses violence on the younger children and the seniors do the same."

"My teachers are not abusive," Tasich says. "But some older children have abused the younger ones." Incidents include a recent graduate returning to attack a young girl and another terrorizing some children with a knife.

In 1991, twenty-five Moscow area teachers were fired for misconduct and at least thirteen teachers were charged with stealing everything from children's private property to orphanage furniture, Semyonov says.

KIDNAPPED! DMITRI'S SOLUTION

One mad day in 1990, Dmitri Karpov, then twenty-six, quit his job teaching at Internat No. 8, an orphanage for children with mild disabilities. But when he quit, he took some of the internat's key elements: ten small children.

"I kidnapped them," says Karpov, who looks rather grandfatherly with his cable-knit fisherman's sweater, bushy beard, and tall, burly physique. "I wanted them to escape a system of perpetual violence."

For the next two years, Karpov was on the run, living on charity and almost single-handedly raising and teaching the children from his one-room apartment. He then moved with them to a dacha outside Moscow.

In a daring, Kafkaesque move, Karpov says he outsmarted the police and beat the system by simply removing the kids' files. Bureaucracy was now on his side.

"I had taken the kids' files, so they weren't registered anywhere," Karpov says. "Officially, they didn't exist. There was a vacuum around them. If the police came and said, 'Give me Natasha,' I could say the girl was Olga. Eventually they said, 'Okay, you'll return them yourself when you get tired of taking care of them.' "

Karpov never did. In the fall of 1991, he moved with the children into four rooms at the Izmailovsky Hotel, near a well-known park and weekend artists' market. The hotel director provides Karpov and the children with free meals and lodging. In return, the children work for two hours each day, doing chores like helping in the kitchen.

I interview Karpov at the hotel, in his small, spotless room, decorated only with an icon of the Madonna and Child. The children rush to gather around him as he explains the problems he encountered with the internat system.

"The main problem is the teachers," Karpov says. "Most of them are lost souls who couldn't find themselves in life. They were broken, not normal themselves, and very often sexually perverted."

Again I hear that children the staff couldn't handle were often sent to the psychiatric hospitals where "the doctors would inject them with drugs that are usually used on criminals. They couldn't walk or move for three days."

Sergei Alexander, thirteen, who spent one full year and another two three-month stretches in a psychiatric hospital, says he's "nearly forgotten" the episodes, as if they were just "bad dreams."

"Now it's completely different," he says with a big smile. "There, we couldn't have a place for ourselves. Here we can study and learn to make sweet cakes in the kitchen."

By the time I meet Karpov, in April 1992, the Moscow government has decided to grant him permission—and funds—to establish a small, alternative orphanage.

"We just had to register the kids," says Valentina Rodenka, director of children's social services for the city.

THE RUNAWAYS

The main places they head for are the train stations. Children like Sergei Glinia say they are fast welcomed into a new "family," with their own initiation rules.

"First," says Sergei shyly, "the older teenagers strip us. They take our money and whatever possessions we have. Then they give us new clothes."

The young runaways are then in the gang's debt. Many are or become addicted to alcohol, narcotics, and/or nicotine. To earn their keep, the runaways do everything from selling gasoline and ice cream to prostitution.

Some of the child prostitutes are six years old or younger, say Russian doctors who treat them. The children are so well guarded by the gangs that their stories rarely make it to print. *Time* magazine once ran a large "investigative" story that included photographs of such children. But the photographs—taken by a Russian teenager—turned out to be fake.

Police are supposed to patrol the stations, on the lookout for runaways who work for organized crime gangs. But the police are too often on the gangs' payrolls themselves.

Far from the railways, outside the Nefto Agip gas station on Leningradsky Prospekt, Dima Buzdanov, thirteen, and Roman

Simiontovsky, ten, work part-time for the gangs, along with twenty-five other children. The kids cut class to make money, but still live at home.

In May 1992, Dima and Roman say they make two hundred rubles a day wiping windshields, while older teens earn up to four thousand rubles a day—at a time when the average salary is fifteen hundred rubles a month—filling gas tanks and washing cars around the corner from the gas station. This year, gas stations are often closed or besieged by long lines of impatient drivers. Black market gasoline is a popular alternative, even if the quality is questionable.

Dima and Roman pay twenty rubles for every one hundred rubles they earn to the local "tax collector," seventeen-year-old Sasha, who, in turn, gives most of the money to middle-aged leaders of the local mafiya.

"It's dangerous biznes," says the tight-lipped Sasha, a small, Winston chain-smoker with scared blue eyes and a new leather jacket. An entourage of aspiring young hoods shuffles behind him.

Taxes are enforced with threats, knives, and guns. "Everyone pays," says Sasha. "Last year, when the biznes was just taking off, there was a shoot-out at the gas station between us and the gas-station workers." (Sasha's gang won.)

Back at the Yaroslavsky train station, I meet Volodya, a friend of Sergei Glinia. Caked in dirt, Volodya, thirteen, is so malnourished he looks much younger. But his eyes are ancient.

Volodya washes cars on a main thoroughfare for the station's gang. According to Sergei, he is also a prostitute. I ask around the topic but Volodya is uncomfortable. I'm not going to push.

Volodya and Sergei come from small towns outside Moscow. They both lived in special internats.

When asked about his family, Volodya looks down at the ground, reluctant to talk. Sergei plays tough and shrugs.

"My mother sent me and my two sisters to an orphanage. She couldn't afford to take care of us," he says. "Sometimes I visit her and my stepfather." (He hasn't seen his father since he was two years old.)

As for his mother, he says, "She knows I'm not hungry and I'm making good money. Sometimes I give her half."

But Sergei always comes back to the railways. It is the gang—not parents—who are referred to as family.

Both Sergei and Volodya shrug off the violent aspect of their lifestyle. "The station is safe," Sergei says. "The bosses are my friends."

Still, he admits, he's had "some trouble" with the family. "Once," he says, "my own company accused me of stealing. But I paid fifty extra rubles and the incident was forgotten."

Yet for the past few weeks, there has been a bright pink scar— the unmistakable mark of a cigarette burn—on the back of Sergei's neck that is harder to explain.

"Somebody was smoking," he says. "It was an accident with the wind. I was with my good friends."

Another day there are more marks. I express my concern. "They're not burns," he says. "They're bruises. I fell out of a car by accident."

When Sergei was younger, he dreamed about being a train conductor. Now, when he's lucky, he lives in a railroad car. "I know life better from living here. But I never think about what I *can* do anymore, what I will do in the future."

Sometimes, Sergei and Volodya are caught by police and placed in a prison-like holding cell. Most runaways, though, aren't. There are too many children—and too many police on mafiya payrolls.

THE HOLDING CELL

When police detain children, they often spend the night in a cold jail cell at the train station. One night I meet two thirteen-year-old provincial girls, scared and grimy, who were picked up for prostitution. If the children refuse to identify themselves, or if they live with parents who don't want them, they are sent to a bleak five-thousand-room holding center, the Moscow Reception-Distribution Center for Minors, a dumping ground for runaway and unwanted children, aged three to eighteen.

Runaways are grouped by sex and age in the dreary concrete compound north of Sheremetyevo Airport. They are watched over by uniformed guards, and often not even allowed to make telephone calls. They stay here for weeks, or months, until they are identified and placed elsewhere.

"All too often, the children run away again and the cycle continues," says Igor Markov, the center's deputy director. Sergei Glinia says he can't remember how many times he's been here. He boasts that he and Markov know each other well.

The younger children, like Klara, a wide-eyed seven-year-old in a bright red dress with Peter Pan collar, are less hardened. Klara is here because her mother doesn't want her.

"My mother is very ill," Klara whispers. "When she is ill, she gets very angry with me. When she is better, she'll take me home."

The government is placing Klara in an orphanage that, she is promised, will be "better" than the abusive one she ran away from.

Other runaways are sent back to parents who demand them—even if they are abusive.

"We have to give the children back—even to parents who are alcoholics," Markov says. "It's easy to say no if the child's father shows up drunk. But he will come back sober the next day and take the child."

Not surprisingly, as the breakdown of Communism's social system continues, nothing replaces it, and anarchy rages. The number of runaways continues to increase. By November 1992, seven months after my first visit, the number of children here has doubled to a record high of 300. More than 3,700 children pass through the center in 1992. That's up significantly from 1,500 runaways in 1987. The numbers continue to skyrocket. About 80 percent of the runaways are from Russia. The rest are from the old empire.

Cases of sexually transmitted disease among runaways have also doubled during the same period, says Dina Silkina, the center's chief doctor. "The children regard such diseases as status symbols," she says. "Many of the runaways work as prostitutes and suffer venereal disease, drug and alcohol addiction."

Children who grew up with rape, violence, and abuse face the same perils in the holding center, from older children and from guards, Silkina tells me. In 1992, six Interior Ministry guards were fired for such abuse.

"Unfortunately, there are bad apples everywhere," says Markov, who has a large book on his desk about love and Jesus Christ. "When we discover guards like that, we fire them. It's all we can do."

The level of violence among runaways is also rising. More than a hundred criminal cases were opened at the center in 1992, says Lyubov Ulyanova, a criminal investigator there. Such behavior mirrors that of adult Russians.

Many of the runaways are desperate for psychological help. But the center only recently hired a social worker—one for all of the children.

That's just not enough. There are too many children like Natasha, sixteen, who has already experienced more than most people do in a lifetime.

Natasha, a pleasant, pudgy blonde clad in a blue skirt-and-jacket uniform, with bare legs and yellow socks, ran away from her home in Ukraine to Moscow, where she became a prostitute. "I needed money to buy drugs," she says. "My boyfriend back home got me addicted."

Like many young runaways, she was taken in by a gang that set her up in a flat with five other teenage prostitutes. Her life changed when she witnessed a brutal murder in the apartment. "Police picked me up and brought me here for my own protection," she says.

Natasha has not recovered from the trauma. But no one takes the time to talk to her. "It's like a prison here," she says in a soft, shaky voice. "You may be alive, but it's awful."

During my talk with Silkina, I discover that three of the girls are pregnant. Although the average Russian woman has seven abortions in her lifetime, these girls want to keep their babies. "Their children will be coming to stay with us in ten to fifteen years' time," Silkina says.

BACK ON THE STREET

Once released—often to abusive parents or orphanages—many runaways end up back on the street, where they often meet up with internat graduates like Alexei of Internat No. 98.

After graduation, the state is supposed to provide each orphan with a flat and a monthly stipend. But the stipend, drowned by inflation, Alexei says, "isn't enough to buy food."

Alexei lives in a crumbling state dorm where the toilets don't work and there's no hot water. The building is now mainly filled with refugees from ex-Soviet republics, who fill up alternate floors like different layers in a rotting cake.

Only a small percentage of such internat graduates attend postsecondary institutions.

"Nobody helps us to study further. Everybody tells us we'll only be able to do manual work," Alexei says. "Before I tried to study a lot. Now I feel like I won't get what I want. Maybe if somebody would tell me I had hope and give me some extra help and lessons, I would study."

Instead, Alexei is looking for work as an unskilled laborer. But jobs are scarce. It's not surprising, then, that a large percentage of internat graduates end up in criminal institutions.

JAIL

Aleksin, Russia

I want to see where teenage convicts go after the holding center. I can't believe labor camps for teenagers still exist. Now, in April 1993, I'm heading out of Moscow to the Aleksin Correctional Labor Camp, 100 miles south of the city. I am with Viktor Shumilov, a chain-smoking Interior Ministry official who helps supervise the juvenile labor camps. On the way, he tells me about some teen crimes, from stealing to rape and murder.

Since the empire's collapse, teenage crime—and the intensity of violence—has increased dramatically: Two thousand more teens were convicted in the first four months of 1993 than in all of 1992, Shumilov says.

"One of the worst crimes this year involved a group of young boys who raped a sixteen-year-old girl and burned her to death in southern Russia," Shumilov says.

The camp is surrounded by rolling hills, onion-domed churches, and the general serenity of rural Russia. But the camp, with its 221 teenage prisoners aged fifteen to twenty, has the same concrete, iron, and dogs as every other Russian prison institution I've been to. It is part of a network of fifty-eight labor camps for seventeen thousand juveniles, aged fourteen to twenty-one. Three of the camps are for females.

Sergei Makarov, seventeen, has been here for two years. He has another six months to go. His crime: "Stealing from a government store."

Sergei's story is like many I've heard: alcoholic mother, absent father, orphanage abuse. Now criminals like Sergei are joined by those from relatively stable families who have been hit hard by the "transition" to the market, says Shumilov.

Vadim Solamatin, a lanky nineteen-year-old, is one such teen. He's serving a three-year sentence for raping a sixteen-year-old girl. He was first charged with stealing at age fourteen.

Under the guard's watchful eye, Vadim and his group wolf down —the sitting is timed—their meal of thin porridge, bread, a slab of cold meat, and compote, served on metal plates.

"I hate the guards more than prison itself," Vadim says. "They're so tough with us. Some speak to us like we're in the army. The others don't even speak to us like we're human."

Vladimir Stepanishin, head of the Moscow-based Association for the Rights of Children, says the labor camps are dehumanizing.

"We have to organize a system that will choose better teachers and officers to work with the children," he says.

Teens dress in somber prison blues and browns, marching to and from school and work with arms swinging, boots pounding concrete in unison. Some faces are covered with thick scabs, from disease and malnutrition picked up while the boys were in adult holding centers, waiting to be transferred here.

"They were put in real prisons first. The conditions there are terrible," says Pavel Chechumaev, director of the Aleksin camp.

The teen camps, though, seem only marginally better. Intellectually, the teens are starving. "They're here to work," Chechumaev says. "Art, music, sports, and drama are not part of the school curriculum."

Work, in a metallurgical shop, is filled with the clank of metal and whir of machines. Teens earn three hundred rubles a day to turn out farm tools. But the money doesn't go far. "They must use it to pay for goods they stole, like cars," says Shumilov. If any money is left over, it's often spent on cigarettes, even though some teens are too young to buy them legally.

Access to alcohol, and sometimes drugs, is easy—if the kids have enough money to bribe the staff, some teens on a cigarette break out in the cold tell me.

Some also amuse themselves by getting tattoos, a key part of prison culture, although getting caught often means a stint in solitary, as Vadim recently discovered.

Officials say they are trying to reform the system to more "humane" post-Soviet standards. But Russia's current chaos has only brought further deterioration.

And although the maximum sentence for juveniles was reduced from ten to seven years in 1991, the state no longer ensures jobs and flats for ex-convicts. Unlike Soviet enterprises, private businesses can't be forced to hire ex-cons.

"Before, the labor camps and local authorities were obliged to find them jobs, but now nobody wants them," says Shumilov.

The new market malady of spiraling unemployment makes it worse. Those who can't find jobs often return. The recidivism rate jumped to 25 percent—up 5 percent from 1992 to 1993—and higher in later years.

"Let's retreat to my cabin. Dinner is waiting," Chechumaev says at the end of the day. We drive with some prison officials to a secluded cabin in the woods. Typically Soviet, it is simple but luxurious: an elite state dacha hidden away for the private enjoyment of the Communist *nomenklatura.**

Inside, a feast is waiting: fresh fried fish, salads, smoked meats, chickens, vegetables; vodka and champagne. With each glass, the toasts get longer, until Chechumaev descends into a lengthy speech about the breakdown of the labor camps, and Russia in general.

"Children are languishing in jail because society and their families don't need them," he says. "All of the politicians and businessmen making money must give some back to the people. Businessmen forget this very simple thing. Otherwise, tomorrow the teens will come with their knives and ask, 'Where are your millions? Please give us some.' "

---

* While *nomenklatura* originally referred to top Communist Party brass, it now means any privileged official in Russia.

◄--►

CHAPTER 4

The Homeless

The Killer, the Grandmother, the Mad Poet, and the Discoverer of the Cure for Cancer— Who Could Invent Roommates Like This?

> Do not judge a house by its appearance,
> but by the warmth of the welcome.
>
> — Russian proverb

Entire families sleep in chairs on the upper floor of Paveletsky Train Station, hanging clothes out to dry while commuters rush by. There is even a television, droning endlessly, for commuters and homeless, who are captivated, like the rest of Russia, by a twenty-year-old Mexican soap opera, "The Rich Also Cry." (When the show's most popular star, a much older "Mariana," visits Moscow—and meets with the mayor and thousands of Muscovites at a crowded public rally—the newspaper *Izvestia* counts down the days to her arrival on its front page.)

While reporting for the *Moscow Times*, I write about gangs who steal children from homeless families to sell on the black market. Newspapers carry ads from couples who want to trade their children for bigger apartments. Police tell me about one mother who sold her child for eight dollars' worth of rubles. "I didn't sell her. She was stolen by Gypsies!" cries the woman, a bundle of rags and tangled black hair, when I find her, drunk, slumped under a broken escalator in the station.

Over the next few months, I meet many families whose children have been stolen from them at the railway station. The children are often sold into black market adoption rings or else, say some families, they are trained as professional beggars, thieves, and prostitutes. "Maybe," says one police officer, "some are stolen by sympathetic women who can't have children of their own and want to provide them with a better life."

Mikhail and Natasha Vinokurov's two-year-old, Zhenya, was recently snatched from Paveletsky. The Vinokurovs, once private farmers, moved into the train station in 1990, when their home near Volgograd was destroyed by fire.

"I'm terrified Zhenya may no longer be alive," says Mikhail, a small, withered forty-two-year-old with washed-out, sleepless eyes and a gray, stubbled face. At 1 A.M., Natasha, thirty-two, is fanning one of their four remaining, sleeping children as she gossips with Galina, her homeless neighbor, who fled an abusive husband in Baku. (Galina's brother is in Moscow, though he refuses to help her and her six children, one of whom is now in jail; another is in the hospital.)

Natasha and Mikhail's kids, aged seven months to eleven years, each sleep on three chairs put together to make beds. Their black-soled feet peek out from under scratchy blankets without sheets. A yellow baby jumper lies out flat to dry on a chair, under which is shoved a cardboard box stuffed with children's clothes.

"The station is dangerous, and I don't always make enough money begging to feed my family," Mikhail says. "But I refuse to put my children in an orphanage. My wife was an orphan. She knows exactly what goes on there and doesn't want her children to have the same experiences she had. It's even more dangerous there. It's not easy here, but we're doing the best we can. And now that there's democracy, I'm going direct to the White House [Russian parliament] for help."

Natasha is less hopeful. "I feel I'm losing strength each day," she says. "And the police don't care. I know it would be different in our hometown."

Anatoly Muraviov, head of the city police's teenage unit, says he is so alarmed by rising reports of child kidnappings that he has opened a special investigation. "But there have been no results so far." In Russia, the state is so disorganized and the homeless so disenfranchised, there are no public campaigns as in North America — on milk cartons and television stations—to help find missing kids.

"I don't understand how the government can allow this," says one officer, frustrated by his inability to protect homeless children. "What kind of citizens can these people become in a few years?"

Now that Communism is being dismantled, there is even less help for those most in need. There should be shelters, I think, somewhere for these people to go. I know the situation is bad, but what I discover is startling. In December 1992, there is only one homeless shelter in all of Moscow. More than one hundred thousand people live in Moscow's streets. The shelter has room for twelve of them.

Much to my surprise, I find the shelter on the ground floor of a psychiatric home on the outskirts of northeast Moscow, at the end of a lonely road. I expect to see a depressing vision from Goya. Instead, I encounter the unbreakable fighting spirit of rebellion.

In the first room, I meet a tiny Georgian grandmother war refugee sitting on her cot, dangling legs so short they do not reach the ground. Beside her is a burly ex-convict and killer. In the Far East, newspapers report, ex-convicts sent to live in an old-age home end up terrorizing, robbing—and killing—their elderly roommates. Here, though, the proximity produces friendship.

There's an artist who writes poems to Yeltsin, an inventor from the Far East who holds three patents and "discovered *the* cure for cancer," a gray-bearded professor who studies "Soviet forms of psychological torture." I've never met more sane, lucid, inspiring people.

Even the nurse, an older woman in white who worked here before the shelter existed, is friendly, in the most nonbureaucratic way.

The room of the killer fresh out of jail and the grandmother is small and stark. Two army cots are neatly made. The green walls are bare, except for one religious painting. Mariya Dagbarsheva, seventy-two, has just escaped a war that is killing thousands and displacing 250,000 people, as Muslim Abkhazia tries to separate from Georgia.

"The people who come here want to renew normal lives," says Lyubov Sukhareva, the administrator on duty one night at Psychiatric-Neurological Institute No. 23, home to 508 psychiatric patients—and the twelve homeless residents.

Sukhareva says she is also impressed by their spirit. "There is no violence," she says. "They try to help each other, sharing food. There are no greedy people here."

I think of the fate of the elderly in the Far East, of rising murder rates, of Russians' growing desperation. The spirit here is rare. In these times, extraordinary.

Most of the shelter's residents have been regulars since it opened in June 1992. Unlike the tens of thousands of homeless on the streets, these twelve receive individual counseling to help them find jobs.

"Five of them have already found flats and will move soon," Sukhareva says proudly, adding that the homeless receive no financial assistance from the state.

Alexander Veremeyev, forty-five, who spent the past twenty-one years in jail, lost his apartment when he was convicted of murder in 1972. ("It was in self-defense," he explains.) Hunching his shoulders and holding a cigarette to his deeply lined face, Veremeyev looks more like a petty thief than a murderer, especially considering his kind manner with Dagbarsheva.

"Now all I want is a job and a place to live," he says softly. "I want a corner or a room to sleep—not even a flat—and a job where I can make some decent money."

While the homeless socialize among themselves, they have little contact with the psychiatric patients. "They are really sick, different people. I don't understand them," Veremeyev says.

Nikolai Ostasha, the fifty-eight-year-old painter-poet, likes to think of the shelter as some sort of cultural exchange. Ostasha, dressed chicly in black, his shirt buttoned to the top, with wavy gray hair and thick black-framed glasses, looks like he should be on the bank of the Seine with an easel. But, he says, he's spent his life "identifying" with the dispossessed.

"I have always fought against the Bolsheviks and the fascists," says Ostasha, clutching a large satchel. After repeated requests, he opens the satchel and shows me some of his paintings, bold charcoal portraits that reveal talent, and poems that perhaps reveal less. "Some of the poems are dedicated to Yeltsin and the new democracy," he says.

Nikolai Sederenko, fifty-five, the sloppy but suit-clad inventor, gave up his flat in the Far East to discover Moscow. "Somehow, I ended up here." He smiles.

"I may be homeless," he insists, "but I *have* invented the cure for cancer. I was supposed to have died twelve years ago, before

I found, and patented, the cure." With that, Sederenko rummages through a bag to show me the patent papers, creased and almost worn through, but carefully folded, with all the stamps and seals of Soviet officialdom, to "prove" it.

"Anybody with real ideas always has trouble," he says.

"We're just beginning to consider this problem," says Yelina Yulikova, director of homeless programs for the Ministry of Social Welfare. "We never had homeless before. They were taken care of by the state."

Under Communism, police roamed the streets and picked up vagrants—anyone who did not have residence papers. They were placed in prison-like hostels, where they were at least sheltered and fed. "While about two hundred and sixty thousand people still live in such hostels, police stopped picking up the homeless in 1990," Yulikova says. Since then, their numbers have increased dramatically, though, she says, there are no accurate statistics.

"It's all political," Yulikova says. "There is more freedom now, but there is more ethnic turmoil, unemployment, and trouble within families. Many homeless are not regular tramps but just people trying to get by."

The government is now trying to deal with the problem of homelessness, Yulikova adds. But her ministry can only afford to help around thirty thousand people who are considered to be "social outcasts," even though there are more than triple that on the streets.

On top of the domestic homeless, the Russian government is also trying to shelter refugees from ex-Soviet conflict zones. More than 460,000 of these refugees are now in Russia. In one shelter I visit, Armenian and Azeri orphans are placed on alternate floors, so they won't kill each other trying to avenge their parents' deaths. I've seen shelters for the allies of the old Soviet state, from countries like Afghanistan, who are now plotting the downfall of new governments.

Third World and Middle Eastern asylum seekers are also sheltered by the Russian state. I once visited Somalis housed in a small town outside Moscow, where racial intolerance was high. Some African students have been killed by Moscow street toughs.

While these shelters for foreigners are far from adequate, they are more than what the government provides for its domestic homeless. "Of course one shelter isn't enough, but at least it's a start," Yulikova says. "More shelters are expected to open across the country." They do, though there are still far from enough.

In the meantime, international aid groups are also starting to help. Médecins sans Frontières tours Moscow train stations a few nights a week. Russian doctors see between five and sixty people nightly and hospitalize about five weekly, says Christophe Hambye, the group's administrator. The program, funded in part by the European Community, began in the summer of 1992. The team includes four expatriates, eight Russian doctors, and some support staff.

One night at Paveletsky Train Station, about forty homeless get in line for checkups. Some patients have blistering, bleeding sores and red, bumpy rashes—skin diseases, fleas, and lice from poor hygiene. Tuberculosis, cancer, and ulcers are also common. The midnight crowd includes two young girls with matching pink scarves and mittens and dirt-stained men with bloody, infected legs and feet, ragged thin jackets over bare chests.

Fyodorov Klatov, forty-five, waits in line with his dog, a straggly mutt who seems to be in better shape than he is. "I just left my wife; he's all I have left," says Klatov, his pants rolled up to reveal swollen legs and large, festering sores. "It's so bad I can hardly walk."

Lyuba Bachodinaya, eight, and Alisa Serovarova, ten, hold hands as they run to hug the foreign nurse, Patricia Kormoss. Expert scammers, they immediately hug me, the newcomer, and ask for cash while they peer at the sick and the old people around them.

"Aren't you afraid here?" I ask, knowing too well what can happen in this place.

"Not at all," says Lyuba, the more talkative of the two. "It's good here. I have lots of friends in the station. I'm not afraid at all."

CHAPTER 5

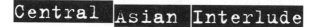

Central Asian Interlude

On Coups, War, Black Gold, and White Gold—
A Nine-Hour Cab Ride through the
Kara Kum Desert

White on a throne or guarded in a cave
There lives a prophet who can understand
Why men were born: but surely we are brave,
Who make the Golden Journey to Samarkand....
We travel not for trafficking alone:
By hotter winds our fiery hearts are fanned:
For lust of knowing what should not be known
We make the Golden Journey to Samarkand....

> — JAMES ELROY FLECKER, "The Golden Journey
> to Samarkand: At the Gate of the Sun,
> Bagdad, in Olden Time"

Oil and camels, extravagant carpets, Eastern fragrance.

The Old Silk Road linked East and West for centuries before Marco Polo "discovered" it in the late thirteenth century. Closed to the West for so long, Central Asia, rich with oil and gas, gold and uranium, is still a mysterious region, bordering Russia, China, Pakistan, Afghanistan, Turkey, and Iran.

Dozens of empires have battled over Central Asia, where the lands of ancient Greece, Rome, India, and China once met. By late last century, when Russia had crushed the Muslims of Central Asia, Russian expansion was threatening British interests in India. The region swarmed with spies in what was called the Great Game, which sometimes spilled into Afghanistan, China, Persia, and Tibet.

Now, flushed with independence from the FSU, the Central Asian republics—Turkmenistan, Uzbekistan, Kyrgyzstan, Tajikistan, and Kazakhstan*—are once again in geopolitical demand. The Americans see the region—which has already exploded in post-Soviet ethnic wars—as an extension of violence in a hot zone from the Middle East to the Balkans and Kashmir. Like much of the FSU, Central Asia is undergoing a spiritual rebirth. Thirty million Muslims live in the region, which is bursting with new mosques and Koranic schools. That makes Washington, which fears a bunch of "hot-headed mullahs armed with nuclear weapons,"** nervous.

China, with six million ethnic-minority Muslims on its side of the border, inspired by their neighbors' newfound independence, is also tensely watching the region's development. Iran, Turkey, Saudi Arabia, Pakistan, and Libya are involved, too, while Japan and Korea are keen to invest.

My first foray is into Turkmenistan, which borders Afghanistan, Iran, Uzbekistan, Kazakhstan, and the Caspian Sea. The cost from Moscow, if you have a Russian passport or foreign media accreditation: seven dollars. Return. (Prices rise so fast that thousands of travelers can't afford tickets home.)

The Soviets cemented their empire with cheap air travel, from the fifteen republics to Eastern Europe, Africa, and Cuba. Aeroflot carried the Soviet flag to 102 countries. Its mandate was to provide mass transportation to 138 million citizens as cheaply and as extensively as the Moscow metro system.

Now the ancient caravan route, which brought Chinese tea, china, and silks—the making of which the Chinese kept secret for thousands of years—to Rome and the Mediterranean, is opening up again.

Natural riches, like oil and gas, brought the United States, Europe, and Great Britain to Kazakhstan. Iran also wants in on the pipelines. Russia and the West fear the rise of Iranian-style Islamic fundamentalism. But for now, Iran is negotiating with Russia on

---

* There is no general agreement whether Kazakhstan—twice as big as Turkmenistan, Uzbekistan, Kyrgyzstan, and Tajikistan combined—should be considered part of Central Asia.

** Peter Hopkirk, *The Great Game* (New York, 1990), xv.

nuclear sales. In return, Tehran is keeping its distance. At least on the surface.

Turkey also wants more regional influence. Its claim is cultural as well as geographic. The Azeris, for example, separated from Central Asia by the Caspian Sea, are a Turko-Tatar race; Uzbeks, the largest ethnic group in the region, are related by language and origin to the Ottoman Turks. Turkey is so popular in some ex-Soviet republics that, in Azerbaijan, portraits of the Turkish president hang in offices and stare from street walls, fast replacing those of Lenin.

Nevertheless, Islamic fundamentalism is growing in regions like the Fergana Valley, where Kyrgyzstan, Uzbekistan, and Tajikistan meet. About one third of the Uzbek population lives in the Fergana Valley. In recent years it has been the site of some bloody battles: between Uzbeks and Meskhetian Turks in 1989, and in 1990 between Uzbeks and Kyrgyz—leaving some two hundred dead and hundreds more wounded, according to Human Rights Watch/ Helsinki, a New York-based international human rights group.

Central Asia is also a hub for growing, manufacturing, and trading in narcotics, especially heroin. Loose border controls allow for easy drug movement, perhaps with the participation of the Russian army, from Central Asia and Afghanistan into China and the East, and through Russia to the West. Drug money is often used to buy weapons from the Russian army, which are then used in ex-Soviet ethnic wars: in Chechnya, Georgia and Abkhazia, Azerbaijan and Armenia, Tajikistan and Afghanistan, Moldova and Trans-Dniestria. Such instability enables the Kremlin to deploy "peacekeeping" troops throughout the old empire.

Ashgabad, the capital of Turkmenistan, means "lovely settlement" in Arabic. It is where the Kara Kum Desert meets the daunting Kopet-Dag Mountains. Prosperous during the time of Alexander the Great, Ashgabad fell to Turkish rule before it was decimated by Genghis Khan in the thirteenth century. When the Russians conquered it in 1881, they rebuilt the city from scratch.

Turkmenistan is rich in natural gas—it has the fifth largest gas reserves in the world—as well as oil, cotton, petroleum, and raw minerals. The president, Saparmurad Niyazov, a Gorbachev protégé, renamed the Communist Party the Political Council of the Democratic Party of Turkmenistan in late 1990, and gradually developed his own secular cult of personality modeled more on Lenin than on Lincoln. He is known as Turkmenbashi, leader of all Turkmen, and was reelected president with a whopping 99.5 percent of the vote in June 1992.

While Turkmenistan's tiny population of 3.9 million has enough natural resources to make it independent and wealthy, the country's survival is still inexorably linked to Russia. All of Turkmenistan's natural gas pipelines go north into Russia or other countries in the Commonwealth of Independent States (CIS). It needs money to build pipelines into Iran, Turkey, Pakistan, Afghanistan, and China. And it is still owed hundreds of millions of dollars from FSU republics—which are paying for oil with bartered goods instead of desperately needed cash: pickled eggplant from Moldova; green tea from Georgia.

Today, Ashgabad is a Russian creation of wide, tree-lined avenues and concrete monuments. It is Kiev, Odessa, Moscow recreated on Asian streets. Only when I see such Asian peoples— men with tall hats, long, pointed white beards, and robes; women in colorful head scarves, quarter-covered faces, forbidden to look you in the eye—all speaking Russian, do I realize how well the Russians conquered.

On my first trip, with Adam, an American colleague from the *MT*, we stay in the only hotel available to foreigners, Hotel Ashgabad. The four-day trip—hotel, food, and airfare—costs about thirty dollars each. The hotel flows with vodka, quenching ex-Soviet thirsts and those of the Iranians flooding in from the nearby border, where drinking alcohol is strictly forbidden.

The hotel restaurant serves the same generically greasy chicken and potatoes found in Soviet Intourist restaurants from Siberia to Samarkand. Middle Eastern music plays to a full house: men in suits; women in frills, spikes, and scarlet lips, glitter, green eye shadow, thick mascara, and Cleopatra cat's eyes. Between courses, guests dance. Women's arms wave gracefully in the air.

The first night, I sleep in a tiny room on a threadbare sheet with a bright orange bedcover. There is a hole in the door, right beside the dime-store lock. The walls are so thin I am awake most of the night listening to pounding music, drunken laughter, and thundering footsteps from a private party above me. I hear men shouting, running up and down stairs, fighting. Because this is an old Soviet hotel, there is a *dezhurnaya* on each floor, a woman who, in Soviet times and presumably still today, keeps watch over her floor. I don't think she'll be much help if anything happens, though.

The next evening, the hotel restaurant is closed for a wedding. "We're starving. Can't we please get something to eat?" I ask a large, blonde Russian. "No," she says, with more than a hint of a smile. She is, I realize, part of the power-crazed class of bureaucrats created by Communists who take pleasure in maintaining absolute control over even the smallest of fiefdoms.

After being unexpectedly confronted with Soviet Attitude, Adam and I take a cab to Ashgabad's two other small hotels, not on the list for Westerners. On the way, we get a tour of downtown Ashgabad. It takes a few minutes. The beauty—mountains, desert, camels on the side of the road—is best found outside the city. The other hotels are also closed for weddings.

"Why don't you come to my house?" asks our young cabby. "My wife would be most pleased to make dinner for you." The offer is tempting, but it's late. I don't think his wife would appreciate it.

We stop at a tea house with mud coffee, which reminds me of what the Druze drink in Israel. As at an Italian bar, midday in a small village, there are no women. We dine at the local kiosk, the only one open, outside our hotel. It's far less well-stocked than its Moscow counterparts: Snickers bars and a vile-tasting, mineral-rich German fruit drink. We go for a walk and discover a carpet museum. The guard offers us a private evening tour.

The next morning, we check out Ashgabad's monstrous department store, where Turkmen buy everything from Soviet teacups with the ubiquitous orange polka dots to the material women use to sew their robes and veils. The "ready-to-wear" section of the store is just as bad, the lingerie department depressing. We do, however, find stolen Moscow police caps for pennies, and fake icons. Food in state stores is limited but plentiful, the heavy sausage of Moscow juxtaposed with the thick flat breads of Central Asia.

Next is the market. Stalls of fresh and dried fruits, spices like saffron and anise. (At the time, none of the fruit is regularly available in Moscow during winter.) There's another section for meats and cheeses; even stalls of cheap clothes.

From the market, we head to an incredible underground mineral lake outside the city. "I've got to fill up for gas first," says our cabby, "and stop by the house to tell my wife I'll be gone for the day."

The house, outside town, is one room. A little girl in a bright floral robe, all cheery reds, pinks, and greens, is out front. Animals roam. More girls run out, along with older women in the same robes and quarter veils. The driver's wife silently presses pomegranates into our hands. She does not speak Russian.

On the way to the lake, we are stopped by police. Our driver is nervous. "Just say we're friends," says our cabby. "You're not paying me."

The officer saunters over. "You're driving in a restricted zone, off limits to foreigners," he says. A Soviet-era ritual ensues. The driver transforms into a humble, faintly sycophantic comrade; the policeman intimidates with glee.

Adam joins in, with a by-cooperating-we-can-all-help-foster-peace-between-nations-in-the-new-world-order routine. Finally, I look at the police officer and say, "Is this how you'd like your daughter to be treated if she was traveling through North America?"

Somehow, it all works. Entrance to the lake is a few rubles. We descend an eternity of slippery stone stairs. The warm water smells like sulfur. The swim is sublime. My passport, which I left on some rocks, falls in and becomes permanently water-stained.

Climbing out to reality, I sit on a primitive swing hanging from a thick, ancient tree and watch the sun set, fuchsia and red, in absolute silence. It's hard to believe so much chaos, so much war, comes from ex-Soviet countries like this.

The next day is Sunday. Once-a-week bazaar day. It's what I've been waiting for. I wake with a sharp pain ripping through my gut. "If you're feeling sick, you should stay at the hotel," Adam says, his brother having recently suffered some nasty illness from backwater ex-Soviet travels. "It's our only day to see the market and I'm not going to leave early to take you back."

We are warned to leave around 7 A.M.; *everybody* goes to the market outside town on Sundays. We leave at 8 A.M. and end up in a traffic jam in the middle of the desert, a lonely line of bumper-to-bumper beat-up cars striving to get to the market in the chill of early morning light.

The market overwhelms me, so rich with color, commerce, and people. I can barely move. This is where you can buy *papakha*, the tall woolly hats Turkmen wear, winter and summer, made from astrakhan, wool of the karakul sheep and named for the town where it is sold. Here are rows of luxurious antique carpets, ancient (and new) Turkmen jewelry—thick silver with orange stones— antique daggers and coins, necklaces made from century-old coins, and cheap manufactured fakes.

The market buzzes with barter and gossip. Iranian women, shrouded in black, scout the carpets and look like death next to the Turkmen women in bright florals. Old men with long white beards and young boys in shirtsleeves sit cross-legged selling watermelons big enough to have been irradiated at Chernobyl. Women sit by towering bags of popcorn, which they sell for pennies in newspaper cones.

Turkmen who don't speak Russian bargain by drawing numbers in the sand. Suddenly, amidst rows of exquisite carpets, the illness hits me. Adam takes me to a line of cars parked in the sand, near the stalls of bleating goats and camels. I lie down in the sand, by some goats. Finally, a driver agrees to take me to the hotel. The ride is interminably long. The driver refuses money.

I almost black out as I reach the hotel. I struggle to open the door, and sit down in the lobby to gather strength for my next move: the elevator. Close to blacking out again, I get to my floor and collapse in the arms of a startled dezhurnaya, who leads me to my room. The dezhurnaya checks on me every few hours. She brings me green tea and, later, bread. I'm queasy, but I get better, angry and frustrated at the helplessness of being ill.

By December 1992, my second visit to Central Asia, much has changed. Some Central Asian countries, like Uzbekistan, are already in their second phase of "independence." Flirting with democracy is over, if it ever began. Presidents continue to plaster their own faces all over their countries as new cults of personalities solidify, following Turkmenbashi's lead. The suppression of human rights, thought to have relaxed with the collapse of Communism, increases. Political opponents, activists, Islamic leaders independent of the state, and journalists are beaten and jailed. Some disappear. Newspapers are shut down. This year, the Uzbek chapter of the Islamic Renaissance Party was banned and its leader, Abdulla Utaev, disappeared. Human Rights Watch/Helsinki, which has offices in Moscow, will soon be banned from visiting the country.

This time I plan a road trip with another *MT* colleague, and an American human rights worker and her Russian boyfriend. Flights between Uzbekistan and Turkmenistan are limited and unreliable. Why not drive it, I think, a nine-hour ride across the Kara Kum Desert. I want to return to Turkmenistan—and visit Uzbekistan's mystical Silk Road cities of Samarkand and Bukhara.

It's difficult for journalists to get visas to Uzbekistan. Western journalists have been rousted from bed at weird midnight hours and kicked out of the country for lacking proper accreditation. Of course, getting the accreditation is next to impossible. One American journalist in Uzbekistan has already been expelled. Others will follow.

"You must fly to Tashkent [the Uzbek capital] in order to get an Uzbek visa," says the Uzbek consular official in Moscow. But we plan to fly to Samarkand, and do so. Somehow we talk our way in. It takes a few hours. We meet an Uzbek-KGB official and change some dollars with him at a favorable rate.

Samarkand, a city of elaborate turquoise domes, was the bustling hub of eleventh-century Persia. For a time, it was also home to Omar Khayyam, the great sage, poet, astrologer, and mathematician. Khayyam helped reform the calendar and did unique work in algebra and astronomy. (The remains of one of his observatories is still standing.) But he is best known for his magnificent *Rubaiyaat*, a literary genre of epigrammatic verse quatrains, or poems. Khayyam is said to have begun the *Rubaiyaat* in 1072, in Samarkand, which, he wrote, was "the most beautiful face the Earth has ever turned towards the sun."

Khayyam also wrote, prophetically as it turned out for the region, "Both Paradise and Hell are in you." Another wanderer in Samarkand during this era was Hassan Sabbah, who founded a secret order of Muslim Shiites known as Assassins, before he moved to his famed mountain fortress, Alamut. The Assassins killed people for causes, often sacrificing their own lives in the process: Martyrdom was not avoided, but sought. The word has come to be synonymous with murderer, especially for political motives, in many European languages.

In the fourteenth century, Samarkand rose again as the ancient capital of Tamerlane's great empire. It is also the site of his tomb, the splendor of which impressed me as much as Napoleon's. Not until the twentieth century was his skeleton found there, buried in a deep crypt.

As his power increased, Tamerlane—also known as Timur Leng, or Timur the Lame—began to harbor blood legitimacy fantasies, and by 1370 he claimed that he was a direct descendant of Genghis Khan. The empire began with Turkestan and swallowed Persia, Ankara, parts of southern Russia, and India up to Delhi. It is said that up to seventeen million people died violently during the time of this tyrant. After capturing some cities, he slaughtered thousands of their defenders—allegedly up to eighty thousand at Delhi—and built pyramids of their skulls. He mixed some heaven in with the hell, though, and was a big supporter of the arts, literature, and science. What remains is the beauty, the mosques, built with thousands of slave laborers, and schools. Tamerlane died in 1405, as he was about to invade China.

In Samarkand, we tour some tributes to this rich history: the museums, mosques, and new Islamic schools. As we walk, the confident, self-affirming hum of renewed prayer chants—banned for more than seventy years—rings through the cold, mud, and rain-soaked streets.

From the city, we hire a cab and drive four hours to Bukhara. So many carpets used to be traded here that some are now called Bukharan carpets. We spend the day before Christmas at the two local synagogues. One is for the Ashkenazi Jews, mainly European, many of whom were moved to Central Asia by the Soviets during World War II, which Russians call the Great Patriotic War. The move saved their lives, although Stalin later sent some Jews to the gulags for alleged collaboration with the Nazis—even if they had fought in the war, especially if they had been captured and somehow managed to survive. (Stalin also accused and punished Chechens, Ingush, Kalmyks, and other ethnic groups for alleged Nazi collaboration.)

"My father fought and was captured by the Nazis," says Josef, a local I meet, who was shipped to Central Asia with his mother and siblings during the war. "None of his fellow prisoners ratted on him. The Germans never knew he was Jewish. But instead of getting a hero's welcome upon his return, he was thrown into the gulag—for surviving. Stalin thought it was impossible for a Jew to survive Nazi imprisonment without collaborating."

We also visit the Sephardic synagogue. Some of these Jews came from Persia and have lived in Central Asia for centuries. Even their skullcaps look similar to those worn by Central Asian Muslims.

That evening, Christmas Eve, we return to our hotel, where we meet up with some other *MT* colleagues and a group of retired teachers, mainly from Britain. The teachers now *live* in Uzbekistan. Some of the women remind me of Agatha Christie or Merchant-Ivory characters. Their passion for life is inspiring. We share their imported plum cake and spirits, toasting Christmas and the New Year.

Next morning, we visit the Sephardic rabbi. His family lives in one large room. The rabbi's wife looks after the mikvah, the pool in which women immerse themselves in a ritual cleansing process, monthly after menstruation and also before the marriage ceremony. "Please stay for tea," she insists after our tour of the mikvah.

While Central Asian Jews survived the Holocaust and maintained their religion during Communism, they are leaving the region in droves. Israel air-lifted Jews out of war-torn and potentially unstable regions of the old empire, like Uzbekistan, Chechnya, Tajikistan, and Georgia. Others flock to "Qveens," New York.

Every Bukharan Jew we meet has relatives who have just moved to Israel or America. Many would have left under Communism if they could have. Now they can. The economies around them are collapsing. Some fear war and growing nationalism. Others say they haven't been persecuted, but, like most emigrants, they just want a better life for their children.

The flight is hard on those who stay. "We're celebrating fewer and fewer marriages. Soon, there will be no one left," says one musician.

The Central Asian Jews who move to the States usually end up in Queens, near the center of an international Orthodox Jewish sect, the Lubavitchers, who follow the teachings of the Russian-born Rebbe Menachem Schneerson. Some Lubavitchers proclaim Schneerson the Messiah. It is quite a shock to step into a room in mystical Bukhara and see a large photo of Rebbe Schneerson, still alive at the time.

We leave Bukhara in a chilly predawn mist to drive the nine hours across the Kara Kum Desert, which comprises 90 percent of the country. Destination: Ashgabad. No traffic lights, no drive-by diners. Just desert and one single dusty road; lucky we don't run out of gas. Young boys sit by the side of the road, watching cars and camels go by. Our driver talks about the Aral Sea—an oasis in the Uzbek and neighboring Kazakh desert wasteland—which is dying and turning to salt. Since 1960, it has dropped from the world's fourth to sixth largest lake, losing 40 percent of its surface area—one and a half times the amount of water in Lake Erie. It's a direct result of the Soviet decision to cut off its water supplies—the Amu Darya and Syr Darya rivers, feeding into the Aral Sea for the past ten thousand years—to irrigate millions of acres for cotton production, which the Communists called "white gold."

Ninety percent of all cotton grown in the FSU comes with the help of these two rivers, which are also used to irrigate melon patches and cereal fields. But the cost has been deadly. There are no more fish in the Aral Sea, so Moscow ships in frozen fish from the ocean to be canned in the old fishing villages, which are now miles inland. Not only the fish are dying. The Aral may soon be a newborn Dead Sea, Uzbeks are dying of throat cancer from the dying sea's dust while area children are born with scores of illnesses directly attributable to the Aral's death agonies.[*]

I think about the sea as we drive through the vast, endless desert. (There's not much else to do.) We eat bread and drink sulfurized mineral water, passing time with games, singing, and sleeping. Squeezed into a typical small, bumpy Lada, we are cramped and uncomfortable. The ride is long, monotonous—and peaceful.

Ashgabad is just as I remember, the hotel just as run-down. This time, there is only one wedding. I still barely eat and almost avoid getting sick. We go back to the market, but there's no time for the underground lake. I buy my first old carpet; dusty rose, softly faded, almost Aztec in design. Law is you can't take carpets out of the country. Law is so unrespected that I carry the carpet, over my shoulders, onto the plane.

---

[*] William Ellis, "A Soviet Sea Lies Dying," *National Geographic*, 177, No. 2 (1990), 73–93.

From Ashgabad, we drive to the ancient town of Nissa, fifteen kilometers west of the capital. Nissa, founded in the third century B.C., was the Parthian capital after the time of Alexander the Great. We wander through the ruins of two grand temples, circular and tower-shaped.

Then it's back to Moscow, first time-zone change; then Paris and Toronto. It's my first visit home in ten months, the longest I've ever been away. It feels good to be home. But after three weeks I'm anxious to get back to Moscow. I thought Russia was going to be temporary. I can no longer see an end.

A few days after I arrive back in Moscow, Adam and I fly to Baku, the capital of Azerbaijan, filled with flat-roofed, white-washed clay buildings, haphazardly stacked, that remind me of Jerusalem's old city. The Russians captured this ancient town from the shah of Persia in 1806. A stone tower looms in the background; a boy on his bicycle stares. Sheep wander. Women roll antique carpets out of shops in winding back alleys while men sip cups of tea.

We dine in one of the private rooms of an old castle, warmed only by brightly colored carpets. A band plays outside, as we feast on black Caspian caviar and spicy meat *plofs*, or pilafs. The setting—the old city, tower, castle—would make for a great James Bond film, we think. Real intrigue—a coup, a monstrous oil deal, CIA-KGB plotting—is in the works, but of this I am, at the time, still (blissfully) unaware.

We write about some oil drilling on the Caspian Sea. The project is run from a concrete, man-made island named Oil Rocks, which, in its heyday, employed five thousand people; there was even a disco on the island. We fly there by rickety helicopter with some of the island's employees, including a Soviet-style older woman with fiery orange hair. "Why are you all in black if no one died?" the air-traffic controllers ask me.

Baku and the Caspian Sea surrounding it have been steeped in oil since Persian fire-worshipers, amazed by flames blazing from earth more soaked with oil than tiramisu oozes alcohol, founded a holy city here. In the summer of 1992, the National Front of Azerbaijan, a nationalist-democratic movement created in 1989, replaced the Communist Party in parliament. But Abulfaz Elchibey, the elected president, was considered too independent and Western-leaning for Moscow—especially with the valuable oil fields at stake. In early 1993, Russian-backed Armenians attack in the disputed region of Nagorno-Karabakh, a (Christian) Armenian enclave in (Muslim) Azerbaijan where at least fifteen thousand people have been killed since 1988.

In June 1993, Elchibey is about to sign a contract with British Petroleum, negotiate with some American oil companies, finalize a new pipeline from the Caspian Sea to Turkey, establish an Azeri currency, and leave the ruble economic zone. Under Elchibey, Azerbaijan rejects the CIS founding treaty and becomes the first ex-Soviet republic to kick out the Russian military. But plans crash when two hundred people die in a military coup. Elchibey flees to Turkey, where diplomats charge Russia with planning the coup and turning over bases and perhaps even weapons to coup leaders. Gaidar Aliyev, the first secretary of the Communist Party of Azerbaijan until 1988, is named interim president and "elected" president that fall—with an unbelievable 98.8 percent of the vote. Azerbaijan then rejoins the CIS, and Lukoil, the Russian state conglomerate, is added to a consortium of Western oil companies. Career Communists like Aliyev are replacing Soviet dissidents turned into democratic nationalist presidents in ex-Soviet republics as Yeltsin begins to implement his Greater Russia policy, classifying ex-Soviet republics as the "Near Abroad," and re-staking Russia's claim. The return of the empire may indeed be on its way.

CHAPTER 6

Gulag Ghosts and Arctic Coal Mines

Where Darkness Really Is before Noon

> Heart's memory of sun grows fainter.
> What now? Darkness?
> Perhaps! This very night unfolds
> the winter.
>
> — ANNA AKHMATOVA, "Heart's Memory of Sun"

"Vorkuta is built on graves," says Vitaly Troshin, the city's chief architect.

A coal-mining town of 220,000 people 100 miles north of the Arctic Circle, Vorkuta was built by Stalin's prisoners. The gulag heartland became one of Russia's most prosperous coal-mining regions. In 1989, coal-mining strikes helped spell the end of the Soviet Union. But as the mines downsize to become more efficient, miners are forced to cut back their working hours; avoiding direct firing is the government's way to stave off wide-scale social unrest. Most miners haven't been paid in months and inflation renders their late paychecks worthless. Now the miners are threatening a nationwide strike. In typical Soviet fashion, the miners stage underground sit-ins—protests so dangerous that men have died in them. One coal-mine strike in Vorkuta has already begun.

The Communists lured miners to the Arctic the only possible way: pure capitalist incentive. Workers flocked to this coal-mining center for *za dlinnym rublyom*, the big ruble. Work was harsh in this land where the winter sun can set before noon and summer lasts less than eight weeks. Pay was high. Pensions could begin after fifteen years. By then the miners, if they survived, looked far more than fifteen years older. Young, still in their thirties, they had saved enough money to fulfill a Soviet dream: to move out of oppressive communal flats to the south, to buy a home, even a car. The empire's collapse changed all that. After Yeltsin freed most prices and inflation skyrocketed in January 1992, families about to leave the Arctic lost their life savings. The phenomenon hit millions of families across Russia. But families here are trapped: They can't afford to leave.

When I visit Vorkuta in January 1993, about 700,000 families are stranded in the Arctic, according to the Russian Federation's Committee of Social and Economic Development of the North. The cost of moving out of the Arctic is about 350,000 rubles ($350), while the monthly salary, even though it is higher than average, is still only 50,000 rubles ($50).

"Before, when people retired, they bought cars and dachas. Now fifteen to twenty years of their life's work has been wiped out," says Alexander Segal, the mayor of Vorkuta, in a large office with red carpets, a large portrait of Lenin looming behind him, and an American flag on his desk.

Segal, a trim, mustached forty-seven-year-old, moved here sixteen years ago. He is from Yekaterinburg, Yeltsin's hometown in the Urals. "About forty thousand people can't afford to leave Vorkuta," Segal says. "It's a crisis situation."

At the same time, there is a massive struggle for control of Russia's social security and pension funds, which used to be administered by the only legal trade union allowed under Communism, which every worker in the empire had to join from Stalin's time on. As you can imagine, the union was unbelievably rich. It still controls billions of dollars through the Social Insurance Fund of the Russian Federation.

In addition to the social security and pension funds, the union, now, perhaps misleadingly, renamed the Federation of Independent Trade Unions (FITU), owns property around the world: a five-building complex in Moscow where five thousand people once worked, offices and vacation resorts across the empire, as well as its own consulate-like buildings in foreign lands, seventy-eight newspapers, sixty press centers, think tanks, transportation networks, and more. The value of these holdings is estimated to be in the billions of dollars.

After the empire collapsed, new trade unions began to sprout up. All want a piece of FITU's assets. One of the first unions to split is the Independent Miners' Union. Some of the new unions that broke from the old monolith tend to be more reform-oriented, while FITU supports centrists and Communists. Since the collapse of Communism, new trade unions in ex-Soviet republics have also claimed their share of the union's material wealth. Not surprisingly, FITU leaders, grimly determined not to relinquish any part of the union's portfolio, have called for the restoration of the Soviet empire.

While following the money trail of the social security fund—in which the Russian parliament investigated corruption charges—I am drawn by pictures of miners with jet black faces; they haven't received salaries for so long that they can't afford to buy soap. Safety conditions in the mines here are as bad as in prewar America.

When the mines close, so will the towns. Under the Soviet system, employers, like coal-mine directors, were responsible for almost all aspects of their workers' lives: schools, stores, roads, and hospitals, even summer vacations for workers and their families. Shutdowns of these mines will mean social trouble on a national scale. That is why I have come to Vorkuta.

White is all I see when my translator Kolya and I arrive. Parents tow children wrapped in fur behind them in sleighs. Crisp, sparkling snow is piled higher than people on roadsides. It is pristine white, unlike Moscow. Men sell slabs of raw frozen salmon on the street.

Vorkuta is *rich* with coal. But under Communism, the mines supported too many employees and depended on state subsidies to survive. Now the subsidies—if they are not siphoned off—arrive late, if at all. It's the same with workers' salaries. Mine directors also sell directly to the West for hard currency, which can be deposited in Swiss bank accounts—bypassing the workers altogether.

While sophisticated Muscovites think of Vorkuta as an Arctic outpost, it is considered the height of luxury, a big-city getaway, by those who work farther north. When these adventurers want a break, Kolya and I discover, they come to our hotel.

The first night, we dine in what appears to be a workers' cafeteria. I have the usual Intourist fare: chicken. It's the only item available, a spoon the only cutlery. There are no napkins on the table, but there is a sink at the entrance to wash your hands. The men drink substantial glasses of vodka, as if it were water.

The next night we discover the other restaurant. "Real Russian gourmet food. I don't believe it!" says Kolya, as his eyes devour the menu.

"I'm sure they'll be out of everything," he adds.

The prices are outrageously cheap, perhaps the reward for making it this far. Kolya, the seasoned Muscovite, does the ordering. Salmon in cream, baked mushrooms and cheese, cold smoked fish, and caviar.

Before I head to the coal mines, I interview Alexander Marmalukov, head of the Independent Miners' Union. "Safety conditions are so bad, deaths are frequent. I've been to too many friends' graves," says Marmalukov, forty-five, a small, gangly man with drooping mustache who worked as a coal miner for fifteen years. He speaks to me in his office under a large portrait of Lenin.

Soon I meet Afanasy Prasalov, the mine director, a large, balding, comfortable-looking man who also sits under a portrait of Lenin. Prasalov, sixty-three, was born in Arlovsk, a rural area south of Moscow. He moved to Vorkuta twenty years ago.

"It was a chance to change my life," he says. "I planned to stay, make some money, and go home, but this city is magical."

Prasalov introduces me to Leliyah Gordieko, who helps me change into coal-mining gear. Leliyah, forty-six, has worked here for seventeen years. After clearing the men from an orderly locker room, we strip down and add layers of clothing: thin cotton, then heavy padding. We wrap our bare feet in cloth before putting on thick boots. I hang equipment from a belt slung on my hips, an electric light on my hat. The equipment and clothing make movement awkward. We descend into darkness, cold, and damp. I hear water dripping and the voices of workers in the distance. Up ahead are the tracks of a miniature train. Dozens of workers with black faces and glazed eyes hunch over inside the low-roofed carts, which are scrawled with obscenities. They are taking a brief break. Some play cards. They look so old. We walk along some planks, single file, watching our way.

After our descent, Leliyah and I scrub and sauna in the director's private quarters. I pass on female bonding, which would mean letting this woman hit me with birch-tree branches until it hurt.

The director has prepared a lunchtime feast, far from typical workers' fare. There seems to be no end to Prasalov's appetite—and toasts. First, welcoming the "American" to Russia. ("It's all the same," he says, when I explain that I'm Canadian.) We drink to the first "American" to visit the mine and, he says, in an additional toast, "to top it all off—you're a woman!"

The toasts continue. "To Russian and American friendship! To the end of the Cold War!"

I ask about miners' salaries. The highest-paid miner receives seventy thousand rubles, about seventy dollars, a month, far above the national average.

Nikolai Karelin, one of the managers at the lunch—a working-class Ukrainian who made his way to management—then asks me a direct question.

"What is *your* salary?"

At first I answer diplomatically: "A lot compared to Russian salaries, but modest by North American standards."

He doesn't let me off that easy. Karelin has been direct with me. I owe him the same. Still, I feel awkward. I say what my starting salary was, which, no matter how low for the West, causes astonished silence here.

It's a few weeks after my twenty-fifth birthday; I'm just three years out of graduate school. Karelin, twice my age, earns seventy thousand rubles a month. It is a sobering moment. Then he starts drinking again.

"I'd like to invite you and Kolya to my home for dinner," Karelin says.

"We'd love to."

Children toboggan outside in the dark, too close, I think, to cars.

Although Karelin is one of the mine's top managers, he, his wife, Alla, and their seven-year-old daughter, Anya, born in Vorkuta, still live in a two-room communal flat. "We're still waiting for our private flat," he says. "It was promised *eight* years ago," Alla adds.

She pours us strong Russian tea and a sticky sweet liqueur, and offers us thick white slabs of *salo*—pig fat. Salo is such a popular snack in parts of the FSU that it is nicknamed Snickers, after the chocolate bar.

The flat is crammed with electronic goods and Anya's drawings. Inflation is so high that the Karelins spend money as fast as they can. We watch a movie on their new video machine. The film is *Cabaret*.

Anya, the small, blonde, blue-eyed angel, stares wide-eyed at the screen as she seraphically sings "Money Makes the World Go Round" with Liza Minnelli.

Before we leave, Vitaly Troshin, the chief architect for the city, takes us on a bumpy jeep ride to see the remains of the gulag. "Vorkuta was built by Stalin's prisoners from the Soviet Union, Eastern Europe, and Germany," he says. When coal was discovered, the prisoners helped build the mines, the railway, and the city infrastructure. Thousands of prisoners were also executed here: as many as 1,300 a *day*.

"If poltergeists really exist, we're in for trouble," Troshin says. "Factories and schools were built directly on graves—like everything in Vorkuta. This was the main center for prison camps in the Arctic region."

Troshin, whose wild-eyed look, frazzled hair, bushy beard, and intelligent eyes give him the air of a nineteenth-century novelist, is also the unpaid local representative of Memorial, a human rights group created during perestroika by gulag survivors to document atrocities and help victims' families.

Ten minutes outside Vorkuta, the barren white landscape begins to reveal itself and yield its skeletons: piecemeal gates and barracks peeking out from shrouds of snow. Though it is early afternoon, the sun is already veiled in a misty gauze, a blanket of iridescent white. Suddenly, so much snow kicks up, bleaching, purifying the scene so blindingly, we can barely see. "[Rutskoi, the vice president of Russia,] got lost here once," Troshin chuckles. "We spent eight hours looking for him."

As the unheated military jeep flies on ice, Troshin tells us more about a project that combines both his talent, architecture, and his passion, human rights.

"I want to create a monument in memory of the thousands of gulag victims who were shipped here," Troshin says. More than one million political prisoners passed through about eighty camps in the Vorkuta area, mainly between 1934 and 1957. "Some of them may have been Americans," Troshin says.

He also wants to build a "humanitarian religious center" for all religions, a gulag museum, and a center for human rights. "I want the memorial to be an inspiration for people to fight against totalitarianism," he says, adding that fund-raising has already begun. When we talk, Troshin, with the support of Segal and the city administration, has raised 140 million rubles ($140,000). He estimates he'll need 2 billion rubles ($2 million).

We stop in front of the remains of a prison camp for "women and foreigners." Years from now, I will still think about this camp, and about a Russian film documentary I see about the gulags. In the film, a Russian journalist interviews an old man who worked as a gulag guard. The guard says he knew all along that the political prisoners were innocent. When asked if he feels remorse for his actions, the guard says no. "There were mines and railways to build, and work to do. *Somebody* had to do it."

Only one large memorial has been built so far. It is surrounded by a field of crosses, blurred by snow in the middle of nowhere. It was created in the fall of 1992 in memory of the gulags' Lithuanian prisoners. It's easy to miss: small crosses, like memory, buried under an avalanche of history.

After Stalin's death in March 1953, prisoners launched strikes and refused to continue forced labor. But by 1968, when most political prisoners were freed, that rebellious spirit had perhaps frozen to death. Many freed prisoners continued to live in their cells. They had nowhere else to go.

"It's a strange and awful city," Troshin says. "Prisoners continued to live in the same place. Only the fence and soldiers were gone."

By then, many of the prisoners' families had moved to Vorkuta. They're still here, joined by those who can't afford to leave, and by Anya, whose rendition of "Money Makes the World Go Round" still haunts me, like the small crosses, buried in snow.

CHAPTER 7

--->

Cars and Drivers

Learning the Rules of the Road—On Guns, Cars,
Drivers, Bribes, Cops, and, of Course, Robbers

He who fears wolves will never go into the woods.

— Russian proverb

Having a driver in Moscow is not as decadent as it sounds. While Ivy League gangsters ride in *Chaikas*, Russian limousines, my drivers usually have beat-up Ladas, except for Sergei, who drives an eight-year-old white Mercedes. Sergei received the car, with red Tajik diplomatic plates, from an old boss who couldn't pay him. He loses it when he lends it to a friend. (The mob blows it up.) My drivers' cars also tend to break down in the cold, at the end of a long day, or when I'm late for a plane. That's when they heat up, on the verge of explosion.

Still, in Moscow, a good driver is indispensable. My first driver, Valery, helps me learn Russian and shops for my dinner parties. Good drivers know how to obtain hard-to-get goods, even guns and Mace, and how to put up mosquito nets and screens in summertime. In 1992, when buying and selling hard currency is officially still illegal, drivers carry suitcases stuffed with money. They are our private mobile banks. The drivers' rate may not be the best, but the bankers are reliable and trustworthy. (When I first arrive, the rate is ninety rubles to one dollar. By 1996, when I leave, it's more than five thousand rubles to the dollar.)

One of the best ways to understand a city is to study its internal arteries, the roads, and get to know the people who drive—and regulate—them.

In Moscow, the roads are lawless, like the country. Everyone makes illegal turns. Streets are changed from two-way to one-way — and back—too fast to remember. The potholes are like Cambodian minefields. I have heard gunfire more often than anyone would expect in a European capital in peacetime. Especially at night.

More than 1.7 million cars clog city streets. Overcrowding is one reason why accident victims litter the roadsides. And ambulances take their time arriving. One colleague—who broke her ribs in an *avariya*, an accident, alive only because she was in a Volvo instead of a tinny Lada—waited forty-five minutes in a blizzard for an ambulance, which never showed. She then hitchhiked to an American clinic, whose X-ray machine was on the blink. "They sent me to a Russian hospital," she says wryly, "which is what I was trying to avoid."

I would hate to drive in this city. It is such a *koshmar*, a nightmare. Cars are stolen so often I cringe thinking about owning one. Forget the radios. Muscovites take the windshield wipers off cars when they park.

Then there are the cab drivers. Even with personal drivers, I take lots of cabs. Especially at night, when I send my driver home. Cab services are rare. You have to call to reserve a cab at least one hour in advance, and they're often already completely booked.

Some of the cabs are legit official old Soviet taxis, run-down white or blue Volgas. More often they're gypsy cabs, strangers who stop for extra rubles. They only take you if *they're* going your way, depending, of course, on the price. (Russians rub their middle finger and thumb together to signify cash.) Practically every Muscovite with a car is a part-time driver. Gypsy cabbing through Moscow is the best way to sample the population, and to practice Russian. The downside is danger. Think about it. Would you get into a strange man's car in the Bronx, or on Fifth Avenue for that matter?

I have been driven by old men with gold teeth, and old men with no teeth, in cars that break down, and in cars that don't brake at all. I've been driven by young and old biznesmeni and mobsters in Porsches and Ladas who refuse to take money; and their chauffeurs, who ask for as much as they can.

I've also had drivers who were sailors; vodka-soaked men who I didn't realize smell like distilleries until it was too late; young couples who, like me, were on their way home from dinners; scary men in combat fatigues; smugglers, soldiers; an Armenian diplomat whose wife had just had a baby; fur sellers; and a retired acrobat with the Moscow circus who had toured the world.

I have encountered raving anti-Semites, an old man who spoke Yiddish and was born near my grandmother's village, KGB agents, ambulance drivers, hard-core Communists, potential psychopaths, thugs, black market dealers, fun-loving students, and the oddest assortment of personal drivers.

At first, I don't speak Russian and can barely pronounce where I'm going. I get into cabs late at night, unable to give directions, just the address of my flat. No one has maps. We often get lost. The drivers, incredibly good-natured, get out of their cars in snowstorms and sometimes ask dozens of people directions before reaching our destination. They never complain. Sometimes I'm so frightened I keep my hand on the door handle, ready to jump out. Sometimes I do—though not when I should.

"You're going the wrong way. Please turn around," I tell a middle-aged man who is taking me from the Slav to my flat. "No, this is a shortcut." I ask him again. Again he refuses. Spooked, I run with my instinct and jump out. I stand on a deserted road, at night, waiting for another car. No one stops. Finally, the same tinny car returns. "Please get in," the man says.

"Why are you afraid of me?" he asks, explaining the shortcut he wanted to take.

"Don't take it personally," I say. "Taking cabs at night can be dangerous." He drives me home and refuses to take money.

"I'm a professor at the university. I have a family," he says. "Please don't think all Russians are bad people."

I remember one of the first cabs I took at night. I was wearing jeans and carrying a knapsack. If anything, I looked like a student. "So, you're a journalist," said the cabby, with an ever-so-polite, slightly supercilious smile. His English was perfect. Too perfect. I just said yes, fast learning not to be surprised by anything.

"Coincidences" like this are common, especially for arriving diplomats and journalists. One young diplomat friend says the week he arrived the same cabby stopped for him every day, and is now almost his regular driver. "I don't care who sent him," the diplomat says. "He's cheap and personable. Besides, I have nothing to hide."

Other drivers are less sinister. I once have a toothless man insist on teaching me two essential Russian phrases: "I love Russia," and "The Russian people are very kind." He makes me repeat the phrases over and over, correcting my accent.

I take a lift from a guy in a broken-down blue car. He charges me five thousand rubles, five dollars and relatively expensive at the time for the short distance. He looks desperately poor. I have a ten-thousand-ruble note. He opens a large shopping bag to get change. It's stuffed with *hundreds* of American one-hundred-dollar bills. Fishing amidst the American hundreds for five thousand rubles, he looks up, embarrassed.

"I'm a waiter," he says, naming one of the big hotels. "I get some of the best caviar in Russia, and run a biznes on the side."

"So that's why most restaurants in Moscow are so often out of caviar!" I say.

"If you ever need some, give me a call," he says, scribbling down his number. He looks at me, then again at the bag of hundred-dollar bills, and hands me back my ten-thousand-ruble note.

Another driver, distinguished and fortyish, dressed in Armani and driving his Mercedes, proudly shows me his new Italian passport. "I own a textile factory and have two homes in Italy. I only come to Moscow on business now," he says, leaving me his card after I politely decline his dinner offer.

Soon the Slav starts a twenty-dollar-an-hour taxi service, which fast rises in price. Shiny cream Mercedes line the drive, taking up precious parking space. They are part of a rather dubious city government-linked monopoly. "There are so many idle drivers, you can usually bargain with them," a friendly, fur-caped doorman tells me. It's still more than the streets, but the drivers are slightly less likely to be psychos. By 1996, there are even sunny yellow cabs that look like they're direct from New York City. I tell the driver of one I'm delighted to take it. Then he tells me the price.

By now, I no longer say I'm in a rush. The last time I did, the tattoo-knuckled, aviator-sunglassed driver turned on a flashing blue light on top of his car, and proceeded to speed down the wrong side of the road.

"Are you a police officer?" I asked, a nervous bundle of naïve skepticism.

The man with the walrus mustache just laughed.

"The goal," I reminded him, with as much of a smile as I could muster, "is to drive to arrive alive." (It's a favorite expression of my father's.)

By the time we did arrive, I was shaking. The Slav doorman who opened the car door was impressed. Car and driver were apparently from the presidential guard.

By now, I've been here so long that I start getting cabbies who know the same people as I do. There are also now some people who shun cars and drivers altogether—whether for legitimate reasons or eccentric, mad whim stemming from living here too long. One biznesman, who used to be chauffeured around town in a cream-colored Mercedes, invites me out and then shows up on foot. Two mean-looking bodyguards lurk behind him. Besides not adding much to the general conversation, and cramping their boss's, uh, style, they're not the most reassuring types to travel with: If the bullets come, you know you're the last one they'll decide to defend.

"What happened to your car?" I ask.

"I've ditched it. I'm sick of being followed," he says, sweat streaming down his face from subwaying and walking across Red Square to my flat in the midst of a killer heatwave.

The newborn pedestrian is Paul Tatum, a forty-one-year-old American and part owner of the Slav. He is a bit obsessed, you could say, about a well-publicized, ongoing battle with a Chechen biznes associate. The feud, which has been going on for years, is filled with intrigue, police, padlocks, a stabbing—and, ultimately, murder.

"It's much easier to lose your tail in a crowded metro. Besides, I'm rediscovering the city," he says, "though the stress is killing me."

Then there's the dreaded GAI (pronounced guy-ee), or traffic police, who can be as corrupt and dangerous as the gangsters who rule the taxi stands by Moscow hotels, airports, and train stations. Russians share the worldwide lack of respect for law enforcement officials. "Police are called *musor*," says Kolya, who later tells me the word means trash. The GAI stand on street corners blowing whistles, or loom above roads in lookout posts. They look like overstuffed penguins, in their thick-belted coats and shapkas.

When I arrive, the big story is bribery. The poorly paid GAI are prone to stopping cars with foreign plates. This is such a control freak-oriented country that the Communists labeled foreigners by their license plates: different colors for journalists, executives, and diplomats, different numbers for each country. The "democrats" continue the practice.

The 1992 game of harassing foreigners is to accuse them of drunk driving. When the driver protests her innocence, she is threatened with a dirty needle: a blood test. In horror, the driver pays whatever she can. I know Westerners who budget for this and keep some cash with their driving papers to hand over to the GAI. Others stash bottles of vodka in their trunks. Some simply say, "How much is the fine? It's okay, I don't need a receipt."

Diplomats, though, are immune from prosecution. (Some use their status to smuggle out art.) Their special privilege creates a new word in our own Russian-English patois. *Razvernyis* means "U-turn." A *dipraz*, or "dip-turn," means any illegal turn, which is often necessary because of the proliferation of one-way streets.

The maf, of course, enjoy their own special status. Once, on an unasked-for and terrifying joyride with a mafiya millionaire, I ask, then demand, that he slow down. It is past 2 A.M. and he is running red lights. The roads are slippery. "The police will give you a ticket," I say. "Hah!" he brags. "The police *salute* me when they see me."

When I first arrive, a Western colleague drives me home from a dinner at the Spanish bar, at the time one of the only hard-currency restaurants in town. (It turns out to be the start of a Russian food empire—from formal French and authentic Spanish, to American subs and Oreo milkshakes, Tex-Mex, and more.) The problems begin when my friend doesn't immediately offer a bribe when, inevitably, we are pulled over.

At 1 A.M. we are escorted to a local police station. The police take my friend away, I think to another room. Nobody anwers my questions, rattled off in miserable broken Russian. I stare at the officer behind the desk. He ignores me, pretending to do paperwork. I hear laughter from a back room, where the policemen are watching a porn video. Outraged, I cool off in the car, expecting my friend any moment.

When my toes are on the verge of freezing, I barge back in and, in awful Russian, demand to know what's going on. "I'm a journalist!" I threaten, hoping this will instill fear, or at least interest, in their guts. The captain merely looks up, then goes back to his silence and paper. I move into a second, fearful stage beyond the original *inconvenience* of it all. There should always be a witness, I keep thinking.

I hear the television and cackles of male laughter. More cops rush in, rifles tossed sinisterly over their shoulders.

Hours later, my friend returns. "They took me to a hospital for a blood test," he says. (The police showed some mercy by not administering an on-the-spot test with the vile and fearsomely dreaded dirty needle.) Results confirm he is not drunk. We're on our way, though there's no guarantee we won't get stopped again.

Another expatriate is attacked and professionally beaten up by some traffic police on his way home from a meeting with associates of some Russian émigrés who soon make headlines in a corruption scandal that rocks the government. "I speak fluent Russian," he says, "but before I opened my mouth or showed them my documents, they started to club me." Perhaps it is a warning.

As strange is replaced by familiar, the GAI become a source of amusement or, at worst, a nuisance, instead of dread. Humor and patient good-naturedness help.

If I'm with a Russian driver, I let him deal with the GAI, even if it means being held up while driver and GAI haggle before parting with the ever-present male handshake (and sometime cash exchange). There are two rules I've learned to live by in Moscow. (Others will follow.) The first is, Never explain. The second: Never let them know you're late. The key is to look like you've got all the time in the world. The corollary: Don't be uptight about arriving on time.

If I am stopped while with friends, we often just smile, thank them, and ask for directions, as if we are lost, which we often are. Once, when I'm with a new correspondent, driving in Moscow for the first time, I tell the GAI he is a big *nachalnik*, or boss, and how dare they stop him. Somehow, perhaps because in 1992 there is still some innate instinct to obey authority, whatever authority, it works.

One of my favorites is a third-hand story about a journalist who uses the same expression whenever he's stopped: "*Ya ni ponedelnik*," which means "I'm not Monday." The phrase is similar to "*Ya ni ponemayu*," or "I don't understand." The GAI usually wave him on his way.

Although the country is falling apart, some Russians still live in style, just as others did under Stalin and the tsars. While Moscow roads are notorious for potholes, some roads leading out of the city—for bullet-proof Mercedes driving to the exclusive guarded dachas of the new rich and old Communists—are smooth and perfectly paved. Militia are posted every few miles, ensuring that this part of Russia is as peaceful as a stretch of French countryside, without the strikes. (Unless someone has orders to run you down.)

NASTY URBAN MYTHS

Besides making good companions, drivers are also impromptu bodyguards, when need be, shoppers, handymen, and language teachers. The secret is to get someone who doesn't speak English, like Valery. This is how I learn Russian. I point to cars and learn the names of colors. We recite basics, like the days of the week and how to conjugate verbs, such as "to write." Once a basic level is achieved, Valery brings me a newspaper each morning. I struggle to read the headlines without knowing the words. He explains until I understand.

Valery is a heavyset Russian in his forties. Because he helps with my personal, as well as professional, errands, I share his cost with the *MT*, which recommended him. His uniform of choice is a mauve shirt, sleeves rolled up and front unbuttoned to reveal a large gold cross. He reminds me of a Russian Elvis. He is good-natured, with a kind face and a hearty kind of laugh. I think we'll get along, despite his beastly orange, rust-speckled car. Valery later trades it for a white Lada with a fractured windshield that could shatter at any moment. It takes months before Valery heeds my requests, fixes it, and buys a map. (For some reason, drivers think maps un-macho, and prefer to spend hours lost, on roundabout routes, asking clueless "brothers" and "sailors" for directions.)

Valery fast becomes my right-hand man. ("He's so proud you call him that, he told all the other drivers," a colleague later tells me.) He knows my quirks, doesn't complain when I oversleep, and waits downstairs for long stretches, even after I have insisted that he arrive early. He never lets me down, even when I need rides to the airport at 5 A.M. I give Valery afternoons off when I don't need him, hear all about his children, and help him choose a birthday gift for his wife. He brings me flowers, apples, and bags of walnuts from his dacha.

Valery also drives me to the markets. I soon stop buying meat there. I don't like the display of bloody carcasses, and preparing it makes me queasy. "When I took my meat home, it was riddled with maggots," says Euan, an *MT* colleague. Russian newspapers report that *human* flesh containing bullets has also been sold at the markets. Soviet rule was too strict for such incidents, but now there's so much else to deal with that food quality seems to be one of the last concerns of the authorities. Russians sell expired milk outside the markets, raw fish on crates near subways.

"How much did you pay for the garlic, the tomatoes, the smetana?" asks Valery when I return to the car. Whatever I say is too much. "Hmph!" he exclaims. "I could get that for"—a few rubles less. Finally, I give up. Valery does the shopping, but he goes to so many places that it fast loses its original, cost-effective purpose.

After a year, I almost stop patronizing the markets altogether: lack of freshness, questionable quality control, and unknown radiation levels in the produce come at prices that are often higher than the ever-increasing selection of fresh, imported food in the shops.

When I have dinner parties, Valery goes to dozens of stores to get everything I need, including fresh *lavache* dough from a Georgian bakery. "Have fun while you can," Valery says. "Soon you'll quit work, get married, and start having babies!"

Valery is also a doctor, of sorts. "Have some raw onions, garlic, and vodka," he says as soon as I start to sniffle. "It's the only way to cure a cold." He proudly tells stories about his family "gang," which shook down (literally shook the foundations of) a kiosk after a mobster ripped off one of their own.

Once, when Kolya and I are stuck all day at the holding cell for children, Valery goes home for lunch. When we finally emerge after dark, Valery is waiting with delicious fresh liverwurst sandwiches and a still hot flask of coffee, in a colorful Russian matrioshka-style container, prepared by his wife.

Like all drivers, Valery is a tireless gossip. Once, in response to his eternal question, I say that of course I plan on getting married. What I mean is: someday. This transforms into an office rumor about my upcoming marriage. The rumor starts in the drivers' room and spreads to the publisher. Valery doesn't understand why I *want* to work, why I don't *want* to get married right away. (Neither does Kolya: "Some foreigners come to Moscow for money, because they can't get jobs elsewhere, or because they're trying to escape someone, or something. But none of this applies to you. I still can't figure out why you're here!")

Ambulances are also popular modes of transport. The drivers are so poorly paid they're often looking for ways to make extra money. They also have reputations for safety and trustworthiness. At least until the Moscow urban myths come along: Never take a ride from an ambulance is one. The drivers will inject you with drugs, perform weird experiments, or take some of your vital organs to sell on the black market.

Russian urban myths far outdo their North American counterparts. The best North American ones are usually about New York sewers filled with alligators, drunken frat boys who discover they've gang-raped their sisters or who awaken after a one-night stand to discover a message scrawled in red lipstick across the bathroom mirror: *Welcome to the world of AIDS.*

Moscow urban myths are more creative. There is the underground city for forty thousand elite in case of nuclear attack, with shopping malls, movie theaters, swimming pools, and fresh food brought in daily. (This could be based in fact. One respected British paper even printed a map of the underground city, although foreign journalists who brave the depths encounter only sewers and, sometimes, knife-wielding homeless.)

One of my favorite urban myths is about Yuri Gagarin, Russia's first cosmonaut. My Russian teacher swears she read about it in a letter-to-the-editor of a well-established newspaper, from one of the doctors involved. The story, which reflects Russians' classic Communist paranoia, goes like this: Gagarin didn't die during an experimental plane test crash in March 1968, as is believed. Instead, after he snubbed Soviet leader Leonid Brezhnev at a party, Brezhnev placed him in an insane asylum, not unusual for political prisoners then. Gagarin underwent reconstructive facial surgery. He emerged a different person, to live a long but cursed life. The more he declared himself Gagarin, the more doctors confirmed his "insanity."

A GUNPOINT TOUR OF MOSCOW:
TVERSKAYA STREET, FEBRUARY 1993—7 P.M.

Valery is sick, so Pasha, another driver, drops me off at Tverskaya. I'm going to do some errands, including food shopping at one of my favorite hard-currency stores. An out-of-town friend is coming to visit.

"Do you think I should get a gas gun?" I ask Pasha, as I'm about to step out of the car. I don't believe in guns, but just this morning a Russian colleague was robbed outside a hard-currency store. Gas guns shoot tear gas. They cost around one hundred dollars.

"If you want to buy one, just let me know," says Pasha. Like all drivers, he is versatile, enterprising, and knows where to obtain *anything* in Moscow, no matter how difficult.

At least half the foreigners and even some Russians I know have become targets lately. Two friends, a Scandinavian and a Russian, were severely beaten by some drunken soldiers. The Scandinavian, wearing a soldier's coat, was buying cigarettes at a late-night kiosk. The soldiers thought he was a Russian *pretending* to be a foreigner. They beat him unconscious. Another friend was beaten when he visited an apartment advertised in a newspaper. An American journalist was robbed and beaten in a cab; an Italian friend was robbed *three* times; an American we call the "friendly giant," because he is so tall and good-natured, was rolled on his way out of the Slav. One Western diplomat tells me about unpublicized, and violent, rapes. Foreigners have even been murdered in random attacks and gangland hits.

Several diplomats have offered to teach me how to shoot at an old KGB rifle club. Even some U.S. Marines want to teach me. I have always refused, on principle. "Now I'm thinking about it," I tell Pasha, who drops me off by the Intourist Hotel across the street from Yves Rocher.

Men and women are trudging home in the dark after work. Their heads are bent, chin to neck, as they brace against the cold. Loaded with parcels, Russians still buy most goods on the street. Coming up the *perekhod*, or underground crossing, there is a particularly nasty ice patch. To be initiated into Moscow winter means a rump-landing ice flip at least once a season.

I go to Yves Rocher and then buy bags of Norwegian salmon, Russian caviar, American shrimp, French cheeses, and Italian wines. Back by the Intourist, I wait for a cab. I refuse the first that pulls up. He looks a little too rough. Then a young, clean-cut blond man in a regular old Soviet taxi stops. I get in.

We are driving up Mitchurinsky Prospekt when we reach a red light. From the shadows, three gun-wielding young men in leather jackets run toward the car. "Step on it!" I yell, shaking the cab driver. "Let's go!" What a close call, I think, what a story to tell.

But the story has just begun. My driver doesn't move. The thugs reach the car. They open the door. One man pulls me out and puts me in the back seat. Two men are on either side of me, so close I can't move. One thug puts his arm around me. His grip is tight, but if anyone peered in, it would look like we're all friends. The third man is in the front seat, beside the cab driver—their partner.

We drive in silence. I don't open my mouth. I don't want to give them an excuse to be violent. I stare straight ahead and surprise myself by keeping so calm.

The car-jacking seems like a setup. Maybe this is some sort of warning, related to a story I'm working on. I've also been investigating kidnappings, which are on the rise. Silently, I add up all the money I have in the bank. I think they'll be disappointed if they're trying to trade me for money.

I think about the book I have just finished reading, Margaret Drabble's *The Gates of Ivory*. It's about an award-winning British writer who leaves the calm safety of England, which he calls Good Time, for Cambodia, which he calls Bad Time. The prophecy becomes real, for him, when he's captured by the Khmer Rouge. "Beware what you read when young," thinks Stephen Cox, Drabble's hero, as he's about to die. "Beware what you feed upon. It may bring you to this shore, this brink, this bridge."

Now I, too, have entered Bad Time. What the hell am I doing in this insane, lawless country? I'm leaving tomorrow, I think. If I get out alive.

Finally, I say one word: "*Pochemu*?" Why? "Money, money," says the ringleader, turning his head. His looks are striking: dark eyes, crooked nose, shiny black hair that flips stylishly. I'm surprised he's not masked. I know I'll always remember his face. One of them says "Ramenky." That's where I live.

The thug on my right checks my pockets and even my cowboy boots for money. He is professional, and does not harass me. The thug on my left tries to do the same. Instinctively, I push him away. "He's already done that," I say. He taps me, softly, on the arm. "Leave her alone!" the first one snaps.

We pull into a deserted parking lot behind an apartment complex. Silently, I freak. The gangster up front goes through my purse. He finds some Somali money, a souvenir from a fellow journalist. "What is this?" he asks. "It's not worth anything. It's from Somalia," I say. He doesn't believe me. They take my Swatch watch, my sheepskin gloves, my purse. (They leave my boots, sheepskin coat, mink shapka, tiny diamond studs.)

"Get out of the car," says the leader as he hands me back my press card, which was in my wallet. I'm terrified to get out. This is when they shoot me, I think, or worse.

"Get out," he says again. "It's over."

I can't believe it.

"Can I have my purse back without the money?" I ask, thinking about my address book, my keys, my glasses, a Central Asian silver bracelet, a minor fortune in Chanel lipstick, which you can't buy in Moscow in early 1993.

"No!" he says.

That's when I run. The car speeds away.

I run to the first apartment building I find, and knock on the first door. It's a risk, I think. I'm in a bad neighborhood, but what choice do I have?

"Who is it?" cries an old woman.

"I'm a foreign journalist," I say, trying to steady my voice. "I've just been robbed. Could I please use your telephone?"

The old woman creaks open the door, but keeps the chain on. I show her my press card.

"Stay there," she says, in a voice without sympathy. "I'll call the police."

I'm not too keen to stay out here. The thugs, or anyone, could show up at any time. "Please," I say. "Could I please come in until the police arrive?"

The apartment is old and musty, like its owner. I call the *MT*. The editors are wonderful and offer to do whatever they can. "I'm on my way to the police station," I say, "and then I'll drop by the office." After my locked-out incidents, I keep a spare set of keys there.

Two plainclothes policemen come in an unmarked car. I'm reluctant to get back into a strange car. "The cab driver wasn't really a cab driver. How do I know you're really police?"

"I'm so sorry," one of the officers says. "This never would have happened under Communism."

"I bet they were Chechens," adds the other officer, who seems upset when I say I think they were Russian.

At the station, I phone Olivia Ward, the new *Toronto Star* bureau chief. When I hear her voice, I lose it. I was so calm, controlled, when dealing with everyone from the thugs to the old woman. Emotion finally returns. Tears gush as I tell her what happened. Such raw emotion seems to embarrass the police. They want to help but don't quite know what to do.

The police take me to the *MT* and then my apartment. I am surprised by how seriously they are treating the robbery. My neighbors are in the halls, near panic-stricken by the commotion. Let a foreigner in and look what happens, I can hear them thinking, afraid that the building will now become a crime target. Natasha, my neighbor, asks if I'm all right.

Pasha, the driver, and Irina, an *MT* employee, meet me at the flat. Irina is a young champion ice skater who had a demanding but privileged life in Communist days. Now her funding is cut to nothing and she works as the *MT* receptionist, giving skating lessons to foreigners on the side. Irina helps write up the police report while I pack.

"The robbers have my address book," I tell her. "They have my keys and they know where I live. I can't stay here. They could come back at any time." Even if I changed the locks, I'd never feel the same here. I've lived on Ramenky Ulitsa for almost exactly one year. I love the flat, but I take this as a sign. It's time to move on.

"You're very lucky," Irina says. "You can pick up and move when you want. That's a luxury most Russians don't have."

Pasha helps take my bags to Olivia's apartment; she has kindly invited me to stay with her while I look for a new flat.

The police stake out my apartment building overnight in case the thieves come by. "Would you have any food for us?" one officer asks. "It's going to be a long night." I'm happy to oblige.

Olivia nurtures me with wine and cheese. Talking to her calms me. So does the Colette novel she thoughtfully leaves for me in the spare room.

The robbery is in the Russian papers the next day, though I don't know how they got it, or why they're interested. When colleagues ask if they can quote me in their stories on rising crime, I say no. I don't even want to write about it. It's still too close.

I spend most of the day steeped in bureaucracy, applying for a new passport and otherwise reestablishing my existence.

Moscow police are notorious for their inefficiency. But, surprisingly, they treat my case as a priority, even though they don't for other foreign journalists in worse shape—robbed and severely beaten. I arrive at the *MT* late in the day, only to discover a police officer waiting for me. "I'm so exhausted," I say. "Can't we do this another time?"

"Please," says the young officer. "The chief is staying late at the station. He's waiting for you." The police chief and his deputy are in his office. I tell them again what happened. We drive to the spot where the thugs jumped into the cab. "I promise we're going to do everything we can to find these men," the chief vows.

Two weeks later, a police officer calls. "I think we've identified the criminals. Are you available this afternoon?" Two officers take me to the heavily guarded police headquarters downtown. Ironically, I've been here recently, investigating a special police unit that still monitors foreigners.

Past the guarded entrance, we walk upstairs to a small, stuffy room. Eight detectives, shirtsleeves rolled up, are puffing away. The windows are closed, the room smoky. They look like detectives all over the world: yellow, pasty faces from too much vodka, too many stale cigarettes, and bad coffee. They stand up and invite me to sit down.

A man pulls out some pictures. I pass on the first black-and-white mug shot. The second photo is easy. A group of young people celebrating somebody's birthday. That's him, on the end. The same black eyes, black hair flipping over one eye, crooked nose. "*Eta on*," I say. "*Tochna*." That's him. Exactly. The room electrifies.

Next surprise. "We've caught him," an officer later calls to tell me. "He's head of a Chechen gang that robs people, mainly single women, with a taxi mafiya outside some of the big hotels.

"You see," he adds, "we knew the robbers weren't Russian!"

The police want me to identify the young gangster in court. But unlike in the West, I'd have to do it face-to-face, knowing that the rest of his gang is still on the streets. "I think the robbery was an attempt to frighten you off a story," says one top Western diplomat.

He and other diplomats advise me not to testify. "If we were in North America, it would be different," one says. "But it might put you in danger. It's not worth it." I do, however, identify the thief on paper. I'm impressed with the police. It's good to know they can be so efficient. I just wish they were more often.

News of the robbery gets around. Months later, when I meet people on assignment, they ask if I'm all right. For me, the robbery is a turning point. A year ago, Muscovites worried about where to find food. Now they're terrified of crime. Democratic disillusionment has set in.

I try not to travel on my own at night anymore. Still, I refuse a night driver or bodyguard, although many people I know have one or both. I can't afford it. I also can't live that way. Women I know who live alone have informal "buddy systems" so they can always let someone know where they are.

Still, there are times where I'm unavoidably stuck traveling alone at night. "Here, take this," says one photographer friend, who invites me parachute-jumping with a KGB pal after the robbery. It's late at night and I'm taking a cab home, alone. My friend shoves some sort of electric-shock contraption into my hand. "You can zap the cab driver with it if anything happens," he says. It's called a stunner, and the device is quite popular in Moscow these days. But holding it repels me. I'll never carry it again.

CHAPTER 8

Ukraine, Human Trafficking in the Baltics, and the Black-Booted Thugs of Memory

Odessa Relatives, the Diva in Riga, a Bejeweled Russian Priest from Manhattan and the French Riviera, and His Dwarf Sidekick— Pamyat Pals Flying in for the Trial

Richter, one of the drivers, brought in a handful of leaflets accusing the Jews of the murder. They had been printed, Yakov saw when he examined one, by the Black Hundreds organization. Their emblem, the Imperial double-headed eagle, was imprinted on the cover, and under it: SAVE RUSSIA FROM THE JEWS. In his room that night, Yakov, in fascination, read that the boy had been bled to death for religious purposes so that the Jews could collect his blood and deliver it to the synagogue for the making of Passover matzos. Though this was ridiculous he was frightened.... His own father had been killed in an incident not more than a year after Yakov's birth.... But the son had lived through a pogrom when he was a schoolboy, a three-day Cossack raid. On the third morning when the houses were still smoldering and he was led, with a half dozen other children, out of a cellar where they had been hiding he saw a black-bearded Jew with a white sausage stuffed into his mouth, lying in the road on a pile of bloody feathers, a peasant's pig devouring his arm.

— BERNARD MALAMUD, *The Fixer*

As the MT grows, we move into new offices in the *Pravda* building—the heart of Communism. We are a Western capitalist newspaper. For some, our invasion is sacrilege. Die-hard old Communists from *Rabochnaya Tribuna*, the *Workers' Tribune*, stage a sit-in. Our dollars have bought some of their office space. We take over a floor, construct a Western newsroom, even renovate bathrooms and keep them locked because reporters on other floors steal the soap and toilet paper.

MT staff sometimes refuse, or forget, to respect Communist convention, like showing a special pass to get past the lobby, even though the same guard sees us every day. I smile and say good morning—without showing my pass—to a babushka at a side entrance. She smiles back and lets me through, though I've seen her give hell to men her age.

Visitors are supposed to walk in the cold to another building, to a small room, where a clerk phones the *MT*, gets permission, and writes out a special entrance pass. The wait is often long. The clerks, bodiless heads in ancient wooden booths, often shut their windows inexplicably for various lengths of time, just as you're about to approach them. We simplify the process, though it's still a feature of most government buildings in the country. Russians I work with, especially young ones, have more patience. They sympathize with the clerks in the booths, paper tigers who once demanded respect and are now often too old and ill-prepared to adapt to the new world their country has unexpectedly plunged into.

Our attitude is so un-Soviet that Derk Sauer calls a staff meeting soon after we move in. "I know that some of the rules here seem antiquated and absurd, but we are guests here. It's hard enough for people to get used to us. Please try to show some respect," he says. We soon integrate into the building, and mingle with fellow journalists over vodka in the bar.

A few weeks after I'm robbed, in February 1993, I head to Yalta, in what is now the Ukrainian Crimea, for a short break. The site of the 1945 conference of Roosevelt, Stalin, and Churchill, where plans were made to divide Germany, Yalta is now a summer playground for the nouveaux riches zolotaya molodezh, the golden youth. I go to Ukraine without the officially required visa. Later the border controls will be stricter, as Russia and Ukraine fight over the Black Sea Fleet and Russia's only access to a warm seaport.

I have visited Ukraine before, in the summer of 1992, with my parents. We met our last living relative in the FSU, a forty-four-year-old engineer named Josef, who lives in Odessa. When my grandmother came to Canada, one half-brother, the eldest, stayed behind. His son, Josef's father, served as a captain in the Red Army during World War II.

Now history has repeated itself. In 1989, when more Jews were allowed to emigrate, Josef's brother and his family moved to the United States. "I didn't go," Josef said, "because my parents were still alive. They refused to leave, so I stayed to take care of them." Although his parents are now dead, Joesf stayed on. "It's hard for a man my age to begin again—and it's not so bad here."

Josef's wife and teenage daughter thought otherwise. The couple divorced. Wife and daughter emigrated.

Josef remarried and now had a beautiful second wife and baby daughter. ("We had a large flat, but I had to give it up after the divorce," he said.)

Landing in Odessa, the air felt fresher, full of warmth and sun. The city descends in terraces from a hill to the sea. It's beautiful. Josef had no car, so he came with a friend to pick us up at the airport. Right away he felt like family. He brought flowers for my mother and me and filled his flat, even the bathtub, with roses. The family lived in a small apartment in a wide, fragrant, tree-lined street in the center of Odessa. Josef's wife, Ina, had prepared a feast, which was out cooling on the porch. (There was no fridge.) We ate at a small coffee table. Ina made beet borscht *exactly* as my grandmother did—I've never tasted it that way anywhere else.

Like many Ukrainian Jews, Josef and his friends considered themselves ethnically Jewish and spiritually atheist. "I've been discriminated against because of my religion, even though I was brought up as an atheist, like all good Communists," Josef said. "I never believed in God, and I'm not going to start now." However, his friends' children said the younger generation was interested in learning about Judaism.*

---

* Despite pogroms and the Holocaust, Ukraine's Jewish population of 500,000 is still the fifth largest in the world, though Odessa's Jewish community has shrunk from 100,000 people in 1990 to 40,000 people today.

We spent our days at the Greek beach, Arcadia, reputedly the best of the cosmopolitan city's many ethnic beaches, saw the Odessa Steps—unchanged since Sergei Eisenstein filmed them for the famous massacre sequence in his 1925 *Battleship Potemkin*—and attended a concert in the nineteenth-century Viennese-designed opera house reminiscent of the old Paris Opera. A hotbed of activity during the 1905 revolution, Odessa often serves as a backdrop in the works of Sholem Aleichem and Isaac Babel; Pushkin lived here in exile during the 1820s.

Yalta, I discover in February 1993, is another seaside center rich in literary history. Nestled between the Black Sea and the Crimean Mountains, the resort capital has the feel of the French and Italian Rivieras. Tsar Alexander II summered in nearby Livadia. Aristocrats built lavish estates in Yalta, where Chekhov met Tolstoy and wrote *The Cherry Orchard* and *Three Sisters*—and where Rachmaninoff played piano. After the Revolution, the estates were transformed into spa-like resorts for workers. However, the Communist elite continued to build their private dachas nearby. Like Odessa, Yalta was, over the centuries, a multicultural center. The Romans introduced Christianity to the Crimea. Yalta then became an outpost of the Byzantine empire—until 1243, when it was conquered by Tatars. Russia did not possess Yalta until 1783. The resort town was fiercely anti-Red. During the Nazi occupation, Yalta lost almost half its population; Stalin deported the remaining Tatars —about 250,000 of them—after the war, to Uzbekistan. Almost one third died on route. Now Yalta is the playground for the new elite —Russia's new rich.

After a brief rest (hotel and restaurant standards are still Soviet as opposed to Western), I'm back in Moscow. But I leave almost immediately for the Baltics. The last republics swallowed by the Soviets, they were the first to revert to capitalism. Even the airfare is expensive.

Riga, Latvia, is a charming old city of cobblestoned streets that resembles both Eastern Europe and Germany with the earthy comfort and efficiency of nearby Scandinavia. The city was founded by an order of German knights, the Livonians, in 1201, and used as a base to spread Christianity through the Baltics. (Churches throughout the Soviet Union were transformed by the Bolsheviks into ordinary state buildings. There's a church on Solyanka Street in Moscow that became a Communist health and beauty salon.) I can still hear the voice of a Swedish opera singer resonating through a spiraling, fifteenth-century church in the old section of Riga. I've never heard such intimate, haunting beauty.

In neighboring Tallinn, Estonia, I climb a steep road of winding cobblestone, topped by a medieval cathedral, to sip coffees at loft cafés where potters practice their craft. This port town on the southeastern coast of the Gulf of Finland was also founded in the early 1200s, but by Danes, who sold it to the Livonian Knights in 1710. The city's upper town is joined to a lower town, which is surrounded by a medieval wall with massive round towers. Hotel staff are friendly here and understand service—no dzhernayas, in-your-face prostitutes, or spook-doormen (that you can see).

But all is not well under this picture-postcard-perfect surface. World War II wounds still gush, and Baltic discrimination against ethnic Russians is rampant. Newspapers show Estonian pensioners putting on their World War II "independence" uniforms, posing with Hitler-style salutes. (Many Balts fought with the Germans to gain independence from the Soviets. In their quest for "freedom," many also enthusiastically helped the Nazis murder Jews, and other minorities, for the sake of a "Judenfrei" Nazi empire.) Germany is now talking about giving *pensions* to Baltic veterans of World War II. *Fuck off all Estonian Nazis* is spray-painted on a wall.

Once despised colonial masters, ethnic Russians are now barely tolerated. Estonia and Latvia are introducing a controversial law requiring all residents to pass a language test to qualify for citizenship. That means ethnic Russians, whose families have lived in the Baltics for generations, can be turned down for citizenship. When a Russian comes to town and asks a Balt for directions, the story goes, she is directed to the city dump. The new language laws violate human rights and incite Russian ultra-nationalists to call for the military "protection" of twenty-five million ethnic Russians now outside Russia's borders in the "Near Abroad"—and the restoration of the Soviet Union.

By the spring of 1993, the Baltics—the FSU's closest ports to the West—have also become a center of smuggling, particularly metals, from Russia and other parts of the old empire to the West. "National treasures," including icons that are illegal to ship out of Russia, are also exported here. In addition, I discover a network of human trafficking: Illegal immigrants, mainly from Africa and the Middle East, are smuggled from Russia to the Baltics, and then to Scandinavia and Western Europe.

The trade began under Communism, when old mafiya bosses brought Soviet prostitutes to the Baltics, where they married foreign sailors and moved abroad. The women, called *inter-deyavushki*, or inter-girls, would then invite their "relatives," Soviet crime bosses, to the West, where they could then apply for citizenship.

As the empire disintegrates, the crime lords begin a new type of human trade. Desperate refugees from Africa, Afghanistan, Pakistan, Vietnam, and the Middle East bribe their way into Russia, hoping to move West. But Western airlines refuse them because of laws imposing severe financial penalties on carriers found to be transporting illegals. Many of the refugees end up in the Baltics, where they pay thousands of dollars to be smuggled to Sweden from small fishing villages along the coastlines of Estonia and Latvia.

"They box the refugees together like chickens," says Sandis Metuzans, spokesman for the Latvian Defense Ministry, adding that they can be smuggled out on "former" Russian military ships. The refugees often begin their journey in Iraq and Turkey, where they cross the Black Sea into Ukraine. From there, they move to Russia and into Latvia by train, according to Colonel Laimois Liepinch, head of the Latvian Interior Ministry's Criminal Division.

Driving from Riga to Tallinn, I stop in Salacgriva, a small seaport. A rusty, beached ship lies at the end of an unpaved road by the shore. Aqris Zaqrinch, an ancient-looking forty-two-year-old with a large red face as lined and weathered as the ship, comes out of a small building and introduces himself. Zagrinch is the customs official. "The town can't even afford uniforms for its customs officers, let alone a boat to patrol the waters," he says. "If people were being smuggled through here, we'd never know."

Back in Moscow, the battle between Yeltsin and his reactionary opponents, led by Vice President Alexander Rutskoi and parliamentary speaker Ruslan Khasbulatov, is heating up. Yeltsin storms out of parliament after the Congress of People's Deputies votes against expanding presidential power. Yeltsin—who rules by *ukaz*, presidential decree, instead of law—hints that he may have to invoke his Emergency Powers. Rutskoi refuses to support such a decree; the constitutional court says it must rule on the constitutionality of the decree. Parliament votes on whether or not to impeach Yeltsin.

In March 1993, the democrats, headed by economic guru Yegor Gaidar, gather in the frosty air by Red Square. The Communists group nearby, in Manezh Square. Russian politics is increasingly simplified, like Clinton's foreign policy toward Russia: Support Yeltsin, no matter what. Yeltsin is portrayed as the Great Reformer, Russia's Only Hope, Rutskoi as an enemy of reform. A giant statue of Lenin, hidden by curtains since the collapse of Communism, is again on display at the Great Kremlin Palace of Congresses.

Foreigners living in Moscow get frantic calls from friends and families. We know they're overreacting, but how can they not when newspaper headlines scream, "Russia on the Brink of Civil War"? Tanks are on the outskirts of Moscow. Cars are stopped and searched. Even a helicopter or two circles the city.

I head to Red Square to watch Gaidar and, later, Yeltsin address the reform crowd; then I climb up to the rooftop of the Hotel Rossiya with an American network's television crew, equipped with plenty of beer and cellulars. The angle from the rooftop makes the crowd look even bigger. "Some schmuck in New York does a lead-in by saying, 'Gee, the crowd looks as big as it did during the 1991 coup, doesn't it?' and I have to nod foolishly and try to back out of it as best I can," says one angry correspondent. The crowd holds up effigies of the pipe-smoking Khasbulatov, a Chechen economics professor who was once Yeltsin's reform ally.

I walk to Manezh Square to see the red-brown protesters, their monarchist and Communist flags, young black boots mixing with yellowed and gold teeth. The crowd is smaller than the democrats'. Many have been paid a few hundred rubles to show up. "Down with the Zionists!" an old woman spits while an engineer tells me that Yeltsin is a Jew in cahoots with the Zionist government in Washington. "Even Chernobyl is the result of a Zionist conspiracy," he says. I used to regard these crowds as archaic. But their numbers are growing, along with the smell of alcohol on unemployed youth.

Outside the Kremlin, the crowds tense, waiting for the result. Yeltsin wins, narrowly surviving impeachment, even though his relations with the constitutional court are now over, and everyone waits for the April referendum,* which will basically be a popularity poll on Yeltsin's leadership, a blank check. Like a lumbering giant, drunk with vodka and power, Yeltsin proves he can still keep the crowds' favor and hold the country together—barely. But it's far from the great-and-only-hope-for-democracy image America had in mind for him.

Yeltsin's shift to the right has already begun, whether the West acknowledges it or not. Most reformist politicians have been ousted. The security services are being strengthened.

There is also a noticeable shift among the population. Two years of disenchantment—with democracy, the decline in living standards, and the rise in crime and corruption—are taking their toll. Instead of setting Russians free, democracy has made most more destitute. Only Communism's privileged seem to be profiting from privatization. Apathy and cynicism rule. Maybe Communism wasn't so bad, people think. Maybe what Russia really needs is *order*.

I conduct a random survey of Moscow kiosks. Almost all of the young people I talk to, aged sixteen to thirty, say that although they defended the White House, Russia's parliament, in 1991, they wouldn't do it again.

"I risked my life for democracy," says Viktor, twenty-three, hanging out with two young women in the back of a kiosk. "But I'm no further ahead than I was, and the country is in chaos. We need someone who can bring in order, like Zhirinovsky, maybe, or Rutskoi."

Soon Rutskoi and Communist Party leaders, like Gennady Zyuganov—the presidential candidate who will receive 40 percent of the Russian vote in 1996—will be seen openly drinking with

---

* The referendum poses four questions formulated by parliament: Do you support the president of the Russian Federation? Do you support the social and political policies of the government? Do you advocate early elections for the president? Do you advocate early elections for the parliament? Sixty-four-and-a-half percent of the population apparently vote, although the free and fair nature of the election is later open to debate. The results are as follows: 58.5 percent in favor of the first question, 52.88 percent in favor of the second, 32 percent in favor of the third, and 41.4 percent in favor of the last.

and regularly participating in conferences with outright fascists. In the spring of 1993, the fascist, anti-Semitic group, Pamyat, whose name means "memory," is out of control.

Pamyat is a paramilitary group of black-booted, ultra-nationalist, anti-Semitic thugs, who talk about restoring Great Mother Russia. In October 1992, they stormed the offices of *Moskovsky Komsomolets*, a popular Russian daily, and threatened the editors. Yeltsin issued a statement of public outrage, although he had met with Pamyat before he became president.

The *MK* is a liberal paper with talented investigative reporters who aren't afraid of dangerous stories—even though reporting is becoming an increasingly hazardous profession. Dmitri Kholodov, twenty-eight, an *MK* investigative reporter, will soon be murdered by a suitcase bomb while investigating army corruption; other reporters are beaten after staying on stories they were warned off. Because some of the reporters are Jewish, the *MK* is often displayed with a Magen David star scrawled across it by red-brown neo-fascists outside the Lenin Museum. The red-brown coalition is an odd mix. Hard-line filmmaker Stanislav Gavorukhin claims in *The Russia We Lost*, in a sinister-sounding voice-over, that Lenin was part Jewish. Gavorukhin also names some of Russia's Jewish bankers, without, of course, mentioning the Russian Orthodox ones.

Following the storming of the *MK* offices, Pamyat's leader, Dmitri Vasilyev, sued Moscow's bimonthly *Jewish Gazette* for thirty thousand dollars for slander. Vasilyev claimed he was "offended and deliberately defamed" by the paper, which called Pamyat anti-Semitic. He was playing a word game. In part, Pamyat argued that "Semite" applied to various ethnicities, such as "Arabs" and "Babylonians." Consequently, Pamyat could not be "anti-Semitic."

"The case is outrageous," says Tankred Golenpolsky, editor of the *Jewish Gazette*, over coffee and pastries in his Moscow apartment. Golenpolsky says he included Pamyat's newspaper in his annual list of anti-Semitic publications because in 1991 Pamyat published the *Protocols of the Elders of Zion*. The infamous text, completely forged by tsarist officials in 1905, has been used to justify anti-Semitic slaughters from tsarist pogroms to Hitler's concentration camps. Pamyat serialized the *Protocols* under the new name *This Is What Threatens Russia*.

Judge Valentina Belikova decides there is enough evidence for a trial, which will be based on determining the definition of *Semite.* "In civilized countries," Golenpolsky says, "this case would never have made it to trial."

This time, Yeltsin is silent. It's drizzling, the first day of the trial, an evil, damp cold that bites into skin, a sinister kind of day even before I reach the suburban courthouse in southwest Moscow. An angry mob is outside, like a movie lynch mob. About two hundred Pamyat supporters, mainly old and disaffected, shout "Down with the Jews!" and other anti-Semitic epithets. They are led by a group of young men with crew cuts, who link arms, blocking entrance to the courthouse.

The crowd reminds me of another Communist demonstration, in the spring of 1992, when Yeltsin was addressing deputies in an assembly hall by the Hotel Rossiya. Demonstrators with red flags locked hands to keep reporters out. The crowd spit at some reporters, tossed coins, and physically pushed us. It was the first time I saw a crowd move from yelling against the "dirty Yids" to actual physical contact. This crowd seems to be even more menacing.

Then, there were no police to help journalists enter the assembly hall. This time, there are plenty of police. They stand, ominously, at the top of the courthouse stairs, with submachine guns and barking dogs. But they are standing with Pamyat leaders, who seem to be telling the police whom they can allow in. It's not supposed to be this way. At least, not so openly.

"Golda Meir go home to Israel!" the crowd shouts when I try to push through the locked hands, the air tainted by vodka fumes. For this crowd, any foreigner is a Jew. A vile drunk tries to put his hand in my coat pocket, where my keys are.

Finally I get inside the courthouse. A police officer admits that the police have openly solicited Pamyat "to help keep the peace."

Next battle: to get inside the courtroom, which is guarded by even more police, guns, and dogs. After shouting matches with police, and a private interview with Pamyat's pimply-faced young public-relations man, who invites me over to watch a film about the organization, I finally make it inside the courtroom, where, Russian-style, Vasilyev sits in a cage.

Before entering the courtroom, I am mesmerized by the show in the hall. A well-dressed gang of Pamyat thugs prances, clamoring for front-row seats. More Pamyat types pile up the stairs. In the midst of the Pamyat sea is a group of *MK* journalists. I watch as young hoods try to trip Alexander Minkin, one of the *MK*'s star investigative reporters, attempting, unsuccessfully, to provoke him into a fight.

Next is a vision from a gothic horror novel. In a corner lurks an older man in a black flowing robe. A large cross, studded with rubies and other jewels, hangs from a long gold chain down his chest. Hard, sharp eyes peer from ancient wrinkles and a long, gray-white, wise-man beard that flows from the Middle Ages to Judgment Day. The priest is accompanied by a middle-aged dwarf, with frightened eyes and threadbare clothes, who follows him like a puppy.

The priest is part of the White Russian anti-Communist Diaspora. He lives a fabulously wealthy, jet-settingly luxurious lifestyle. "I used to live in a villa in the south of France. I now live in New York," he says. "I have followers around the world. I came here to show my solidarity with Dmitri [Vasilyev]."

A bejeweled anti-Communist priest and his dwarf, resident of the French Riviera and Manhattan, who flies to Moscow to show his solidarity with the leader of Pamyat. These are some of the characters who make up the post-Communist landscape. I couldn't have imagined them if I'd tried.

The Russian Orthodox Church within Russia has refused to take a stand on the trial. The Baltic-born Russian patriarch is currently under attack for being too close to "reformers," "foreigners," and "Zionists," while the metropolitan of St. Petersburg—the second most important church leader in Russia—has publicly *promoted* the anti-Semitic *Protocols*.

In December 1993, the *Jewish Gazette* finally wins the case. The same month, Zhirinovsky wins the largest single bloc of votes in parliament.

◄---►

CHAPTER 9

The New Rich

Wild Growth, Madness, and Fear—
After-Hours with Volodya, the Teenage
Mafiya Millionaire

> When money speaks, the truth remains silent.
>
> — Russian proverb

After more than one year of writing mainly about the poor, it's time for me to focus on an equally disturbing phenomenon: the new rich. As the great American journalist H. L. Mencken claimed, the point of journalism is to comfort the afflicted and to afflict the comfortable. It's about time I dug into the second half of this equation.

Some of the new Russians are honest businesmen and women who in the past were persecuted—others executed—for common capitalist practice. Now their work is legal, although they often still pay government bribes and mafiya "protection" money.[*] Some of the people I meet will end up in jail or in hiding. Others will be murdered.

Some of the honest capitalists are young entrepreneurs who tell their parents they are still in school or working. "Anything is considered more safe, more honorable, than biznes," says Viktor, a twenty-three-year-old T-shirt seller who tells his parents he's working in a local factory.

---

[*] By 1996, up to 80 percent of all local and foreign businesses are believed to have received extortion demands, according to a report conducted by Control Risks, the British-based security consultants.

When I moved to Moscow, the Old Arbat was filled with artisans and hustlers. Outside antique, linen, and book stores, before the Italian pizzerias, Benetton store, and even sushi restaurants, kids sold everything from paintings and T-shirts to cheap souvenirs, caviar, and tinted glass ashtrays. Mayor Luzhkov later banished most of the sellers, who moved to a giant outdoor flea market and arts center by Izmailovsky Park, in northwest Moscow.

At Izmailovsky, tourists and Muscovites eat shashlik, washed down with vodka or red wine, while artists get drunk in the cold by their paintings. This is where to find Azeri carpets, Uzbek pottery, Russian birch baskets, Red Army uniforms, Nazi medals and Hitler matrioshkas, Baltic amber, Russian shapkas, first editions of Molière; kitsch art, and bronze Lenin and Tchaikovsky busts, all of varying quality.

Over time, I watch the sellers—the new Children of the Arbat, to borrow the title of Anatoli Rybakov's novel—learn more about economics and capitalism than they ever would in school.

"It took months before I understood that if someone buys a lot of T-shirts, the price should go down," says Viktor, in front of his stand, getting stoned with his friends.

Viktor now has sale signs, and even Kmart-style blue light specials. Like the street kids, he pays taxes to the mafiya for his stall. "Most of it ends up with city officials," he says. Young Pioneers turned entrepreneurs, like Viktor, are the first generation—perhaps in seventy years—to be *less* educated than their parents.

"Sure, I regret dropping out of school, but it's just not practical now," Viktor says. "I need money to survive, to provide for my family." Viktor works hard. He's also honest. Others are less so.

MILLION-DOLLAR MADNESS

In the spring of 1993 an American takes me to dinner in a trendy jazz club, hidden in an alley not far from the classical pillars of the Bolshoi Theater. He is a friend of a friend, whose visit seems to be mysteriously linked to the April referendum. It is before gun-checks and bodyguards, when some nouveaux still hide their wealth in a self-preservation instinct held over from Communism.

My escort is a gray-haired whiz kid whose work friends study in graduate school. I'm not really sure why he's in Moscow. We walk past the Bolshoi, where young men wait for rich johns, past the Metropol Hotel, and down a narrow alley, by a first-rate Russian restaurant with crystal goblets and a band. Nearby is our jazz haunt, guarded by men in combat fatigues.

We are accompanied by "Benjamin," whose job is not to let the American out of his sight. Benjamin is a Russian Ivy League grad who received his degree during Communism: unusual, for those without KGB links.

In his early thirties, Benjamin has thinning hair swept sideways and sports nondescript clothes as bland as his conversation, though he's a hawk-like observer.

When the jazz club first opened, it was almost trendy; in a tucked-away but prime location, still unknown, a tad shabby but offering decent Russian food, and jazz. Then it was discovered, ballooned out of the reasonable price range, and became a new hangout for the zolotaya molodezh. Now the patrons are large young Russian biznesmeni with Western suits, scruffy faces, and leather jackets, black turtlenecks, cranberry cashmere. Well-dressed young men wait for us at a table. Biznes, encompassing artists and politicians on both sides of the Atlantic, is discussed between mouthfuls of zakuski—cold appetizers, including smoked fish, salads, caviar, and meats, sort of like Italian antipasto. And, of course, vodka.

One man, with pale blue beady eyes and a blond tuft of hair on a balding head, glances at me from the corner. He is silent, the only Russian not drinking.

I think he's a driver, or bodyguard, though the others seem to defer to him. He leaves suddenly, dragging his gaunt frame with impudence, before the meal is over, without explanation, like a spoiled tsar tired of court. Another young man skulks after him. More drinking. The American keeps up.

On the drive home, Benjamin tells us about the young man who left early. I'll call him Volodya. "Volodya is nineteen years old," Benjamin says, "and he's already worth at least several million dollars."

"I can't believe it," I reply. "He looks forty." I don't think Volodya ever sleeps. His sunken eyes are circled with bags. His face seems to be twisted into a permanent scowl. It shows fearlessness, but also the ever-present belief, awareness, that betrayal is everywhere.

"Hold on a minute," I say. "I've heard about this guy. The nine-teen-year-old millionaire. But I had no idea that was him. Why didn't you tell us?" Benjamin just flashes a guilty smile.

The American is dropped off first, "for convenience," Benjamin says. This makes the American uneasy. He doesn't trust Benjamin, but is reluctant to say so, afraid to jeopardize this new, shaky Gringo-Russky alliance.

I don't mind at all. No matter how wretched Benjamin may be, his job is to take care of the American, and, by extension, me. While I don't exactly trust Benjamin, I don't think anything will happen. As soon as the American leaves, Benjamin looks at me conspira-torially. "Volodya went back to the office. Would you like to meet with him?"

Nothing surprises me anymore. "Why not?" I say, even though it is 1 A.M. The office is in a fancy part of town, by a discreet lux-ury hotel. The building looks like any other run-down low-rise. We walk up concrete steps in near-darkness. As usual, lights and ele-vators don't work.

Suddenly I see a gang of men standing guard. With machine guns. We open a door to a small, bare corridor. A man sits at a small desk. Bodyguards muck about in the background. A televi-sion blares.

We walk into an adjoining room that's a mix between the Louvre and "Romper Room." Volodya, wearing a green blazer, red-and-khaki silk tie, and striped shirt too big around the collar, poses behind a sprawling desk covered in papers. Somber, antique red rugs line the floor; precious icons hang on the wall in heavy gold frames. A page of *Hamlet*, "To be or not to be," boxed in a blue-and-gold frame, rests prominently by Volodya's chair. Empty and half-filled chocolate boxes, plates of half-eaten cookies, and imported apple-juice containers litter the room like casualties of war.

Volodya is an apple-juice fanatic. Like most serious power- and money-crazed Russians I meet, who are intent on maintaining or expanding their empires, Volodya doesn't drink.

"I'd like to set up a time to interview you," I say.

"No problem," he says. "We'll have lunch together at the hotel next door." Before we arrange a time, Volodya challenges Benjamin to a timed game of chess. Volodya grabs a timer from behind him. Chess pieces fly. The clock ticks loudly. The rest of the room is silent, except for the pounding *whacks* of marble pieces hitting the board.

Volodya and Benjamin plunk their pieces down with vigor, like judges with gavels, the cultivated mobster's equivalent of a duel. Benjamin wins. He smiles, but, for a moment, seems nervous.

Volodya's eyes roam to a shotgun delicately nestled on an antique chair between two icons on the wall. He grabs the gun and aims at the wall, which, I now notice, is already riddled with bullet holes.

I stay calm, displaying no emotion whatsoever. Another Moscow survival rule: Never let anything surprise you. Just don't think about the obvious: What if the bullets ricochet? What if he misses? What am I doing here?

"These are Soviet cartridges," Volodya grins. "I put an iron plate in the wall so I can practice shooting."

"We just put new wallpaper on yesterday," he adds as he proudly points to the bullet holes in the wall. He smiles as he boasts about his gun, an antique Mauser from 1904, and his collection of one hundred Kalashnikovs.

Shooting, I later discover, is a way some men try to impress women. But at twenty-five, I feel old enough to be Volodya's grandmother. I am wearing a light linen blazer and short skirt, a "career suit" that I think is sophisticated. It also makes me feel old, responsible—conservative, even. I can't imagine that Volodya thinks of me as anything but a Western, if somewhat eccentric, reporter.

"Why don't we go clubbing?" Volodya says. It's the last thing I feel like doing. A flimsy, thin wisp of a girl, in skinny T-shirt and off-white pants, nervously edges into the room and approaches Volodya, who barely acknowledges her. She whispers, he yells, though I have no idea about what. They embrace.

"That's his teenage wife," Benjamin whispers. She is not introduced. Nor is she invited along.

By clubbing, Volodya means gambling, the "in" sport for mobsters and nouveaux. We are accompanied by a bodyguard. Volodya drives a dark blue Jeep. Like many of the new rich gangster set, Volodya lives, and drives, with an ever-present entourage, for physical and perhaps psychological protection. His life may be in danger, but it also seems as if he doesn't like to be alone.

Another car, filled with armed young men high on testosterone, follows. Volodya drives like a maniac. Speeding, he tails other cars, refusing to stop for red lights. My heart is in my mouth. My gut sinks. "Slow down!" I say, trying to remain calm. (I think he's trying to frighten me.) Onion-domed churches and the brightly lit White House whiz by.

"The Jeep is my fourteenth car this month. I smashed all the others," Volodya jokes.

We arrive at a club with no sign. We walk downstairs, where a burly man greets us. Volodya is welcomed like a regular. Some high heels are on the prowl, but we mainly seem to be in a gentlemen's club for gangsters. There are no foreigners here. Volodya sits down by a roulette table. I sit beside him. He pulls out a wad of American one-hundred-dollar bills, which he loses while chain-smoking Winstons. He keeps tossing the bills, losing them, and tossing some more. I don't see the fun, the adrenaline rush. If anything, the gambling seems to be a compulsion that bores him.

"I spend two to three hundred dollars a day gambling," Volodya says. "Sometimes, I gamble as much as five thousand dollars. I have so much while others have nothing. Most people are in need. It's so depressing." Whitney Houston, then George Michael ("You Gotta Have Faith") blare as I watch Volodya gamble. The rest of his entourage sits on a sofa, feasting on salmon, party sandwiches, vodka, and champagne that he paid for.

Volodya says his philosophy is pretty simple. "I don't see films and I don't read much," he says. "I'm afraid my life may seem boring later—but I may not be alive then, so I don't think much about it."

"I'm worth seven million dollars," he adds. "But I need to make more."

"Are you helping your brother fighters from Moscow, since you're not fighting yourself?" I ask, imagining him as some sort of arms seller, runner, negotiator, as I try to find a logical explanation for his money. Volodya is from Abkhazia, on the Black Sea.

"I'm just an honest, independent businessman," Volodya says with a smile. "I swear it. I'm just trying to hide my money from the mafiya and the government. Money appreciates because of inflation. I get interest for doing nothing," he explains, as if he's still amazed by the concept.

"So how did you make your money so fast? Communism didn't end all that long ago."

Volodya began life as a journalist, publishing his first piece, on the human rights group Memorial, in a prestigious literary magazine when he was fourteen years old. He then worked as a journalist in various ethnic war zones: Karabakh, Ossetia, Moldova, Georgia.

At the same time, he began to wheel and deal. "First I sold small things, like music cassettes and records," he says. "Then I met some foreigners while I was working as a radio journalist in Georgia. I began to trade in currency when it was still illegal. The profit margins were high. I invested well." Part of the profit went to bribe bank officials to give him a huge credit line.

By the summer of 1992, Volodya had made $1.5 million. By then, another friend of his had created the first young Russian millionaires' club. Volodya invested his money in clubs and, he says, "with a man who makes films with my money."

Still, now that Volodya has money, he says it's not so easy to get to it—because it's all wrapped up in investments and Swiss banks. Nevertheless, he says he is a patriot. He does not want to leave Russia, even though that may be the only way to protect his fortune, life, and freedom.

"I could make more money outside Russia," he says. "I have new ideas every day, but it's difficult for me to get my money from Europe. I've been to America—New York, Los Angeles, Miami, Boston—and I hate it. It's not interesting. And I don't like Europe. I think Russia will normalize with time.

"I don't think there will be a revolution in Russia," he adds. "But if there is, I'll give all my money to Yeltsin. I'm a journalist, not a war man. Yes, I have guns and pistols, but that's just biznes."

It's been well over an hour since we arrived, and I'm exhausted. At last we're leaving. Volodya is speeding again but this time I am less good-natured when I tell him to slow down. "Don't worry, be happy," he says with a smile. He drops me off at my new flat, on Frunzenskaya Naberezhnaya, on the Moscow River embankment. Volodya walks me to the door. We say good night.

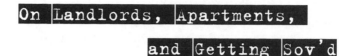

CHAPTER 10

On Landlords, Apartments, and Getting Sov'd

By the Moscow River Embankment—Lilacs
on Frunzenskaya, My Hippie Landlady and
Tangerine Kitchen

> When a peasant becomes a landlord, he flays the peasants.
>
> — Russian proverb

My new apartment is a high-ceilinged, spacious flat on the sixth floor of a building just ten to fifteen minutes—by foot, car, or boat—from the Kremlin. I am across the river from the Ferris wheel of Gorky Park, near a well-known apartment building where many high-level party hacks disappeared, one at a time, in the middle of the night, during Stalin's purges.

If it weren't for the robbery, I might never have left my first flat. It wasn't in the most fashionable district, but it was safe, quiet, and pleasant. It was also cheap, and stayed that way. Despite occasional vandalism, there were never any dangerous incidents. Not far away, though, a friend's nephew was killed by some teens who wanted his leather jacket; another friend was attacked by thugs outside his front door.

The day after the robbery, my landlord, Alexei, came by with his wife. They were always so kind to me. I think they were afraid they'd have a hard time renting the flat. "Don't worry," I promised, "I'll find you a new tenant." All it took was one ad in the *MT*. I was sorry to say good-bye. I knew that finding my next flat wouldn't be so easy.

But I've been lucky. Frunzenskaya is my favorite residential area in Moscow. It's along the river, on a shady, tree-lined street, sheltered from Moscow's noise and grime. The area is filled with Stalin-era Communists who survived, and Jewish dissidents.

"Under Gorbachev, refuseniks started an underground synagogue here," says one old-time journalist. Kolya and his wife want to move here for their daughter, because the schools are good.

My building is beside a *diplomaticheski korpus*, a diplomatic building, and around the corner from a police station. Dip domes, as we call them, are specially guarded complexes. They were the only places foreigners could live under Communism. The guards reported on the foreigners, the buildings were bugged: Not much has changed.

Down the street are tennis courts, and there's a mysterious mansion up a grassy hill across the river that I dreamed about before seeing. In spring, the air is fragrant with lilacs, which I pick for my kitchen.

Up the street is a private club for Russian artists and journalists. There are a lot of egos in cramped quarters but no gangsters, no maf molls, just the usual trophy mistresses. I meet hungry Russian journalists with a racist diplomat, who buys them drinks and trips to exotic war-torn locales.

One of Moscow's first private restaurants, Le Châlet, which serves Moscow's best Caesar salad, is also nearby. So is an incredible store for fresh fish, a bakery, even a furrier and an antique store. On summer weekends I walk up the riverbank to the Kremlin and beyond, to the Slav, about forty minutes by foot, for a good swim and/or brunch. On the way, I pop into all sorts of stores, watching old, ugly state boot stores transform into French boutiques, perfumeries—even, finally, a bagel shop—while more homeless fill the streets.

As cowboy capitalism has progressed, unscrupulous landlords have been known to raise rents by the month—even if you signed a contract (unenforceable by law) and paid in advance for a year. It's so common that a colleague at the *MT* calls it "getting Sov'd."

"You pay two hundred dollars a month for a year. All of a sudden, the landlord says, 'Next week, the rent increases to six hundred dollars. If you can't pay, I want you out in two days.' You're lucky if you get a week—another tenant has already been lined up," says the American, who has just been Sov'd.

While conducting my odyssey, I stay at Olivia Ward's, raiding her bookshelf, eating healthy breakfasts, and go out to look at flats, each more awful than the last. I see big malodorous flats owned by cat ladies who haven't cleaned since Trotsky's assassination, and tiny, cramped flats where the landlady wants to visit for an hour at a time, every day. It makes coming back to Olivia's luxurious Western flat even more difficult.

I begin to realize how lucky I was with Alexei, as I see that the landlord horror stories I've heard were no mere aberrations. Russians are still so unfamiliar with renting to foreigners that they don't know how to act. The women usually want to clean the flats they rent out. Understandable, but I refuse outright because I have Katya.

Cleaning is often an excuse to keep an eye on the flat—and to invade a tenant's life. "My landlady calls me at six A.M. on Sundays," one friend complains. "Mine barges in with her key, unannounced, weekend mornings to do the laundry!" cries another, upset about the effect such unsolicited visits have on his love life.

I am seriously considering one apartment until the woman says, "My husband and I will be moving to our dacha, but there's no room for our things, especially the books. I'll be coming by every Thursday—to clean, water the plants, and to study at *my* desk."

Finally, a friend tells me about the Frunzenskaya flat. "I think you'll really like it," she says. "But the landlady's kind of strange. She's a hippie, into horoscopes and stuff."

When I knock on the door, an attractive round woman in her early thirties invites me in. "What sign are you?" she asks as we sit down on a burgundy sofa. A Russian version of an American hippie, Irina has the sea-blue eyes and blonde hair of a porcelain princess. Her figure, draped in Indian floral prints and shapeless caftans, is as thick and shapeless as a babushka's.

These apartments were built for the elite. Irina's father is a well-known artist now living out his retirement on the Black Sea. Spooky black-and-white photos, including one of a gray-bearded, severed head of a man floating through clouds, haunt the apartment. I take them down after I move in.

Irina has added her own special touch to the flat. Dried flowers, plants, and elaborate vines crawl up the majestic heights of the kitchen Irina painted tangerine, Matisse-style, in a flash of inspiration. There are no cupboards, just a rack for a few plates. Irina lived spartanly. I'll make do. (I won't be here long enough to remont.) Part bohemian, part pared-down simplicity. I like it.

Like everyone, Irina asks about my marital status. She seems to approve of my single state. She is also one of the few Russian women I've met who has never been married.

The flat is similar to my last one, but with more light and space. A large living room is filled with typical, heavy wooden furniture. Irina proudly shows me some Russian china heirlooms. A big window looks down onto a courtyard where children play. Sketches of women in floral prints, in Chinese brocades, line one wall. There is a large entrance and hallway, complete with telephone stand and winding phone cord that can stretch to anywhere in the flat.

Irina moves into a communal flat near the Kremlin. She uses the first month's rent to buy a new refrigerator for me. Second month's rent buys a television for the flat. I've never heard of a landlord doing anything like this.

Irina and I become friends. She comes by for tea—and to check on the flat. She is even respectful of my housekeeper Katya, whom she seems to mistrust, or resent, at first.

Irina and I go for coffee, to a new Russian café, the Kafé Kappuccino. Valery drives us. Irina is taken aback by the notion of a driver. Then there is a flood of questions: "Does your mother work? Do you have a dishwasher in Canada? Do you have a house? How many cars do you have? Do you have a housekeeper? Does your mother?"

Many of the residents here grew up in the neighborhood. This time when Irina warns me against talking to the neighbors, it's not because they're potentially dangerous, but because they talk too much. Across the hall is an old woman who lives with her middle-aged, unmarried daughter. Another woman down the hall, with two children, is Irina's close friend.

"Okay, Jennifer, it's time I showed you the real Russia," Irina says, and takes me on an *exkursia*, excursion. "This is my treat, so we do things *my* way," she emphasizes as she declines my offer of driver or taxi. We go to an imperial estate on the outskirts of Moscow—and spend hours on the metro and buses getting there.

At the end of the metro line, we emerge in a desolate area and wait for a bus. Irina buys us fresh blueberries, wrapped in old newspaper, from a babushka outside the metro. An old man with a white beard shuffles by, a bag of wilted vegetables in his arms.

I know this man. I met him yesterday while writing about Moscow's first kosher restaurant, which sells veggie burgers. He's the kosher food inspector. (The restaurant is popular with Moscow's small but growing kosher community, including Israeli and American Hassids coming to reawaken the Jewish community.)

I love bumping into people in the middle of nowhere. It makes me realize I've lived here long enough for Moscow to be more than an "experience." It has, in a sense, become home. Irina and I wander about the estate. Elaborate, gold, Versailles-like inside; beautiful grounds outside. We take in the sun by a large pond where children swim, and stroll through immaculate gardens. Russia may be falling apart, but, when they want to, the Russians know how to take care of beauty.

CHAPTER 11

Meditations on
Translators and Buddhism

Getting Mistaken for a Princess
in the South Gobi Desert

Never forget that the Russians are an Asiatic people.

— ALEXANDER SOLZHENITSYN

Summer 1993: one in the morning. The Hermitage. Not Catherine the Great's museum in St. Petersburg, but a Moscow nightclub, on Karetny Ryad, near police headquarters. No flashy techno-junk, just expats and Russians in T-shirts and jeans. I have just left the *MT*. I'm about to begin freelancing full-time. (I was writing for a variety of newspapers while I was at the *MT*.)

At the bar, I bump into Georges, a French photographer. "I'm off to Mongolia, the land of Genghis Khan, to shoot *Naadam*," he says, referring to a traditional summer festival of horse races, wrestling, and archery. "Princess Anne will be there with her new husband."

"I've always wanted to go to Mongolia. I was planning to go for my next vacation," I say.

"Call one of the British papers," says Georges. "You write for the *Daily Express*. They love this stuff."

Georges spent years on Fleet Street and sums up tabloid headlines in a snap: "Princess Anne swoons under the hot Mongolian sun," he ad-libs. "It's morning sickness. The princess is PREGGERS!"

At the Hermitage, I talk to a colleague who, now that I'm leaving the *MT*, tells me my nickname: Lenin's Angel. I love it, and don't ask him to explain. To me, it sounds uplifting. The name sticks with me. I think about all the connotations "Lenin's Angel" could have. In practice, Russian Communism may have turned out to be a totalitarian tool for continued, state-sanctioned oppression, imperialism, and anti-Semitism, but in theory it wasn't so bad. There's a lot of good to be found in *reading* Lenin. Maybe that's what's left of Lenin, that angel, ghost, hallowed husk of good. Maybe Lenin's spirit, or his guardian angel, still hovers over Russia, within some souls, trying to protect a people so prone to suffering.

Lenin's Angel is also better than some of the nicknames unknowingly worn by other writers, like Lizard Lips. Just knowing I have this nickname mysteriously transforms my mood.

What is the Russia I have come to know? It's vodka and tears. People drink. When they're depressed, when they're happy, when they're tired, when they have something better to do, when they have nothing left to do, rich or poor. After drinking, Russians cry. Tears of laughter, tears of sadness, of what might have been for the poor, of how many have been tortured and murdered for the rich, for those with any tears left to give.

In Lenin's Angel, I can also pretend, hope, at best, that this warped, twisted country that writhes in hatred and greed may survive the empire's collapse and prosper without reverting to the bear's paw and peasant's boot that kill without tally, that kill without remorse, that kill without reason.

I can hope, but my gut instinct is more foreboding. I am fearful for what happens *after* Russia's Weimar Republic, *after* the Gianni Versace bought by the new rich have gone out of style and the last coins have been looted by some other democrat-gangster or gangster-democrat and smuggled out of Russia, and the army decides that now, now that there's nothing left to loot, it's time to establish some order.

I leave the Hermitage around 4 A.M. A friend walks me to my door. (I try to take precautions now.) "Good night," I say, and lock up. There's a knock at the door. I rush to open it.

"*Kto eto?*" Who is it? I ask. No answer. A louder knock.

"Who is it?" I ask again. I hear men whispering outside.

The incident is unsettling, so soon after the taxi robbery; it spooks me. I won't sleep much tonight.

One foreigner was recently robbed this way by a drunken driver he had fired. The doorbell rang. Sleepy and disoriented, the Westerner opened the door. The driver beat him and tied him up in the kitchen with the gas turned on. (He managed to escape.) Another Western executive opened the door at 3 A.M., thinking it was a neighbor in trouble. An unknown assailant beat and robbed him at gunpoint.

In October 1993, Laura Binkley, a thirty-three-year-old Canadian missionary, is murdered in her Moscow flat—apparently by people she knew who wanted money. By then, the Canadian embassy reports, at least one out of ten Canadians in Russia have already become victims of crime—sometimes more than once.[*]

It's a crime trend, like gangsters who ring the doorbells of business partners, shoot them in their living rooms, and leave their wives or mistresses alive and whimpering in the bedrooms. "It's considered classy, even more than gutsy, to leave a witness," says Scott, an American, after his thirty-year-old best friend, a Russian "in the oil business," was murdered this way.

"He was making so much money, I told him I wanted in, but he said no way, it was too dangerous," Scott says over submarine sandwiches one day in his office—a hotel where biznesmeni and bodyguards mix with FSU refugees. "I found out they were smuggling oil through an ex-Soviet republic and getting arms in return. After that, I stopped asking questions. I don't want to know."

After the 4 A.M. knock on the door, I know it's time to move again. I love the space, but I no longer feel safe.

"I have a flat, fully remonted, by the American embassy," says a YILG I know. He used to live there, and offers to rent it to me at cost.

Other expats also live in the building, which is like a Russian version of "Melrose Place." Overlooking the Ring Road, the flat is noisy, but large and secure. (And comes with a piano.)

---

[*] Olivia Ward, "Woman Held in Strangling of Aid Worker," *Toronto Star*, October 15, 1993, A2.

The week before I move in, someone tries to break in. "I think I know who did it," says the YILG. "They thought I was still living there." I take it as a bad omen and pass on the flat.

For now, I'm frantically preparing for Mongolia. Flights and hotels are already booked for the festivities. I travel with Georges and two other photographers. One of their assistants, Masha, helps with the arrangements. It is the start of our working relationship—and friendship.

ON FEAR AND TRANSLATORS

Masha is nineteen, with short, straight hair dyed red, then spiky black, sort of like Liza Minnelli. She was born in Vladikavkaz, in the Caucasus, to a Russian father and Jewish mother. At seventeen, she moved to Moscow to attend Moscow State University's prestigious journalism program. That's where another friend first found her.

"I wanted a part-time translator and fixer, a student who would be cheap and eager to learn," says Heidi, a twenty-seven-year-old Alaskan photographer. You can often spot her in a scrum of male photographers. In 1992, most Russians weren't used to working with foreigners. Those who did often had work ethics severely out of sync with the Westerners'. Masha, however, was a godsend.

Masha is hardworking, with spunk, brains, charm, and initiative. She began to work with foreign freelancers, then big news organizations. She saves her money and invests, when many Russians I know lose their savings in pyramid scams. "I give my savings to a very good friend I trust," she says. (Interest rates are high in Russia.) The friend goes to Turkey, buys leather coats, and sells them in Moscow. The interest rate she gets is good: Banking is still so primitive in Moscow that such arrangements are quite common.

Another young translator-journalist, who comes to work in a snazzy double-breasted blazer, seemed to be equally enterprising. Fiercely intelligent, he can't, however, seem to shake his ingrained Soviet mentality. He's driving the American journalist he works with insane.

"He takes a week off for the slightest sniffle, even when I'm working with the flu," says the American. "He also takes the longest breaks and lunches, no matter what kind of deadline pressure we're under."

Many Soviet-trained translators and journalists also lack a certain, well, aggressiveness. (Though some pick it up fast.) I ask an Interior Ministry official some specific questions after a carefully scripted press conference. "You just can't ask those questions!" says Galya, a twenty-four-year-old translator.

I mention the Freedom of Information Act, and say that journalists believe the state has a public obligation to provide what information it can. Whether the state lives up to its obligation, whether the information it provides is true, and whether the journalists ask the tough questions, is the subject of another discussion. Galya is amazed at the very concept of a Freedom of Information Act.

When I ask another translator to help get basic information—the number of juveniles arrested this year, not nuclear secrets—she is skeptical and condescending, as if I'm naïve, and the information is impossible to obtain. (It's not.) And even if I don't get everything, I usually get more than the translators expect. If information is refused, that, too, can be a story, I explain.

Russian officials are good at stalling. "Could you please fax us your request?" A few days later: "I'm sorry, we never received it. Could you fax us again?" The official I want to interview is then on extended vacation or sick leave, or booked for interviews "indefinitely." Finally: "Minister X will agree only if he can approve your story before it is published." I explain this is considered unethical in the West, and no, unlike Japanese and American television networks, I won't pay the minister for the privilege of his public paid-for time.

Usually, though, I find that with patience and persistence, I can wear down the roadblocks and get what I want. However, information is easier to obtain in the early Yeltsin years, before the post-Communist security services regroup.

When Masha leaves for one of her first trips abroad, I look for a replacement.

Not too tall, with faded acne scars across his small face, Misha has extraordinary, slightly shifty green eyes. His smile is a little too eager. But he speaks impeccable French and better-than-average English. He's been to Paris and wants to move there. He loves Russian jazz.

I hire Misha, who becomes my fixer. Although he is only twenty-three, he has a distinctly Soviet mentality, which is based on fear, a fear that has decreased—but not yet disappeared—since the empire's collapse.

At first Misha is afraid to make calls to some top officials. "They'll never speak to you," he says. But he soon gets used to making the calls—and setting up times for the interviews, which I think he enjoys.

Yet Misha refuses to make the calls from his apartment (and save himself a trip to my place). "I live with my aunt," he says. "When she heard me calling the prosecutor general's office, she got really nervous. Some of the calls I make for you are to very important people. My aunt still remembers Stalin and all the disappearances. She just doesn't want any trouble. She doesn't want any calls that can later be traced back to her."

Two years after the empire's collapse, Misha and his aunt are still skeptical of reform. "Perestroika and democracy were organized from above, not below," Misha says. "Reform may be just a temporary phase, like Brezhnev's thaw," which could be followed by an Arctic gulag chill.

Like a typical Russian, Misha then tells a joke: "Comrades, you now have the freedom to speak freely. Just remember, the KGB is listening."

IRKUTSK

The trip to Mongolia is so rushed that I receive my visa from the Mongolian embassy on the way to the airport. We are flying to Irkutsk and from there to Ulaanbaatar.

We land in Irkutsk after dark. Our flight is so late—typically, we sat in the airport and on the plane for hours before taking off—that we miss the connecting flight and have to spend the night: a problem, without hotel reservations. Many hotels throughout the FSU are still so steeped in Communist tradition that they refuse to grant rooms to foreigners unless Intourist cables them in advance.

We go directly to the only hotel for foreigners. "So sorry, but the hotel is full up," says a blonde, middle-aged woman. The hotel is too large to be full.

"Is it a question of money? Do you want money, then?" says one of the photographers. Bribing may be a part of life in Russia, but Russians still have pride. The woman is insulted. Now there is no way she will help us. No matter how much we offer.

I try to explain our predicament. "I'd love to help," she says. "Really I would. But we're fully booked. Yeltsin is arriving tomorrow with Helmut Kohl. The rooms aren't full," she explains, in typical Soviet logic, "but they *will* be." She refuses to budge even though she knows there's nowhere else for us to go.

"Where can we find a place to sleep then?" I ask.

The woman motions for me to follow her behind the front desk, and shows me her room. It is the size of a cupboard: single cot, sheet already turned down, small television. "If you're really stuck," she says, "you can sleep here. For a price, of course."

Deciding to bypass the woman altogether, we skulk through corridors, going directly to the source. Maybe a dezhurnaya will rent us a room privately. No such luck. The hotel manager is losing patience when the doorman takes pity. "I know a houseboat," he says. "It's not much, but at least it's a place to sleep."

The houseboat is about twenty minutes away by foot. The tree-lined, silent route is lit by stars and the flickering of a flashlight.

Small and dilapidated, the houseboat is charming by moonlight. It, too, is full up. "There is one place where they never turn anyone away," the doorman says. No, not the prison, but the refugee hostel, which really can be called a "fleabag" hotel. The building may have been grand in some pre-Bolshevik stage, but now only bugs seem to be prospering. A worn red carpet limps down the once-grand staircase. A woman takes our passports for registration and leads us upstairs to one large room with six cots.

The pale green paint is peeling. Evil beings cling in clusters to the wall above my bed. The shower is a small square with a drain. I dream about diving into the clear water of Lake Baikal.

ULAANBAATAR

We land in a mass of green surrounded by mountains. The sun crushes the air with cruel July heat. "Welcome," says a young state official in a perfectly white, pressed shirt. He delivers our more wilted selves to the hotel by way of a bright new military jeep. Like most of Mongolia's elite, the official says he was educated at a top language institute and KGB training ground in Moscow.

"Minder" speaks perfect English and Russian, but he prefers English. In fact, he seems to feel a vehement and most undiplomatic hatred toward Russia, one that his countrymen have harbored for centuries.

"Don't speak Russian here," he says, his stoic face twisting, for a moment, in passion. "You might get beat up."

The hotel swarms with the inflated egos of journalists. Australians filming a documentary, more print journalists and photographers. Lots of "I haven't seen you since the last war/revolution in _____."

As I registered late, Minder is unprepared for my existence. Fortunately, my name has been hastily scribbled by hand on the bottom of his computer printout. "I know the hotel is overbooked. I'm happy to share a room," I say.

"You'll do nothing of the sort," he says, and arranges a single room.

After registering, it's almost time to go back to the airport, where the princess and entourage descend from their royal plane. Print journalists aren't even allowed on the tarmac. Anne waves with her new husband, Commander Timothy, extending gloved hands for the pictures, and is whisked off, by motorcade—soldiers in aviators and combat gear.

We return to the hotel, which is Chinese. Unlike in Soviet hotels, the rooms are modern and the food at dinner is spicy, surprisingly good.

Mongolia, with its mainly nomadic population of 2.2 million, has spawned a haute couture trend, surprising for a remote country sandwiched between Russia and China; photos of its people, landscapes, and Buddhist temples are now in French *Vogue*. Designers like Jean-Paul Gaultier are celebrating Mongolian fabric and design.

But despite its sudden popularity, Mongolia's transition to the market hasn't been smooth. In fact, Mongolia's lack of capitalist experience reached near-mythical proportions in 1990–91. That's when Mongolia's central bank—including a group of teenage bankers—lost the nation's foreign-exchange reserves: all $82 million worth.

The money was "lost" when the inexperienced group, some out of school a mere three months, tried to play the international stock market with a single telex machine and Mongolian operator-assisted phone calls—in a business where seconds cost millions.

Two former governors of the bank, including the brother of the twenty-nine-year-old head of the Mongolian Stock Exchange, and three other bankers, are facing criminal prosecution at the time of my visit.

Without hard currency, there is a severe shortage of fuel, which has forced about half the rural schools to shut down. Hospitals have also closed, and many families are desperate without electricity in the winter, when temperatures plummet to fifty degrees below zero.

Now that Communism has collapsed, Mongolians are reexamining their social system. When Mongolia turned to Communism in 1921, only monks were literate. Under Soviet rule, literacy reached 97 percent. The Communists took children out of their natural, nomadic environment and placed them in schools. Now many parents are deciding to keep their children at home, believing that Soviet education was just another form of cultural imperialism.

Mongolian land has long been communal—both before Communism and after. The country's vast green steppes, filled with roaming horses and surrounded by mountains, are an eco-tourist's dream. So are Mongolia's wild, rare animals, like snow leopards, the mazalai bear, the khavtgai wild camel, and the red wolf. But as schools close and the social system declines, more children are running away to the streets of Ulaanbaatar, which has become a drug haven on the smuggling route from Central Asia to China.

Mongolians elected their first post-Communist president the month before I arrive by reelecting a former president, Punsalmaagiyn Ochirbat, who defected from the ruling Mongolian People's Revolutionary Party. But Ochirbat's impact is still limited by the

Great People's Hural, or parliament, which can overrule him with a two-thirds majority. And parliament—comprised of seventy-six members, seventy-one of whom are ex-Communists—will continue to block attempts at privatization, press freedom, and other democratic and free-market practices.

After dinner, we go to the hotel bar, which seems to be the late-night watering hole for the expat community: a cross-section of diplomats, Peace Corps activists, and international-aid advisers. Only one expat journalist, a young Brit working for a wire agency, lives here full-time. It reminds me of Evelyn Waugh's *Scoop*.

The bar is where I find a gray-haired, pinstriped banker and a hippie-like international-aid adviser, who brief me over drinks. People are often more forthcoming over drinks at 1 A.M. than they would be in their offices at noon the next day—in a foul mood from a nasty hangover.

The festival we're here to see, *Eriyn Gurvan Naadam*, or Three Men's Games, began when feudal lords gave feasts to celebrate the birth of a son, the launch or end of a battle, a wedding, or other major event. It was a chance for warriors to show off their skills.

Today, hefty men in loincloths, high boots, and traditional hats with gravity-defying cones compete in wrestling matches, the most popular sport in the country.

The biggest event, held in districts across the country, is an eighteen-and-a-half-mile children's horse race. I buy a book in the hotel lobby that tells me the race is first mentioned in *The Secret History of the Mongols*, a thirteenth-century classic. Back then, the race was for adult warriors. Today it is a rite of passage. Mongolians learn to ride as early as the age of four. Thousands of children, aged four to ten, train for months. Horses race without stopping until the end—even if their riders fall off. The brave little warriors, clad in traditional clothing, chant war cries, high-pitched, staccato shouts, while they ride.

Naadam's opening festivities include traditional dances and a procession led by a man dressed as Genghis Khan. The Communists, who ruled Mongolia from 1921 to 1991, knew they couldn't abolish Naadam, so they tried to incorporate it the way early Christians adopted pagan rites, like tree worship, into Christian ritual. Similarly, Naadam was renamed the People's Revolution

Day—though Genghis Khan's influence has far outlasted Lenin's. Mongols are now trying to reclaim their own history, including the legacy of Genghis, who ruled the world's largest land empire— stretching from Hungary to Mongolia and Turkey to Korea—in the thirteenth century.

At the festivities, I meet the British ambassador and his charming wife. She has long brown hair and is wearing a big picture hat and flowing skirt. Jumping out of her Range Rover, she exudes a spirit of both careless adventure and decadence.

"The princess had no hot water last night," she says, like a schoolgirl sharing a secret. "No one had hot water, so there wasn't much we could do."

The next morning, I am abandoned by the press jeeps, off to meet the president and the princess. I'm on my way to the lobby when the elevator gets stuck. My colleagues think I've slept in (we all had a late night) and leave without me. The shaky elevator has stalled before. I had a feeling this would happen. But why now? Why me?

I am with a Mongolian couple. We look at each other in horror. The woman pounds on the door and shouts. I join her. I'm probably not missing more than a photo op at the palace. But if something happens and I'm not there to cover it, I'm really in trouble.

Finally someone hears us. Soon a hand is extended from the ceiling of the elevator and we climb up the elevator shaft. I run down flight after flight of stairs. The press jeep's long gone, I hitch a ride in the first car I find.

Shouting and pleading, I somehow manage to get the presidential guards to let me, unexpected and unescorted, inside the palace. My heels click on shiny floors as I run down gilded halls, alone, looking for the pack.

Finally, I arrive at an outdoor courtyard a moment before the gloved princess and the grim-faced president emerge from an elaborate, decorative yurt, called a *ger* in Mongolian: the nomadic, felt-covered tent most Mongolians still call home, which looks sort of like an upside-down teacup.

End of photo op.

I go for a short walk on our return to the hotel. Ulaanbaatar is a Communist creation, seeming out of place with the rest of the country. The main square, Sukhbaatar Square, even looks like Red

Square. The leader of the Mongolian Communist revolution, Sukh-baatar, is as glorified as Lenin was in the Soviet Union.

Fleet Street is panicking. Princess Di is in Africa. British journal-ists scramble with byzantine intrigue to make sure our story gets coverage.

The Fleet Street set is young. Money is no object in the pursuit of British royalty. The set's expense accounts are huge. But, after watching them in action, I can say they do work hard. The London-based contingent includes print journalists and cameramen with monstrous lenses and satellite hookups, who travel the world on the royal beat. They are competitive in a clubby sort of way and masters of the pack mentality in a manner that is more, well, hon-est than North Americans'.

At first, as an outsider, I am treated with skepticism. "You're not here to hang with us, gain our confidences, and then write an exposé about Fleet Street journalism, are you?" asks "Roger," a bespectacled journalist, as he buys a round at the bar. "An Aus-tralian did that to us once," he adds, with a slightly menacing undertone.

Joining the royal beat is like joining a cult. There are all sorts of weird and illogical rules to follow. You're only allowed to cover royals from afar, trailing after them at a tactful distance. In order not to be frozen out of the palace's information hub, you're not even supposed to speak to a royal unless she addresses you first. If you are engaged in royal conversations, females are addressed as "mum." (It's not unlike the Washington press corps, who are afraid to ask tough questions for fear of being frozen out of the White House.)

Each day, the Fleet Street journalists get together for an unof-ficial meeting. What will be the agreed story line of the day? Maybe it's Commander Timothy taking a strong dislike to *ariq*, the Mongolian name for slightly alcoholic mares' milk given to guests as a symbol of hospitality.

British diplomats in Mongolia are faxed our published stories each morning, more up to date than we are. One diplomat chas-tises me for the "tone" of an article, as if I were a PR flak for the palace. I was startled by the clip, which, while accurate, bore no resemblance to what I had filed the night before.

After a full day of following the royals around official ceremonies—from Buddhist temples and horse farms to orphanages—I return to file by dictation. That means waiting hours for an international operator. I'm often not through until midnight. That's when I go to the bar, to find out what's really going on.

Up at dawn, we charter a plane to the South Gobi Desert, where the princess will be making her next appearance. When I get off the plane, dozens of Japanese tourists who appear to have been waiting for us jump up and down, clapping their hands and shrieking wildly.

I turn to Georges in bewilderment. Crazed Japanese tourists on a desert airstrip in the middle of nowhere are not exactly what I expected.

"Who are these people?" I ask.

"Oh, that is just the way they greet visitors. It is their custom," says Georges, ever the French sophisticate.

All at once, the Japanese begin to snap our pictures. Georges puts his arm around me and smiles. Other Japanese jump in to pose with us, their shouts and cries filling the desert.

They think I'm the princess.

The news that I am in fact *not* a princess spreads slowly. I am sorry to disappoint them. They take it well.

"We knew a British princess was on her way, and you look like a princess should," says one of the women consolingly, though the early morning flight and my wrinkled clothes make me feel more like a bag lady.

One woman sprays me with Japanese mosquito repellant, and then gives me the can, perhaps as a consolation prize. It comes in handy. The bugs are vicious here.

The Japanese are here for an eco-vacation. They sleep in gers, with only the stars for entertainment. As we leave, their guide is preparing lunch: freshly killed mutton over an open fire. I have this sinking feeling they're being obscenely overcharged for it.

From the landing strip we ride to a nature reserve. Linen and mules may be appropriate for following around a princess, but they're not exactly practical, especially when the job entails hiking across glaciers and jumping or wading through streams on the South Gobi Reserve.

We hike through the reserve, running ahead of the royal delegation, since we can't travel with them. We are accompanied part-way by a guide on horseback. We reach layers of glaciers, refreshing in such sticky heat. The view is majestic. The photographers set up their cameras like hunters. We run back and forth, trying to monitor the royals as we wait, listening to their laughter approach from afar.

The most sensible princess is clad in 1970s-style safari gear: khakis and hiking boots. (The *Express* wants me to do a piece on her wardrobe, which is unbelievably prim and proper, to be juxtaposed with a piece on Princess Di's extravagant African safari wardrobe.)

From the reserve, we go to visit a wealthy private Mongol farmer who breeds horses and camels. Perched on a camel, Anne, scarf wrapped tightly around her face, asks knowledgable-sounding horse questions, while Commander Tim, in a smart-looking anorak, hams it up. The photographers run to take *his* picture until Anne snaps, angry, perhaps, that he's getting so much attention.

We also ride camels and sip ariq, unpalatable to most foreigners, served in ceramic bowls as it has been for centuries. We are invited into the host's ger, which is surprisingly roomy.

Gers are easy to reassemble when families move with their cattle. Although their exteriors are modest, they are not just casual tents to be pitched any old way. Gers are always set up in a strict order. The floor, made of wood covered with felt, helps retain heat in the winter. The fire in the center of the ger symbolizes ties to ancestors. To show respect, legs cannot be stretched toward the fire, nor can garbage be burned there.

The fire itself is mounted on three stones that symbolize the host, hostess, and daughter-in-law. It also divides the ger into three separate areas: male and female living quarters—the host and hostess sleep in the female section, guests in the male—and the *khoimor*, where prized possessions like weapons, horse bridles, furniture, and photographs are displayed.

Back in Ulaanbaatar, we tour the famous Gandan Monastery, filled with young boys and men in colorful bright orange robes with burgundy sashes. Inside, I walk through rooms thick with incense and bursting with thirteenth-century gold statues, brilliant silks, and ancient texts. In one corner, monks pray. The deep-toned chants, combined with the rich smell of incense, are soothing.

After seventy years of Communism, Mongolians are experiencing a resurgence of religion. Like Tibetans, Mongolians follow the Dalai Lama, whose name comes from the Mongolian, not Tibetan, language. In the 1930s, the Communists shut down almost all of the country's more than seven hundred and fifty monasteries. About thirty thousand monks were executed. Others were jailed.

"It's much easier now," says T. Naksrai, an eighty-three-year-old, raisin-like bundle of bright orange robes whose hands constantly caress the green glass worry beads in her lap. "The number of monks here has risen from about five under Communism to two hundred and fifty."

Our Moscow-educated minder is particularly silent at the monastery. "Are you a religious man?" I ask.

"No, I'm not a believer. At least I never was," he says. "But my father is. He prays every day."

Back at the hotel, my editor calls in a panic. "There's a rumor that someone tried to kill the princess when she was in Moscow, on her way to the airport to get to Mongolia, and that the KGB stopped it," he says. "Check it out."

Excited at a chance to do some investigative reporting, I rush off to the British embassy, where a small party is under way. It's somebody's birthday. Diplomats and the royal plane's crew are sipping champagne. The pilot is quite charming. Someone hands me a glass of champagne. I am in the midst of asking questions when two other journalists rush in. We find out as much as we can, which isn't much. A car swerved too close to the princess's car. The KGB protected her, and that's all anyone's saying.

The princess will leave for Central Asia at the close of Naadam, which ends with the children's horse races. Thousands of Mongolians attend these races, which occur across the country. Families arrive by horse and cart, as well as car, lining the route and shouting.

When it rains during one race—a torrential, bone-chilling downpour—green fields are transformed into dangerous mud slides. The winner is a rain-soaked nine-year-old girl. Elders surround her. They bless her and the four runners-up while they dance. The winning horse is called *Tumny Ekh*, which means the Leader of

Ten Thousand. One of the elders then sprinkles Tumny Ekh and the horses of the runners-up with ariq.

Elders also sing in honor of the horse that places last. The rider was too young, the song goes, the racetrack was filled with stones and pits. But the little rider should not worry because next year the horse's fame "will rise like the sun to glitter like gold."[*]

The winners are then loaded with gifts, from school notebooks to a Chinese-made television: too much to transport back to the ger easily. (While Ulaanbaatar is filled with apartments, like many Soviet-influenced capitals, most Mongols who live outside Ulaanbaatar still live nomadically, in gers.)

On the way back to the city, traffic—in narrow lanes surrounded by green fields—is at a standstill. The royal entourage is about to pass. Cars are backed up for miles. A noticeable number of men get out of their cars to attend the call of nature publicly. Quite a sight for the princess. (From public toilets to public transport, infrastructure in Mongolia is sorely lacking. Only one north-south railway links the country, which is about half the size of India.)

With the close of Naadam, the princess takes off. So do we.

On our way to the airport, we stop at the tiny flat of the hotel receptionist. It's in a typically shabby Soviet building. The woman sells cashmere sweaters on the side: half the price of that at the hotel gift shop. (Mongolia is known for its cashmere—the country has thirteen million sheep, mainly in the Gobi region.)

Of course, now that we're really late, the run-down taxi we're in finally decides to break down. Fortunately, we arrive just as the plane begins to board.

As we're about to run out onto the tarmac, a young boy pounds on a window. He is from the hotel. In my rush, I left my credit card at the hotel reception desk. This little boy traveled all the way out here to try to return it—a truly royal gesture that will stay with me.

---

[*] Ya. Yunden, G. Zorig, and Ch. Erdene. *This Is Mongolia* (Ulaanbaatar, 1991).

CHAPTER 12

Kalmykia, Europe's Only Buddhist Republic

On Monks, Priests, Cats, and the Biographies
of Dictators and Chess Champions—Touring
Impoverished Collective Farms in a White
Stretch Cadillac, Barren Steppes at Sunset,
Turning a Cash-Strapped Republic into a
Billion-Dollar Corporation

A rich president cannot be bought.

— KIRSAN ILYUMZHINOV

Almost as soon as we return from Mongolia, Georges and I leave for Kalmykia, Europe's only Buddhist republic, on the Caspian Sea. Kalmykia's new president, Kirsan Ilyumzhinov, is a thirty-one-year-old multimillionaire who looks like a cross between a gangster and a rock star. He is celebrating his first one hundred days in office.

Kirsan—that's what everyone calls him—rides through his republic's poverty-stricken steppes decked out in designer silk suits, in a white stretch Cadillac. His slick, full-color campaign posters of himself, still plastered throughout the parliament building, carry the slogan A RICH PRESIDENT CANNOT BE BOUGHT.

During the campaign—in which he surprisingly beat a long-time Communist Party boss and a highly decorated Afghan war hero with 65 percent of the vote—newspapers reported that Kirsan promised one hundred dollars, more than the average *yearly* salary, to everyone who voted for him. When asked, he says it was "just a joke."

First Kirsan declared Kalmykia's independence from Russia. Then he said Kalmykia was going to become a tax-free zone, like Cyprus or Luxembourg.* Now he's got this crazy plan to turn his republic into what he boasts will be a "billion-dollar corporation" called Kalmykia Inc. He's asking all of Kalmykia's 320,000 citizens to *hand over* their privatization vouchers, worth about ten thousand rubles, or ten dollars each. The vouchers, recently issued by Gaidar's reform government, are supposed to give citizens a share in the privatization of state-owned businesses.

On our flight to Kalmykia, some Kalmyks from Paris are also on board. Their families fled Kalmykia during the Bolshevik revolution. It is their first time back.

Deplaning, they are welcomed by a throng of Kalmyks armed with roses. We are greeted by the glamorous Alexandra, a tall, long-legged Kalmyk, with short mod hair, a fashionable blazer, and hot pants. Alexandra, twenty-eight, stands out in any crowd. Especially here, in Kalmykia's backwater capital of Elista. Alexandra is a local television celebrity, on her way to national fame.

"I've booked rooms for you at the local hotel and arranged for you to follow Kirsan around when I'm filming him for local television," she says. Some of Alexandra's reporting is already shown across Russia. She will soon make headlines for becoming the first Asian news announcer on state-run Russian television. (Most Russian television faces are ethnic Russian, due to the colonizing role television played in Russifying the Soviet empire—and despite the ultra-nationalist Vladimir Zhirinovsky's claim that Russian television is dominated by Jewish faces.)

Alexandra joins us for dinner at Elista's best restaurant, a large space offering stringy fried cutlets and soggy potatoes, cucumber and tomato salad, and fresh-from-the-Caspian black caviar. "I'm

---

* Kirsan will go on to support parliament in its bloody showdown with Yeltsin during the October 1993 rebellion. After parliament's defeat, Kirsan undeclares his republic's independence, and toes Yeltsin's line. During the 1996 presidential election campaign, Kirsan, an avid chess player, arranges for Kalmykia to host the World Chess Federation Championship. Then, in the manner of a feudal lord, Communist Party boss, or Chicago Party boss for that matter, he also promises Yeltsin he'll deliver "ninety-nine percent" of his republic's vote.

sorry, but I have to get back to the television studio," she says. We stay and talk to some young women out celebrating a birthday.

"We see you know Alexandra," one says wistfully.

"Do you know her?" I ask, provoking a cackle of giggles.

"Everyone knows Alexandra," she responds. "She's famous."

Kalmykia, 1,100 miles southeast of Moscow, is known, if at all, for sheep, some oil, semi-arid steppes, and bitter-tasting tea mixed with butter and salt, which tastes slightly better than Mongolian ariq. According to legend, Kalmyks are descendants of one of Genghis Khan's four sons. They migrated from Central Asia to the North Caucasus in the seventeenth century. Like other ethnic groups, including the Chechens and Ingush, the Kalmyks were exiled to Soviet outposts by Stalin in 1943 for alleged collaboration with the Nazis. Many died there of cold and starvation. Those who survived returned to Kalmykia's flat steppes, where the Volga River meets the Caspian Sea, in 1958. Kalmyks now make up 45 percent of the population, Russians 37 percent. The remainder is split among fifty different nationalities.

Russia has assimilated Kalmyks more successfully perhaps than any other ethnic group. Like Alexandra, most Kalmyks born after the Revolution don't even speak Kalmyk. They also don't eat Kalmyk food—bland mutton and mares' milk.

But while the young Kalmyks I know, like Alexandra and her friends, prefer to study English and French instead of Kalmyk, they are rediscovering Buddhism—late-twentieth-century-style. "I've got to go into the hospital for an operation," says Mariya, a young businesswoman and friend of Alexandra's. "Before I go, I'm going to get a blessing from the monk, as is customary." What she doesn't tell the monk is that the operation is an abortion—Buddhist sacrilege.

In his first one hundred days, Kirsan is already treating Kalmykia like a bankrupt corporation he has just raided. He has wiped out the old KGB, slashed the number of ministries from forty to five, and downsized parliament from one hundred and thirty to twenty-five members by buying people out, or, as he puts it, offering "interest-free loans" to deputies who want to quit and start their own businesses. He also gives "loans" to political parties so they can quit politics and transform themselves into private business enterprises.

In his office, filled with shiny new furniture, in the decrepit parliament building, a picture of Genghis Khan sits to the left of Kirsan, while Buddha looms behind him, where Lenin used to be. A soccer ball is to the right. "My biggest achievement so far," says Kirsan, who speaks English and Japanese, "is to give people hope. Before, people were so depressed they didn't believe in anything.

"We need more independent politicians, like me," he adds, emotion lighting up his narrow, expressionless face. Kirsan represents a new type of Russian leader, a capitalist who succeeded because of the changing order, but one who still admires the old system. "My favorite books to read are biographies of strong personalities, like Genghis Khan, Winston Churchill, and Stalin." Kirsan, named after his uncle, a Kalmyk World War II hero, graduated from the prestigious Moscow State Institute of International Relations, though he passed over diplomacy in favor of working with a Japanese-Russian joint venture. Somehow, he got really rich, really fast.

Along with his capitalist blueprint, Kirsan is also trying to introduce a spiritual dimension to his republic. But he is doing so in a most undemocratic way. Kalmykia is the first republic in Russia to change its constitution to unite Church and State. Russian Orthodoxy and Buddhism are now the official religions of Kalmykia.

"The Bolsheviks were wrong to separate Church and State in 1917," he says. "We must unite them again. It's probably the only ideology to bring people together in this difficult time."

At the local Russian Orthodox church, a gap-toothed babushka hangs the priest's clothes out to dry by a sun-washed blue wall. While the priest is young, his congregation seems to consist of elderly women and stray cats. "We're having a hard time gaining a young following," he admits.

The handsome young Buddhist monk, however, is having great success. I run into him at the parliament building. Although of Kalmyk descent, he was born in Philadelphia, my old stomping grounds, where many Kalmyks emigrated. In the Tibetan Buddhist tradition, also followed in Kalmykia, he is believed to be the reincarnation of an ancient god. Like the current child Dalai Lama, he was plucked from his American parents at a young age and brought up in a monastery in India, though he still speaks English with a Philadelphia twang. He seems out of place in Kalmykia, and yet that makes him fit right in, sort of like Kirsan, who is also something of a mystery. No one knows how much he's worth, or how he became so rich: most private commercial activity was illegal until not too long ago. Kirsan is rumored to own fifty different companies, including restaurants, textile factories, and car dealerships, with a combined turnover of $500 million a year. Some say he made money mediating oil deals. There are also rumors, unsubstantiated, of course, that Kirsan laundered money for the Russian mafiya after graduating from the Moscow international relations institute.

I ask one of Kirsan's good friends about his mysterious wealth. Tamerlan Gasanov, Kirsan's former biznes partner, is now Kalmykia's industry minister—even though the solid, tough-looking lawyer of Russian-Azeri background never lived in Kalmykia before. "Like Kirsan, I'm forgoing my salary," says Gasanov, an extraordinarily altruistic biznesman. "Kirsan has high analytical intellect and he knows how to work with people. He's a very smart man."

Kirsan says by creating Kalmykia Inc.—of which he will be CEO —he'll be able to get credit from foreign banks to invest in state businesses that are now being privatized, and to develop resources, like unexplored oil. Gasanov adds that 30 percent of the company's profits will go to social welfare programs—although the details are "still being worked out." The rest of the profits will allegedly be reinvested in the company.

Alexandra, Georges, and I tour the barren, scorched countryside with Kirsan, who is cruising in his famous white stretch Cadillac. We trail behind him with some aides in a modest black Volga.

We visit Russian peasants who still toil on unyielding collective farms that are barely self-sufficient. During the election, Kirsan subsidized dairy and bread prices. They have since soared. The head of one collective farm prepares an elaborate feast for us, with fresh vegetables, caviar, and shashlik. Judging from the appearance of the farmers, the meal is far from typical. Yet even here, where people spend their lives working hard and rarely see results, there is hope. Democracy is still new.

"For us, nothing has changed yet, but I hope it will get better," says Lyuba Ivanovna, thirty-two, a kerchief wrapped around her head as she shovels mustard-seed-oil sludge from one useless pile to another. Lyuba's job, obsolete in more technologically advanced regions, pays four thousand rubles (four dollars) a month, which she uses to support herself and her two-year-old son.

Like many Russians, Lyuba doesn't understand much about capitalism. She has no clue what to do with her privatization voucher —despite the Russian government's and the U.S. Agency for International Development's expensive program for an American advertising agency to "educate" Russians about privatization. (And, at the same time, to drum up their own private business.)

So when Lyuba hears that Kirsan wants her privatization voucher, she says she'll give it to him. "My voucher is at home, of no use to me. I will give it to the president," she says, before excusing herself to get back to her Sisyphean task.

"I want you to come for dinner to my parents' house," Alexandra says on our third and last evening. She has shown us around Elista with pride and gets ruffled when Georges teases her about its provincial nature. Alexandra's parents live in a one-story home that they built themselves after returning from Siberian exile.

At the house, I meet Alexandra's husband, a heavyset, tall, serious man who has a good job in the local power structure, and their beautiful eight-year-old daughter. I also meet Alexandra's older sister, a single "career woman" television producer in Moscow, and another sister, who is visiting from Germany with her husband —they met while he was an East German student here— and their children. Alexandra's parents are warm and hospitable. I am immediately made to feel at home. Alexandra's father seems to be both proud of and amazed by such exceptional daughters. Alexandra's mother sometimes sells clothes that Alexandra brings from Moscow. (There isn't one decent store in Elista. When I bring Alexandra the French *Vogue* with the section on Mongolia and some other magazines, they are devoured by a circle of women in days.)

Tonight is a family reunion, a night of celebration. I am honored to be a part of it. Other guests include a local professor and his wife, and lots of children. The women prepare and serve most of the food, except for the shashlik, which is prepared by the men, just the way, I guess, American men like to barbecue. The feast is delicious, and puts the local restaurant to shame.

The mood is warm, relaxed, and festive; this is a dinner both Georges and I say we'll never forget. "One day you'll be head of a table like this, grandchildren clustered around you, telling stories about these days," Georges says to me.

After dinner, Georges, Alexandra, the sisters, husbands, assorted others, and I go to the local nightclub. It's not exactly packed, but it is filled with Elista's golden youth. There's even more food. I never gamble more than twenty dollars as a rule. Tonight, I gamble even less. But it's in rubles. The money lasts all night.

CHAPTER 13

An American Murder Mystery

Tbilisi, Georgia: What's the CIA Doing in
Russia's Sphere of Influence Anyway?
On Moonlit Terraces, the Bullet-Riddled
Piano Lounge, and a Cocktail Waitress with
Flawless English Who Trades Her Combat
Fatigues for a Long Black Slit Skirt

> See how love and murder will out.
>
> — WILLIAM CONGREVE, *The Double*
> *Dealer*, *Epistle Dedicatory*

August 1993: To me, sitting on the floor overwhelmed by the product of countless murdered trees, the electronic revolution seems years away. I'm surrounded by reams of Teletype, wire stories spit from rickety, noisy machines twenty-four hours a day. Most foreign correspondents, along with everyone else who can, leave Moscow in August. This is one reason why coups occur in this month and rumors that more coups are planned for fall abound.

It's a busy time for freelancers, some of whom live in authentic Russian flats, like me, and now get to house-sit for kind, generous, vacationing bureau chiefs. I move into Olivia's flat, grateful for Western comfort, an entire library, even videos and the wires.

Wires can be useless. I go days without reading them and then get depressed about information overload, about how nobody reads anymore because there's too much out there and not enough synthesis. But the wires are like rottweilers when it comes to certain topics. They just don't let go, keeping track of wars and politics. When I'm gathering raw data, hungering after a certain story, I turn into a news junkie. Like now. Then the wires become indispensable.

It's another wet, gray day, sort of like winter without the snow. I'm preparing for a trip to sunny, war-torn Georgia. The wires, blessed with the work of some talented young British and American journalists who live in Tbilisi, the capital, keep me updated on the latest troop movements, cease-fire negotiations, violations, and casualties in this tiny country of five million people.

Georgia, north of Turkey on the Black Sea, is a country with a sophisticated culture that mixes Europe and the southern warmth of the Mediterranean with the spiritualism of Byzantine orthodoxy and the nearby Muslim world. It's almost mystical, with its ancient history and acres of orange groves and vineyards. The Old Testament records that Noah's ark settled here, onto Mount Ararat, after the Flood. The Greek myth of the Golden Fleece of Colchis is set here, where, according to legend, the god Prometheus, who gave people fire, was chained to a mountain. Georgia's unique alphabet and distinct language emerged even before its fourth-century conversion to Christianity, which occurred well before that of Greece or Rome.

But for all of Georgia's culture, history, and beauty, her ancient mountains are etched with centuries of warfare. Historically, the Transcaucasus was the "Euro-Asian bridge" for East-West trade routes, a crossroads between Europe and Asia. Arabs, Mongols, Persians, Turks, and Russians fought for this land, which, in 1879, gave the world Stalin.

Now about 15,000 people have died and more than 200,000 people have been displaced in the war between Georgia, which is Eastern Orthodox, and Muslim, separatist Abkhazia. (Although Abkhazians are Muslim, Christian Georgians now make up the majority of the population in Abkhazia.) On the Black Sea, Abkhazia used to be one of the most popular vacation resorts in the Soviet Union. During the war, which began in the summer of 1992, the Abkhazians have been unofficially encouraged and aided by Russia, fearful that Georgia, which is refusing to join the ruble economic zone, is getting too close to the West.

As I'm drowning under paper in a country that doesn't recycle, breaking news comes off the wires. The CIA station chief in Tbilisi has been murdered. Fred Woodruff, forty-five, a twice-married father of five, was returning home from a luxury hotel on a Sunday evening with Eldar Gogoladze, Georgia's head of security, and two young Georgian women. No one else was injured.

It was all rather embarrassing. Woodruff was listed as a regional affairs officer with the American embassy in Tbilisi. But it is CIA director R. James Woolsey who will fly to Tbilisi to meet privately with Shevardnadze and to bring Woodruff's body home.

The Georgian and American governments say he was likely killed by "bandits"—before the investigation has even begun and even though he was murdered by a single, execution-like shot. The Georgian government later says Woodruff was killed by a young man, Anzor Sharmaidze, in a "random act of violence." But Human Rights Watch/Helsinki believes that Sharmaidze "confessed" under torture.

A murder mystery. The first post-Cold War murder of a CIA career man in an ex-Soviet republic considered by some powerful Russians to be edging too close to the West. Died on his way back from a weekend stay at a luxury hotel with two unidentified Georgian women and Gogoladze, the head of Georgia's national security. Not only was the style of the murder identical to an execution, the timing is also noteworthy. Woodruff was murdered shortly after news reports revealed that the CIA was training Georgian head of state Eduard Shevardnadze's security troops in the United States and Georgia. It was the first time the U.S. government was caught directly intervening in FSU affairs since the end of the Cold War. The background is a war that pits Georgia against Muslim separatists supported by Russia. An American murder in a country in Russia's backyard. The Americans helping Shevardnadze, at war with his own people; Russia aiding Abkhazia. The equation doesn't necessarily spell stability for the region and —if it is part of a larger trend in the FSU—the post-Cold War world. Murder, sex, war, and politics—with potential worldwide political implications. I decide to move up my trip and fly to Georgia the next day.

That night, before I leave, I go to dinner with a distraught colleague of Woodruff. My dinner companion is shaken by the news. I've never seen him so angry. "His death was no accident," he says. "When you're in a car with the head of a nation's security forces, that man is responsible for you. Why would the head of Georgian security travel at night in a deserted area, notorious for armed bandits, without protection? The usual practice is to travel in convoys.

"Washington is completely out of touch," he adds. "We're regularly in these hot spots. Nobody in Washington understands the volatile nature of the Caucasus. America wants to help Russia control its borders so Yeltsin doesn't lose face. The region is going to explode. Yugoslavia is just the beginning. But nobody wants to see it. They're afraid of the region. They don't understand it."

I think about his words often.

Shevardnadze is best remembered as Gorbachev's Soviet foreign minister and co-architect of perestroika. Westerners think of Shevardnadze as a respected, freedom-loving democrat. Georgians remember him as chief of KGB terror in Soviet Georgia. Shevardnadze came to power in Georgia only after Gamsakhurdia, a Soviet-era dissident, Georgian nationalist, and popular, democratically elected president, was violently overthrown in January 1992. Shevardnadze was then "elected" head of state with a stunning 90 percent of the vote. His name was the only one on the ballot.

Gamsakhurdia fled to nearby Chechnya, which had already declared independence from Russia. At the time of Woodruff's murder, Gamsakhurdia is fighting to regain power. His interests happen to coincide with those of Abkhazia. Both want to destabilize the Shevardnadze regime. Gamsakhurdia's forces have cut off Tbilisi and central parts of Georgia from vital food and fuel supplies: it looks like they could win.

Although Georgia is small, it has geopolitical significance because it is considered to be one of the last buffers between Christian Europe and the Muslim world. "The United States wasn't neutral. That's why he was shot," Woodruff's colleague says. "His death is making the U.S. government rethink its policy in Georgia."[*]
My contact is right. The situation is potentially explosive.

---

[*] Others, with links to the American government, will be killed later. In November 1993, Michael Dasaro, a Harvard-educated Russian studies expert who loves to dance in Moscow nightclubs, is found dead in his bathtub of a "heart attack." He is thirty-five years old. Dasaro, believed to be a CIA agent, worked, on contract, for the American embassy's economics section in the late 1980s. He was later hired by an

I think Tbilisi will be swarming with American journalists.

I'm the only one to show up.

The flight to Tbilisi is full, but my dinner companion gave me the name of someone at the Georgian embassy who can arrange a seat for me. "No problem," says a Georgian on the telephone. "Can you be at the embassy in twenty minutes?"

I throw some stuff into a knapsack, and flag a cab. By the time I arrive at the embassy, it's 11:30 A.M. The flight is scheduled for noon. The airport is an hour away. I don't see how I'm going to make it. But this is Russia. The man I spoke to on the telephone introduces himself, then disappears. I wait in the lobby. Finally, I board a van with some diplomats. We stop to pick up some Georgian businessmen who have just returned from a luxury biznes tour of America, and then stop at an Aeroflot office on the Moscow River. I give the driver my money and passport. He buys tickets for a flight that is supposed to be full—and already in the air.

In Georgia, the machismo factor is even more prevalent than in Russia, so while we wait for the tickets I am pleasantly surprised to meet Nina, a tall, dyed-blonde, chain-smoking Georgian diplomat. Dressed in a tight fitting business suit and white high heels, with heavy eye makeup and red lips, Nina does most of the talking. That she is thirty-six and never married is a rarity in this part of the world.

Even in the van, before the flight, Nina pulls out a bag and offers me some cookies and juice. Most former Soviets still travel with heaps of food and drink, no matter how short the flight, partly because Aeroflot food is so vile and also because flights are often delayed for hours, if not days.

The van drives straight onto the tarmac and pulls up outside a special VIP lounge. Once inside, I quickly call a friend in Moscow. Luckily, she's in and gives me some Tbilisi contacts, which become invaluable. The trip is so rushed I've had no time to prepare.

American accounting company in Moscow that was administering contracts for the U.S. State Department and U.S. Agency for International Development's privatization programs throughout the FSU. (Seymour M. Hersh, "A Death in Moscow", *Atlantic Monthly*, June 1994, 61.) In the spring of 1995, Frederick Cuny, a humanitarian aid expert who knows Clinton disappears behind Chechen rebel lines. (See Chapter 20.)

On the plane, Nina describes Tbilisi. "People are lining up before dawn to buy bread," she says. It's so cold I sleep in my winter coat. But the worst part is the climate of fear."

By day, Tbilisi is a ghost town, stores and cafés on the main boulevard, Rustaveli Avenue, closed since the December 1991 civil war. By night, Tbilisi is so violent that most of its one million residents and refugees stay in after dark, respecting an unofficial curfew. The streets turn into battlegrounds. Too many roaming bands of drunken soldiers returning from war, roving armed bandits, and mafiya gangs of factionalized, political bodyguards.

As Nina talks, the businessmen surrounding us insist on buying us sodas, chocolate, and nuts after we decline their offers of champagne. Most Georgians I meet go out of their way with southern hospitality.

But despite their warm, generous nature and ancient, sophisticated culture, the legacy of Stalin is in their blood. Everyone knows someone who's been shot, even killed, by random bullets. Nina was robbed recently on her way out of her well-guarded government office.

The Georgian currency is practically worthless. Food is scarce. Yet although Nina could live more comfortably in Moscow, she refuses to leave. Like most Georgians I meet, she is possessed of fierce if somewhat irrational pride and love for her homeland. "Tbilisi is my home. I couldn't think of living anywhere else," she says.

I remember watching Georgians blow themselves up on CNN during the two-week civil war, shortly before I moved to Moscow. Watching that war woke me up. It was one of the reasons I rushed to Moscow. The entire Soviet empire seemed like a tinderbox just waiting to explode. Now Georgia is flashing me another warning signal. The balance of power in this part of the world is so fragile. With the collapse of Communist order and the Red Army's warehouses turned into open-house garage sales across the old empire, regional conflicts are exploding like wildfire.[*]

---

* After the collapse of the Soviet Union, war continues in Armenia and Azerbaijan; and begins in Georgia and Abkhazia. War also erupts in North and South Ossetia, Ingushetia (a massacre), Russia and Chechnya, Moldova and Trans-Dniestria; a coup

War in Georgia began in 1990, when South Ossetia, an autonomous region in the northeast, decided to separate. Moscow backed the South Ossetians in an attempt to weaken an independent Georgia, which had not yet joined the Commonwealth of Independent States.

When Gamsakhurdia was overthrown and replaced with Shevardnadze, the career Communist, in January 1992, it was part of a larger pattern throughout the FSU. In Georgia's case, Shevardnadze was the democratic front for a group of political thugs led by a feared demagogue, Jaba Ioseliani.

Gamsakhurdia launched his terrorist war from western Georgia, with some of the separatist Abkhazians on his side. He bombed key transportation centers and took over some strategic towns and ports. He had unofficial Russian arms, soldiers, and intelligence on his side. Independent Georgia was one thing, but an independent Georgia with its own currency, foreign policy—and control of Black Sea ports, especially now that Ukraine controlled the Crimea—was quite another. Shevardnadze's government has spent so much on the war that people are without heat or electricity, and starving. The entire country is in ruins.

You can smell the war when you land. Young men, like actors or little boys, with shiny aviator sunglasses and AK-47 assault rifles, lounge about like lizards in the hot sun; propped against doorways, leaning on gleaming new jeeps. They are proud of their uniforms, posing with their guns in front of cracked mirrors, thinking American film. Blue-helmeted United Nations peacekeepers also strut about. Women are out of place here, though, I suppose, a somewhat necessary target, and audience.

"My driver will take you to your hotel," says Nina, and we head to the grand Metechi Palace Hotel, a luxury meeting place, and battleground, for the city's gangsters, diplomats, and biznesmeni.

Tbilisi is a sun-baked city that used to make you believe in God. Zigzag clusters of spiraled homes, old churches on hilltops, nearby

---

is launched in Azerbaijan, and border skirmishes pepper Tajikistan, while battles rage in neighboring Afghanistan.

farmland set against a background of awe-inspiring mountains, particularly bewitching at sunset.

There is no traffic in the streets, though. "No one drives anymore, if they can help it," Nina explains. "Gas is too expensive."

The city center is marred with burned-out shells of buildings still unrepaired from the civil war, and the crazed, posturing soldiers returning from war. I see too many women dressed in black mourning. They huddle together at street corners.

Charming old tree-lined streets lead to the Metechi Palace Hotel, a grand, out-of-place structure that looks as if it has been superimposed on the dusty capital. The beauty is staggering.

When we arrive at the hotel, I am startled to see, prominently displayed outside the hotel entrance, a picture of a handgun in a red circle with a giant red X slashed through it. Inside, by the fancy revolving glass door and glassy-eyed doorman, are a metal detector and gun-check. It is sort of impressive, even reassuring, which is what it's supposed to be. But the sign and the metal detector are really just for show, theater designed to soothe the frazzled nerves of arriving foreigners. No one else even walks through the metal detector. You can clearly see the guns and holsters underneath the jackets of many Georgians inside the hotel. Like so much in the old empire, the surface is often deceitful, the reality the antithesis.

I'm greeted by puzzled young Georgians in smart green uniforms who wonder, I can tell, what I'm doing here. The Metechi is filled with lounging mobsters in leather chairs or on the prowl. There is not one guest in sight. Although the hotel is new and modern, it is built in a Communist style: circular, with glass elevators so you can see most of the action from every floor. It's creepy.

I understand that Tbilisi is some sort of frontier. Moscow is becoming more randomly dangerous and chaotic, with fly-by-night shootings. Soon diplomats, parliamentarians, journalists, and bank directors will be commonly gunned down. But here such murders are already so commonplace they don't even garner much attention.

At first I am impressed with the Metechi. Traveling across the old empire, it's rare to stay in a decent hotel. I will soon learn that the one-hundred-and-seventy-five-dollar-a-night hotel is really a bunker for the city's worst criminal elements. But I don't know this—yet. Sure, I see men lurking about the hotel lobby, smoking cigarettes, in black leather jackets or burgundy blazers. Mafiya live in every hotel I've ever been in throughout the old Soviet empire. Why should Tbilisi be different? We lead parallel lives, the gangsters and I. However, without wanting to know, I soon gain some insight into the hotel—and Georgia itself—that is truly horrifying.

I left in such a rush that the first thing I do is fax an article I owe to one of my editors in New York. When the bill comes, eighty-five dollars, I'm in shock, even though the paper is paying. It's far higher than it needs to be for the hotel to make a healthy profit. Still crumpled from the plane ride, clad in grungy jeans, rumpled sleeveless black silk shirt, and ratty jean jacket, I feel like a vagrant, a homeless person, or a biker-gang member. I barge into the hotel manager's smoky office, startling two young, well-dressed European executives.

I tell them that they're charging far more than it costs to transmit the fax, and that the hotel is already so expensive, faxing should be seen as a service offered to guests, instead of as an obscenely high profit-making venture.

The young Austrian with slicked-back hair and a classic, flashy Eurotrash look—starched shirt, Wall Street stripes and cuffs—is not fazed. His colleague, with a pale, longish face and one of those delicate, aquiline noses I've only read about in novels, is more accommodating. This one has a thin, working-too-hard-and-obviously-under-stress, washed-out appearance; he, too, is wearing a well-cut suit with the same impeccable, nervous, edgy type of European style.

He apologizes, and lowers the price.

"Who are you here with?" he asks.

"No one. I'm on my own."

He seems surprised. When I arrive back in my room, a tray with champagne, pastries, and fruit is waiting for me. "Xavier," the thirty-something hotel executive, has asked me to dinner. I already have dinner plans, with Western journalists based here. But I meet Xavier for a drink before dinner.

The next morning I meet "Eka," one of my Moscow friend's contacts. This summer, the average salary in Tbilisi is less than five dollars a month. Salaries are so low that working for foreigners can be a gold mine. Eka takes time off from her job to help me. She is my age, twenty-five, and speaks fluent English and Russian, as well as Georgian. Like Masha, she is an intelligent go-getter who uses her own initiative. She is an invaluable asset—and friend.

For the next few days, Eka and I run from interview to interview. Because I have olive skin and dark hair, people think I'm also Georgian, which may make the interviews easier. I talk to senior politicians and their rivals, the police chief, hospital director, refugees, human rights activists, newspaper editors, international aid workers, artists, soldiers, and gangsters. I also talk to the American ambassador, Western diplomats, and others.

While the war rages in western Georgia, shell-shocked drunken soldiers storm through Tbilisi, using their guns to get what they want. The government seems to sanction them. One soldier fires into a crowd lined up for bread. He doesn't want to wait. His bullets hit a young girl and her pregnant mother. Suddenly the crowd is upon him, seeking revenge, justice. That's because they know the system is so corrupt that soldiers and mobsters are rarely arrested, let alone convicted.

To fight back, citizens are starting to take the law into their own hands—by way of public lynching. More than ten people were lynched during one eight-month period in 1992, Tbilisi's police chief tells me. Five hundred people were murdered during the same period.

At the main hospital, I meet some of the victims of random violence—and witnesses of lynchings. One young hotshot threw a grenade into a crowd to get back at a "friend" he was angry with. About ten people were injured. The crowd then turned—on him. "They ripped him apart," says one of those injured by the bomb, from his hospital bed.

The murder rate is so high that the local hospital director says bodies are dumped on the hospital's front lawn at night.

During my interviews, I ask about Woodruff. One of the women in the Russian car, a Niva, with Woodruff the night he was killed is named Marina Kapankhadze. The other woman in the car remains nameless. Rumor is she disappeared after being interrogated by Shevardnadze's police. Shevardnadze's chief of security, also in the car, was fired. Rumor has it he was arrested.

The Metechi, the city's main nerve center, is also where Woodruff met Kapankhadze, the beautiful Georgian woman who held him in her arms as he lay dying.

"I desperately need to find her," I tell Xavier.

"She works at the hotel," he says. "She's a cocktail waitress at the piano bar. But she's taking some time off now. She's upset and isn't talking to anyone."

Woodruff was apparently a regular customer. Word is Kapankhadze was a soldier, fighting in Abkhazia, and even taken prisoner. I'm fascinated. Xavier says no more. Still, I now know she's in Tbilisi. It's enough to start.

Tbilisi is a small town. Journalists don't have to know everything about every dateline they visit, but they do have to know how to find the people who do. Armed with an address for Kapankhadze, Eka and I drive to a bad part of town. "I'm coming with you," says Gogo, our driver, a student friend of Eka's. "You're not going in that building by yourselves." Elevators don't work anywhere in this city, except in the Metechi. We walk a long way up a fire escape. Windows are smashed. Graffiti covers the walls. For a moment I feel like I'm back in journalism school at Columbia, reporting in the South Bronx.

We ring Kapankhadze's door as we listen to drunken singing and yelling seeping from the neighboring flat. A large, stocky woman, who looks as though she has spent a lifetime working, answers. It is Kapankhadze's mother.

"Please come in," she says, inviting us into a cramped apartment littered with the toys of a young boy, Marina's son.

"I haven't seen Marina for a while," her mother says. "I started worrying when I heard about the murder on television. Marina refuses to talk about any of it." According to Kapankhadze's mother, Marina and Woodruff were quite close. Woodruff was also good to Marina's son. "He was a kind, good, generous person," she says. The mother seems genuinely worried about her daughter. She is kind and hospitable. We don't stay long.

Tableau:

> *Back at the hotel, I sit on a moonlit terrace surrounded by mountains. I am with two young Western journalists who live here. The view is still, peaceful. We are debating Woodruff's murder.*
>
> *"It was a random murder," one says. "They were driving on a bandit-infested road. It happens all the time."*

"But he was with the head of Shevardnadze's security—and no one else was scratched," I say. "I think it's a setup, an obvious political murder: Even the shot was in a clean, execution-like style. There's nothing random about it."

That's when She walks in.

"No, you are wrong," says a beautiful woman as she plunks down the glass of Georgian white wine I ordered. "I know. I was there."

"Marina?" I ask.

As a journalist, this is the moment you always wait for. Outside of the movies, it's not supposed to exist. I've spent so much time looking for this woman and now here she is, serving my glass of wine. *Is* it a coincidence?

Kapankhadze smiles confidently. She has classic Georgian features: long, dark, wavy hair, brown eyes. A former soldier and prisoner of war in Abkhazia, she tells me. The twenty-nine-year-old cocktail waitress with the perfect English has replaced her soldier's uniform with a long black slit skirt.

"I've just come from visiting your mother at your apartment," I tell her.

Now it's her turn to be shocked. I ask her some questions, but she soon excuses herself to get back to work.

"Why don't you go talk to her?" one of the journalists says. "If we all interview her, she might get nervous and freeze up. You're a woman. You might have more luck getting her to open up."

Kapankhadze agrees to meet me after midnight, when she finishes her shift at the piano bar. A man she calls her "best friend" died of a gunshot to his head in her arms less than a week ago, but it does not seem to be affecting her work.

We talk for more than an hour. I know she's not telling me the whole story. Small details keep changing. It's a strange feeling, watching someone you're interviewing lie to your face. I've now had ambassadors, ministers, even important figures I used to admire do that. It's even weirder when they know that you know they're lying.

"We met in the piano lounge," Kapankhadze says. "He came in every day and always drank red wine. He used to joke that he felt like Sean Connery, because he, too, was balding."

Sometimes she talks in a straight, cold voice. Sometimes she cries. "He was my best friend," she says.

Kapankhadze won't give me the name of the other woman in the car. She says the car was stopped by "bandits" on their way home from the luxury hotel. She won't say how the bandits got the car to stop. She remembers one shot being fired, and that shot just happened to slice through Woodruff cleanly, leaving everyone else unharmed. But although the "bandits" shot Woodruff, as bandits are known to do, they didn't do what bandits would normally be expected to have done next—rob everyone in sight. Inexplicably, they just let the car go.

After Woodruff was shot, Gogoladze, the chief of security, in a particularly hapless performance, drove to a local hospital, which was closed because of a lack of electricity. A second hospital was also closed. By the time they made it to Tbilisi's central hospital, Woodruff was long since dead.

Marina gets confused. She remembers, then doesn't remember, how many "bandits" there were, what they looked like, where the shot came from, where Woodruff was hit and how he fell. When I try to get the story straight, she gets upset. "It's so confusing. A lot of it is just a blur."

If Kapankhadze's story seems too fuzzy, her English is too flawless for a local "cocktail waitress." Perhaps Woodruff's death is a message to the Americans: The Cold War may be officially over but Georgia is still in Russia's orbit.

The next day I attend Woodruff's memorial service, at the Metechi. His colleagues at the American embassy pay tribute to him as a well-loved family man who doted on his children, his work—and Georgia. Western and Georgian diplomats also speak. No one directly mentions the possibility that the murder was political, although a European diplomat gives a stern between-the-lines message. Kapankhadze does not attend.

Many young-to-middle-aged American men, well built and with that square chiseled-jaw look, fly in from Frankfurt for the memorial service. No one will talk about why they're here, how they know Woodruff. Almost a year later, I read a six-line wire story that the Russians have shot down a small American plane flying from Frankfurt to Tbilisi. (There's no further explanation, or apparent connection.)

Once the CIA is exposed as directly intervening in FSU affairs —by training bodyguards in the United States and Georgia—and after Woodruff's death in August, Shevardnadze's fortunes change. Five days after Woodruff's death, Washington quietly gives Tbilisi most favored nation trading status. But the war seems to speed up, and Gamsakhurdia appears to be winning.

While the battle for Georgia rages, Shevardnadze travels to the United Nations in September to beg for help. (He omits the fact that he has already received some covert American help. The question is, How much?) His request is denied.

By late October 1993, Gamsakhurdia's forces gain key towns, including the strategic Black Sea port of Poti. Newspapers carry pictures of the gray-haired Shevardnadze risking his life in the besieged resort of Sukhumi until zero hour before it is captured by Abkhazian separatists. Just when it begins to look like Shevardnadze is finished, he finally agrees to join the CIS. The tide turns again. Better-equipped Georgian soldiers begin to recapture opposition-held territory.

In the winter of 1994, Gamsakhurdia disappears and dies in mysterious circumstances, reportedly a suicide. He is buried in Grozny.

Russian peacekeepers try to "stabilize" the region. Peace negotiations are linked to financial aid from Russia. After arrogantly declaring Georgian independence, Shevardnadze humbly returns to the Russian fold.

I fly back to Moscow in a panic. An out-of-town friend is arriving today. The Tbilisi–Moscow flight is delayed. (A new Georgian airline is aptly named Chance.) I've made alternative arrangements in case I'm not back in time. I struggle to get on the plane with heavy bags; I bought some Georgian pottery from an artist Eka knows.

An old man yells at his teenage son because (the nerve!) he does not immediately rush up to me, a stranger, and offer to carry my bags. Father and son are part of Georgia's aristocracy. The father owns a vineyard. His boy is off to school in London. Like most Georgians, the boy is a soccer player. He teaches me Georgian phrases, asks if we can be pen pals, and hands me a small, dashing, black-and-white photo of himself: He is tall, dark, brown-eyed Georgian handsome.

The plane makes an unscheduled stopover in Grozny, the capital of Chechnya, whose independence has only been recognized by one country: Gamsakhurdia's Georgia. More men with aviators and AK-47s lurk about. Some board, although there are no seats and they have no tickets.

Landing in Moscow, I cab across the sweaty city to Sheremetyevo International Airport. I'm only twenty minutes late. A friend and I are off to Sochi, back again near Georgia, a resort town on the Black Sea, near Abkhazia. Refugees fill the region. We hike through Stalin's dacha, much to the dismay of a woman dictator who runs it. The dacha is now a high-priced resort, mainly for the new rich, who fly in on private planes.

We stay at a Soviet-era hotel, with the standard small rooms, orange bedspreads, thin walls, and greasy chicken. Pudgy families, young couples, and high-heeled prostitutes strut about the lobby. The Communists ran so many aspects of their workers' lives that hotel propaganda even includes sun exposure instructions. Meals are also dictated, although Sochi, now the playground of the zolotaya molodezh, also boasts new restaurants. Soon, even an American hotel will open.

CORRUPTION

Back in Moscow, the conflict between Yeltsin and the parliamentary hard-liners, who threatened him with impeachment last spring, has exploded again. Now Yeltsin is on the offensive.

The internal power struggle within Yeltsin's administration was first publicly exposed in March 1993, after Yeltsin appointed Russian vice president Alexander Rutskoi as head of an anti-crime and corruption commission. In a surprise move, Rutskoi said his commission had eleven suitcases stuffed with incriminating documents against top Yeltsin reformers. The "evidence" was never made public.

Now it's Yeltsin's turn. A new head of the commission, Andrei Makarov, accuses Rutskoi of taking a $3-million bribe—from a company linked to the Seabeco Group, a multinational firm founded in Toronto. The evidence supposedly came from a twenty-nine-year-old colonel in Russia's security and intelligence ministries.

The mysterious colonel, Dmitri Yakubovsky, is suddenly in newspapers around the world. Dubbed "General Dima" by the

Russian press, he now resides in a $5-million mansion in Toronto with his fourth wife, a Russian-born Canadian named Marina Krasner.

I'm intrigued. But I'm on my way to Afghanistan, for the *Toronto Star*. I have just gotten my shots and visa when another editor at the *Toronto Star* calls. "Someone tried to kill Yakubovsky in Toronto," the editor says. "Three shots were fired into the gates of his mansion. The press is all over the story. Could you find out everything you can?"

It's still August. Olivia, the bureau chief, is still away. Afghanistan, I think, will always be there. I get to work, interviewing everyone I can who knows him. In early September I leave for a two-week visit to Toronto. I end up staying three months to work on this—and a related investigative piece[*]—for the *Toronto Star*.

---

[*] "Canada Tied to $100 Billion Bond Scandal," by the author, *Toronto Star*, November 13, 1993, A1. Billions of dollars' worth of supposedly canceled bond certificates from five New York banks mysteriously made their way from New York to Canada, overseas to Sicily, and into Eastern Europe and the FSU. Western government investigators believe that some of the bonds were used as collateral for loans to start banks in Eastern Europe and ex-Soviet republics. If the scandal emerges and the banks collapse, some newly independent governments could also topple, investigators believe.

CHAPTER 14

Young General Dima

The Communist Party's Missing Billions,
Coup Mentors, Reform Mentors, Corruption
Scandals, and Kremlin Games—From Gunfire in
the Bridle Path to the Metropol, the KGB
Dacha, and the Kresty Detention Center

Graft in Russia is on such a naïvely vast scale that it
becomes almost grotesque.

— JOHN REED, *The War in Eastern Europe*

A cabby once told me that in the Bridle Path, even the faucets
are lined with gold. Some of the richest people in staid, moneyed Canada live in this suburban Toronto neighborhood. But
even by its lofty standards, one mansion stands notoriously
apart: 27 Park Lane Circle, home to Dmitri Yakubovsky.

When General Dima* moved in, life on the Bridle Path sure
livened up. The mansion was transformed into a fortress, complete

---

* In the fall of 1992, Colonel Dmitri Yakubovsky was promoted to a general's rank.
Six months earlier he had been a mere captain. His new job, to be government coordinator of the Security and Intelligence Ministries and to report only to the prime
minister, would be equal to the rank of deputy prime minister. The order was signed
by top officials, including Viktor Barannikov, then Russia's security minister;
Yevgeny Primakov, Russia's foreign affairs minister in 1996, then director of Russia's
Foreign Intelligence Service; and Valentin Stepankov, then Russia's prosecutor general. Although Yeltsin vetoed the promotion, Russian newspapers still refer to
Yakubovsky as General Dima.

with barking dogs and bodyguards. The housekeeper, a slim Filipina named Avel who had worked for the previous owner and stayed on, took to wearing a two-way radio slung low on her hips like a cowgirl's gun and spiking her English with Russian slang.

I had first heard whisperings about the "KGB general" from within Toronto's one-hundred-thousand-strong Russian Jewish community before I left for Moscow. But I don't connect the gossip to events until now. Even Avel could not have been prepared for what happened when the three shots from a forty-five-caliber handgun were fired through the gates of the mansion. One bullet lodged in a white BMW parked in the driveway. In the ensuing publicity, a few details about the mysterious Russian owner emerge. Yakubovsky was a lawyer and a colonel in Russia's Security and Intelligence Ministries, successors to the KGB. He first came to Canada in August 1991 to work for the Seabeco Group, which had extensive interests in Russia.

The night the shots were fired, a cryptic note was left by the gate of the mansion. It apparently warned Yakubovsky to stay away from two men, Boris Birshtein and Alexander Rutskoi. Birshtein, a Lithuanian émigré and the founder of Seabeco, is Yakubovsky's old boss. Rutskoi, Russia's vice president, is trading accusations of corruption with Yeltsin, his one-time ally. No one, however, knows who might have shot at the Park Lane Circle mansion, or why.

The case remains unsolved. In December 1993, Yakubovsky returns to Russia for good, leaving Marina and their child behind, though she will visit him in Russia. Back in Moscow, he lives in an extravagant dacha that once belonged to the last head of the KGB. Officially, he runs a high-profile law practice that grows to occupy the entire top floor of Moscow's historic, ultra-chic Metropol Hotel. It later surfaces that, somehow, from the Park Lane Circle mansion, Yakubovsky played a key role as a Yeltsin loyalist in the corruption scandal that escalated into the parliamentary rebellion of October 1993. That's when a gun-toting Rutskoi declared himself president and Yeltsin, the "democrat," called in tanks and bombarded his parliament.

Over the years, I come to have unprecedented access to this man who, for me, personifies the turmoil and madness of post-Communist Russia. Yakubovsky is a provincial boy who turns the

collapse of Communism into opportunity, ingratiating himself
with both 1991 Communist coup leaders and early Yeltsin reformers. He becomes one of the new and powerful young democrats,
profiled in a *Newsweek* cover story on Russia's "filthy rich" after his
return to Moscow. (Yakubovsky explains his wealth to me this way:
"It came from investments from a thirty-thousand-dollar loan.")

One year later, in December 1994—the month Russia invades
Chechnya—Yakubovsky also becomes the first young reformer to
be jailed, his fortunes inextricably linked with coups and war.

Yakubovsky's new home is a decrepit Russian prison cell in St.
Petersburg's Kresty Detention Center. He has moved to St. Petersburg, it is said, because he has less influence there. Yakubovsky is
charged with complicity in the theft of a historic $130-million col-
lection of rare Far Eastern and antique European manuscripts
from the Russian National Library. His press secretary, Nikolai
Gulbinsky, tells me the charges are ridiculous; one of his lawyers
suggests they were politically motivated. Another one of his
lawyers is murdered in St. Petersburg during the summer of 1995.
By December 1995, Yakubovsky is still in detention, waiting trial.
"I told him not to go back," one person close to him says. "But he
was so young, he didn't listen."

I first interview Yakubovsky in Toronto one Sunday, during the
fall of 1993. When the new, bullet-proof electronic gates open and
close again, locking me in, I feel as if I've left Canada behind, as
if I'm back on Russian soil.

Hulking Russian men in sweat suits lurk about the grounds.
Inside, bodyguards sit on a leopard-print couch (the one anomaly
amidst the nouveau white-and-gilt decor), watching television
beamed in from Moscow. The house is like a collision between a
campaign headquarters and boot camp. Avel, in tight jeans and
scoop-necked red bodysuit, is in the kitchen, making submarine
sandwiches for a steady stream of bodyguards, their women, relatives, and Canadian lawyers.

In a manner befitting an old Communist Party boss, Yakubovsky keeps me waiting. "He slept in," says Avel. At noon, a tall, stout,
baby-faced young man appears, looking dapper and well rested.
His gaze assesses me sharply, though he smiles and talks at an
even, good-natured pace.

Yakubovsky's face is unlined by experience. I'm used to interviewing men like him after they master living in masks, behind public personas. Now I am seeing a man in the midst of the process.

"So this is the woman who writes that I am a janitor," bellows Yakubovsky, referring to a *Toronto Star* article I wrote from Moscow, where some of his former colleagues told me he had once headed a maintenance department at the Moscow city prosecutor's office. We walk outside to the pool. His wife, Marina, also twenty-nine, wearing tight jeans and a clingy designer silk shirt, soon joins us, leaving their one-year-old daughter, Olivia, in Avel's care. Yakubovsky agrees to be interviewed on condition that I don't tape-record him or even pull out a notepad.

"Okay," Yakubovsky suddenly shouts about twenty minutes into our conversation, "it's time to go fishing." Within minutes, three black Mercedes are crammed with people. "Aren't you coming?" I ask Marina. She looks at me as if I'm insane. Yakubovsky drives. I sit beside him, with two bodyguards in the back. We head north to Lake Simcoe, in cottage country about an hour's drive away. By the time we board the cabin cruiser, the gray sky is drizzling. The men drink sodas and munch Avel's sandwiches and *ruggelach*, small rolled cookies filled with jam and nuts. I stand with Yakubovsky in the light rain. He stares out at the water, his back to the entourage. No one fishes.

Back at the mansion, we sit on the leopard-print couch with Alexander, one of Yakubovsky's two younger brothers, as we watch a video of Yakubovsky at a top-secret submarine base. White-haired men in shiny uniforms and white gloves salute him. Others teach Marina, then pregnant, how to shoot.

(Marina is something of a gun enthusiast. When I meet her, she is a member of the Peel Gun Club just outside Toronto and has thirteen handguns and rifles registered in Ontario, including an AK-47 military assault rifle and an M-16 semiautomatic fitted with a scope. "He wanted me to learn how to shoot," she later tells me. "He gets a kick out of it, so why not?")

Yakubovsky excuses himself. "I have to make some calls to Moscow," he says. Marina reappears once Yakubovsky leaves the room. Now clad in old blue-and-gray sweats, hair pulled back into a ponytail, she seems more relaxed as she orders us some hot chocolate with marshmallows, which Avel promptly delivers.

We are now watching a movie starring Meryl Streep and Goldie Hawn. There's a mansion in the film that resembles Park Lane Circle. "I like their gate," Marina says. I realize she may actually get ideas about how to live from television.

When Yakubovsky returns, Marina disappears. Yakubovsky brings out some of his prized possessions, like a photograph of himself with Kim Campbell, the former Canadian prime minister. "There are lots more," he says.

He shows me the gun Pushkin allegedly used in the duel that killed him, a gun from the American Civil War, and rare books in his green-paneled library. "Do you play tennis?" he asks. "We'll play tennis and archery—and I'll teach you how to shoot.

"Why don't you stay for dinner?" he adds. His brother, relatives, a bodyguard, and another young former Yeltsin official also attend. (Before I left Moscow, the Russian government issued a statement saying they were looking for this man. I tried, to no avail, to find him.) Avel serves everything from excellent Russian caviar and smoked salmon to hamburgers and her own spicy noodles. While others drink, Yakubovsky sticks to sodas.

Marina suddenly reappears. "Good night," she says, on her way out the door, dressed for a night on the town.

This is the first of many meetings with Yakubovsky over the next few months. Once he meets me downtown in a gold Mercedes. "What car do you want me to pick you up in?" he asks, refusing to believe that it doesn't matter to me. "Every woman has a favorite car." That day he comes with roses. We drive to his mother's, a pastel, broadloomed, overpriced million-dollar home in suburban Richmond Hill. His mother is a youngish, tough-looking sturdy woman with short, dark, wavy hair. She wears sweat suits and still cooks for her sons: borscht, meat, and homemade apple strudel for me, Yakubovsky, and his ever-present bodyguard, Vitaly.

Usually, though, we meet at the Park Lane Circle mansion, where Yakubovsky lives like a hibernating Russian bear, keeping Moscow time, sleeping in during the day, and playing politics at night by telephone, fax, and modem. His contacts are impressive. During the height of the October rebellion that fall, he calls up top Moscow city police and federal officials, puts them on the speaker phone, and I hear of that day's events first-hand. All of Yakubovsky's predictions, including government postings and firings, are dead-on.

"If Yeltsin is ousted, I'll be killed within days," he says. He often talks by a fireplace, stoking the fire while in his socks, pleated jeans, and a camouflage T-shirt. "You haven't experienced anything until you've been in a war," he once says.

At his mother's, he gets a terrified call from Marina. "Don't worry," I hear him tell her. Within minutes, Russian men zoom up to the house and Yakubovsky disappears. "Some people were acting threatening. I had to bring them to the attention of the police," is all he says about it later.

Yakubovsky likes to spend money, but he often acts like an old-school Communist, uncomfortable in a Western setting. He dresses like a stodgy, middle-aged apparatchik in a leather trench coat and mink shapka. But I once see him hand a parking attendant a one-hundred-dollar bill. When we go out to eat, we are trailed to the restaurant by two bodyguards in another Mercedes. The bodyguards sometimes occupy the table beside Yakubovsky, hands on guns inside their suits, unexceptional in Moscow but definitely out of place in Toronto. Tonight, the bodyguards wait outside. Yakubovsky refuses to speak English, and seems to enjoy creating intrigue.

He is rumored to give people, from lawyers to friends, black Mercedes as gifts. He really is caught somewhere between Communism and capitalism, which is somehow appropriate. "He still thinks like a Communist," a person close to him says. "He doesn't understand the value of money."

Yakubovsky can also sound like Vladimir Zhirinovsky. Both have called for the restoration of the Soviet Union and the execution of criminals on sight. (Although that opinion may have changed since the prison sentence.) At the same time, Yakubovsky acts like an "eccentric who seems to genuinely think he can save Russia for democracy," says a Canadian business acquaintance. In Toronto, Yakubovsky even donates money to a Russian synagogue.

During one of the first interviews, Yakubovsky suggests he could arrange for our meetings to be held in more *private* accommodations. "I could arrange a safe house, or an apartment," he says.

"Out of the question. This relationship is strictly professional," I say.

He then tells me there are other ways for me to get a good story. "I could really help you," he says. Next tactic. He tries to, um, charm me.

"In life, I am a commander, but with you, I want to be your soldier."

No chance, not even a remote possibility, I tell him again. But I begin to worry. What if he's not getting the message?

"Don't worry," he says. "I'm not going to *force* anything. It is only interesting if you want to."

The interviews continue sporadically. He is often temperamental, shouting at those who work for him (so much that they ignore it). Once, when he invites me for dinner at Park Lane Circle, I arrive fifteen minutes late. He storms out in a rage, angered that I kept him waiting. Yakubovsky is unhappy in Toronto. He is in exile here, the mansion a gilded cage. "I can't wait to get back to Moscow," he says. "I feel alive there." He says he is frustrated that events he helped orchestrate, Kremlin Games he calls them, are exploding across the ocean—without him.

In a country used to gray-haired leaders who died in office, Communism's collapse gave rise to a collection of "radical reformers," young people who think fast, many of whom pushed, schemed, and manipulated their way up Russia's political ladder. The fact that the country's sudden transition to—or experiment with—capitalism came hand-in-hand with corruption, violence, and the rise of powerful government-connected mafiya groups[*] made the particular skills of men like Yakubovsky useful. His life story, as he tells it, often differs in detail from the stories told by people I track down in Moscow. Either way, the picture of a fast-talking, hardworking hustler emerges.

The oldest of three brothers, Yakubovsky was born on September 5, 1963, to a poor family in the small village of Bolshevo,

---

[*] By February 1993, government-linked corruption—from bribes for business licenses to media access to the president—was in full swing. That month, Yeltsin told the All-Russia Conference on Measures to Combat Organized Crime and Corruption that an estimated 40 percent of businessmen and more than 60 percent of all the commercial structures were involved in corrupt transactions. Alexander Rutskoi added: "More than half the criminal gangs investigated by federal security bodies in 1992 had corrupt connections with Russian administrative bodies." See Jonathan Steele, *Eternal Russia: Yeltsin, Gorbachev and the Mirage of Democracy* (Cambridge, Mass., 1994), 352-353.

near Moscow. His father, a military engineer, died at age forty-two from a liver disease that likely developed from his work, testing missiles, Yakubovsky says.

After being kicked out of military school for "low moral character"—a thinly disguised act of anti-Semitism, says Yakubovsky, whose mother is Jewish—he studied law. In 1987, he began working with the Moscow city prosecutor's office, continuing his legal studies by correspondence.

Just what Yakubovsky did at the prosecutor's office is still a subject of dispute. Yakubovsky describes his job as an "administrative" post, but according to Vladimir Goncharov, a former aide to the city prosecutor, Yakubovsky's official position was head of maintenance for the economics department—in charge of "cleaning toilets and carpets."

Both Yakubovsky and Goncharov seem to agree, however, that whatever he was doing, it didn't have much to do with the law. His former colleagues say he was principally concerned with currying favor and establishing connections.

"He was very talented but quite insolent," says one prosecutor. "He even posted guards who saluted him. His talent was to be around certain people and to get what he wanted."

In his office in an ornate nineteenth-century mansion in the old merchants' section of Moscow, across the river from the Kremlin, Goncharov pulls out Yakubovsky's old file. It describes how Yakubovsky would try to influence cases by impersonating prosecutors. This behavior sparked an internal investigation, Goncharov says, that led to Yakubovsky's resignation.

By 1989, Yakubovsky was secretary of the country's Union of Lawyers. Along the way, he began to build relations with the Moscow Regional Administration, where one of his ex-fathers-in-law worked. A Yeltsin adviser who knew Yakubovsky then says he really got his start using his connections to help up-and-coming politicians find apartments. "Even if you were a top gun, you still had to deal with the Moscow city council to get an apartment," the adviser says. "This is how he bought his influence. People sell their souls to get flats in Moscow."

When I repeat this story, Yakubovsky laughs and calls it preposterous. By his account, his big break came in 1990 when he found a book of Kremlin classified telephone numbers. He claims he brazenly dialed Dmitri Yazov, then the Soviet minister of defense, and subsequently talked his way into the job of assessing Soviet property in reunified Germany.

Russian military leaders—including then defense minister Pavel "Pasha Mercedes" Grachev, as he's nicknamed by the Russian press—were later accused of illegally selling off Soviet military equipment in Germany for private profit. Twenty-eight-year-old journalist Dmitri Kholodov was murdered while investigating this story. Around this time, Yakubovsky also met Anatoly Lukyanov, the speaker of the Soviet parliament, then the second most powerful position in the Soviet empire. Yazov and Lukyanov, both 1991 attempted coup plotters, became Yakubovsky's political mentors.

"In the end," Yakubovsky says, "Gorbachev accepted compensation for the property in Germany that was much lower in value than my assessment had been." Both Lukyanov and Yakubovsky say Gorbachev was "bribed." Yakubovsky says that by March 1991 his assessment was causing so much trouble that he was "warned" to leave Moscow. He won't say by whom, though the same people who warned him also arranged his job with the Seabeco Group.

Seabeco was founded in Toronto in 1985 by Boris Birshtein, who came to Canada via Israel in the early 1980s. The company got its start with Western fashions, popular in the FSU. After the empire's collapse, Birshtein continued to trade in the ex-Soviet republics. Seabeco also operated a hotel in Moldova, in connection with the Moldovan president's son-in-law.[*] By 1993, Seabeco is reported to have an annual turnover of $500 million.

In March 1991, Yakubovsky moved to Zurich to work for Seabeco Trade and Finance, but Birshtein told the *Financial Post* that after four and a half months Yakubovsky "created so many troubles that we didn't know what to do with him, so we transferred him to Canada." Canadian law enforcement officials say questions have

---

[*] Birshtein was also praised by Rutskoi, who took credit at Yeltsin's expense, for helping to broker—some say buy—peace between Moldova and its breakaway, ethnic Russian region of Trans-Dniestria. By 1996, the political climate in Russia and the West has changed so much that now it is General Alexander Lebed, commander of the Fourteenth Army in Moldova, who is credited—some say by using excessive force—with ending the war.

been raised as to how Yakubovsky entered Canada—and what he did there.

In August 1991, Dmitri Yazov and Anatoly Lukyanov led the coup against Gorbachev that failed miserably. Seabeco came under a good deal of suspicion. A handful of ex-KGB officials, including at least one colonel, were reportedly working for the company in Switzerland.

One Russian investigator, Alexei Ilyushenko, who becomes Russia's acting prosecutor general until he, too, is jailed for corruption in 1996, tells me he believes that Seabeco was set up by the KGB during the Soviet empire's last days. Its mission, Ilyushenko said, was to smuggle natural resources and Communist Party money out of the Soviet Union, and even to finance a kind of Communist Party in exile. (Birshtein has in the past denied such allegations. In addition, there has been no evidence of wrongdoing by Birshtein or Seabeco.) Yakubovsky's move to Toronto and his purchase of the Park Lane Circle mansion, some Russian officials suggest, may have been part of the plan.

(By the time of the attempted 1991 coup, millions, even billions, of Communist Party dollars had been smuggled out of the empire. Nikolai Kruchina, former head of finances for the Communist Party, died after falling out of a window. Did he jump or was he pushed? At least one Russian paper suggested he was murdered for his alleged role in setting up Seabeco to launder money for the Party.)

When I bump into Lukyanov in the parliament, he dismisses the allegations against Seabeco with classic inflammatory Communist logic: "Seabeco is a Zionist organization, so the Communist Party would never use it." By the fall of 1993, Russian officials allege that Seabeco has illegally exported at least seven million tons of state oil and millions of state dollars for the Party. Russia's then justice minister, Yuri Kalmykov, says Seabeco "is looming like a terrible shadow over this country."

Canada has become a magnet for money laundering because, unlike the United States, Canada does not require banks to report large or suspicious currency transactions, and does not require individuals to declare large amounts of cash at the border. Canada accepts more moneyed immigrants, and law enforcement agencies don't ask too many questions about where the money comes from. Poor records in countries like Russia also make it difficult for Canadian authorities to scrutinize criminal backgrounds.

What, exactly, Yakubovsky did for Birshtein in Toronto is still not clear. What is known is that their relationship seemed to quickly sour. And as it did, Yakubovsky appeared to switch sides, aligning himself with Russia's new reformers and with Yeltsin, who had stood on a tank, waving a flag in resistance to the hardliners' 1991 coup attempt. All of Yakubovsky's relationships— with top Yeltsin rivals and supporters—trace the shifting power relationships in Russia.

Though based in Toronto, Yakubovsky spent a lot of time in Moscow. In March 1992, after helping to organize the parliamentary election campaign of General Konstantin Kobets,* he managed to get on to Russia's new committee for military reform.

Kobets, later deputy defense minister, became an influential mentor and business partner for Yakubovsky. Together, they set up the Federal Agency for Government Communications and Information, known simply as the Information Agency. (In an interview from the agency's headquarters on the New Arbat in February 1994, Yakubovsky tells me the agency "has yet to do anything." However, Russian newspapers claim the agency has been selling off state assets—including arms, timber, naval equipment, oil, gas, gems, and timber—for private gain.)

By June 1992, Yakubovsky had become an adviser to Vladimir Shumeiko, first deputy chairman of the Council of Ministers in Russia's new parliament and another Yeltsin-allied reformer. In July, Yakubovsky received an extraordinary promotion, becoming deputy head of the government's communication and information agency—in secret. He drove through Moscow streets in a Mercedes with direct phone lines to the Kremlin. He was accompanied by police escorts, like top Communist-era officials—the style he thrives on.

By September, Colonel Yakubovsky was about to become a general, as well as a liaison between the government and the Security

---

* In his book *The Struggle for Russia*, Yeltsin describes Kobets as an important supporter during both the 1991 attempted hard-line coup and the 1993 parliamentary rebellion.

and Intelligence Ministries. But Yeltsin—advised by Yuri Skokov, an old-time apparatchik and head of the powerful Security Council—stopped the promotion and ordered an investigation. "Within three days I received a report," Yeltsin wrote, "that a frightened Yakubovsky had left Russia and flown off to Canada or Switzerland."

Corruption has always been a way of life in Russia, but never so blatantly as among its post-Communist political class. It was no surprise then, that, given his nose for opportunity, Yakubovsky found his way into the middle of the intrigue.

In the spring of 1993, Vice President Alexander Rutskoi declared that he had suitcases full of damaging evidence of corruption against top Yeltsin supporters.

Yeltsin replied to Rutskoi's charges by starting a corruption war of his own. From the Park Lane Circle mansion in Toronto, Yakubovsky helped to assemble evidence. He was back in Yeltsin's favor. Perhaps he had never been out of it. In any case, most of the alleged improprieties, on both sides, involved companies linked to either Yakubovsky or Seabeco. According to many highly placed Russian officials, most of Yeltsin's evidence came from Yakubovsky. It was his voice on the other end of a taped phone call in which Russia's prosecutor general, Valentin Stepankov, who was later fired by Yeltsin for corruption, seemed to be suggesting the murder of the head of the anti-corruption commission.

Twice in the summer of 1993, Yeltsin had Yakubovsky brought back to Moscow to pore over potential evidence, once even secretly stashing him inside the Kremlin. Wearing only boxer shorts, in a sweltering Kremlin room, Yakubovsky combed a data bank tracing links that implicated top officials in corruption charges.

Within days of Yakubovsky's arrival, the corruption drama became public. Yeltsin fired Security Minister Viktor Barannikov and Deputy Interior Minister Andrei Dunayev over allegations that their wives had gone on a three-hundred-thousand-dollar Swiss shopping spree paid for by Distal, a Yakubovsky-linked firm.

But once Yakubovsky's input was known, Barannikov's friends went after him. Stepankov issued a warrant for Yakubovsky's arrest, on the grounds that he allegedly had not entered Russia legally because he had not passed through customs.

Yakubovsky fled, James Bond-style, in the middle of the night. The adventure began with a car, a stopover at Stalin's dacha outside Moscow, then Sochi and Armenia, where a chartered plane came from Dubai to take him to Switzerland.

The corruption war of 1993 is a complex story filled with byzantine political maneuvers, Swiss bank accounts, and questionable evidence. All the politicians affected had two things in common. Like Rutskoi and Yeltsin, they all used to be friends. And they were all accused of alleged improprieties involving companies linked to Yakubovsky or his old boss from Toronto, Boris Birshtein.

By the time Yakubovsky returned to Toronto, the corruption scandal was in full stride.

By September 1993, top officials had already been fired or forced to resign over corruption charges. Yeltsin then suspended Rutskoi and Vladimir Shumeiko. Next, the democratic president signed a decree to dissolve the democratically elected Russian parliament.

That's when rebel deputies led by Rutskoi, who had declared himself president, refused to leave the parliament building, and Yeltsin called in the tanks. (Officially, 140 people died during the rebellion, although unofficial estimates are far higher.) I was in Toronto and had to make a fast decision: Fly to Moscow and follow the story with everyone else, even though I'd missed the beginning, or stay in Toronto and work on an original investigation. It was a hard decision to make. I stayed.

In December 1993, Yakubovsky is on his way back to Moscow. A new prosecutor general has lifted his arrest warrant. Zhirinovsky's inappropriately named Liberal Democratic Party of Russia is the biggest winner of that month's parliamentary elections, which turn out to be not all that free and fair. One of Yakubovsky's mentors, Shumeiko, is named chairman of the parliament's upper house. Yakubovsky's star is rising again.

I interview the prodigal son at Toronto's Pearson International Airport as he leaves for Moscow, via Zurich. Yakubovsky is with his mother; brother; a Russian friend; and Russian-born, best-selling New York author Eduard Topol. Yakubovsky has put on so much weight he looks decades older than he did in September. Sporting his snug leather trench coat and fedora, he seems nervous but excited. "I want to go work for the Motherland again," he says, "perhaps as a lawyer for the Russian government, if the corruption charges against Rutskoi come to trial."

Before returning, Yakubovsky has taken some precautions. He carries a certified letter from the anti-corruption commission stating that he has not been suspected of any crimes, and an award for "strengthening international ties in the system of Interpol," signed by Andrei Dunayev, the deputy interior minister, before he was fired for corruption.

From the airport, I share a ride back into Toronto, in an outrageously long white limousine, with Yakubovsky's brother, Alexander, and their mother. She seems a kind, unassuming woman, who speaks only Russian. Although she could have maids and fancy clothes, she seems to enjoy cooking for her children and granddaughter, Olivia, whom she calls a real *shayna maidela*, Yiddish for beautiful little girl. She doesn't seem too anxious that her son is returning to Moscow. Perhaps she is used to all the *mishegaas*, the craziness. She raised her boys in a tiny home, lacking all modern conveniences. Now she is learning to drive her new black Mercedes and seems ready for anything. If she is worried, she doesn't show it.

One quiet evening a month later, in January 1994, the telephone in my Moscow apartment rings. A deep voice gives me the license number for a black Mercedes and tells me to go downstairs. It is dark outside, but I can just make out the car. Before I check the plates, the driver says, "Yakubovsky?" I jump in and he slams down the gas pedal, just as I see another black Mercedes, motor running, waiting by the entrance.

The drive begins on icy roads complete with Moscow potholes, stalled cars, and accident scenes, past smokestacks and blocks of dreary old apartment buildings. The cars soon become scarcer, the road smoother. This is the road to Moscow's elite Zhukovo district, to the suburban dacha communities where the nouveaux riches and the old Communist elite (often the same people) live in an aristocratic idyll filled with birch trees, Chekhovian beauty, locked gates, and guns.

Yakubovsky's dacha, seen at night through the Mercedes' tinted windows, is well guarded and impressive; sparkling white snow is piled high on both sides of the road. Yakubovsky refuses to say how much he paid for the dacha or if he paid at all. It previously belonged to Vladimir Kryuchkov, the last Soviet head of the KGB. Yakubovsky's head of security, who overlooks a platoon of body-guards, was also top security for Valentin Pavlov, the former Soviet prime minister and a 1991 coup plotter.

Inside, dressed in pleated jeans and a camouflage T-shirt that grips his ever-widening girth, Yakubovsky perches on a sofa, wait-ing for me, signing documents with a thick fountain pen oozing money and power. The dacha has been transformed into some-thing of a bachelor pad, filled with heavy ornate wood and awful pinks and yellows. "I decorated it all myself," he says proudly. Over dinner, he brings out his newest Russian gun and begins to strike shooting poses like an over-eager preschooler.

"Why do you like guns so much?" I ask.

"You like diamonds, don't you?" he says rhetorically. "Girls like diamonds. I like guns. They're my hobby."

Yakubovsky says he is working as the lawyer for the Moscow Regional Administration, conducting "official regional business." He does not elaborate. One of his employees later tells me that, on one of his first days at work, he made a grand, even absurd entrance. He stunned the staff by appearing in a too-tight jogging suit, the type then favored by Russian underworld figures, a bal-aclava covering his face. He then dramatically unmasked. Still, the quality of office life improves while Yakubovsky is there: His per-sonal cook prepares lunch for the staff.

By the summer of 1994, Yakubovsky has moved from his offices on the New Arbat, beside a Toronto-based travel office, to the top floor of the Metropol. (The Man with the Accent now lives there and I bump into him on my way in or out of the Yakubovsky meet-ings.) Wandering hotel guests who take the elevator to the sixth floor are greeted by armed guards and told to get back on the ele-vator. Those who are expected are invited to sit on plush red leather couches, surrounded by young, well-muscled men armed with guns, telephones, and cigarettes. Older, Soviet-era women in sensible shoes scowl while younger women, armed with heavy perfume, makeup, and heels, prowl. A rather cute *okhrana*, or body-guard, asks if I can teach him English.

"My practice is booming," Yakubovsky boasts when he finally greets me. Two of Russia's richest banks, including Vladimir Gusin-sky's MOST-Bank, with close ties to Moscow mayor Yuri Luzhkov, are clients. There is talk of property in Monaco. His press secretary, Gulbinsky, hints that a government appointment isn't far away. Yakubovsky has even made a movie about his life, complete with grand poses of him thinking inside the Pushkin Museum with classical music in the background. The film, I discover, has gained something of a cult following in Toronto, where it is often sold out in Russian video stores. People even memorize some of the lines. Yakubovsky has also commissioned a top Russian singer to write a song about a gun-wielding Marina, who stars in a James Bond-like video, which has become quite popular in Moscow.

At the office, and at the dacha, Yakubovsky is often trailed by his young cousin, Sergei, eighteen. Large, hulking, dressed smartly in Moscow Gangland Classic—standard black pants, turtleneck, and burgundy blazer—Sergei hunches over his computer, absorbed in a game, looking up occasionally to throw paper balls at an older secretary with dyed-red hair, who treats the teenager with bemused disdain.

"Why aren't you in school?" I ask.

"I'd like to be, but I can't, not now. Dima needs me. It's for the family," Sergei says as if speaking of Don Corleone.

Sergei lives with Yakubovsky at the dacha. He is with us during dinner that January evening. Dinner, prepared by a chef, includes some very sophisticated cuisine. But Yakubovsky sticks to greasy *pelmeni*, a Russian dumpling form of pasta. After dinner, we talk while Yakubovsky sometimes darts looks at the television and simultaneously carries on cellular telephone conversations with family and cronies in Toronto or Zurich.

He proudly shows me his colonel's uniform, still neatly pressed, and uses his two-way radio to demand that a bodyguard bring the latest guns in to show me.

Suddenly, Yakubovsky turns to me and says, "Would you like erotic massage? I am very good, you know."

"No, thank you," I say, as if he had just asked if I would care for a cup of tea.

By one in the morning, Yakubovsky looks exhausted. He downs a few aspirins to soothe what seems to be a constant headache. At that moment, he seems to have so much money, so much power, I wonder why he doesn't just stop.

"When is it going to be enough? When, how, will you ever be able to stop?" I ask.

"I have enough for me, but not enough for all this," he says, gesturing wildly, referring, perhaps, to his crew of bodyguards, women, and children. "If there are no more questions, I'll say good night," he adds. Sergei escorts me to the door. The Mercedes and drivers are waiting.

Yakubovsky dug a foothold into power during the twilight of the Soviet empire, as a faithful servant to the powerful. He kept his footing during the empire's collapse and managed to build from the rubble. He rose with the help of hard-line mentors like Dmitri Yazov and Anatoly Lukyanov, but managed to be out of Russia when their coup attempt against Gorbachev failed and they landed in jail. He switched over and backed the reformers, those who worked for Rutskoi and Yeltsin, when they were taking control, and, when those two allies fell out, managed to land on the winning side yet again, and be out of the country once more when the shooting started. A consummate hustler, he knew how to get ahead when all about him was falling apart.

Yakubovsky may not be Russia's foremost intellectual thinker, but he has a shrewd, street-smart kind of genius. He is an example of how high new Russians can rise—and how low they can fall—when one structure collapses and a new one has not yet fully developed. "He is a symptom of our sick society," says one Yeltsin adviser who has known him for years.

It's a wonder he didn't see the end coming. The electoral success of Vladimir Zhirinovsky—two months after Yeltsin bombarded the parliament—was a clear signal of Russia's shift to the right. In the summer of 1994, Yeltsin issues an organized-crime decree enabling police to lock up Russians for a month without charge. It should be no surprise then, when Yeltsin, accustomed to using force to solve problems, invades Chechnya the month Yakubovsky is arrested, and aligns himself more closely with the loose coalition in the Security and Intelligence Ministries known as the "party of power" and, soon, the "party of war."

Yeltsin also moves closer to General Alexander Korzhakov, head of presidential security, his personal bodyguard since 1985, who now even tries to formulate state policy. In his book, Yeltsin praises Korzhakov's loyalty. ("To this day, Korzhakov never leaves my side, and we even sit up at night during trips together.") It is Korzhakov who sends masked, armed men in paramilitary fatigues —soldiers from his own private army armed with Kalashnikovs and grenade launchers—to raid the offices of Vladimir Gusinsky's MOST-Bank, Yakubovsky's client and Moscow mayor Yuri Luzhkov's ally, on December 2, 1994, shortly before Yakubovsky's arrest. Gusinsky flees to London.

Yakubovsky's arrest in December 1994 comes at a time when two of his allies, Shumeiko and Luzhkov, are rumored to be thinking about running for president in 1996.[*]

After the arrest, I continue to meet with Nikolai Gulbinsky, Yakubovsky's press secretary, at the Metropol. The guards and staff have been downsized. A lone guard listens to Elvis Presley's "Blue Suede Shoes" on an ancient radio. "They're starting to give us a hard time here," says Gulbinsky, who soon runs out of basics like coffee and office supplies.

"Before the arrest, Dima and I were getting tutored from the diplomatic school," Gulbinsky says, pouring champagne instead of coffee while offering me some chocolates to celebrate the New Year. "We were learning Hebrew and North American history. Now Dima continues to study—from jail." (Adds an older friend of Yakubovsky's, "Jail is the best education he could hope for.")

In a typical-but-only-in-Russia scenario, Gulbinsky says a Russian newspaper arrived at their office the day before Yakubovsky's arrest. "The front-page story was on prison reform, a cause Yakubovsky had recently taken up. The photo caption warned readers to be careful, or they, too, could end up in prison," he says. Once, Gulbinsky calls at midnight, sounding genuinely shaken, and as though he's had one too many vodkas. "The police questioned me for hours," he says, "but I had nothing to tell them."

Whether or not Yakubovsky was actually involved in the theft of rare manuscripts is probably less important than the fact that

---

* By the summer of 1995, Gusinsky is back in Moscow, and Shumeiko publicly withdraws his pledge to run for president in 1996—if Yeltsin runs. By the middle of the 1996 election campaign, Korzhakov is on the outs and Gusinsky plays a key part in Yeltsin's reelection team.

Yeltsin now seems to have little use for the man who once helped him crack down on the kind of hard-liners he now courts.

By the time of Yakubovsky's arrest and the invasion of Chechnya, the innocence of post-Communist euphoria is over. Russians who fast profited, like Yakubovsky, are starting to land in jail, exile —or the morgue. The crackdown on the capitalist sweepstakes' first winners has begun. "The brush cuts are now running Russia," says one expat businessman. "The party's over."

Only if Russian politics takes another dramatic swing, or if, as a few of his friends suggest, Yakubovsky gives up *kompromat*, material he may have that might embarrass his allies, does he have any hope of getting out of jail. If he does, he may never return to Canada. The Royal Canadian Mounted Police say they provided Russian authorities with assistance after Yakubovsky was arrested. "He thought he was a lot smarter than he was," says one law enforcement official with thinly guarded hostility.

Back in Toronto during the summer of 1995, I visit Marina at the Park Lane Circle mansion. This time there's only one bodyguard, sitting in the same spot on the leopard-print couch, watching TV.

The house is much quieter now. Marina, dressed in a small T-shirt with a heart on it and tight blue jeans, shows me her paintings, which are impressive. While her husband sits in a jail cell, Marina keeps busy working out, painting, and shopping.

"Before Dima's arrest, I used to visit him in Moscow," she says. "I was with him when he was arrested." Fifteen men with machine guns jumped out of a truck and hauled them away. Marina was later released.

"I came home to a different world," she says. In the past, she flew her friends on a private plane to New York for her birthday while Yakubovsky, though absent, arranged to have their lawn littered with roses tossed from a helicopter. But once Yakubovsky landed in jail most of these so-called friends deserted her, Marina says bitterly.

She is convinced that Yakubovsky is in jail for "political reasons" and that he will be out, perhaps even soon—though by the summer of 1995, his bail hearing has been delayed three times. "He's lost weight in jail," says Marina. "And he's acting as a lawyer for his cell mates."

Yakubovsky is also considering running in the December 1995 parliamentary elections—along with more than one hundred other prisoners. (One of the perks about being a member of Russia's parliament is parliamentary immunity, although it has been vetoed in some cases.)

"Dima and I are now closer than ever," she says. "Marriage, and having a close relationship with a woman, didn't mean much to him before. But in jail he has time to reflect. He's become a born-again Jew, always wearing a yarmulke, and thinking a lot about me and our daughter."

Marina is selling the Park Lane Circle mansion. "I need money to live," she says. She is considering opening up a rock-climbing sports club in Toronto—and maybe one in Moscow. When Yakubovsky gets out of jail, she says, she plans to live with him in Moscow, with another place in Paris.

She runs upstairs to retrieve a gold-painted box where she keeps the small gifts Yakubovsky is able to send her from prison. No more designer clothes and cars. Now it is threads painstakingly wound around an old pencil to spell *Marina*, and a small, ragged gray mouse for Olivia. Marina hasn't actually been allowed to speak to her husband since shortly after his arrest. She says she expects a call soon.

No Fist Fights in the Apartment and Absolutely No Guns Allowed on My Kitchen Table

"Would you tell me, please, which way I ought to go from here?"
"That depends a good deal on where you want to get to."
— LEWIS CARROLL, *Alice's Adventures in Wonderland*

Moscow, January 1994: My new apartment is in an old house across the street from the grounds of the Mongolian embassy, where one of my roommates digs up worms for her pet frogs. The apartment is just off the New Arbat, near Yakubovsky's first office. There are three flats, one per floor. I was supposed to take the empty third-floor flat, which was big, seven rooms, and cheap.

But it gave me the spooks. It was run-down and too large. I knew I'd only use a few of the rooms, and felt like the rest were haunted. Except for a rather grand dining room—complete with crystal, reupholstered chairs, a good table, even a classical bust on a stand—the flat was filthy and falling apart. I don't think the family who lived there ever cleaned. Before that, it was a communal flat.

I turn it down. Then Heidi, a Montreal photographer who is my age, rents the flat with her former roommate at Moscow State University. Lena, still a student, also works at the Canadian embassy. They're looking for a third roommate. I go over for tea. We hit it off. Crime is so bad I no longer want to live alone, and decide to give it a try. The landlord's recently deceased mother used to live in one of the rooms. Her clothes still hang in my closet the day I move in. I think Sergei Nikolaevich, her son, is renting the flat illegally. "There are to be no remonts," he says. "I don't want to call attention to the flat." The kitchen sink juts out of a wall, so small and awkward it looks like a nineteenth-century washbasin. One ceiling has already caved in, while another one collapses after we move in. Fortunately, no one is in the room at the time.

On my way home one evening, I'm about to stop off at the Irish House, a hard-currency grocery store, and pub, across the street. Friends have been robbed outside the store, but I've always felt safe here. I am on foot, when two men in a car begin to follow me. They drive slowly, and shout for me to get in with them.

I ignore them and continue to walk the urban walk, but I just can't shake the feeling that something bad is going to happen.

I almost get run over crossing the busy street instead of using the underground crossing. Just as I am about to enter the Irish House, a group of men from the Caucasus in shiny sweat suits, fedoras, and blazers, leaning against their cars, shout at me in a menacing tone. I ignore them. One of them grabs my arm and purse. He pulls me toward his car, yelling in a language I don't understand. I should yell too, but I can't. I just concentrate on getting away. A security guard outside the Irish House watches, doing nothing. I break free. From behind me, the man hits me, hard, on the back of my head.

"Do something!" I run up to the guard. "At least call the police!"

"I can't leave my post," he says. "I can only help if something happens *inside* the store."

My head is ringing. I run up the stairs to the bar, and bump into the entire security crew from the Canadian embassy. One of them wants to go downstairs and "break heads." I'm grateful for the sentiment, but reason prevails. The head of security, who has been kind and helpful since we met my first week in Moscow, walks me across the street to my apartment, in case the men are still there.

Now, sometimes, walking alone after dark, even if it's early evening, gives me the creeps. But there's not much I can do. Violence, or the fear of it, just comes with the territory.

I like living with my new roommates. But the relationship with our landlord, Sergei Nikolaevich, has got to change. I knew about nightmare landlords, but nothing compares to our man Sergei.

He keeps a locked room in our apartment. It looks like a boudoir, all red and stuffed with old furniture. He has the key and comes and goes when he pleases—without calling first or even ringing the doorbell. People phone for him and leave messages, as if he lives here. He pops by to make long-distance calls. He is often drunk. Worse, he sleeps in "his" room *after* Heidi and Lena move in. An older Russian man living with young women. He's thrilled.

But Sergei Nikolaevich hasn't counted on me. When he barges into the apartment the first day I'm there, I lose it.

I start with an impromptu speech that begins something like this: "The rules are going to change. Starting *now*. You will no longer be able to sleep in the apartment. You must call before coming over and *always ring the doorbell.*" I give him a list of what needs to be fixed. He squints at me, open-mouthed, barely muted hostility tinged with bewilderment.

"Who is this woman?" he asks.

Lena then gives him a lecture on drinking, shaming him in a way that only a Russian woman can.

Perhaps I didn't make the most tactful of speeches. I may even have hurt his feelings, but I didn't have much choice—if I wanted to be taken seriously. Sometimes, especially in Russia, you have to be brutally blunt. Sergei was used to getting his way and bossing around his female tenants, like a regular Russian *muzhik*, man. He acts as if he's doing us a favor by letting us stay here even though we are paying for the pleasure. I want Sergei to understand the complexity of the relationship. As tenants, we have certain inalienable rights. He's got to respect them.

For the first week, I don't think I'm Sergei Nikolaevich's favorite person.

"It was a good speech, Jen," says Heidi, slightly worried. "But if we're not nice to him, he could kick us out for better-paying tenants."

Sergei Nikolaevich may get better-paying tenants, but he won't get better tenants. Besides, I think he likes us. Even me. (Even though he may not know it yet.) I know he'll come around.

For the rest of the week, I'm extra nice to Sergei. He begins to smile. He replaces the cracked window in my room. It's a peace offering. He calls first and asks if it's convenient for him to come around. He rings the doorbell. He treats us with respect.

Lena, Heidi, and I cook cheaply, improvising when we have to. When the spicy Thai noodle sauce I bring from Toronto is gone, we make some ourselves using a monstrous jar of peanut butter Heidi schlepped from Montreal. (It's still a while before all Western staples make it to Moscow.) Lena can't get over the peanut butter. She's never seen it before, and offers it to her Russian friends. We buy our fresh Russian bread from the nearby *khleb*, or bread store, and tea biscuits from the Russian kiosks. Lena discovers Communist Chinese shrimp chips, little dots that expand in oil into fluffy chips in no time. She also buys lots of cabbage, potatoes, and worm-eaten apples.

Sometimes we go downstairs to visit the first-floor tenants, Leonid and Lena. They invite us when they entertain, which is almost all the time. (Lena is an excellent cook.) Leonid always helps, if we need it, with our locks and broken pipes. They both work with computers and speak excellent English. So do their two children, who love Walt Disney videos. In their thirties, Leonid and Lena are typical new Russians (though far from nouveaux riches). They are well educated and live in a huge apartment in a prime location. "We work hard and live well, but we're not rich," Lena says. Their hard-currency salaries go a long way because they live in the ruble economic zone. That means they don't spend money at Western groceries, restaurants, designer stores, or clubs. Instead, they shop in state stores and entertain friends at home with simple but plentiful food and drink, adjusting to the new economy in a distinctly Russian, almost anti-material way.

Leonid, tall and gangly, like a wounded crane, is always hitting on women. Then comes March 8, International Women's Day.

"*S prazdnikom* [Congratulations]. Happy International Women's Day," says Leonid, as all men do on this day. He then kisses me on the cheek.

"It's the only day of the year when there's no sexual harassment," he says.

Living with my flatmates is never dull. Like my old residence suite in graduate school, the flat is a place where people feel comfortable just dropping by. It starts off innocently enough. Students, professors, gifted musicians, wild-eyed artists, photographers, and journalists. The list is indiscriminate. An old lady who loves Stalin, a struggling ex-sailor-turned-translator of obscure literature and self-help books. The list gradually expands to the sons of the famous: Rutskoi's son, who carries fistfuls of U.S. one-hundred-dollar bills and tries to torch our apartment one drunken evening; Stalin's *GQ*-handsome grandson. Each night brings another unexpected visitor. Somehow they all finagle their way inside. Sometimes I spend time I don't have chatting away bored in the kitchen.

One of the men becomes a staple in Heidi's life. "Sasha" is an academic who once, coincidentally, taught Lena. Bland and nondescript, Sasha speaks impressive-sounding Chinese and excellent English. At first he comes by unexpectedly, unannounced. Heidi is not so pleased. He tries to make himself useful.

In his late twenties, early thirties maybe, Sasha is dead-pan straight, though humor comes out once you get to know him. Gradually his presence is a permanent feature.

Basically, he helps Heidi with her work and also has an uncanny knack for obtaining goods that are then still hard to find in Moscow, from faxes and computer parts to obscure videos. Money never seems to be a problem for Sasha.

The night I move in, we launch a series of parties I will never forget. One of Heidi's friends, Betsy, an American who is in computers, is going back to the States. Heidi is throwing her a goodbye bash. Betsy is a friend from "the Hash," a group of expats who meet once a week, in cities all over the world, to go running, or walking, and then drink beer. Most of the Hashers are corporate types, although probably every type of expat is represented. The Hash is a good support network for expats who arrive in foreign cities without knowing anyone. For now, Heidi is a fairly regular Hasher. I have never gone. I just can't believe in any organized form of anything.

Instead of preparing for our first party, Heidi, Lena, and I go out for dinner. Friday nights are hamburger-and-Canadian-beer nights at the Canadian embassy—for those with Canadian or NATO passports.

I am the only one who seems to be worried. "About fifty people are coming to our flat. We don't have any food or drink ready. We're not even home," I say.

We arrive back just as ten Hashers show up, lugging boxes of food and alcohol, like elves. One well-known Russian photographer, who—with glazed eyes, wild hair, and unkempt beard—really does look uncannily like Rasputin, arranges fresh salmon and caviar on trays. A British female oil executive prepares cheese plates. Guests stream in as if on cue.

Our parties are an eclectic mix. Perhaps one of the only places where old and new Russia, YILGs and ordinary expats, meet. Some of the Russian men tend to show up early. Usually with flowers. Poor Russians—artists, musicians, students—who drink bottle after bottle of vodka, gravitate to the kitchen, where someone inevitably pulls out a guitar. They sing for hours, get the drunkest, stay the latest.

Europeans tend to drift toward the dining room; the halls fill with an assortment of Americans, many of them corporate types Heidi knows from the Hash. They tend to have names like Buck and Chip.

The next group are the journalists, and North American, European, and assorted strangers we meet: politicians, actors, diplomats, even U.S. Marines.

I invite some Russian journalists I know, some of whom I met in Toronto when they were covering the Yakubovsky story. One of the younger journalists comes with a rising television star. Both get terribly drunk. Our conversation is most depressing. "Slava" is a good journalist. He's got ambition and he cares about his work. But although he is twenty-three and has a promising job, he—like most young Russians—can't afford to move out of his parents' apartment.

A wealthy Russian recently paid for him and other, older, top Russian journalists to fly somewhere far away, first-class. "Look at what my life is like," he says. "How could I turn down the trip—and how could I write about it honestly and objectively?"

When I look at Slava, I see a handsome young man with energy and passion, all you need, really, to succeed in this business, or any other. But corruption has already begun to destroy him. He knows it's there, like a sickness. "I can't help it," he says. "What choice do I have in these times?" He knows, now, that he will never be a great journalist. Because of this weakness. Because of this country, this moment.

Each party is more elaborate than the last. We have dinner parties, use Sergei Nikolaevich's crystal, and invite a mess of people later. We cater food from Guria, our favorite Georgian restaurant (and a mob hangout), excellent food at prices so cheap it's like they're still subsidized, now by the mafiya instead of the Communist Party. We hire our favorite violinist, a sweet, white-haired man with sad eyes and a droopy mustache, from another restaurant, to come play.

We also get a system down. One person organizes the music, another the food and the serving of it. When we decide the party's over, the party's over. The last thing you want is to see some drunken stranger (it's always the strangers) asleep in your hallway or on your sofa the next morning. We hide at least some of the good wine. The key is to save at least two large bottles of mineral water and orange juice for the morning after. And to arrange to have someone to come and clean very early, so the apartment is spotless by the time we wake up.

THE RUSSIAN LESSON—
MY UNFORGETTABLE NIGHTS WITH THE GYPSY THIEVES
(AND GIPSY KINGS)

It's another Saturday night in February. I'm home, on deadline, finishing a magazine assignment. I've turned down Heidi's invitation to see the Gipsy Kings, a well-known band. (If I went out every time Heidi asked, I'd never get any work done.)

"The band was incredible," says Heidi upon her return. "I charmed my way backstage and scammed us free tickets for tomorrow night, which is sold out. Now you've *got* to come."

The concert is a success. Thousands of Russians are out of their seats, dancing. (In the early post-Communist days, Russians, not used to concerts, sat through shows politely, saying nothing.) After the concert, we go backstage. The band invites us for dinner.

The Gipsy Kings charm me. All of them. They seem so much younger than what I expected. The singers are mostly semi-literate French Roma who sing in Spanish but only speak French. Their backup musicians and light and sound technicians are more sophisticated. Some are French and not Roma at all. The lead singer, Manolo, is as short and round as a butterball—with the most magnificent voice. One of the band's musicians looks very familiar. Maybe it's because he looks like Phil Collins, I think.

The manager is an older, well-dressed Frenchman named Bernard. He is ever so polite and speaks English with a charming accent. The tour's organizer is an American named Howie, with long white-gray hair and a thick Brooklyn accent. The show is complete with a flamenco dancer, in jeans and high heels. "She's the wife of one of the band's Swiss financial backers," Howie says. Her dancing is so simple it looks like anyone could do it. It must be more complicated, more *professional*, than it looks, I think.

The group is accompanied by a man with long, stringy black hair and pointy chin, in a bloodred waistcoat. He's their Russian concert manager, and arranges everything the Gipsy Kings do in Moscow, including tonight's dinner. And he's not too pleased that Heidi, our friend Betsy, and I have come along.

We drive to the House of Gypsies, where Russia's real Gypsy king, called "the Baron," lives. (Every place in Russia is a house of something: house of books, house of artists, house of writers, whatever.) The Baron is a short, squat man with thick ruby lips and thin, longish hair that extends from a shiny balding scalp, sort of like a long-haired, bearded version of Danny DeVito. He is treated with the respect owed a mafia don. His wife is a tall, elegant woman clad in colorful layers, her hair bundled extravagantly high on top of her head.

In Russia, as in most places, particularly large European cities, Roma get a bad rap. In Moscow, many barefoot Roma used to live outside the Kievsky train station by the Slav in the summer. Young kids and mothers with their children often asked me for money. They'd follow others, especially nervous-looking tourists. A few of my friends were surrounded and robbed by the kids. Then the police, using violence, "cleaned" the area up.

But despite the external chaos, the Roma community, at least the one I get to know in Moscow, is tightly organized. The leadership is sophisticated and wealthy. Now I'm in the heart of this community, invited to a private dinner of the Baron himself.

Up the stairs of this large building is a banquet hall and an unbelievably lavish spread for seventy people. When we arrive, the long tables are overflowing with fruit baskets, caviar, champagne, wine, and platters of zakuski. Between courses, a Russian Gypsy or a Gipsy King sings or dances. Children also dance. By the end of the evening, so do we.

When we get home, Heidi discovers she has an old Gipsy King CD. "That's funny," I say. "None of the Gipsies on the cover look like the guys we know, except for Chico."

Chico is the oldest Gipsy King. He says he's in his forties, although he looks much younger. He is a French Arab, with no Roma blood whatsoever. "I guess the band members change a lot," I say. "They're Gypsies, after all."

For the next few days, the Gipsy Kings call and want to get together, but I'm busy reporting, still on deadline. We do, however, invite the Gipsy Kings for dinner their second-to-last night in town. We even get an American embassy chef to do the cooking.

I pick up the Gipsy Kings at their hotel in the middle of a snowstorm. Surprisingly, they are staying at the Cosmos Hotel, a cheap and sleazy Soviet-era hotel with no charm whatsoever. I attribute their poor choice to some dreadful mistake by the man-in-the-red-waistcoat, who reminds me of the wolf in *Pinocchio*.

Back at our flat, twenty people enthusiastically dig into a simple but tasty pasta dinner. We toast the musicians, friendship between nations, and all the rest. Some YILGs show up. Dozens more show up after dinner, when the Gipsy Kings play for us. So does one of Russia's top rock bands.

One of the Gipsy Kings (who is French, not Roma) is only nineteen. He doesn't drink and is instead into New Age healing, rocks, and crystals. When an older Gipsy King has a headache, the young one takes him into a dark, enclosed corner and tries to draw the pain out of him.

"What color is the pain? Blue? Picture that blue completely outside of you," he says.

By 2 A.M., most of the Gipsy Kings are on their way. "We have to be well rested for our final performance," they explain. Manolo, the lead singer, is most nervous. "I need my rest," he says. "I need time to prepare. Thousands of my fans await me tomorrow."

The night after the party, we attend the Gipsy Kings' final performance, dance, and say good-bye. The Gipsy Kings live in Montpellier and Paris. "Next time you come to Paris, call us. We'll come pick you up at the airport," one says. "Montpellier is beautiful to visit in summertime." We all exchange addresses. They give me telephone numbers, but their addresses are in care of other people. I guess they're on the road a lot.

The next month I fly home to Toronto. Imagine my surprise when I find out the Gipsy Kings are playing the night I arrive. I'm exhausted. All I want to do is sleep. But my mother wants to go. (She loved the Gipsy Kings long before I knew who they were.) I drag a poor friend of mine along. We arrive about an hour into the sold-out show.

"I'm a friend of the band's, from Moscow," I say. We're directed to the stage door, where I ask for Bernard, the manager.

A man I've never seen before comes out.

"You're not Bernard," I say. "I'm a friend of the band's from Moscow. I've even brought some pictures for them."

"Can I see them?" he asks anxiously. "May I take them? I'll be back in a minute."

With that, he disappears, and returns a few minutes later.

"What were their names?" he asks. "Was one of them Chico?"

"Yes."

"Chico *used* to be part of the Gipsy Kings—until we kicked him out," the man says. "Now he goes all over Europe impersonating us. The band you met are fakes."

"That's impossible," I say. "I even know Howie S_____, head of Global Productions, who organized the tour."

Mentioning Howie's name really sets this man off.

"Howie S_____ is a *criminal*!" this man says. "We're trying to prosecute him but it's impossible. Russia is so far away."

I am shattered. "What other bands do you think would be popular in Moscow?" Howie once asked. When I left Moscow, Heidi was faxing Howie lists. I even told Howie I wanted to write an article about the Gipsy Kings' success in Moscow. "No problem," he said.

"Look, there are some front-row seats left," the real manager says. "Why don't you stay and enjoy the show, and we'll talk after."

The band is good, but I'm in shock to see a bunch of older men with gray hair playing the same songs that Manolo and company sang so well in our living room. I start remembering all the *little* things: the seedy hotel, the shady man with the red waistcoat.

"I knew they all looked younger," says Sandy, my Canadian journalist pal. "New members," they'd explain. We believed them.

Why not? Some of Russia's top musicians—like Alexander Rosenbaum, whom I adore—came to hear them play. Two more sold-out shows were even added to the tour. In Toronto, the show is also sold out. As in Moscow, people are out of their seats, dancing.

"So what did you think of the band?" the real manager asks in Toronto, after the show.

"They were excellent," I say. "But, honestly, so was the band in Moscow."

The Gipsy Kings experience symbolizes Russia as I know it. This is a country where nothing is as it seems. Where anyone can come with nothing and scam their way to wealth and fame, where everyone is a potential impostor, and no one is the wiser. Believe no one in Russia. That's one of the safest rules.

The people I meet are like Alice in Wonderland characters. Most of the characters I meet in the early chapters—no matter how zany or awful—resurface, often when I least expect it. After the Gipsy Kings leave Moscow, I'm out one night at La Cantina, a semiseedy Mexican restaurant with good food, just off Red Square, on Tverskaya Street, beside the Intourist Hotel.

A man who looks like Phil Collins keeps staring at me, as if he knows me. It haunts me a little, but I don't think much of it. I keep seeing him everywhere after that, like at the Metropol for Sunday brunch. Finally, I remember. He was a local recruit in the Gipsy Kings band-scam; now he's wondering if, or when, I'll remember.

RULE #1:

NO FIST FIGHTS; NO BLOOD IN THE APARTMENT, PLEASE

We continue to throw parties, finding whatever excuse we can. One night "Desmond" comes with a bag stuffed considerably with everything from coffee to wine. A YILG who has trekked around the world, Desmond tells stories, fictional or real, involving near-death experiences, tropical illnesses, and gun-chase scenes in African jungles, Asian swamps, and South American trains. Part of his current job includes making sure that oil (don't know if it's legal or not) makes it from the ex-Soviet empire to the West without being hijacked by alien gangsters or governments.

Desmond is with Barney, a swarthy American in his forties, with laugh lines and hair that flips. After persistent phone calls and declined dinner invitations, Barney wears me down. I turn down another dinner invitation, to stay home and write. He shows up after his dinner, drunk. It's his birthday. We become friends. Like Yakubovsky, he seems to enjoy dining en masse and picking up the group's tab.

Ever the sucker for romance, I fall in love with his story. Barney and Wife fell madly in love. They were young and had loads of children together, escaping the rat race for Europe and the sea. Barney raves about Wife's Great Beauty and Talent, about the Joys of Raising Children. But over time, like a bad character in a Graham Greene novel, Barney trades art, romance, and fiscal restraint for the single-focused pursuit of money. "That's where my real talent lies," he says. "I was never good enough to be an artist."

Making money now seems to be his justification for whatever it is he has to do to make it. He says he doesn't need it to support his lavish lifestyle. It's all "for the children."

But the price of providing is so high, it ultimately costs him the very people he was providing for. "My wife finally left me," he says as he walks me home through snow-clogged Moscow streets one evening. "She didn't like some of the people I had to associate with. And she didn't like the fact that sometimes I had to disappear for a while."

Only in Moscow do I meet people who speak, nonchalantly, of having "to disappear" for a while. No wonder so many of their relationships break up.

Barney seems to have traveled, and lived, around the globe. He is, perhaps, an older version of some of the YILGs I know. He still gets by on charm and decades' worth of contacts, no matter how frazzled he may be by alcohol, who knows what else, and psychological scarring from years of danger and tension.

Once, at La Cantina, Barney bumps into a man his age, with a ponytail. They bear-hug, drink, and reminisce. "We hadn't seen each other since twenty years ago in East Germany," Barney says later, over dinner.

"Just what were you doing in East Germany in the 1970s, during the height of the Cold War?" I ask.

"I was a student," he says.

"Paris I can understand, but East Germany?"

"I went through all sorts of small towns," he says, a few more drinks into the conversation. "It's amazing what East German soldiers would tell you when they were drunk—even though they could have been shot for just being seen drinking with an American."

Overdosing on the parties, Heidi and I decide to issue them sparingly, like a treat, a way to celebrate good news. Otherwise they lose their spunk, their spontaneity. Worse, they begin to turn ugly. Friends start bringing friends of friends, who turn out to be strangers—and trouble.

Then comes an infamous party that fast spins out of control. It starts off innocently enough.

It's late. My recollection of what happens is hazy. One of our guests is an American who now goes by the Russian name of Misha. He is a talented writer, from a privileged background, who seems to be trying to immerse himself in a poverty-for-the-sake-of-art existence. I enjoy talking to Misha more than most people at the party. He's smart, insightful, and funny. I've never heard him say an offensive word. However, he apparently has been approaching strangers at the party and telling them what he really thinks of them—i.e., that they're phonies. His insults may have been accurate, but they have also been needlessly nasty, aimed at men and women indiscriminately. Then he picks the wrong person to mess with.

It's now very late. There is too much alcohol. Some of Barney's crowd are smashing crystal. (It's apparently a Russian tradition, we're told later.) Nothing like this has ever happened before. I'm in the dining room, talking with Maguy and Georges, in a room full of dirty plates and glasses, when something flashes by me in the hallway.

A large man, six foot four, is running down our narrow hall holding Misha, who is quite small. Wham! Crash! Thud! *Blood* is on our walls; glass is broken. Three of the big guy's friends clean up Misha in the bathroom. Others are cleaning up the blood that's splattered everywhere.

"I can't believe there's a *fight* in the apartment I live in!" I yell. Everyone apologizes but they all blame Misha.

"There's no excuse why a six-foot-four man would throw a little guy like Misha down a hallway," I say.

Misha is my guest. The bully is a friend of one of Heidi's friends. Turns out I know him. He seemed like such a nice, unassuming kind of guy. We even went on a sort of dinner date once.

"I'm sorry," he says, apologizing over and over again, "I'm *so* sorry." Apparently, Misha was tormenting him.

"I kept asking Misha to go away, but he wouldn't," he says. "Finally, I told him I thought it would be a good idea if he left the party altogether, and I had friends who would help him leave if he didn't go on his own. You've got to understand. He was more than a nuisance. He was insulting everybody."

Then Misha apparently flicked a cigarette in the big guy's eye.

"I just lost it," he says.

I make sure someone sees Misha home.

By the end of the evening, I am surrounded by plates empty of Georgian food, smashed crystal, Ivy League gangsters, CIA-funded academics, journalists, artists, U.S. Marines. Long past the witching hour, I am getting one drunken friend to drink orange juice and telling total strangers that "fist fights are not allowed in this apartment."

RULE #2:
NO MORE COSSACKS IN THE APARTMENT—AND ABSOLUTELY
NO GUNS ALLOWED ON THE KITCHEN TABLE

Midafternoon, Heidi calls.

"A twenty-five-year-old Siberian Cossack is arriving by train from Omsk," she says. He's a political activist working for Sergei Baburin, a young, charismatic extreme right-wing politician who looks like a cross between Lenin and the Devil.

"I'm running late," says Heidi, who is supposed to meet the Cossack. Would I mind terribly going out into the ice and snow, across the street to Melodya, the record store, where Volodya the Cossack will be waiting?

Heidi and I help each other out. Of course I'll go, though I'm none too pleased. We have certain house rules. Like no fascists allowed in the apartment, after some of Heidi's subjects come calling. Call me crazy, but I'm uncomfortable knowing that bonafide fascists know where I live. I wish Heidi, whose father is Jewish and mother converted, felt the same way.

"How will I recognize him?" I ask.

"Oh, you can't miss him," Heidi says. "He's tall and has a mustache. Besides, he'll be dressed in camouflage fatigues. Oh yeah—he'll be carrying a cane and *walking with a limp.*"

The only detail Heidi leaves out is the medal he wears proudly on his chest, for his service in Moldova. He doesn't want to talk about his limp, though he does say he fought with Rutskoi during the October 1993 parliamentary rebellion.

When he is sober, Volodya is a gentleman. He proceeds cautiously on ice and offers me his arm, worried that I may fall. I take him to the apartment, where I serve tea in the kitchen. I don't even consider offering him something stronger. Turns out he has his own flask. And, as I later find out, he's the type who gets nasty when drunk.

Volodya tells me about his family, about Cossack traditions, about the restoration of the old orders, about digging up his grandfather's old uniform. And I think of my grandfather, who lived in a shtetl, a tiny village in the Jewish ghetto area called the Pale of Settlement, the only area where Jews were allowed to live, and the pogroms he was lucky enough to survive. And now, here I am, talking to a young Cossack who is proudly reviving old traditions.

Volodya chain-smokes Camels and tells me about his experiences in the October parliamentary rebellion. He begins with the following disclaimer: "I am *not* an anti-Semite. My uncle married a Jewess. My nephews are half-Jews."

This is his interpretation of the rebellion: "The Zionists, backed by [Moscow mayor Yuri] Luzhkov, were brought in by Yeltsin to assassinate leaders of the rebellion. I saw it happen."

Moving on, I ask him whom he'll support in the 1996 presidential elections. "I'm not sure. *Maybe* Zhirinovsky." Volodya grins. "My Cossack band votes as a bloc. We'll support whoever we're told to support. It's not my decision to make.

"For now," he says, "my group keeps in close contact with the different leaders" of the neo-fascists, Communists, and monarchists.

It may be at this point, as we fast run out of things to say to each other, that Volodya the Cossack pulls a gun out of the side pocket of his camouflage fatigues. He tosses the gun in the air, catches it, and tosses it again. *This stranger, very likely a psychotic killer, is playing with a gun on my kitchen table.*

Again, I react by not reacting. It's a reflexive instinct by now. Calmly, as if I'm used to such situations, I tell Volodya to put the gun away *immediately*.

"I don't believe in guns *in principle*," I say. "There are absolutely *no guns allowed on this kitchen table*."

Volodya laughs. I don't think he's used to women telling him what to do.

"You don't like guns because you're a girl," he says. It seems to make my demand more palatable. Much to my relief, he puts the gun away.

I decide that it's time to get back to my work, that I have no choice but to leave this man alone in the kitchen, waiting for Heidi. I give him a pot of tea, cookies, and a pile of Russian newspapers. (He soon opens his flask of vodka.)

Before I go, I ask him one last question. "Do you think there will be civil war in Russia? If so, do you think it will be soon?"

"Civil war has already begun," the Cossack says. "I don't feel safe walking around Moscow unless I carry a gun, day or night. Everyone I know feels the same way. We all carry guns. And we use them. If that's not civil war, I don't know what is."

CHAPTER 16

Sexpionage

From Delilah and Mata Hari to Marina
Oswald Porter and Violetta Siena,
U.S. Marines, White Wine, and KGB Colonels

Love ceases to be a pleasure when it ceases to be a secret.

— APHRA BEHN, English Restoration dramatist,
novelist, poet, translator, and spy,
"Four O'clock General Conversation"

An editor I do not know calls with an intriguing assignment: sex-pionage. She wants a piece on the women, known in the field as swallows, or honey-pots, who are used to "turn" the men. I have been fascinated by this topic since I met Marina Oswald Porter, in Moscow, and Marina Kapankhadze, in Tbilisi. Whether these women were swallows or not, they were in positions to be extremely valuable to intelligence services on both sides of the Atlantic. I begin to wonder about the profession. Who finds the women? Who trains them? One contact gives me the name of someone who will be able to put me in touch with the right people.

"Be sure to bring some vodka. He'll also ask you for money," I'm warned. I call a number and mention a name. "Why don't you come over right now?" I do. Much to my surprise, he's exactly who I'm looking for. Other contacts also come through. No one asks for money. In fact, one KGB colonel even gives me a token gift—a small embroidered handkerchief from a recent visit to Japan. It is the winter of 1994. As I do my reporting, Yeltsin restructures the Security and Intelligence Ministries, purging the last elements of reform within. My contacts dry up. I was lucky to have begun the story when I did. Three thousand years after Delilah seduced

Samson as an agent of the Philistines, sexual entrapment remains as alluring a tactic as ever in the search for secrets.

I am sitting in the office of a retired KGB colonel, sipping Spanish white wine and talking about sex. Each time Colonel Alexei Kirichenko's private line rings, he blows the caller off, explaining, as he smiles at me, that he is in the middle of a very important meeting. We are discussing what the Russians call *postelny shpionazh*, bedroom espionage.

The Cold War may be over in name, but Russian spying and recruitment of Western informants have actually increased since the collapse of the empire. The KGB has expanded its targets from diplomats and journalists to more businessmen—who are now flocking to Russia, often without taking the precautions of their predecessors. While they may not know much about, say, troop movements, they do have information that is valuable to industrial competitors. "Human contact is still the most important aspect to espionage," Kirichenko says. And while women play a crucial role, espionage is still, I fast discover, a man's game.

"Espionage is just an adult, military game for grown-up boys," says Kirichenko, his blue eyes waking up as the conversation shifts from formalities to substance. "Of course women are very important. Without them you can't play the game, but in the end, women are just the tools." Until he retired in 1986, Kirichenko, a Japanese expert and former adviser to Gorbachev, worked as a case officer for foreign spies recruited by swallows. Like many Russian officials, Kirichenko quickly finds an excuse to open a cabinet that hides a well-stocked bar. Soon the stories are flowing.

The Russians take sexpionage so seriously, Kirichenko tells me, that they run a two-year program for the KGB women who will direct the swallows. The supervisors are trained at the Academy of the Russian Federal Counter-Intelligence Service,[*] an imposing,

---

[*] By 1994, Russia's security services had changed names thirteen times since 1917. Yeltsin continues to restructure and rename the services. Similarly, the secret service academy also undergoes a variety of name changes. For the sake of simplicity, I will here refer to Russia's foreign and domestic intelligence and security services the way most Russians do: as the KGB.

*All photos courtesy of Jennifer Gould
except where otherwise indicated.*

Young Pioneer with Viktor Aanpilov, a former KGB
operative for Radio Moscow and current leader of
Working Russia, the Communist hardline party, during
a 1996 presidential campaign rally.

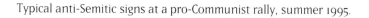

Typical anti-Semitic signs at a pro-Communist rally, summer 1995.

Communist Party leader Gennady
Zyuganov on the campaign trail
in Bryansk, summer 1996.

Young Muscovites gun shopping in the city center.

Outside Lenin's birthplace, Simbirsk, Russia.

Workers in Vladimir, Russia.

On the royal watch:
following Princess Anne through
the South Gobi Nature Reserve.

Camels at the roadside,
Ashgabad, Turkmenistan.

A man and his horse. Somewhere
between Almaty, Kazakhstan, and
Bishkek, near Ulan Bator.

Taking a break in an arctic coal mine. Once Boris Yeltsin's biggest supporters, coal miners at Vorkuta—who haven't been paid in months—fast became disillusioned with the post-Communist regime.

Chechen refugees in the neighboring republic of Ingushetia.

Communist Party headquarters, Dagestan, with a traditional rug portrait as decor.

Buddhist monks and Russian soldiers, Baku, Azerbaijan.

At home with General Dima. Dining with Dmitri Yakubovsky at his Moscow dacha before his December 1994 arrest.

"No guns allowed." Outside the luxury Metechi Palace Hotel in Tbilisi, Georgia, where gunfire has been known to spray the lobby and upstairs piano bar and where a CIA station chief met his woman companion the night of his murder.

(Photo courtesy of Jaime Spitzcovsky)

As the boat slowly pulls out of the harbor, Vladimir Zhirinovsky leans over the rail and waves.

Zhirinovsky supporters Jurgen Zapadalov, a forty-six-year-old psychiatrist and his driver, Zhenya Levin, whom Zapadalov describes as "handsome as a cat."

Young supporters of Vladimir Zhirinovsky.

The Presidential Palace in Grozny, Chechnya, destroyed by Russian shelling. Fred Cuny, American aid worker who disappeared in the mountain foothills of Chechnya, had written, "There were 3,500 detonations a day during the height of the shelling in Sarajevo. In Grozny, there were 4,000 an hour."

Checkpoint outside Mozdok, Russian army headquarters, Chechnya.

Committee of Russian Soldiers' Mothers protesting in Chechnya.

Outside Samashky, eleven-year-old Bislan still clutches the white flag he held while fleeing his village with his mother, grandmother, and siblings. He is the oldest male in his family to survive the massacre. His father is dead. The other men in his family are missing or dead.

Former Soviet leader and 1996 presidential candidate Mikhail Gorbachev.

Russian president Boris Yeltsin in Archangelsk, summer 1996.

heavily guarded building in suburban northwest Moscow. There, the women study the psychology of sexual entrapment, seduction techniques (including acting out potential situations), and how to supervise swallows.

The trainers work with two categories of swallows. The first are well-educated women who are fluent in foreign languages and work as secretaries and interpreters in embassies, news bureaus, and offices. During the Cold War, all nonnational offices had to hire a certain number of Russians from a state agency called UPDK. The requirements, however, were not always reciprocal. No Americans, for example, worked at the Soviet embassy in Washington. The foreigners knew the Russians reported to the KGB, compiling dossiers on their bosses, spying on them, and, in some cases, sexually entrapping them. Now the hiring requirements have been lifted but most offices are still partly staffed by Russians, many of whom continue to cooperate with the KGB. Amazingly, the American embassy in Moscow wants to hire even more Russians because they *cost less* than Americans.

Even high school Komsomol girls, members of the junior Communist Party leagues, were enticed into the trade. During one international festival for youths and students in the mid-1980s, young Komsomol girls were given scanty outfits and told to go to the hotels that the foreigners were staying in. "They were told to write reports about what happened. They could keep the clothes and whatever small gifts they were given, but had to give all the money they made to the Party," says Alexander Minkin, a well-known Russian journalist, over lunch one day.

The second category comprises prostitutes and women with foreign lovers. Some women volunteer to work for the KGB; others are threatened with arrest if they don't comply. "They caught me like a rabbit," says Natasha Kuznetzova, thirty-three, who was pressed into service when the KGB discovered she was dating a young Japanese diplomat.

After the initial sexual contact is made, the man is turned over to a male case officer, who is often introduced as the swallow's "uncle." While the men are rewarded for any success, the women are frequently discarded—without pensions or benefits—once their usefulness ends. "I still get desperate letters from down-and-out older women who once worked for me as swallows," Kirichenko says. "I try to do what I can. I once even helped a woman leave the country so she could marry the man she had been assigned to entrap. Although I love the KGB, I was considered a dissident," he says.

"Are there any famous swallows, like Mata Hari?" I ask, referring to the Dutch dancer recruited by the Germans as their top agent in France during World War I.

"No," he says, "but there is one woman in her eighties who taught at the school for decades."

I can't help but think of another aging beauty, Marina Oswald Porter, whom I met in Moscow in 1992. That summer, I traveled to Minsk, where Lee Harvey Oswald had lived, tracking down his old friends and lovers. It was a topic I had long been interested in. I had heard so many first-hand stories about Marina, and now, here she was, in Moscow, working as an adviser on an American television movie about her life. With her gray hair and cool eyes, chain-smoking Eastern European cigarettes and still speaking English with a thick Russian accent although she has lived in Texas for thirty years, Marina seemed both glamorous and gracious. As we chatted in her hotel room, I couldn't understand how such a woman —so centered, self-confident, radiating with style and presence— could marry someone like Oswald.

"Were you *really* in love with Lee?" I asked.

"No," she said, instinctively, without even taking the time to think about it. "I never loved him."

"So why did you marry him?"

"It was for the children," she replied. (They had two.) She didn't elaborate. I didn't want to alienate her, to have her cut the interview—already far longer than she'd agreed to—short. Marina said she believed Oswald was innocent, even though she had told the Warren Commission she thought he was guilty. (That, she said, was intimidation; she was new and alone in a foreign country, a widowed young mother who had married the alleged assassin of the president of the United States. "I was living in a glass house.") She believed he was still working for some part of the American government. She also swore she had nothing to do with the KGB. She asked after one man in Minsk, the only one to say kind words about her, and pressed some fresh apples from her girlfriend's dacha into my hand as I left.

When I tell Kirichenko this story, he smiles. "Lee Harvey Oswald was the only foreigner then in Minsk," he says. "We always had women report on the foreigners." Other KGB colonels, retired and active, agree.

After a long afternoon of discussion, Kirichenko says he will put me in touch with the school for swallows. We arrange to meet the next day. Kirichenko arrives late, looking as if he regrets yesterday's candor. "I think you seduced me over the white wine," he jokes. "There is no difference between a spy and a journalist."

The official clampdown is on. The meetings that Kirichenko has promised me keep being delayed. Just when I think I will never make contact with the swallows and their trainers, another source comes through. It's nighttime when I meet my contact, Yuri, a man I have never seen, who will take me to an unnamed destination. We meet on the New Arbat. Dozens of people rush by. Only one leans against the designated building.

"Dzhenifer?" asks a young man in the shadows, hidden under a Gap-like knit cap. "*Da,*" I respond, peering at him in the dark. I think he is somebody's assistant. He is, I discover, a KGB officer. "*Poshli!* Let's go!" he says. "We're ready," he adds, speaking into a radio as we walk down icy stairs that lead to a back alley. A driver in a beat-up Lada, motor running, is waiting.

I am told only that we are going somewhere on Leninsky Prospekt, a wide street lined with high-rise blocks and huge gates, behind which stand the state-owned mansions of the old Communist elite. We turn into a residential apartment complex. A man in jeans leads us up darkened stairs to a large, well-lit room, where a tall, slim woman in spike heels, black stockings, tight miniskirt, and sheer blouse motions for me to follow her into a room the size of a closet. "I'm sorry," she says as she frisks me, running her hands down my back, arms, legs—even along the thick wool socks inside my boots. She is checking for wires. When I am pronounced clean, she leads me into an adjoining room. She forbids me to take my camera, tape recorder, even my purse. All I'm allowed is a notepad and pen.

Behind a large desk sits Alla, a young woman with short brown hair, wearing a no-nonsense blazer, rhinestone T-shirt, knee-length skirt, and medium-heeled pumps. "Would you like a drink?" she asks as she presses a buzzer beneath her desk. The woman in spikes instantly appears. I have tea, Alla and Yuri have black coffee. Champagne and chocolate will come later. The three of us are from the same generation, though raised on ideologically opposite diets. I know it is impossible to get this kind of access from the CIA. All a State Department official says is, "We'd never talk about that type of thing. Besides, our women are too intelligent for that kind of work."

When I relay this to Alla, she says, dryly, "Of course the Americans do the same thing. Everybody does." Alla, twenty-nine, is a member of the ruling elite, a graduate of the KGB academy and its little-known female-only training program. Now, in the chill of a Moscow winter, we sit in a warm, bare room. Alla is open to questions. Yuri listens. Occasionally he stops talking into his radio and chips in. Some questions bring tight, coquettish smiles and nyets. Alla looks to Yuri before she answers. He looks rather dapper, now, in a rakish sort of way: black turtleneck and burgundy blazer setting off dark eyes, shaggy hair, and cute, almost impudent nose.

In the past, recruiting someone to spy was as easy as blackmailing them. Just the threat of turning photos and videos over to foreign embassies or news bureaus was often enough. Now, the tactics may be more subtle. Some women tell their lovers they will suffer if the men do not cooperate. Some men may not even know their lovers are KGB until years later. "We know who we want, and then we find the women," Alla says.

Alla is in charge of more than one hundred women who report on foreigners from NATO countries. She got into the business at age twenty-three, when her boyfriend of seven years died mysteriously. "Nobody said how he died but I knew it was because of his work," she says. Her boyfriend was a KGB officer. He was twenty-five years old. "It was a passionate, crazy love," she says, an intense look on her heart-shaped face as she sips a glass of champagne from a bottle she instructed Yuri to open.

"His friends suggested I could continue his work in his memory," she says. And so Alla, a graduate of a technical institute in Moscow, began. "At first, I was happy. I was trying to follow him, to work in his footsteps, not for Communism but for the Motherland." (What does her family think about her line of work? "My mom knows what I do. She doesn't think it's the best work, but she's comfortable with it.")

Alla says she never uses the techniques she studies in her personal life. Nor has she ever entrapped anyone. "It takes a certain type of person to do it," she says, scornfully. "Sex is their life. They don't need to take courses to know what to do." However, she adds, "all women recruits who work for the KGB must be beautiful, intelligent, and able to speak many languages."

Like Kirichenko, Alla believes some nationalities are easier to recruit than others. While Americans are "fairly difficult" to entrap, there have been many such cases, "famous and not so famous." In the 1980s, Sergeant Clayton Lonetree, a young marine, was seduced by a beautiful swallow named Violetta Kosareva, aka Violetta Siena, the daughter of a leather designer and electrical worker. Lonetree was sentenced to twenty years in prison at Fort Leavenworth, Kansas, for espionage. (He served eight years.) I track down his thirty-four-year-old lover, who is unmarried and lives with her mother and younger half sister, Sveta, in the desolate outskirts of Moscow.

Sveta loves Viktor is etched into the door outside the apartment. The first time I visit, no one is home. I knock on the neighbor's door. A man in his fifties, old shirt and gray stubble, invites me in to show me his paintings and stamp collection.

The cramped flat is so packed with possessions, from books to unfinished canvasses, there is barely room to move. The paintings line the walls. They are so wacky, I have to come in.

Religious or secular, the paintings all have one common theme. Cats: crucifixion cats, Madonna and Child cats, abstract cats, jungle cats, portraits of cats, and landscape cats. (His stamp collection is equally obsessive, and yes, it, too, includes cats. I promise to bring him some stamps on my next visit.)

The next day, Kosareva's mother, Henrietta Khokha, invites me in. We chat in the tiny kitchen. Suddenly Kosareva appears, dressed in an expensive mauve-and-blue tracksuit, her shoulder-length hair side-swept into a ponytail. She boils some water and grabs some yogurt from the fifties fridge. "I have talked with Clayton's father, and he has instructed me not to talk about the story with anybody because it may bring harm to Clayton's case. He is currently on parole," says Kosareva, hands on her hips. She reminds me of a cat; defenses up, fur on edge. But she is not my prey. I don't want to intrude.

Kosareva's mother, however, is keen to talk. Over tea at the Slav, Henrietta, sporting a long leather coat, leather suit, and leather purse (she designed them), later tells me that her daughter seduced Lonetree out of "patriotism."

"Violetta loves Russia very much. She never acted against her will or conscience."

Kosareva's career as a swallow is textbook stuff. After graduating from Moscow's prestigious Maurice Thorez Institute of Foreign Languages, she landed a top job as a receptionist at Spaso House, residence of the American ambassador in Moscow. There, in 1985, the five-foot-nine Kosareva caught Lonetree's eye.

Lonetree and Kosareva "bumped into" each other on the metro, which was one of Lonetree's favorite haunts. Kosareva introduced Lonetree to her "uncle," Alexei Yefimov, who asked Lonetree to identify CIA agents in Moscow and to steal U.S. embassy floor plans. When Lonetree was transferred to Vienna a year later, Yefimov followed; Kosareva was transferred to the Irish embassy. Soon after, Lonetree got nervous. He used his bribe money to buy gifts for Yefimov and Kosareva. By December 1986, he'd confessed. Kosareva's cover was blown, her career as a swallow over, although her case officer, a twenty-seven-year-old newcomer, received a promotion.

After spending time with some U.S. Marines, I see first-hand what kind of targets they would make for trained sexpionage professionals. Many marines I know spend much of their time in the embassy compound, watching videos, eating American food, and playing pool in a room that still has a picture of Ronald Reagan on the wall. They are young, lonely, isolated—and almost at war with some diplomats in what seems to be class-based friction. When a friend and I go for dinner with two marines, they say it's their first time in a Russian restaurant, they've never eaten caviar and never been to a Russian museum. "When we go to Western pubs or dance clubs, we stick together," one says. "We're not even allowed to reply to Russians who talk to us." (Although, since the end of the Cold War, they can talk to citizens from any other ex-Soviet republic.)

Seasoned diplomats can also be trapped, even when they suspect the women they are seeing are KGB. For some psychological reason, they enjoy playing such a dangerous game, and end up falling for the oldest trick in the book, like powerful politicians who enjoy tempting fate and end up exposed in humiliating tabloid sex scandals.

Fred Woodruff, the CIA station chief in Georgia, was close to Marina Kapankhadze—even though he knew that the KGB and its counterparts in ex-Soviet republics often place swallows in hotels that foreigners frequent. Still, he avoided taking precautions that could have saved his life.

Many swallows, such as Natasha Kuznetzova, used to be told they must "do their duty" for socialism. "Soviet women don't stand a chance," says Kuznetzova. "They are constantly manipulated. Nomenklatura women can do what they want. They can choose whom they make love to and whom to marry. But even my sexual feelings were being regulated."

Since then there has been an explosion in sex shops and pornography throughout the Russian capital. And while prostitution may be an age-old profession, the real post-Communist change has been the number of well-educated women—doctors and polyglot daughters of diplomats who are flocking to it. The goal is no longer to feed stomachs but to fund monthly shopping sprees to Europe. All of this, says Tatiana Klimenkova, one of Russia's leading feminists, has nothing to do with a sexual revolution like the one the West experienced during the 1960s.

"Our politicians are trying to construct sex differently than in the West," Klimenkova says. It is reduced to being "crude and vulgar and not about freedom. Sexuality, not gender, is discussed. Our politicians are deeply conservative and patriarchal. They are fundamentalists, not democrats."

I remember the second annual International Women's Conference in Dubna, Russia, in December 1992. It was a sign of the emergence of a Russian post-Communist women's movement, but it also revealed divisions within the movement. Young feminists from St. Petersburg and Moscow, who were mainly academics, resented the authority of older nomenklatura women who "administered" women's rights in the old Communist Party power structure. The young looked at these older women as sellouts, or worse. The old, like those who headed the Women's Union of Russia, which used to be part of the state structure and still received state funding, said they were feminist pioneers interested in power not for power's sake but for the sisterhood.

The goals of the conference were basic: consciousness-raising, networking, and compiling a list of women's groups throughout Russia and parts of the old empire. "It's a big step for me just to have told my husband I was coming here—and to leave him and the kids for the weekend," said one woman.

By September 1993, 73 percent of Russia's one million unemployed and 80 percent of Moscow's unemployed were women, half of whom had higher educations. More than 40 percent of these women were under thirty, said Vera Soboleva, international director of the Women's Union of Russia. The now voluntary, government-sponsored organization represented more than two million women. An additional three million Russians were "invisibly unemployed." These people, more than two-thirds of them women, worked reduced hours for lower pay at unproductive factories that would be bankrupt if it were not for the continued state subsidies. Their nominal employment kept out-of-work statistics artificially low, said Molly Meacher, a British labor adviser to the Russian government. As the years go by, the statistics get worse.

"Many women worked in the textiles industry, which was badly hit," Meacher said. "These women are on unpaid or paid leave. Some receive only two thousand rubles [two dollars] a month. They're desperate. These types of people will do anything to make money." Meacher also said many women in the past worked in the research or economics departments of institutes or factories in "almost make-work jobs, even if they sounded good on paper. The jobs were superfluous and they're easily dispensable now."

In the early Yeltsin years during Gorbachev's perestroika era, women who continue to work earn, on average, 38 percent of their male counterparts' salaries, compared to 70 percent, says Klimenkova. But while women bear the brunt of Russia's unemployment crisis, they are also being discriminated against by the government when it comes to retraining and education.

Six thousand out-of-work Russians—a pitifully small number—are now being retrained by the state. Of these, most of the women, including doctors and economists, have been shunted into pink-collar jobs, such as hairdressing, sewing, and cosmetology. Most of the men, however, are retrained for financial or industrial jobs. A beauty salon, Lady Ann, is, for a time, on the main floor of the Women's Union building, just off Tverskaya Street; testimony to the retraining. The Spanish-trained workers in pink are retrained engineers and other professionals. A survey by the Women's Union reveals that only about 20 percent of the students at Moscow business schools are women.

To make it even worse, most employers no longer provide free day care, as they did under Communism. And while there is still access to abortion, there is also hardly any sex education in the schools. Now that the death rate has surpassed the birth rate for the first time since World War II, conservative political groups are pushing for an end to abortion and financial incentives to keep women pregnant and at home.

I question Russia's current labor minister, Gennady Melikyan, about discrimination against women in the workforce. "Why should we employ women when men are unemployed?" he says. "It's better that men work and women take care of children and do the housework.... Russia is the only country with so many working women." While the quotes are picked up in the Western press, the Russians barely blink: Russian sexism is so pervasive that such public comments often go unremarked.

With more women losing their jobs than men, the new Russia can be an even worse place for women to work than it was under the Communists. Then there are women like Natasha, who didn't stand much chance under "Uncle Lenin" either. Dark-haired Natasha, who wears black lace, pearls, red lipstick, and a pillbox hat to our interviews, reminds me of a spunky Holly Golightly, the "fifty dollars for the powder-room" heroine of Truman Capote's short story, which was later turned into the movie *Breakfast at Tiffany's*. Natasha came from the provinces to live illegally in Moscow. "I'm not a prostitute," she says. "I never asked any man for money. For me, the foreigner is not just a dollar bill but a man, the type of man I prefer."

Natasha's story is fairly typical. She grew up in Rostov. Her father was a black marketeer who introduced Natasha to "Voice of America" when she was fourteen. But he was a womanizer who drank their money, leaving her mother "to work her whole life. He did absolutely nothing to help her, just like a typical Russian man," she says. At sixteen, Natasha says, she got into trouble "for asking too many questions and refusing to join Komsomol. I realized I was living in the wrong country." By eighteen, she was working as a secretary in a dead-end job where "women just sat around drinking tea, knitting, and waiting for five P.M. so they could leave. I began to smoke pot. It was the only way I could escape reality. I decided I had to leave Rostov before I really degenerated."

In Rostov, she had already begun to date a few foreigners, but Moscow was big time. "I met a German guy and almost fell in love," she says. "I went to bars and discos and understood what the glittering life was all about. When the German left, he gave me some deutsche marks. I didn't even know how to use them at first. Then I met Kevin, an American from California, who I really liked." Kevin gave her fifteen hundred dollars, fancy clothes, talked about taking her out of Russia—and then disappeared. By then, dating foreigners had become a full-time job. "I'd go to hotels like the Intourist and meet foreigners. They'd take me to fancy restaurants, and buy me clothes and perfume. Sometimes they gave me money. But I wasn't a prostitute."

Once the KGB notices the liaisons with foreigners, such women are told they will be arrested unless they cooperate. Leaving one apartment, Natasha was questioned by a police officer who asked to see her propiska, which she didn't have. "That same night a man called, asking for me," she says. Three mornings later the phone rang again. "A man said he was from the KGB and he needed to meet me. I said 'No way'; I didn't know who he was. He said, 'Would you like us to bring you here?' I said yes, and hung up. Twenty minutes later there was a knock on my door. Three militia men asked to see my passport and told me to get dressed and go with them." After some questioning at the local police station, she met the phone caller—a man in his late thirties "with an ugly smile."

"He took me to the National Hotel, and questioned me in a room there. He lectured me about socialism and asked me to write a report about the Japanese diplomat I was seeing. It was my first experience as an actress," Natasha says. "I started to play the role of a provincial girl. I knew I had to distance myself from my country then, even though I knew nothing about politics."

The KGB set her up in an expensive apartment and tape-recorded her liaisons. "I didn't tell anybody what was happening," she says. "I had nice clothes and money from Hiroki [the Japanese diplomat], and the KGB asked for nothing. But then I started acting oddly. I couldn't lead such a double life. Hiroki even tried to provoke me, saying he knew a lot of Russian girls who date foreigners work for the KGB. One time, as a joke, I said, 'Why not? Maybe I am KGB.' He said, 'Who knows, you might be, but I don't care. I love you.' We never talked about it again."

The relationship continued for four months, during which Natasha also brought other foreigners to the flat. "One night, I was so drunk and crazy from the pressure that I confessed everything to a German I had brought home. I told him he was in a flat that was bugged by the KGB," she says. "He just laughed. He didn't believe me. And the KGB never mentioned the incident. That's when I was really on the edge of insanity. The KGB decided everything for me. I lost control of my inner self. I started drinking more and more."

Finally, Natasha introduced the diplomat to her "Uncle Boris." They shook hands and went into another room, closed the door, and talked for an hour. "After, I was crying, hysterical. He held me and said, 'My poor darling.' That was it. It was like a nightmare for me," she says. Another meeting occurred the next day. Again, the diplomat would not tell her what had happened. "He kissed me good-bye—and never returned. I guess he refused the recruitment effort and returned home in disgrace."

Today Natasha says she is an actress. She is also studying to be a television journalist. For one of our interviews, she rushes in late, with a bag of chocolate wafers and a necklace of dried mushrooms she bought from a babushka on the street. "Foreigners have brought me clothes and other lovers have sent me to Paris, otherwise I'd go crazy," she says. "There are criminals in our country. We're near collapse. Businessmen are killing each other. I'm ready to leave with my mother if Zhirinovsky comes to power, but until then I'm ready to defend the [Russian] White House and give my life if I have to. What else can I do?"

Although spying has now increased, the ideology it once hid behind has been stripped away. Kuznetzova never believed in socialism. But others did. Saying one spies for personal profit just doesn't sound as potent. "The Cold War is not over, even though people who play the game may now drink together," Kirichenko says. "It's not over because the KGB and the CIA don't want it to be. It's worse now that there's no more ideology."

◄---►

CHAPTER 17

The Absolute
Nightmare Hotel

Return to Tbilisi

Oasis: the Metechi Palace Hotel is a refuge
from the war outside.

— The European

T he hotel manager laughs as he hands me the article pulled
from a thick file stuffed with stories raving about this pricey
luxury hotel. But his hands are shaking. It is February 1994, six
months since my last visit. Anarchy has only deepened. Sure,
Xavier still wears his immaculate dark blue suits, well pressed, in
a city where people line up before dawn to buy bread and sleep in
overcoats to keep warm. He still orders his staff to bring us the
very best Georgian wine, famous throughout the world—*almost*
equal to the French, he says. But it's hard to see just what Xavier
is in charge of anymore.

For now, Xavier is the only Westerner working at the hotel.
Some had nervous breakdowns. The rest resigned, including the
new manager—after Georgian staffers put a gun to his head and
publicly humiliated him for his vow to "clean this place up." I can't
believe how downright pasty Xavier looks tonight, completely
stripped of his smug self-assurance. It's not because of the wine,
Marlboros, or late hour. Xavier can't stop nervously running his
hands through his thin, sandy hair. No more stories about his

exploits as hotel manager in Africa, the Middle East, and romantic European capitals. Tonight, defenses are down. Ordinary personal borders are open. The line dividing what you do and don't talk about with strangers is dropped. Xavier gushes fear, relieved, I think, to have someone to talk to. (Even if it is a journalist; almost as bad as a criminal confessing to a cop.)

Tbilisi is still a ghost town by day, exploding into violence by night. Far from being "a refuge from the war outside," the Metechi Palace Hotel is actually a bunker. Even here, the city's fate creeps in, past the metal detectors and gloved bellhops.

The shortages in Tbilisi are the same as before, but it's winter. Even the Metechi can't provide complete shelter against economic, political, and social breakdown. When I arrive, the local phone lines are down (only ten-dollar-a-minute satellite calls are available) and the electricity is out. I can't plug in my laptop and have to work in the shadow of a few eerie candles. I even have to bribe the bellboy for food. I call as soon as I arrive, twenty minutes before room service closes. They phone back forty minutes later to say the kitchen is shut. I'm starving. I ask for anything; I haven't eaten all day.

The bellhop arrives past midnight with whatever he could scrum up: lots of sulfur-water (you get used to it), and enough garlic potatoes, cold chicken, and creamy garlic dishes to feed an army. He leaves me his number.

"If you need anything at all, just call," he says.

The next evening, I am back in Xavier's office, drinking Georgian white wine. On my last trip, he told me some stories, but nothing like this. I think he's reached his breaking point. I just don't know why it didn't happen sooner. He's even developed some sort of illness.

Xavier lives like a man under siege. Although he is scared, shaky even, a secret look of pride, of hidden machismo, escapes as he opens a drawer to show me his gun. "I no longer walk from my hotel room to my office, a few floors away, without it," he says.

Xavier whispers about one of the hotel's expats who had to be flown out for "rest and relaxation." The expat was really in the midst of a nervous breakdown, which occurred when he apparently witnessed the aftermath of torture.

"From the lobby, the expat watched a Georgian employee stumble out of the hotel security's third-floor offices with one eye gouged out, cigarette burns all over his body, and blood everywhere," Xavier says. "The employee was beaten so badly he could hardly walk."

The Georgian hotel worker had apparently been tortured by the feared paramilitary Mkhedrioni, or Horsemen, who operate the hotel's security. The Mkhedrioni, organized in 1989 to help fight for Georgian independence, number several thousand. They are reputed to be fierce fighters in the war with Abkhazia, in which about six hundred of them are said to have died. They are also employed by Georgian law enforcement agencies, like the Ministry of Internal Affairs. Their leader, Jaba Ioseliani—the man who some say is *really* in charge of Georgia—is a convicted-armed-bank-robber-turned-playwright drama-and-art-history-professor. His exploits have captured the imaginations of his romantic mountain people, steeped in the twelfth-century writings of Shota Rustaveli and his notion of heroic death. Ioseliania spent seventeen years in Georgian prison, where he allegedly ran one of the country's largest organized crime gangs during the 1970s.

(Ioseliani is also heading Georgia's peace negotiations with Abkhazia and the United Nations, despite fierce objections by human rights activists like Erika Dailey, head of Human Rights Watch/Helsinki's Moscow office, who calls Ioseliani's appointment a "disgrace.")

The Mkhedrioni tortured the employee because he had apparently "stolen" a three-thousand-dollar bracelet a guest had left in the hotel safe.

"It's a ruse they often use," Xavier says. "Georgian staffers are accused of stealing large amounts of money or jewelry. They are then told they have a certain amount of time to 'return' the stolen goods—or to replace them with cash." In a country where the average salary is less than five dollars a month, staffers are lucky to leave with their lives if they don't come up with unobtainable sums of money.

As Xavier tells me this story, a tinge of something, faded outrage, perhaps, weaves in and out of his voice. Perhaps that's what compels him to talk. As for the expat, Xavier says he never got over it.

"He went to the bar and drank. For *days*," Xavier says. "He was a nervous, drunken wreck. Management had to ship him out."

"I've seen torture before," says Xavier, who grew up in North America and Europe, and speaks many European languages, as well as Arabic, some Hebrew, and Georgian.

"I've seen men burned alive with rubber tires around them when I worked in Africa," he adds. "But nothing compares to this. I came to Georgia expecting to find such a *civilized* country, so close to Europe, with such an ancient history. But the violence, the savage barbarism, is worse here than anywhere else I've ever seen in the world."

When I first arrived in Tbilisi, I thought the Metechi was the safest place in town. It is, after all, where the foreign diplomats, biznesmeni, and journalists stay. I remember being surprised by the luxury, so rare in the FSU. I *liked* the metal detector and the lobby, even the local maf, who gave the place *character*, I thought.

The night I hear Xavier's stories, I push a chair to the door, put the phone by my bed, and barely sleep.

I remember asking him if *I* would be okay.

"Don't worry," Xavier says. "They don't usually touch foreigners. And they've seen you with me. They know you're a friend. You look Georgian, so just don't dine alone. And make sure you chain your door at night."

"But my room doesn't have a chain."

"Oh yes," he says. "It's the only floor without them."

Georgian head of state Eduard Shevardnadze is trying to clean up violence *outside* the hotel with a campaign to curb crime and de-gun his population (though at least one of the leaders of the crime purge has been murdered, shot at point-blank range.) The campaign comes at a time when local and international human rights groups[*] say wrongful imprisonment and torture by law enforcement agencies is widespread in Georgia. Meanwhile terror inside the hotel is out of control.

"Nothing can be done," Xavier says, "because the violence is government-sponsored." The hotel is a joint venture between an

---

[*] An August 1994 report conducted by Human Rights Watch/Helsinki charges Georgian authorities with illegally jailing and torturing political opponents as well as journalists and the children, spouses, and parents of the late Gamsakhurdia's imprisoned supporters.

Austrian company and the government of Shevardnadze, darling of the United Nations. As part of the joint venture agreement, the Georgian government ensures the hotel's security with its own guards, the dreaded Mkhedrioni.

Shevardnadze supporters say he was forced to make the alliance because he can't maintain power without the Mkhedrioni guns. If Shevardnadze ever forgets this, there *are* ways to remind him.

"All the hotel, and Western diplomats who live in Tbilisi, can do," Xavier says, "is to meet with Shevardnadze when senior Western officials pass through town—staying at the hotel—and request that the Mkhedrioni violence be toned down that *week*." Then the terror resumes.

This trip, I arrive shortly after Gamsakhurdia's mysterious death. Some sporadic fighting is ongoing. Ioseliani heads cease-fire negotiations while his Mkhedrioni carry out violence throughout Georgia —and inside the hotel, from their third-floor offices.

"You can't write about any of this," Xavier says. I don't, though I do tell the stories to some diplomats and human rights workers I know. I only write now, years after Xavier left Georgia.

Xavier himself has witnessed four murders at the hotel. "The workers are used to cleaning messy bloodstains from the carpets," he says. Gunfire has often sprayed the hotel's lobby and tenth-floor piano bar. Sometimes, the Mkhedrioni get into wild turf-war shootouts with their competitors.

"I recently had to close the pool and saunas because there was too much blood in the pool and too many murders and rapes in the saunas," Xavier says.

"More than twenty-four Georgian women who work here were raped this month," he says. The women, cleaners and waitresses, are trapped when they enter the rooms of mafiya leaders.

"They are lucky if they're just raped," Xavier says. "They come to me with their eyes cast down, too embarrassed to look at me, and ask for some time off because they're not feeling well. There's nothing I can do because they're afraid to go to the police. If they do, they know the Mkhedrioni will go after their husbands, brothers, and fathers."

By witnessing such flagrant human rights abuses, which occur under the auspices he helps to manage, and by keeping silent,

Xavier has become an accomplice. I often ask him why he stays. He mentions his contract.

"They respect me," Xavier says, referring to the Mkhedrioni. He speaks proudly about the last Georgian New Year's Eve. Seems Xavier mingled with the Mkhedrioni leaders, getting drunk and consuming vast quantities of Georgian food. "After dining, the men, completely bombed, shot loaded AK-47s into the air," he adds.

Once, when Xavier closed the hotel's health-club membership to non-hotel guests—because of all the blood, murder, and rapes—a large, burly maf creature came to see him, angered that he was refused membership.

The mobster made his way up to Xavier's office, which is guarded by his secretary, a young, perfumed Georgian woman in heels. The maf was threatening Xavier when two Mkhedrioni guards appeared.

"They beat him so badly," Xavier says. "They even shot him in the leg. *I had to beg them not to kill him.*" This, Xavier says, is loyalty.

I try to reconcile this violence with the people I know. The same Georgians capable of such terror are the teenage soldiers who offer me their chairs and bring me a hot cup of strong coffee even after I decline; the babushka who lives without electricity and insists on giving me fruits and other delicacies with tea even though she is rationing for her family; my driver, an academic, who brings me a map of ancient Tbilisi and an illustrated book of Georgian poetry; and a young, talented artist who lives with his mother and struggles to paint, brilliantly, when he can afford it—and when there's enough sunlight, since they have no electricity.

Seven months later, in September 1994, I'm back again, traveling last-minute, as usual. I have come with Jaime, a Brazilian friend and colleague, to interview Shevardnadze.

I spend the Jewish New Year in an old Tbilisi synagogue. Georgians were reknowned for their religious tolerance under Communism. Now some ultra-nationalists and a "Georgia for Georgians" campaign, combined with a nonexistent economy and the instability of war, are pushing some minorities, including Jews, out of the country. Attendance at the synagogue, never high, is

down to two dozen worshipers, including only a few in the upstairs section where women must worship.

I sit beside a young Israeli woman who is here with her husband, a Russian Jew. "We met in Israel five years ago," she says.
"We're now here to teach Hebrew and Jewish studies. But I'll be
happy to go home. I wasn't expecting to live through winters without heat, locked in at night because of all the guns and crime."

From strolling down a beach with his friend Gorbachev, helping to
think up perestroika to—at age sixty-six—risking his life, with his
troops, by staying in besieged Sukhumi until zero hour before the
Abkhazians captured it—Shevardnadze remains a fascinating figure.

Wearing a gray suit with red-and-blue striped tie, Shevardnadze
looks like the classic elder statesman, especially with his mane of
white hair and the devilishly charming way he has of squinting his
right eye when he laughs.

Having just returned empty-handed from the United Nations
during a critical period in post-Soviet Georgian history, Shevardnadze blasts UN peacekeeping policies. "The United Nations failed
Georgia and [the former] Yugoslavia," he says. "UN peacekeeping
needs to be entirely restructured."

I ask if he feels that the West has let him down. That's when he
does that narrowing of the right eye thing, and laughs.

"Last year I had more hopes from the Security Council, but since
it was such a long process, we decided to choose the other way," he
says. "Georgia requires immediate action. I wouldn't say the West
let us down, it's just that they couldn't do anything else.

"We are on the verge of economic catastrophe and disaster," he
adds. "It was natural to resume our links with Russia. Georgia's
relationship with Russia is more important than its relationship
with the United States now, but that could change."

So far, it hasn't. I ask Shevardnadze about Fred Woodruff's murder. He smiles again, and says Georgian investigators concluded
that Woodruff died in a random shooting. However, he does criti-
cize Washington for focusing too much, economically, on Russia
at the expense of the other ex-Soviet republics.

On the way out of our meeting, held in the parliament building, Jaime and I bump into Ioseliani's top aide.

"I would love to meet your boss. I've been trying for some time," I say.

"His gold Mercedes is waiting outside. But he's still in his office. I'll see what I can do," the young Mkhedrioni says, smiling.

We're invited into a small room adjacent to Ioseliani's office. A large man with a two-way radio waits with us. More bodyguards, who speak of Ioseliani in glowing terms that smack of father-figure worship, wait outside our door.

Ioseliani is a trim, disciplined-looking man who, at sixty-seven, looks like somebody's grandfather.

"Are you the one who really rules Georgia?" I ask.

"There's no doubt about it," says Ioseliani, clad in a smart Italian khaki suit. "Frankly, I am the one who brought Shevardnadze to power. He would not be president without me.

"Shevardnadze wanted to return," Ioseliani adds ominously. "But it was also *necessary* for him to return. He is internationally famous for his democratic activities. We needed Shevardnadze to persuade other countries to recognize our independence."

"Is your power based on fear and terror?" I ask.

"Our power is justified. We kept our word and our promise. We fought in war and now we have peace."

When I press him, Ioseliani admits that some "individual" Mkhedrioni have abused their power.

"If anyone commits any human rights abuses, they are suspended or fired—but only if they are convicted," he says.

"But the courts are so corrupt, there are hardly any convictions," I respond.

"There were several cases [of Mkhedrioni committing human rights abuses] and there may be others we don't know about," Ioseliani says. "But there was war. There were no laws. Even now there are no laws introduced. There was economic hardship."

He adds that he would "never punish soldiers for minor offenses *because we need the soldiers.*"

Along with jailing and torturing political opponents, the Mkhedrioni have been accused of extortion rackets and other criminal activity, which Ioseliani denies.

Like Shevardnadze, Ioseliani is critical of American foreign policy in the FSU. "After the collapse of the Soviet Union, the United States didn't play an active role in rebuilding the republics," he says. "They thought that after the collapse of Communism, there was no more danger, so they focused on domestic policy. But their policy of noninterference helped new Russian imperialism. Now it's too late."

Ioseliani's relationship with Shevardnadze remains tense. "I know you support Shevardnadze, but would you call him a friend?" I ask.

"We're both striving for the welfare of Georgia, but I put serious meaning into the word *friendship*," Ioseliani says. "That's more deep than my relations with Shevardnadze. I can't say we're not friends, but we're not real friends. If I found out he was doing something that was not in the interests of Georgia, I wouldn't be his friend anymore. That's why it's not friendship."

I ask Ioseliani about the contradiction within Georgians—the warmth of spirit and hospitality mixed with brutality. He explains it as part Communist legacy, part Asian heritage. "We don't have the experience of democracy. We're moving from feudalism to capitalism, gaining freedom and individual rights—*before* there are laws for people to abide by."

Cultivating Kalashnikovs, machismo, and terror is as ingrained in this culture as cultivating vineyards and orange groves. Gun culture was fast incorporated into official post-Soviet Georgian politics. Every serious politician (male, of course) is surrounded by his own personal army of young men. All soldiers I interview, from rival gangs and politicians, have a hero-worshiping admiration for their leader, whoever he happens to be.

Ioseliani's group just happens to be the largest and best organized—and best paid. At least forty Mkhedrioni live in the luxury hotel when I am there. "We guard the Metechi, which is why it stayed intact and survived the war," Ioseliani says.

This is the first time I come to Tbilisi with a colleague, instead of on my own. Xavier was right. Now that I am dining with a male foreign journalist, the rules have changed. Mkhedrioni crawl out from the leather couches and approach. I now see the Mkhredioni's hospitable side.

When I sit down with Jaime, two bottles of Georgian champagne arrive at our table, compliments, the waiter says, of two young men seated nearby. We tell the waiter to thank them. Soon "Nick," tall, dark, and fairly drunk, saunters over. He bows, hands me a red rose, kisses my hand, then shakes hands with Jaime.

Before we know it, Nick sits down, calls his friend over, snaps his fingers for the waiter, and orders our meal. We were planning on the buffet. "That's out of the question!" cries Nick, who is sporting a droopy, theatrical mustache. "The chef makes the best spaghetti bolognese in town. You *must* have it!"

Soon the table fills with food, vodka, and Coke to go with the champagne. "I'm part Italian," explains our Horseman, with pride. "Spaghetti is hard to find here. My grandmother was Italian. I want to be a godfather, like Don Michael Corleone."

Nick downs vodka after vodka. Spaghetti is followed by desserts, more alcohol, and Turkish coffees thick as mud. Much to my surprise, Nick's friend, "Stas," turns out to be seventeen years old —one of the Mkhedrioni's youngest, though he looks older. Stas is well dressed: jeans, button-down shirt, new black leather vest. He is also polite.

"Isn't your mother afraid for you? How can she sleep at night knowing what you do?" I ask him.

"She understands," Stas says. "We live better than anyone in Tbilisi. Jaba [Ioseliani] takes care of us."

In August 1995, a car bomb explodes outside the Georgian parliament building, almost killing Shevardnadze. Ioseliani is Shevardnadze's prime suspect. Ioseliani's weapons cache, which he stores in his parliament building office, is raided. But Ioseliani can't be arrested because of parliamentary immunity. Tensions are running high over a multinational oil deal* and the upcoming November 1995 presidential elections.

---

* Azerbaijan controls three major oil fields under the Caspian Sea that could be a real alternative to the Persian Gulf—four billion barrels of recoverable reserves. An eleven-company consortium, including five U.S. firms, will develop the oil fields and build a pipeline. Russia wants the pipeline to go through Russia; the United States wants it through Georgia to Turkey. The August 1995 assassination attempt on Shevardnadze comes a few days after a top Turkish official, Emre Gonensay, meets with Shevardnadze in Tbilisi to discuss the pipeline. (See "Pipeline Politics," by Thomas L. Friedman, *New York Times*, September 13, 1995, A23.)

Following the assassination attempt, Shevardnadze outlaws the Mkhedrioni in an attempt to "put an end to the era of legalized gangsterism." Igor Giorgadze, a former head of Georgia's security service—accused of masterminding the assassination attempt with the Mkhedrioni—moves to Moscow. Now Shevardnadze wants Moscow to arrest Giorgadze and extradite him. But Moscow says there isn't enough evidence.

In an interview with a Russian newspaper, Shevardnadze suggests that his political opponents are being "given a helping hand" by their former KGB colleagues, and suggests that "certain Russian politicians" may have been "privy to the plans" for the assassination attempt.[*]

"Georgia has been through six years of hell," Shevardnadze says. "But it will emerge from it clean. My purpose is not to pave my way back to the presidency, but to create a situation by the time of the elections in which blackmail, harassment, and bribery will be eliminated. Georgia is saying farewell to terror, hopefully forever this time."

As soon as Shevardnadze wins the election he arrests Ioseliani. On national television, Shevardnadze calls the assassination attempt "the last act of terrorism" in Georgia.

As of 1996, Ioseliani is still in jail, charged with trying to assassinate Georgia's head of state. The maximum penalty he faces if convicted is death. Around two hundred Mkhedrioni were also arrested with Ioseliani, on drug, terrorism, war crimes, and "banditry"-related charges, says Emil Adelkhanov Shteynberg, of the Tbilisi-based Caucasian Institute for Peace, Democracy, and Development.

"Only two or three Mkhedrioni—out of two hundred—have been released so far," Shteynberg says. "The crackdown has put an end to their activities."

After flirting with independence, Georgia, like many ex-Soviet countries, has replaced its nationalist (now dead) president with Shevardnadze, a career Communist. Back to the future, again.

---

[*] N. Broladze, "Georgia Says Farewell to Terror," *Nezavisimaya Gazeta*, October 7, 1995.

←- →

CHAPTER 18

Zhirinovsky:

Mister Kurtz of the Volga

Portrait of a Dysfunctional Russian
Family—Zhirinovsky on Tape: The Horror,
the Horror. A Love Boat Cruise Down the
Soul of Mother Russia.

Ultimately a journalist anxious to know something of the fate of
his "dear colleague" turned up. This visitor informed me Kurtz's
proper sphere ought to have been politics "on the popular
side..."

"But heavens! how that man could talk. He electrified large
meetings. He had faith—don't you see?—he had the faith. He
could get himself to believe anything—anything. He would have
been a splendid leader of an extreme party."

"What party?" I asked.

"Any party," answered the other. "He was an—an—extremist."

— JOSEPH CONRAD, *Heart of Darkness*

August 1994: *Playboy* is hungry for Vladimir Wolfovich Zhirinovsky. Ever since he won the December 1993 parliamentary
sweepstakes, this crazed, neo-fascist madman has become an international media gigolo. Hurling flowerpots and spitting at Jewish
protesters in France; kissing a naked man on the mouth in a Slavic
sauna; threatening to nuke his neighbors, restore Russia's imperial borders, invade Turkey, and use giant fans to blow radioactive
waste into the Baltics. Zhirinovsky is so overexposed that the *New*

York Times Magazine even runs a cover shot of him in the shower.

But the profile doesn't include an interview. Though he feasts on publicity, Zhirinovsky hates reporters so much he charges up to fifteen thousand dollars an interview.[*] When, after weeks of negotiating, one American magazine agrees to a five-thousand-dollar interview fee, Zhirinovsky ups the price. "That's five thousand dollars *a half an hour*," he says, pulverizing the journalist's ethics—and story—in one greed-busting tizzy.

Playboy's freelance assignment is tricky. My first challenge is to get the interview. (I know I'll get it. I just won't go away until he agrees.) The real challenge will be to go beyond the headlines and sensationalist stunts: This is a politician who will even try to choke a female member of parliament and rip the cross off a priest. Is he really a madman or is he a talented strategist whose seemingly spontaneous gestures are expertly calculated?

A *Playboy* interview requires hours and hours of taped sessions—perhaps more time than Zhirinovsky has ever given to one journalist. I will start by asking what has already been asked. My plan is to go beyond the sound bites of short interviews to reach revealing, new territory—unprecedented, character breaking insight and all that.

But first I've got to get him to agree to the interview. Zhirinovsky is spending most of August on a cruise down the Volga, the longest river in Europe and, some say, the soul of Russia. It is the launch of his 1996 presidential election campaign. I know I've got to get on that boat. That way I'll know I've got him. What I don't realize is that I, too, will also be trapped.

Surprisingly, I arrange the interview easily—too easily—over the telephone, a few weeks before the cruise.

"No problem," his aide says even after I stress my refusal to pay.

A week before the trip, the aide reneges, gleefully saying the same interview will now cost fifteen thousand dollars.

---

[*] Even post-Communist Russia's first prosecutor general, Valentin Stepankov, got caught up in the capitalist euphoria. In 1992, he charged one thousand dollars per interview, according to the Foreign Correspondent Association's list of corrupt officials who wanted money for interviews—before he, too, was fired for corruption. (See Yakubovsky, Chapter 14.)

I attend Zhirinovsky's monthly rally, where I meet a senior political adviser. I explain how much I'd like to interview Zhirinovsky.

"Don't worry. I'm sure we can work it out." He smiles, and invites me to a press conference Zhirinovsky is holding with Gerhard Frey, a German neo-Nazi. The presser is held at the Praga, a winding, multistory Communist-era restaurant on the New Arbat. Outside the restaurant, two kitchen staffers are in a vicious fight. A crowd gathers, hungry for blood, to cheer them on.

Past the gruff bodyguards with the slicked-back hair, up in an ancient elevator, the top floor swarms with hungry journalists and fascists submerged in overstuffed tables of food: caviar, salmon, white fish, vodka, beer, even ice cream and coffee. Zhirinovsky thugs hand out books. Instead of taking notes, the journalists, mainly Russian, indulge. After Zhirinovsky talks, the crowd, including journalists, cheers. I half expect their arms to go up in a "Heil" salute.

"It was like they were hypnotized," says one colleague. The crowd includes balding men flashing their virility and the overwhelming aroma of liquor mixed with hypocrisy. The German contingent is out on the balcony, dressed in better-textured seersucker, pinstripe, and plaid. A perfectly coifed middle-aged German woman sits frostily on a throne in the corner, where politicians pay homage to her as she sips tea like an evil queen.

Zhirinovsky is surrounded by a swarm of television cameras. He has the intelligent face of a well-to-do lawyer, a raspy voice that could be Caligula's, and the half-moon eyes of a mean-spirited snake.

I slip through to the front of the scrum.

"Don't you think it's ridiculous to charge fifteen thousand dollars for an interview?" I ask, finally, face-to-face.

"Oh no," he says, touching my arm, cameras rolling. "That's for companies, not individuals. How much can you pay?"

"In my country," I say, "it's unethical to pay for interviews." He agrees to do an interview for free, and tells me to arrange it with his press secretary, Grigory.

"He didn't mean it," Grigory says. "He only said it for the cameras." He looks at me, then adds, "I'll see what I can do."

"I will also be covering the cruise for the *Toronto Star*," I say. Grigory cringes.

"Canadian women are trouble," he says. "We've gone through hell because of a Canadian photographer named Heidi."

"Heidi *who*?" I ask and beg off before he connects me to my *sosedka*, or roommate, who has just taken a rather gruesome photo of Zhirinovsky sprawled on a bed in his briefs at his dacha.

Zhirinovsky attacks ethnic minorities for "stealing" jobs from Russians, then leaves in an entourage of Lincolns and Mercedes for the luxury Baltschug Kempinski Moskau Hotel.

A few days later, my friend Masha, the translator, and I arrive at Moscow's Northern River Port with small overnight bags, not knowing whether we'll get on board or not. A brass band in red and gold plays "*Proschaniye Slovyanki*" ("Farewell of the Slavic Women"), which was popular during World War II military parades when soldiers left for the front. Yeltsin set sail from here a few hours ago, on his own cruise down the Volga.

The port has potential. It's quiet, out of Moscow's city center, on the way to the airport. In a few years, it could be transformed into a summer playground for yachts, with old-fashioned inns and a charming country club, if the new Russians can get past their obsessions with flash and immediate gratification. If the new Russia lasts that long.

"Please wait outside until we decide what to do with you," says Zhirinovsky's half brother, Alexander, an older man with a sharp, hawk-like face who checks the names of everyone who boards. Like American Republican presidential nominee Pat Buchanan,[*] Zhirinovsky's party is a family affair. Two half sisters, also on board, are senior members of his party, the Liberal Democratic Party of Russia. Zhirinovsky's twenty-one-year-old only child, Igor, works as his parliamentary aide, salary paid by the Russian government.

While Zhirinovsky is head of the LDPR, there is nothing liberal or democratic about this party, which recently voted its dictator head of the party until the year 2004. On board, Zhirinovsky is worshiped like a combination of a Communist Party boss, a duplicitous gangsta godfather, and a Greek god of decadence.

---

[*] That's not all the two have in common. Zhirinovsky so identifies with Buchanan's "family values" campaign (and perhaps its hypocrisy) that he sends a letter of support to him in February 1996.

Finally Alexander returns.

"There are some rooms left," he says. "Welcome aboard."

Campaigning down the Volga is better than any whistle-stop campaign tour. The Volga *is* Russia. It has natural beauty, in the process of self-destruction. The dams, built with slave labor under Stalin, are actually destroying the environment.

The river is so wide I often feel like we're at sea. When it narrows, pre-Revolutionary mansions float by. A young girl in a mangy T-shirt leans out of a cracked window. She waves with the defiance of poverty born from fertile soil; a nation of Buddenbrooks. I think of lost empire and decay. Russia, Mann, and Faulkner, crumbling, eccentric, and ageless.

The cruise lasts twenty days, and takes us from Moscow to the Caspian Sea and back. I am on board for eight days.

The Volga, home of the singing boatmen, flows twenty-three hundred miles from the Valdai Hills northwest of Moscow to the Caspian Sea. Germans and Mongols, Vikings and Cossacks fought for it. The Romanovs, Russia's last line of tsars, emerged from the Volga town of Kostroma, while Lenin, responsible for their murder, was born five hundred miles downstream in Simbirsk (known as Ulyanovsk under the Communists).

The farther downstream we go, the more I learn about Zhirinovsky. I begin to realize that the Volga and Zhirinovsky are intertwined. The farther we get from Moscow, the more of Zhirinovsky's own soul, or lack thereof, begins to reveal itself.

Zhirinovsky already reminds me of Mr. Kurtz, Conrad's ivory trader corrupted by greed, environment, circumstances, long descended into madness. My Volga has transformed into the Congo and I, too, am going downstream into a post-Cold War Heart of Darkness. This voyage down the Volga becomes a symbol of my personal and professional odyssey through Russia and the FSU. Zhirinovsky is a success (at the time of our cruise, he holds the largest number of seats in the Russian parliament) because his personal madness is symptomatic of Russia's political state. Slice open a part of Russia's collective unconscious, the gray, sticky stuff we call brain matter, and Zhirinovsky—in all of his laughable, highly intelligent, sadistic, fascist, control-freak sides—is there. He is as Russian as vodka and tears.

Zhirinovsky explains his success this way: "It's a coincidence," he says, "in which the personal qualities of one man meet with new times. If I had appeared twenty years ago, nothing like this could have happened. Or twenty years from now. It just coincided. It's chance. Luck.

"If you tear off the leader of this country, he will appear abnormal in the West," he adds. "But return him to this sick, abnormal country and there is harmony."

Although we're on board the *Alexander Pushkin*, there is nothing poetic about this ship, which I rename the *Hunter S. Thompson* after the creator of 1960s-era American gonzo journalism. The *Pushkin* was built in the 1970s for Brezhnev. It's now run by a private Russian company, which rents it to everyone from Richard Gere (now why couldn't I have gotten *that* assignment?) to Zhirinovsky and German travel agencies. The boat is three floors of heavy wood paneling, complete with a large restaurant and bars. The small shop at the front of the boat—a small glass-covered table displaying a few tubes of toothpaste, razor blades, cheap notebooks, and matrioshka dolls—is still from the Soviet era.

So is the hidden radio in the cabin I share with Masha. When we arrive, it is turned on, Communist-style. There is only one station. It blares music, propaganda, and 7 A.M. wake-up calls. I turn it off.

Each day, party members attend seminars, learning how to run local chapters, recruit members, give speeches, and adhere to party unity. They're getting down to the basics—loyalty, unity, recruiting, and following orders—though the way Zhirinovsky speaks, it sounds like they're joining a cult.

The 175 passengers on board fall into four categories: Zhirinovsky's money men and political advisers; the rank and file; young bodyguards and aides; and spouses and children. Stringy boys and potbellied men with armbands, the in-house police, huddle in corners playing checkers. They lurk self-importantly, and smell like freshly starched, or soiled, brownshirts. The boat's stairs, bars, and passageways give it the feel of a medieval castle filled with forbidden rooms and intrigue.

I expect the cruise to be some kind of bizarre party boat. The first meal surprises me. Vodka is not served, though there is a cash bar. Meals tend to be rather subdued, even family affairs. They occur in two sittings, with military authority, like a Communist boot camp. Waitresses deliver many plates, including smoked fish, mayonnaised appetizers, greasy meats, and globs of potatoes. There is sugared water-juice, called *soc*, and fattening desserts.

"The food reminds me of Pioneer camp," says Masha.

We stop in one or two towns a day. Zhirinovsky waves. Crowds, numbering from one hundred to a few thousand people, cheer. Zhirinovsky and local party members give speeches. All the boat's passengers, wives and children included, carry banners and flags. Party activists from the boat set up booths to sign up new members. They even give out their own party cards, just as the Communist Party used to, as well as their own newspapers and books. Zhirinovsky slightly alters the same speech for each town. I am struck by the campaign's organization. I have seen nothing like it before in Russia.

Midafternoon, I watch Russia pass me by under a sun the color of a faded peach. It's a lazy, hazy, midday moment. I'm munching peanuts with a sadistically inclined world-famous hypnotist. He is playing Rasputin to Vladimir Wolfovich, Russia's new tsar of neofascist imperialism.

Anatoly Kashpirovsky, the hypnotist, and I are at the bar. His new wife soon joins us, but she speaks neither Russian nor English, only her native Czech, so her participation in the conversation is limited. A plump young woman spread into a pair of tight white pants, she polishes off the nuts and then goes for vanilla ice cream, which she devours with admirable speed. The Czech native is far younger than her fifty-year-old faith-healer-turned-member-of-parliament husband. "We don't need to speak the same language in order to understand each other," he says as he gives her the most lascivious of grins.

A woman asks Kashpirovsky if he can help get rid of her cough. Russian women tend to swoon over this small, swarthy Ukrainian psychologist. During the height of perestroika, two hundred million people in the FSU tuned into his television show, which was also broadcast in countries like Poland and Vietnam. Kashpirovsky induced Soviets to do all sorts of unorthodox stuff, like undergoing stomach surgery without anesthesia, like getting teeth pulled without painkillers. One of the operations performed without anesthesia was actually nationally broadcast. He claims to cure everything from sterility to tumors, to be able to make 350 pounds of fat disappear in ten months without the aid of liposuction.* I don't understand how this squat little man sitting beside me in a dark, baggy tracksuit, his flat face etched in sun-splashed wrinkles, can have such an effect on people.

When we pull into some Volga towns, it is Kashpirovsky, and not "Mad Vlad" Zhirinovsky, who gets top billing. Hundreds of women chant Kashpirovsky's name. He has a power that Zhirinovsky incorporates, since he cannot replicate it. When we get off the boat in Lenin's hometown, Simbirsk, also the home of some Zhirinovsky relations, hordes of women flood up and engulf Kashpirovsky. They are as desperate for a blessing as if the pope, or Divinity itself, had just sailed into town.

Kashpirovsky is an expert at cashing in on the Russian love of mysticism. Mysticism carries concrete political weight in Russia today. It implies an ability to encourage the dispossessed to eschew potential uprisings by reshaping their belief system so that they are able to either transcend their natural desire for justice or to equably postpone its fulfillment to the afterlife.

Kashpirovsky, as Russian mystics go, is something of a piker. He'll never match the high-society status of Mme. Blavatsky, the international following of Gurdjieff and Ouspensky, or the sheer craziness of Rasputin. But he's the best they've got.

Zhirinovsky's wife, the scientist Galina, is also playing her part. A postgraduate student of chronic viral infections, Galina seems to be genuinely smitten with this late-twentieth-century lady-killer. Somewhat greasy black hair snaked above heavy blue eye shadow, in one of those sleeveless dresses that never fail to reveal bra straps, Galina smiles demurely from a nearby table. Her face is shiny from the sun, her hands used to holding limp red bouquets and waving on deck, as if she is already First Lady.

This tsarina is currently in the midst of an intense hand and arm massage from a khaki-clad colonel who retired long ago. In

---

* David Remnick, "Soviets under a Spell," *Washington Post*, October 12, 1989, C1.

between strokes, she flashes more secret, pink-lipped smiles Kash-pirovsky's way, as if he has transformed her from spurned and abandoned wife into light-headed teenager.

Galina and Zhirinovsky met when they were students in Moscow. Zhirinovsky entered Moscow State University's prestigious Institute for Oriental Languages, a top KGB recruiting pool usually reserved for children of the nomenklatura, in 1964. While still a student, he interned as an interpreter in Turkey. He was arrested there in 1969 for allegedly distributing Soviet pins. His speedy release from jail and repatriation were widely believed to have been arranged by the KGB.

After graduation, the young couple moved to Tbilisi, Georgia, where he became a Soviet army officer. Zhirinovsky then attended law school, graduated, and joined a state firm that specialized in pension and inheritance cases. He left in 1983 over allegations that he had accepted an improper gift—which he denies—and had bad-mouthed his superiors after they failed to approve his request for Communist Party membership. Zhirinovsky then joined the Mir Publishing House, one of the Soviet Union's largest, as a lawyer, and began to dabble in politics.

On board, Galina and Zhirinovsky sleep in separate bedrooms. As everyone on the boat knows, they haven't lived together for years. Their arm-in-arm embraces are strictly poses for the cameras. Close up, you can feel the tension. Zhirinovsky spends time with his bodyguards. He's photographed with strippers in international publications. Galina, well, she smiles and lets the retired army officer massage her arm.

While this cruise may resemble some warped and twisted Russian version of the *Love Boat*, I'm having a hard time finding a Russian version of Julie, the symbol of innocence. Instead, the boat is cast with shadows of young women dubbed the ghosts of the boat. These pale-faced, undernourished creatures appear only at night. They spend most of their time in one of the more dimly lit bars with the hard-drinking bodyguard set and at least one of the boat's pre-teens, if he can sneak away from his parents.

The bodyguards are more than the ship's gofers. They are its lifeblood. Young men, sometimes in suits, or loud Hawaiian shirts. Two are brothers. Their large faces, hidden by aviator glasses, still reveal fierce, almost savage pride mixed with boredom. Andrei, with the classic blond, blue-eyed, chiseled Russian features, high cheekbones and all, whispers self-importantly into a two-way radio. That Zhirinovsky is surrounded by middle-aged deputies and silver-haired advisers is a given. But that he has cultivated his own personal army of young men dedicated to his cause and injected it with all of the anger, madness, and confusion of post-Communist Russia, is not.

Youth is Zhirinovsky's target. The young are the voters he needs and caters to, more than any other Russian politician. At his office in Moscow, a small head shop sells rock paraphernalia. Zhirinovsky goes to clubs frequented by skinheads in Moscow and gives speeches. He also recruits young Russians to fight in foreign wars, especially Bosnia, and throughout the ex-Soviet republics.

"There are some young guys who really need war," he says. "It is some kind of a patriotic need to defend the orthodox Slavic world. It's also profitable for us, in an economic and military sense."

The Russian *Love Boat*'s captain, of course, is Zhirinovsky, surrounded by his phalanx of bodyguards. Today, Zhirinovsky—who speaks fluent Turkish, as well as English, French, and German not too badly—is wrapped in a snazzy green plaid sports jacket. It gives him a different persona than his blue worker's cap, the image plastered on his own name-brand vodka bottles. He will later tell me that he never smokes and he doesn't even drink, although he does pose with booze, like a real Russian muzhik, for the cameras.

As the boat slowly pulls out of harbor, Zhirinovsky leans over the rail and waves. The action, a simple wave of the hand, seems to whip the crowd into a hypnotic frenzy of adulation. It is a scene that plays over and over again. The bodyguards, hair cropped, arms crossed, hover in a semicircle around the Great Man. Zhirinovsky waves. Over and over again. His face is expressionless. It is as if he is amazed that the people have come to cheer for him, as if he is thinking about what to do with the cheers, the waves. He waves, but there is no connection. It is a methodic, lost movement, a permanent moment. Only the sky varies. Blue to gray, sun to storm.

The white- and silver-haired men, the men who stand behind the young bodyguards, the gray cardinals of this new Russian phenomenon, are pleased by the applause. But Zhirinovsky finds it boring. So boring, he says, that it makes him feel like he is dying. Fear. Hatred. These are emotions he respects and understands. But love? Worship? Popularity? For Zhirinovsky, these thoughts are anathema.

"I used to address crowds much better when they were hostile," Zhirinovsky tells me. "Now, with all this applause and flowers and praise, I'm decaying, decaying. It's better with resistance. Thousands of voters are standing there waiting for me. . . . It dampens my ardor."

Force, says Zhirinovsky, with a late-twentieth-century take on Machiavelli, is necessary with both women and politics. "Eighty percent is talk and twenty percent is force. If you do it vice versa, it will be a dictatorship. We need democracy. But some violence is required. Just a little bit, sometimes, eh?"

In 1991, Zhirinovsky was an unknown lawyer from Kazakhstan who ran for president. His promises—flowers for the women, no more food lines, and cheap vodka for men—were laughed at. But he came in third, behind Yeltsin and the former Soviet premier Nikolai Ryzhkov, with 6.2 million votes. By December 1993, no one laughed when Zhirinovsky's party received 12.3 million votes, or 23 percent of the ballots cast, more than any other party running in the parliamentary elections.

Russians have long romanticized the underdog. Under Communism, it was Yeltsin, picked on at the Party congress by then Soviet president Gorbachev. At this moment, it is Zhirinovsky. He understands that most of Russia is far from elite Moscow and St. Petersburg, that emphasis in the rest of the country is on survival. He also knows that he doesn't have to deliver his promises, that boasts like having Russian soldiers "wash their feet in the Indian Ocean" are, as he tells me, "more symbolic than concrete."

Zhirinovsky also knows how to exploit racism and play on people's fears. Never mind that he is in all likelihood the son of a Jew named Volf Isaakovich Edelshtein. When asked, Zhirinovsky says his mother was a Russian and his father a lawyer. He calls a birth certificate, unearthed in Almaty, that proves his Jewish heritage, a forgery. Zhirinovsky also applied to move to Israel in the 1980s and participated in a Soviet-era Jewish cultural group in

Moscow called Shalom. He says he joined to practice his oratorical skills; there is speculation that he was a KGB informer.

Comparisons have been made to Hitler's beginnings. Zhirinovsky also unexpectedly got votes by stirring up ethnic tension in a shaky democracy, even though he is at first dismissed as lunatic fringe. In a *Time* cover story that featured a menacing Zhirinovsky in combat fatigues, the United States librarian of Congress, James Billington, says Zhirinovsky's autobiography, *The Last Thrust to the South*, is "in some respects psychologically an even more unstable work than *Mein Kampf.*"

Zhirinovsky's 1993 success also helped shift Russia's political spectrum—including Yeltsin's policies—dramatically to the right. Surprisingly, Zhirinovsky tends to back Yeltsin in his battles with parliament, prompting some analysts to speculate that he is really working for Yeltsin.

Touring with Zhirinovsky, I experience first-hand what office-chair political analysts never get to see: how he interacts with Russians in villages across the countryside, where the Communist system of coupons and collective farms still thrives. National politicians rarely take the time to come here and explain what democracy and free elections actually mean.

I watch as he tells an open-mouthed crowd in a dug-out amphitheater that *they* are the ones who elected *him*.

"I'm your *elected representative*," he says. "This is what democracy is all about. I'm the only one who cares about your interests."

"Yeltsin's boat just came by," he says in Nizhny Novgorod, one of Russia's oldest cities, and the first to launch privatization. "Yeltsin had time to play tennis with your governor, but not to come talk to you, the people."

For now, Zhirinovsky distances himself from the Communists and democrats, blaming people's poverty on the collapse of the old system, the new politicians, and the ethnic minorities—including Jews and darker-skinned people from Central Asia and the Caucasus.

He is also a master entertainer. I've heard him say that Yegor Gaidar, the heavyset young economic guru, looks like a well-fed suckling pig. "Why do you think you have no summer vacations this year? Why are you unemployed? The Communists haven't helped and neither have the reformers," he says. Once, he singles me out in the crowd, points directly at me, and launches into a tirade about the evils of Western journalists.

"He's a surrealist politician," says one of his advisers, Vyacheslav Shishelin. "He speaks aloud what's whispered in the kitchen." Shishelin, an academic, then tells me that most of Russia's current politicians, from Yeltsin to Gaidar, are Jewish. "You can tell by analyzing the roots of their last names," he says, as he blames Russia's current problems on the "international Zionist conspiracy." Ironically, none of the politicians he mentions, like Yeltsin, are Jewish.

Zhirinovsky himself knows how to change the message for the audience. He tells me he is a great friend of Israel.

"I think Israel should pay me a ten-million-dollar honorarium just for writing my book, *The Last Thrust to the South*," he says. "It's about the salvation of the state and an immediate weakening of the Islamic world. But only Russia can do this. . . . That's why Israel should look at our party differently."

His notoriety is enough to draw crowds, whether they are activists, curiosity seekers, or the truly desperate, looking for a savior, any savior.

Tableau #1:

A crowd meets us at the harbor. Old people, middle-aged, their children and children's children. Some carry the black, yellow, and white flag of Imperial Russia. Zhirinovsky, in his brown suit, and Galina, carrying flowers, descend like royalty, accompanied by a crush of aviator sunglasses, hidden guns, silver hair, and blonde flips. A small child with an angel's face, white-blond hair, and blue eyes runs behind them. The boy's pug nose, nostrils flared, makes him look like a little Hitler Youth. He is carrying one of the tsarist flags. Other boys rush up to him. Giggling, they snake through the crowd. We march through a forest to the village square, where the rally will be held. An old, tattered woman rushes up to the boys. "Fascists!" she cries.

"I'm an old lady," says Anya Pushkina, seventy-four, whose late husband was a World War II veteran. "I've worked all my

life at two jobs. Just look at my hands. I work all day in the garden trying to get something to sell. But we don't believe in Zhirinovsky. He's the embodiment of fascism. If he could, he'd bring civil war here. If he gets real power."

Another toothless old woman rushes up to Anya. "Speculator! Speculator!" she yells. "She's been going into the forest, picking flowers, and selling them to us for twenty years. Why are you talking to her? She's a speculator."

Resenting those who try to do better, even if it's not by much, is a Russian tradition. There's an old Soviet joke about a collective farm and a private farm across the road. The private cow gives more milk. Instead of asking the private farmer his secret, the farmers on the collective poison the cow.

When we get off the boat, I talk to everyone from local leaders to passersby. One of Zhirinovsky's men follows me, and scowls when he hears me ask questions he doesn't approve of. After a while, perhaps because it takes too much energy to follow me, or because I completely ignore him, he stops.

Back on board, Zhirinovsky and Galina are on deck, taking up position to wave. They are surrounded by a semicircle of bodyguards. I duck under one of the larger bodyguards. Caught with a tap on the shoulder, I move back, then duck under again. I now lean against the rail with a waving Zhirinovsky. The bodyguards back off.

"Don't you think your campaign is similar to a grass-roots American political campaign?" I ask.

He answers and elaborates in a later interview. "Today one hundred and fifty people signed up to become members of our party," he says. "We are winning part of the local administrations. It's like an army division fighting a small war to get quick results. Everything about the style and actions of the leader and the party is different."

Zhirinovsky agrees to my request for a longer interview the next day. Then he keeps me waiting. When we finally meet, he is serious, courteous, professional. And surprised when I ask for yet another interview session.

At first, Zhirinovsky's words contain an inherent logic, even if I don't agree with the premise. Each day, the more we talk, the more he loosens his guard. His words become more tangled and confused. Then the sex talk begins. A completely irrational, obsessive, self-destructive side takes over. His calculations give way to a twisted beat warped by position, power, poverty—the extremes of Russia, from tsar to Stalin to Yeltsin. I become journalist, priest-psychoanalyst, and woman, a symbol of all Zhirinovsky is attracted to and repelled by. Upset that he gives in so much, reveals too much, he tries to exert sexual as well as professional control, over me, the journalist, and Masha, my translator, as well as his bodyguards. If that's not fascist, I don't know what is.

We begin to meet each day. Every interview ends with him promising it is the last session. Our second interview, on deck, is fairly relaxed. We discuss politics. Zhirinovsky is in a shiny Reebok tracksuit, the zipper undone to reveal gray chest hair and a large paunch. He sips imported orange juice with a straw. Blue eyes, tired but sharp, squint out of narrow slits under a white NBC "Meet the Press" baseball cap.

Despite the relaxed atmosphere, the interview is straight, his responses stiff. The raspy voice lacks humor, warmth. He answers without thinking about the questions, with a voice that says he has done this too many times before.

I try to provoke him, to get him to *feel*, to talk in an interesting, engaging way. I ask why he has such hostility, and lack of respect, for women. Why he hates all journalists, especially Western ones.

"I have the same attitude toward all journalists," he says. "I'm sick of them. Everyone, foreign or Russian. They've asked the same questions for five years. I'm sick of repeating the same stuff like a parrot. You know they'll always write lies anyway. They'll always distort the truth and write some of their own."

Trying to gauge his misogyny, I ask Zhirinovsky if he thinks women are just as intelligent as men, if women can also be presidents.

"It's hard for women to think globally," he says. "The president should be a military person; he should understand problems of war and peace. Women aren't drafted into the army.... Women would feel pity for the criminals. Women have some natural minuses. They are more tender, modest, loving. You need to be tough in the state." Yet he believes women are tough enough to push men to crime: He says Mikhail Gorbachev and Bill Clinton both compromised themselves in order to be able to buy presents for their wives.

Our interview sessions usually occur before or after dinner. Masha and I wait in a corridor that leads to the private chambers of Zhirinovsky and some of his bodyguards. Beyond the rooms is a large conference room with a piano, where most of the interviews occur. Bodyguards with walkie-talkies and hidden guns hover in the background.

The bodyguards, known as Zhirinovsky's "falcons," have a don't-mess-with-me reputation. They have been known to grab journalists' tape recorders and cameras, throw them out of rooms, and worse. But as the days progress, they become more friendly. We begin to greet each other by name.

First is Andrei, tall, blond, godlike, who starts off stern and ends up waving to Masha and me if he gets off the boat first to do advance. Then there's Volodya, a twenty-six-year-old giant, who gives me ruggelach, jam-filled cookies his mom baked for him, when we stop in Simbirsk, the hometown he shares with Lenin. Volodya is friendly, but not the brightest. He says he was always late for English class and only remembers one phrase: "May I please come in?" which he'd have to ask his teacher every day. And Vitaly, a tall, gangly nineteen-year-old. Vitaly wears a Red Hot Chili Peppers T-shirt and asks what the words mean. He's never heard of the band. Another knows only one English phrase: "How many submachine guns do you have in your arsenal?"

After one interview, I run into Igor, whom I first met when he was shielding his father from the sun at one Moscow rally. Zhirinovsky told the crowd their jobs had been stolen by southerners. He spoke at an open-air market run by Central Asians, who kept working as his voice boomed from the speakers.

Now, at a table by the bar, Igor, tall and gawky with stringy, dirty-blond hair, invites a young soldier, fresh from Moldova, to join us. Igor orders one, then two bottles of champagne and charges them to me. He speaks fondly of his father. "I'm proud to be more of an anti-Semite than he says he is," Igor says.

One night Masha and I are at the bar, where a group of young Russians and two photographers, Georges and the Alaskan Heidi, who are on board for the first few days of the trip, are gathered.

Conversation descends into a drunken attack on the evils of the Western press. Anti-Semitism is somehow brought up. Much vodka has been imbibed. The scene has the potential to turn ugly.

The bar then plays the songs of Alexander Rosenbaum, one of Russia's best-loved, most brilliant folksingers. All of us—including anti-Semites and me, a Canadian-born Jewish journalist—descend into song.

We are invited to the birthday party of one young army man with a pencil-thin mustache who gives intense anti-Semitic speeches. Now he holds doors open for me, and pours me a glass of champagne.

After repeated requests from the bodyguard set, we—the Western journalists—finally give in and go to the top deck. That's where the disco is. No one over thirty ventures here at night. Bodyguards stroll about with young women in hand. There is none of the crude, pseudo-sophistication of Moscow's nouveau riche set and the flashy, fifty-dollar-entrance-fee clubs of the capital here. The music is far more backward than in Moscow: mindless Russian techno pop mixed with the Beatles and some reggae blasts from a poor-quality sound machine. No, they don't have the Rolling Stones or, it seems, any other Western band since. Even the Zhirinovsky crowd, I gather, has their own politically correct code. Many of these young Russians are from the provinces. The women are dressed nicely but primly, in frocks no Moscow club princess would be seen in.

The effect, surprising for a Zhirinovsky boat cruise, is almost charming. On deck, under the stars, there is almost a sense of some "Twin Peaks" form of surface innocence. I don't think many of these young Russians understand the implications of their political allegiances, the potential consequences of their actions, beyond the free cruise and the sense of family and belonging. We all move into a circle, dancing under the stars, on a boat cruise down the Volga. For a moment, we are just dancing. That's all.

At one point we are held up for hours on the river. Yeltsin's boat is ahead of us. Zhirinovsky takes advantage of the delay to jump aboard a nearby cruise ship, also marooned, packed with Defense Ministry employees and their families.

"Quick!" Zhirinovsky shouts. "Get some vodka!" Soon trays of vodka and champagne—as well as Zhirinovsky and most of his passengers—are aboard the neighboring ship. Zhirinovsky gives an impromptu speech, his campaign song plays—and dozens flock to sign up as new party members.

> Scratch the Russian and you will find the Tatar.
> — attributed to JOSEPH DE MAISTRE

When we reach Kazan, the capital of Tatarstan, the crowds turn hostile. Tatars are a Turkic people who were part of the Mongol Golden Horde. The Russians annexed Tatarstan in 1552. The Tatars never forgot. Today, Tatarstan, with its population of 3.7 million, is an economically wealthy republic the size of West Virginia. Together with two adjoining Turkic republics, Chuvashia and Bashkortostan, it has called for greater economic independence—and even, like Chechnya, independence, although so far, Chechnya is the only republic to declare it. Understandably, the Tatars are not about to give Zhirinovsky a gracious welcome, even though one of his party's founders, its gray cardinal, is a Tatar.

Kazan has one of the highest crime rates in Russia. Its people are Muslim, and they, like the Chechens, terrify ethnic Russians. The Russian collective memory still harbors fear from centuries of Tatar yoke and oppression. It took the Tatars just three short years, from 1237 to 1240, to conquer Russia.

The boat is met by angry Tatar women in white head scarves. They carry anti-Zhirinovsky signs and chant, "Fascist, fascist!" The Zhirinovsky men refuse to let their women off the boat. Men yell at me for descending. "Don't wander off on your own like you normally do," warns a bodyguard. "It's not safe here."

Instead of walking into town, we are met by buses. "You shouldn't be here," yells an old man on the bus. "It's dangerous. You should be on the boat like the rest of the women." I ignore him, pretending I don't understand.

The crowd is held back by machine-gun-toting soldiers, who kneel in front of them, under a light rain. There is an ugly, foreboding feel in the air. Some of the Zhirinovsky group seems excited. Action, finally. Local journalists are out in full force.

Tableau #2:

A new, chanting crowd gathers by the side of the demo, blocked by a fence. The crowd, while unruly, is peaceful. Suddenly, an older woman swathed in a white veil begins to scream. It's a haunting scream that carries centuries of injustice and oppression. The woman beside her takes up the cry. Then the women laugh uncontrollably. So does the crowd. Turns out a policeman accidentally touched the woman's hand. She is Muslim, and this is sacrilege. Not knowing what else to do, she began to scream. This is the essence of the opposition Zhirinovsky encounters. It is explosive, lit from spontaneous combustion, and dissolves just as easily.

We depart without incident.

In another town, I meet some of the money behind Zhirinovsky. As I stand in the rain, watching him give yet another version of the same speech, I spot Jurgen Zapadalov, a forty-six-year-old psychiatrist, with the police and security cars at the side of the rally.

He is comfortably seated in his shiny new black Jeep Cherokee. A trim, balding man with close-cropped hair and olive skin, Zapadalov is dressed in a black-and-white tweed jacket with a tsarist armband wrapped around his sleeve. It matches his canary yellow tie.

Despite the get-up, it is not Zapadalov I notice first but Yevgeny ("Zhenya") Levin, his twenty-four-year-old bodyguard/driver, whom Zapadalov accurately describes as "handsome like a cat." Levin is leaning out of the Jeep away from Zhirinovsky and the stage.

Although he has an engaging smile, it's not Levin's looks that first attract me, but an enormous dragon, in brilliant reds and greens, tattooed across his flat, broad, hairless chest. The dragon is hard to miss, since Levin's burgundy checked shirt, tucked into loose cream pants, is open to his navel. The jewelry is also striking. Not the heavy gold chain around his neck (body piercing has yet to make its way to the Russian provinces) but a huge gold ring in the shape of a dollar sign, on a finger tapping away to Russian techno on the Jeep's window ledge. I cautiously approach.

Zapadalov and Levin, ever the gentlemen, are delighted to be of service, pleased, even, to be interviewed. As it is raining, I get into the back seat. I don't want to conduct another interview while soaking in a cold August rain, watching my hard work drizzle away, smeared into illegible runny inkspots down a limp, soggy page. The Jeep smells like new leather, cheap cologne, and sweat mixed with beer. I turn down the offer of a cold one and get a kick out of watching Zhirinovsky's team shiver in the rain.

"I'm a close friend of Zhirinovsky's," says Zapadalov. He adds that he knows, and doesn't mind in the least, that Zhirinovsky is a *Zhid*, or "Yid," slang for Jew, like *kike*.

"Of course he has Yiddish blood, but that's no problem," Zapadalov says. "He's very clever. We don't make problems among different people. If you can work and live, what does it matter?" As our conversation progresses, Zapadalov explains how his biznes works. He says he "employs" about fifteen hundred young men, aged twenty-two to thirty. He calls them sportsmen, expert in karate and other martial arts, who patrol the town's stores and cinemas, scraping up protection money. As Zapadalov sees it, he's actually helping the law enforcement bodies by keeping order in the town.

"Our government isn't strong," he says. "The political and social atmosphere in Russia is so chaotic that, with the help of my young friends, I help the city government, the police, and the KGB." Zapadalov, like his friend Zhirinovsky, also blames the country's problems on non-Russian "criminal elements"—even though he is part Georgian. "There are many people from the southern Caucasus here," he says. "We control the criminal situation." Like most mafiya bosses I meet, Zapadalov has a tendency to moralize, and thereby justify some aspect of his job. "We also sell stolen cars but never drugs. I don't like drugs. I'm a doctor."

What strikes me most about both men is the level of their education. Zapadalov is a doctor; Levin was a student before turning to crime. Zapadalov knows Levin's family; both his father and grandfather were well-respected doctors. It reminds me of a *Vanity Fair* article that quoted one law enforcement official as describing the difference between the Russian-Jewish mafiya and the Italian mafia this way: "The Italian mobsters play boccie ball, the Russian gangsters play chess."[*]

---

[*] Robert I. Friedman, "Brighton Beach Goodfellas," *Vanity Fair*, January 1993, 28.

Levin's biggest accomplishment appears to be the creation of his dollar-sign ring. "It cost three thousand dollars," he says proudly. "I melted the gold down myself."

Levin, who says he is "one-quarter" Jewish, was baptized two years ago. After the breakdown of Communism, a fierce competition for the souls of Russia began. Russia, reembracing the Russian Orthodox Church, was awash in baptisms. The country was then flooded with foreign preachers with enough cash to pay for conversion, offering potential converts everything from food to computers and education. It got so bad that the Russian Orthodox Church, which didn't have the funds to compete, tried to ban foreign preachers.

We move from talking about religion to discussing Zapadalov's town. Ever the gracious gangster, he invites me to return there whenever I like. "I'll send a limo to Moscow to pick you up," he says. "I'll make sure you have a wonderful time."

Until then, Zapadalov will continue to support Zhirinovsky. "Some of Zhirinovsky's words are real," Zapadalov says, grinning. "We *can* help the poor people. We can give them money."

Back on board, Zhirinovsky waves good-bye. We lean against the rail and watch the people fade. Zhirinovsky's wave is on automatic pilot. Sometimes as he waves his head turns from the water while he talks about schedules with his aides. Often we stand without talking.

"When can we continue the interview?" I ask after the waving is over.

Zhirinovsky then makes a crack about my clothes. At first, he agrees to the interview but stipulates that I cannot wear my jean jacket: It is too informal. After that, the clothing directions are more specific.

"I'll agree to the interview only if you wear less layers, if you wear a bikini, if you come in topless," he says. His entire male entourage breaks into laughter.

As the interviews continue, the harassment increases. He says he resents the fact that he is "giving in" to me, consenting to the interviews even though he says he doesn't want to. I've paid nothing, after all, and the interviews may be the longest he's ever given.

One session begins with him angrily exploding with the insane notion that I am raping him.

"This is the last time you can interview me," he says. "You're raping me all the time. You're raping all these men around you and they are reacting. Are you leaving tomorrow or today? You will leave tomorrow and that will be the end."

Interviews are always about power. A journalist has questions she wants answered. A subject has issues he wants to discuss no matter what question he's asked. If a stranger talked to me the way Zhirinovsky did, I would tell him off or walk away. But this man could become the next president of Russia. If his words don't shame him, I'm not going to let them intimidate me. As I continue the interviews, Zhirinovsky begins to slip in sex talk. Instead of telling him off, I try to turn the situation around and get him to explain why he acts the way he does. As Zhirinovsky says, he is only a reflection of all that is sick in post-Cold War Russia.

The sex talk explodes during our last interview. It is my seventh day on board. My colleagues are long gone. Zhirinovsky's half brother, Alexander, wants to know why Masha and I are still here. One or two more sessions, I think, and that's it. Around 9 P.M. Masha and I are summoned into the conference room. Zhirinovsky is seated, wearing his favorite blue sweat suit with the pink Nike logo. A Russian book on Tatar nationalism rests on his knees, his reading glasses are on the table.

He begins with a provocation. He likes Masha.

"I have a feeling she's a virgin," he says. "I like her more than you. I haven't seen such a pure girl for so long. She makes such a womanly impression, so very sexually developed. She's kind, mild, meek. This is the style I love. The more contact I have, the more desire I have to touch her hand, to stroke it, to kiss it. And then you can write that I am inclined to be a womanizer. *Then you'll conclude in your article that everything ended in group sex.*"

Later, going over the tapes, I realize Zhirinovsky had this plan from the start.

"Do you enjoy flirting?" I ask.

"I don't have enough time, but of course I love it."

I then turn the conversation back to where we left off last session: the use of force with women and politics.

He continues to flirt with Masha.

"Are you really a womanizer, or is it all just talk?" I ask.

He assures me he is, but more so when he was younger. "Every new woman was a little victory," he says. "That's the psychology of young men. The more women he has, the stronger he is considered to be. Like a hunter. The more you kill, the luckier you are."

He talks so much about his past achievements that I ask whether he feels, at age forty-eight, dead, or at least past his prime. He responds by saying that ages forty to sixty are the Golden Years "when a person achieves wisdom." He says that if he were a little younger, he would have already entered into "an intimate relationship" with Masha. If he were over sixty, he says he'd offer her chocolate. (This is exactly what he does.)

He also boasts about his sexual achievements. "I've had more than two hundred women, and with every woman I've had it several times. And if you add masturbation, I've climaxed probably ten thousand times. I started when I was fifteen. Now I'm forty-eight. How many years is that? Almost thirty-five? Thirty-five years, one hundred times per year. Multiply: three thousand five hundred."

We move to espionage, the mafiya, and Communists who are still in power. Zhirinovsky says he never worked for the KGB, despite evidence suggesting otherwise. In 1991, his party was the first to register since the Communist Party's monopoly in 1917. Russian and American analysts speculate that the Liberal Democratic Party of Russia was created by the KGB to give the illusion of a multiparty system.

When I ask why Zhirinovsky denies his Jewish heritage, he again swears he is not Jewish. I also want him to respond to rumors that he is gay and has been known in Moscow's underground gay community since the 1960s. I ask around this question delicately, knowing that he may cancel the interview. Zhirinovsky says homosexuality is a "satellite" of human sexuality, but refuses to be more specific.

We return to politics. Suddenly restless, Zhirinovsky blurts out: "Let's turn to the sexual part, because Vitaly can't stand it anymore. He's a maniac. He is actually nineteen, at the height of his sexual power. And yes, Jennifer, yes—it's good. He has lost his mind for Jennifer."

I am sitting at a boardroom table across from Zhirinovsky. Masha is on my left. On my right is Vitaly, his favorite bodyguard. Vitaly is tall, thin, and rather forgettable, although vaguely sinister despite his outwardly shy demeanor. Sergei, another young blond bodyguard, sits by the door. He has a shiny, sweaty face, slightly marked from adolescent acne.

Every so often, Vitaly's leg brushes against mine. I move away. I think it's accidental. Then the wheels of my chair begin to move, ever so slowly. Again, I think it's an accident, or the immature prank of a teenager trying to screw up my interview. I turn to Vitaly and, in louder than conversational tones, ask him to stop.

We return to politics. I ask Zhirinovsky if there is anyone in the world he depends upon, whom he can't live without. He says no. I ask if he gets lonely, not being able to trust anyone fully.

"In my younger years," he responds. "But when a person enters a more mature age, he has a much calmer attitude about everything. All the rest are just dreams, dreams, dreams."

In another interview, I asked him about Galina: Has she been a great support in his life? "No," he responded. She was "just the opposite—a counterforce"; she didn't want him to get into politics, although she is pleased now by his success.

The conversation continues its bizarre orbit. When I ask Zhirinovsky if he wants to meet Castro, he begins to ramble illogically about his father.

"I've never met [Castro]. It's a mistake to express opinions about people you've never met," he says. "Some people express opinions about me here and abroad and they've never spoken with me. I think that's obscene. They write that I refused to acknowledge my father, but I am probably the most tender, loving son. Nobody has boasted to the world about their father and mother the way I have."

Zhirinovsky shouts for a bodyguard to bring him his autobiography, *The Last Thrust to the South*, and wildly flips to pictures of the man he calls father. "They're always saying Zhirinovsky is so bad, refusing to acknowledge his father. But they've never talked with me." He points to a photograph. "This is my father. I'm proud of him. I love him. Then suddenly some mean people wrote that I refused to acknowledge my parents. I published the best picture of my mother. You can't have more respect and love toward your parents. It's the same with Fidel Castro."

When asked again if he'd like to meet Castro, Zhirinovsky says, "I'm always in favor of making contacts, no matter with whom. For example, if you want to surrender yourself to me, I could enter into an intimate relationship with you. If you don't want to, I won't even think about it. I'll just enter into an intimate relationship with your translator. And if she doesn't want to, then I won't do anything at all . . . I have no fanaticism at all and I win because of this." In his autobiography, Zhirinovsky writes that when he fell in love as a teenager, he learned that when a woman says no she really means yes. "Women frequently deceive by not saying what they think," he says. "Consequently, you also have to deceive them, not telling them what you want but what they want to hear. I transferred this concept to politics and achieved great success."

Finally, the conversation lands on Mars. I am asking Zhirinovsky about his political advisers. Instead of answering, he looks behind him, to the rain pounding on the window.

He turns back as if in a trance.

"Rain," he says, in his slow, low, raspy monotone. "When it rains this way it's good to make love. It's quiet, it's warm, not to think about anything. And you, Jennifer, you've been bothering me for such a long time."

After a moment of uncomfortable silence, I ignore the comment and return to my original question. But he persists.

Zhirinovsky: "Right here, now. You'd like to make love in this weather? Right now, the four of us. You don't need anything else. Such calm weather."

The room electrifies. I look at the tape recorder with its small red light, on the table directly in front of him. I feel like I'm listening to a killer's confession.

Me: "Have you ever done that before—with four people?"

Zhirinovsky: "It's best when it's with a group."

Me: "You've tried it?"

Zhirinovsky: "Of course. I love to watch more."

Me: "Why do you like to watch?"

Zhirinovsky: "To see how the others do it. To see the mistakes. Plus, I'm lazy. It inspires me to see the passion of youth."

I'm just trying to find the ballast I need to weigh Zhirinovsky down, to draw out more from him than base vulgarity. I ask if the passion within him has died. He says yes. Pro: He doesn't get as disappointed and suffers less. Con: Life becomes more "gray." I move the conversation back to politics, then music. Again he drifts back. To memories of a woman he seduced when he was twenty years old in Budapest.

"I love silence, silence," he says, rambling. "*I become calm by [the sound of a] woman choking on her tears. She is like...such suffering! This pleases me.*"

I think of this man's finger on the nuclear button.

Then: "I'm tired of questions. I want to cry a little bit. You laugh too much, and they [the two young bodyguards] will make you cry. And this will be ecstasy."

They don't teach you how to deal with situations like this in journalism school.

After an hour, Zhirinovsky says the interview is over.

I ask if we can have one more session tomorrow.

"Through there," he says, pointing to his private chambers. "We'll just pop by my cabin for half an hour. Then tomorrow, probably, we'll have something."

> It was as though a veil had been rent. I saw on that ivory face the expression of somber pride, of ruthless power, of craven terror—of an intense and hopeless despair. Did he live his life again in every detail of desire, temptation, and surrender during that supreme moment of complete knowledge? He cried in a whisper at some image, at some vision—he cried out twice, a cry that was no more than a breath: "The horror! The horror—!"
>
> —JOSEPH CONRAD, *Heart of Darkness*

We walk to Zhirinovsky's cabin, just a few doors away. The men enter the room, which is just like the one Masha and I share, only twice the size. Zhirinovsky sits on a sofa. Masha and I stand outside, peering in.

While Zhirinovsky's words are abusive, at no point do I think Masha and I will be in physical danger. This is still Russia. I'm still a foreign journalist. Zhirinovsky is not yet a tin-pot dictator. (When I ask whether he wants to be a dictator or president, he responds, "It will all be explained when we win. It will depend on what will be more efficient.")

"Look, Jennifer, Masha, what are you afraid of?" Zhirinovsky says.

Cautiously, we enter.

Zhirinovsky: "Come in, come in. A little bit of chocolate, a little bit of liquor. Sergei, lock the door. Sit down, sit down, sit down. Pour some liquor for the girls. Give them chocolate, sweets. Have you locked the door, Sergei? Or someone will peep in and Jennifer will be embarrassed."

We all hold cups of sweet, sticky brandy. No one drinks. Vitaly hands us chocolates from a large box. "Give them the box. They have to take them themselves," Zhirinovsky says. "Oh, greedy Vitaly. Now, sit down and caress her legs. Excite her. Work on her. Drink, drink, Jennifer. Drink, drink, drink. Relax, relax."

It seems like Zhirinovsky has done this before. But considering that he's an internationally known politician, no matter how mad, I can't believe how self-destructive he is. I have often read about politicians with bizarre sexual predilections—and their urge to get caught and have their sordid perversions trumpeted on the front pages of cheesy tabloids. Now here I am with a man who is consciously, willfully hanging himself—even after I give him a break and ask if he's sure he wants this on the record.

Zhirinovsky continues to encourage Vitaly to seduce me, telling him to sit at my feet, like a puppy. Now I really feel like I'm in a weird movie. But when Zhirinovsky orders Vitaly to "embrace the girl," Vitaly doesn't move.

"He's scared," I say. "For good reason." I try to be diplomatic. Vitaly is sweet, I say, but far too young for me. What most upsets me is subjecting Masha to this. I did not hire her to be harassed. She handles the situation exceptionally.

Zhirinovsky has told me about one woman he wanted to rape, about being calmed by the sound of a woman choking on her tears, about how it's necessary to use force with virgins. I ask him if he has ever talked to a doctor about this stuff. He says I'm the crazy one for not wanting to be with two healthy young bodyguards. When his words become too much, I tell him to stop, that he's frightening us.

I'm with a man who controls—and participates in—even the sexual activity of his young bodyguards. "Don't you feel bad about all this?" I ask him.

The bodyguards spook me. Maybe this is how Hitler Youths started out. A bunch of young guys who give you cookies their moms bake and have found a group to belong to, a leader to obey.

I want to get Zhirinovsky talking about the connections between sex, power, and politics. About fascism. But first, psychosis with a sense of humor.

Zhirinovsky: "Work, Vitaly. Look at this young passion, Jennifer. Do you want him to throw himself into the cold river water of the Volga? Where is your kind feminine soul? Start, Vitaly. Oh, please me for a little while, so I can fall asleep. There are four of you here. You have to show me love for four."

Me: "Why?"

Zhirinovsky: "Four hearts should start to beat together. To see the flow of life."

I don't understand, I say. It's not such an ordinary desire. Does it give him some sort of rush of power? He explains that instead of drugs and alcohol, it enables him "to see real life here, to look, to see lots of emotions."

"Isn't this the type of thing that's best kept between two people, so you can feel a genuine closeness and love?" I ask. "Besides, this isn't about love. It's about power."

"It's an observation of the process of life.... Start, and I will tell you. You can't understand this way. During coitus, I love to lecture."

Zhirinovsky says he can never have a relationship with one particular woman. I say that power has warped and twisted him. When he says he is helping his bodyguards, I respond by saying he is ruining them for life, that they'll never be able to have normal relationships with anyone.

Zhirinovsky: "We'll understand one another better if you undress right now. Masha also. You will lie on these little beds, and these boys will caress you. And I will be listening to you and continue talking myself."

Me: "I could never do that, and neither could Masha. We're not like that. It's simply outside the realm of our personal experience. It's just impossible. It's not even an issue. I'm really just trying to understand you, and I can't."

I ask if this is the kind of attitude that produces fascism.

"I haven't yet reached the state that I can do whatever I want," is his response. He then says our refusal violates the rights of the bodyguards.

Zhirinovsky: "Look how selfish you are. You say to go and see a psychotherapist. Yet you are two healthy women and you don't want to enter into a healthy relationship with two healthy men. You push them toward war by not letting them enter an intimate relationship. Today all Chechnya is in an uprising. If each Chechen had a woman there would be no war. That's why you're the source of war on the planet. That's why I never fall in love that deeply, so you can't control me, I won't perish as an individual."

I tell him that some people don't look at sex as a power issue, that some believe women bring love, humanity, nurturing, and warmth to the world. "That's an eternal idea. You want it to be like this, but it never happens on this planet. Never. There is war on the planet and you are the main source of it. Men take bribes because of you. They don't need money themselves. They need it for expensive presents, and you make them take bribes."

"Are you serious about this, or are you just trying to shock us?" I ask.

"I'm telling you about real life," he says. Again he tells me I'm violating his bodyguards' rights. "[Vitaly,] having gotten angry, will offend another woman. These are the vices of life. We hinder the lives of others. Vices, vices, vices, everywhere. Fraud, fraud, fraud, everywhere . . ."

When the balance between insight and insanity is so skewed, it's time to leave. I ask again if we can have one last session tomorrow.

Zhirinovsky: "Tomorrow we won't finish anything. Tomorrow at eight A.M. in Balakovo you will leave the boat and take a cart over a bumpy road—one hundred and fifty miles. In a week, you'll get to Saratov. On your way you'll be attacked by bandits. They'll rape you. Then you'll get to Saratov, with great effort, all scratched up, without any money. They will destroy all your cassettes. There are bandits everywhere on the road. . . . I will forget you two minutes after you step off the boat in Balakovo, unless you give me joy here. Let me hear the pulse of life. I have to feel it. I have put you all together here. Such passion. It's like war, a little war. . . ."

"A compromise should be made. . . . You torture [Vitaly] and think you are something. . . . Let the two of them get pleasure, too. My presence here won't disturb anything. Anyway, in this sense, [Jennifer] is also violating my rights. She alone is violating the rights of three people—three people! Is that any better? It's like the way the white race usually dominates the whole world, and then the world rebels, rebels against that."

"Let's finish tomorrow," I say. We slowly move to the door, unlock it, and head to the bar. There is silence as we enter.

"Are you satisfied?" asks an older aide, chuckling. "Have you gotten everything you need?" He is Zhirinovsky's chief of security. He used to work for Brezhnev.

"Do you agree with and respect everything he does?" I ask.

"Not everything, of course. But it won't affect his presidency."

I move to one of the sofas outside the bar for a quiet moment to reflect. The corridor is empty now. Suddenly, Vitaly walks by. He looks at me sheepishly.

"Are you, um, okay?" he asks.

Vitaly is back to being the nervous, gangly teenager I first met a few days ago.

"I'm fine," I assure him.

Masha and I agree to leave first thing the next morning, as soon as the boat pulls into the small town of Balakovo, hours away from any airport. Our leave will be unexpected: It would make more sense to wait until we reached a city.

We take a bus into town and hire a gypsy cab to drive us to Saratov, where there is an airport. On the way, we stop off at that morning's rally. I jump onstage, shake hands, and say good-bye to a startled Zhirinovsky. Despite his predictions, our trip back to Moscow is uneventful. Although it is only August, summer is over. A gray half moon floats above the Volga.

CHAPTER 19

Under Fire in Chechnya,
Part I:
Massacre in Samashky

"This Is War, You Know"; Cigarman and
Lipstick; America Understands, Says Clinton.
We, Too, Had Our Own Civil War

There are bloody great oil fields in Chechenia, even if they've
been screwed up by lousy exploitation. Minerals, timber, all the
goodies. There's the Georgian Military Highway, and Moscow
intends to keep it open whatever the Chechen and the Ingush
think...

— JOHN LE CARRÉ, *Our Game*

April 7, 1995: The ancient TU-154 Aeroflot plane sags from the
weight of bullet-proof vests and refugees. Women in head
scarves and sheepskin are jammed into the aisles, arms stuffed
with baggage and food and babies crying too close to my ear.
Unshaven men in leather jackets lurk by the back, smoking foul-
smelling unfiltered cigarettes. A shouting battle erupts between
the blonde flight attendants in smeary red lipstick and the dark-
haired women. The plane is overcrowded. The Chechen and Ingush
women won't budge. Tough-looking soldiers in blue combat gear
climb on board. But the soldiers are Russian. Like the flight attendants, they are no match for Caucasian women. We sit in the
cracked, broken seats for an hour before takeoff. It is a stare-down
match and the women win. Survivors of bombings and the deaths
of children, they are not easily intimidated. I can't imagine why

anyone would want to fight to get on a plane to return to what is, at the moment, one of the world's hottest war zones.

Parcels are stuffed into every crevice of this broken-down plane. The food, sausage and sulfurized mineral water, is slightly better than on Aeroflot flights to other parts of the old empire. Caucasian hospitality has already begun, with bags of fresh pistachios from nearby Turkey. Food, at least, abounds, as can be discerned from the tight-fitting seventies-era uniforms of the attendants.

I am traveling with Olivia and "Chris," a British translator in his twenties, with short hair and a nose stud. Chris—who irons his shirts even in the Caucasus—speaks fluent Russian; he only recently arrived in Moscow, though he has traveled through here before.

We fly over snow-covered mountains too magnificent for war. As we land, a distinctly American voice booms over the loudspeaker.

"*Welcome to Sleptsovsk. The weather today will be wet and cold . . . and thank you for flying Aeroflot.*"

An American voice on a Russian plane? Thank you for flying Aeroflot? The world's worst airline? The concept, the thank-you, the English, are unexpected and absurd here in the republic of Ingushetia. The culprit is a tall man with a smoothly shaven head as bald as a newborn baby's. Perched on top of it is a bright skullcap of intricately woven Azeri design. Just under his bushy brown mustache, clenched on the side of tobacco-stained teeth—he is also a Marlboro man—is the chewed-up end of a stubby cigar.

Stubby Cigarman is something of a legend among foreign correspondents in the region. He is, perhaps, the ultimate freelance war correspondent. (He has even written, rumor has it, for *Soldier of Fortune*.) After some prompting, Cigarman remembers Olivia from Azerbaijan. But she is a woman and, I gather, not warified, or tough enough, for his liking. He then nods hello to Chris. They are previously acquainted.

Finally, Cigarman turns and leans toward me.

"And who do *you* work for?" he says in a voice that dismisses as it disdains.

This is no conversation between colleagues of equal stature. Rather, it is a well-polished stone tossed from Hardened War

Correspondent to Schoolgirl in Kneesocks In over Her Head. The condescension is accompanied by an up-and-down once-over look that sizes up a lot more than my reporting skills. I mumble something about the *Village Voice*, which has sent me to Chechnya.

He is not impressed.

"I didn't even know they had a foreign editor," he scoffs.

"They don't," I reply.

Expertly chomping away on what could pass as the charred remains of a rocket fragment picked up on the bombed, explosive-riddled, corpse-filled streets of Grozny, the capital of Chechnya, Cigarman briefs us on what he's been up to.

"I've just spent three weeks filming a documentary in Samashky," he says. As we speak, at least two hundred of Samashky's inhabitants are being brutally murdered in one of the worst civilian massacres of the war so far.

He talks about a big network interested in the film, his agent, big-name magazine pieces, and a book. About assignments and treachery in the North Caucasus, Central Asia, Turkey, and the Middle East. About pit stops home to America, big meetings in Washington and New York, and conversations with spies on bar stools. "I was back in New York at my favorite bar in Soho," he says. "The guy beside me started talking about 'the big picture' in Russia. When I hear that, I know I'm obviously talking to a spook. He was saying that the war is in Washington's interests because it keeps the Russkies busy in their own backyard."

Used to living in conflict zones, Cigarman has the look of a wandering adventurist. Eking out a living in hot spots around the globe that most people can't pronounce, let alone locate on a map, can be as profitable as it is dangerous. Information is a valuable commodity for intelligence, as well as for news agencies. It is online gold, its procurers info-scavengers, modern-day gold diggers. It is the FSU as artist/con man/adventurer's canvas, the last frontier on our surfed-out highways. If Cigarman dabbles in more than mere journalism, that, of course, is pure speculation.

We negotiate a taxi and, cutting the conversation short, drive from Sleptsovsk to Nazran, the Ingush capital. The drive, cast in stunning light, is flat, hills and mountains in the background. Ice is gone and muck that stopped cars during the winter is starting to dry up. The wind is cold. Sheep graze, horses run wild.

Russian checkpoints, soldiers, tanks, and helicopters never let you forget where you are. We pass small houses in pastel mauves, yellows, blues, and greens, intricate iron roofs and high patterned gates. All of the designs display unique skill and creativity. The gates, originally put up to keep out Russian invaders, are as individual as the people. It's a breathtaking change from Moscow.

We also pass enormous mansions, of brick and marble, with pillars. Most were built recently, financed by some form of nefarious activity, from oil, arms, and narcotics smuggling to bank fraud. The mansions have even more intricate roofs and gates than the small houses. The designs include Arabic inscriptions.

Some of Russia's greatest writers and poets, from Tolstoy to Lermontov, have fallen in love with this region, but—perhaps because of all the bad press—I didn't expect it to be so beautiful.

Russia cut flights to Chechnya around the time it invaded in December 1994. Journalists fly to the neighboring Russian republics of Ingushetia or Dagestan, and drive in. During the winter, the nearest flight could be up to six hours away by car, on icy roads under constant attack.

Russia's 1.5 million Chechens and Ingush are like cousins. Both groups are Muslim. Chechens say Ingush are a lazy version of themselves while Ingush say Chechens are a bunch of wild and crazy Ingush. The Ingush president, General Ruslan Aushev, named a Hero of the Soviet Union in 1982 for service in Afghanistan, and Chechen president General Dzhokar Dudayev, an air force general who also served in Afghanistan, were both distinguished Soviet pilots, renowned for bravery. Aushev is now delicately trying to negotiate with the Russians on Chechnya's behalf—while not rising to Russian provocation to enter the war. Russia has already bombed inside Ingushetia and Dagestan, and repositioned the map to "legally" bomb heavily populated Chechen villages that, up until December 1994, were officially registered in Ingushetia.[*]

---

[*] In early December 1994, just before the Russians invaded, Moscow transferred Assinovskaya, a largely Chechen village, from Ingush to Chechen territory, and subsequently attacked it. Other Ingush villages with large Chechen populations, such as Arshty, were also attacked. By 1996, Ingush border villages, like Sernovodsk, are attacked as well.

Under Communism, the Ingush and Chechens made up the Chechen-Ingush autonomous republic. In February 1944, the Soviets rounded up the entire Chechen population in freezing cattle cars and deported them to Kazakhstan and Siberia. Almost half of the four hundred thousand Chechens exiled died of cold and starvation. Stalin had accused the Chechen and Ingush, as well as other groups from the Caucasus and the Crimean peninsula, of collaborating with the Nazis, even though many fought for the Russians. Members of those ethnic groups who survived, or were born into exile, like Aushev—born in Kazakhstan in 1954—could not return until after Stalin's death in 1953. The Ingush returned to find Christian Ossetians in their homes, unwilling to leave. Some political analysts say this was the start of the current war, which could keep expanding and exploding, as in the former Yugoslavia.

The official Chechen-Ingush union ended in 1991, when Chechnya declared its independence from Russia; Ingushetia declined Chechnya's invitation to join the breakaway republic.

By the fall of 1992, Communism's collapse coupled with rising nationalism had emboldened the Ingush to try to reclaim their homes from the North Ossetians in the tiny, disputed Prigorodny District. The North Ossetians were unofficially armed and assisted by "neutral" Russia. South Ossetians, part of, and often at war with, independent Georgia, came in to help the North Ossetians fight; the Chechens helped the Ingush. A massacre of the Ingush by the North Ossetians, unnoticed in the West, ensued, displacing about fifty-three thousand Ingush. It was the first ethnic battle to occur on post-Soviet Russian territory. It symbolized the potential for the Russian Federation to fragment the way the Soviet Union did.

Although Chechnya declared independence in 1991, Russia did not invade until December 1994, when forty thousand troops stormed Grozny. In the interim, the republic had transformed into a customs-free zone where midnight planes—from Central Asia, Turkey, and the Middle East—landed with contraband cargo, including narcotics and even fugitives. Thanks to the retreating Soviet army, Chechnya had become a giant arms bazaar. Kremlin politicians were undoubtedly profiting. Bordering Turkey, Russia, and Iran, with outlets to the Black and Caspian seas, the oil-rich Muslim republic was also a strategic Russian center for oil refining. A valuable oil pipeline ran through Chechnya, from Azerbaijan's

Caspian Sea and Kazakhstan's Tenghis field to Novorossisk. Chechen independence also set a dangerous precedent inside Russia, where rich autonomous republics were already refusing to pay central taxes. And Islamic fundamentalism in the region was growing.

Zhirinovsky called Chechens "blacks" and "bandits." Yeltsin referred to Chechnya as a "criminal state." Chechnya's gangster image fast spread West, especially after the 1993 murder of two Chechen brothers in London, who, according to Scotland Yard, were trying to sell missiles to Azerbaijan. There was another well-publicized Chechen scam to swindle millions of dollars out of Russia's central bank. Such incidents helped vilify Chechnya's image abroad: a quirky region filled with trigger-happy mobsters in fedoras. The 1930s American gangster style was best captured by President Dudayev himself, with his pencil-thin mustache, passion for pinstripe, fedoras, and fleets of machine-gunning, Mercedes-driving bodyguards.

Most of Chechnya's population of one million were, of course, hardworking villagers, far from this gangster image. They came across as warm and hospitable, with a strict code of honor.

Shortly after Chechnya declared independence, then vice president Alexander Rutskoi tried to storm the region, but his planes were surrounded at the Grozny airport. They were forced to return, humiliated, to Moscow. Kremlin geniuses then tried to stir up, and fund, local opposition, some of whose severed heads Dudayev later displayed in Grozny's main square.

By December 1994, the young reformers were all out of power and hard-line hawks were entrenched in the Kremlin. Yeltsin's chief bodyguard, Alexander Korzhakov, wrote a memo about state policy on oil. One of Korzhakov's top aides, Giorgi Rogozin, the new Rasputin, consulted astrology and cabalistic charts to shape Kremlin policy; he even moved Yeltsin's bed to give him a better energy field, according to a *Moscow News* investigation. Soon the party of war ruled. Defense Minister Pavel Grachev boasted that Chechnya will fall to "a single paratrooper regiment" in two hours.

Now Kremlin games, as Yakubovsky calls them, are being played out deep in the Caucasus Mountains.

Chechen fighters are unofficially aided by some Ingush, Abkhazians, Caucasian mountain tribes, and Chechens from the diaspora, mainly Turkey and Jordan. Chechnya has been practically abandoned by its Muslim allies and Western democracies. Afghanistan has its own internal troubles and a border war with Russian-backed Tajiks; Russia has cut off potential Iranian support with a nuclear deal. Turkey, torn between NATO and its urge to exert regional influence in oil-rich, ex-Soviet Muslim republics, unofficially does what it can, which includes sheltering Dudayev supporters. Rich, autonomous, independent-leaning regions within Russia, like Muslim Tatarstan, have sent Chechnya humanitarian aid. And the West, well, the West still lets Yeltsin get away with murder.

And yet. While Washington claims to want a stable, peaceful Russia, maybe a weak Russia, consumed by war, is also in America's interests—as long as an unforeseen madman doesn't unexpectedly sweep into power and change the plans, which is what often happens.

By the spring of 1995, Chechnya has become a bizarre international breeding ground with people from far beyond Russian and Chechen territory. Go deep into the mountains, and you'll discover a mishmash of Iranians, Israelis, Jordanians—and Americans.* Chechen rebels train in Pakistan and buy American arms—with closed-eye, unofficial approval from the United States—via Turkey, confirm Western diplomats I talk to.

There's an exchange in John Le Carré's *Our Game*—a book about a spy who disappears in the Caucasus—that uncannily reflects what is really going on right now.

> "Maybe they both sent you. The British and the Russians. In the great new spirit of *entente*."
> "No."

---

* One Chechen rebel fighter, who used to work in Dudayev's foreign ministry, tells me he met with Western diplomats—including American—before the war. Americans, the fighter says, helped Chechnya set up "information centers" abroad to publicize their cause. Western diplomats also gave Chechnya military and economic advice, including how to establish a new currency and passports. In addition, American intelligence was advising American oil companies that had begun to do business in Chechnya—and advising Dudayev as to which companies he should be dealing with.

"Maybe the world's only superpower sent you. I like that. America the great policeman: Punish the thieves, quell the rebels, restore order, restore peace. There will be no war, but in the struggle for peace not a stone will remain standing. You remember that very funny joke from the Cold War?"

I didn't but said yes.

"The Russians are asking the West for peacekeeping money. Did you hear that joke also?"

"I believe I read something of the sort."

"It's true. A real-life joke. And the West is giving it. That's an even better joke. For the purposes of peacekeeping in the former Soviet Union. The West supplies the money, Moscow supplies the troops and the ethnic cleansing. The graveyards are full of peace, everybody's happy."

As we approach Nazran, the country roads are dotted with shashlik stands where mutton marinated in fresh garlic is roasting. We are to stay in a presidential guest house, down the street from the presidential palace, which is a large square building with guards posted out front—grand from the outside, run-down within. We drive down a muck-plagued dead-end road lined with decrepit apartment buildings and children playing. On the left is a blue wooden structure known as the Blue Hotel. Médecins sans Frontières is here. A new building is also under construction.

The three brick guest houses are at the end of the road. The one on the left currently houses the Open Society Institute (OSI), part of Hungarian-born American billionaire George Soros's empire. On the right is a fancier guest house, designated for visiting government officials.

Our guest house is in the center. Associated Press occupies the top room. Other journalists, Russian, Georgian, Chechen, Spanish, Swedish, and North American, also stay here.

"As soon as you arrive in Nazran, you must meet a woman named Galina," said a friend of mine in Moscow the night before I left. "She knows everything there is to know about Chechnya."

Galina works for the OSI. As soon as we drop off our stuff, I head over.

"Galina's not here," says a grumpy, unshaven man. "She's with the American in the mountains."

"Do you know when she's expected back?" I ask.

"She should have been back days ago. We expect her any day now."

From Nazran, we head to Sernovodsk, near the Chechen border. Before the war, drivers charged a few dollars a day. Now some foreign correspondents pay up to three hundred dollars a day. Ingush and Chechen drivers are reluctant to drive after dark because of a curfew. Many Caucasians disappear at Russian checkpoints, day or night. One driver we meet lost most of the sight in his left eye to shelling while driving an American network crew around. Passengers in cars ahead and behind him lost their lives. The network, he says, did not compensate him beyond the daily rate.

In Sernovodsk, we visit "Shamil," a friend of Olivia's from an earlier trip. Because Shamil is twenty-six, fighting age, he is often suspect at checkpoints. Shamil videotapes what he can of the war, and smuggles the tapes to Russian and Western journalists.

We are immediately welcomed by Shamil, his parents, and a dozen relatives, who, like all Caucasians, insist on feeding us. We leave our boots, covered in mud, at the door, near barking dogs. The house is two large rooms, full of lots of women and babies. A table is quickly laid out with salty cheese, fresh honey ("Too much is bad for your heart," Shamil cautions), bread, tea, and jam. We see some of Shamil's video footage.

Western journalists bought him the expensive camera he uses. He jokes that we could be American spies. It is a new level of paranoia, but makes sense in a context we will soon understand.

The family talks about a massacre in the next town over, Samashky, a small farming village in western Chechnya. "The Russians have been pounding Samashky for days," Shamil's mother says. "Our windows were shattered by the explosions." Refugees have been pouring out, and are gathered at the end of a road that leads from Samashky to Sernovodsk. Black smoke still smolders over the village.

SAMASHKY

Thousands of refugees throng around our car, desperate for news. The crowd is so thick we can't move. At first we are the only journalists around. The Russians have closed off Samashky. Refugees still flood out of the village, twenty miles west of Grozny.

Slowly, we steer the car through the crowds that swarm us until we can go no farther. Rock music pounds from an armored personnel carrier (APC) that guards the entrance to Samashky. Young Russians in fatigues, looking bored, tell jokes or glare menacingly. One soldier stares through the telescopic lense of his automatic rifle, aiming at live targets. He agrees to a picture only after putting on the mask that guards his identity.

Some of the first group to get out are barefoot. They fled at dawn with their cows and sheep. A dozen refugees describe the same sight: two children, aged ten and twelve, hanging from nooses in the center of town. Snipers shoot at villagers who try to remove the bodies and bury the dead.

Everyone crowds around us, anxious to tell their stories. Raya Umarova, a Belorussian farmer who lives in the mainly Chechen village, rips open her blouse to show me the fresh blood of her sixteen-year-old son, Rizvan, murdered in front of her. "The soldiers tried to run over my seven-year-old son with a tank," she says. "I ran in front and managed to save him."

Umarova and others describe masked soldiers, with glazed eyes and slurred voices, injecting themselves with mysterious substances. "Some of the soldiers tried to inject me with their needles," Umarova says. Vials and syringes litter Samashky's streets, near fresh shallow graves and charred corpses.

(When journalists are finally allowed into Samashky, a week after the massacre, a few pick up some of the vials and syringes. Although Russia's Interior Ministry denies villagers' accounts of drug- and alcohol-crazed soldiers, the ministry does confirm that all soldiers carry emergency kits of Promodol, a powerful narcotic, and Dimedrol, an antishock tranquilizer. Independent analysis reveals that the painkillers, when mixed with alcohol, can create "extremely aggressive" antisocial behavior.)

Witnesses describe soldiers stacking bodies in between mattresses and then burning them. "I watched them burn the corpses of two young girls and two old men," Umarova says. "I'm now trying to find my brother. They took him away. I don't know where he is or if he's alive."

Umarova and others say special OMON and SOBR troops, older, elite trained contract killers from Russia's Interior Ministry, went from house to house, tossing grenades in basements where people were hiding. The young teenage recruits followed behind them. One soldier begged an OMON soldier not to shoot an old woman. The OMON turned and shot the young soldier instead. Other villagers describe a young woman who threw her arms around her father and begged the soldiers not to shoot him; they tied the father and daughter together and flamed them to death.

The army insists that only thirty-two people were killed and that they were all *boyeviki*, rebel fighters. But some of the four thousand refugees who fled tell horror stories about masked soldiers dragging unarmed men, women, and children from their homes. Some were doused with gasoline and set on fire, along with their homes. Others were hanged, run over by tanks, set upon by dogs. At least two hundred civilians—including many ethnic Russians—were killed in the massacre. About eight thousand of the village's population of twelve thousand, including many refugees from Grozny, were trapped.

The attack began the way it often does. The Russians gave the village elders—the community's spiritual and political leaders— an ultimatum: Hand over fighters and weapons or the village will be destroyed. The elders told the Russians all the boyeviki had already left for the mountains.

The massacre, some refugees and local officials say, was really payback time for Samashky, which had been fiercely anti-Russian since the war began. On January 31, 1995, the Russians tried to enter Grozny through Samashky, but the villagers cut them off, leaving a battlefield littered with destroyed or abandoned APCs. The Russians didn't forget.

For the next few days, thousands of refugees gather outside Samashky. Russian troops sit on an APC, listening to rock music and refusing to let anyone except the villagers back into Samashky. Those who return, like Aminat Ilsanova, thirty-six, say they are still shot at.

"I hid my children in the forest and fled on foot with my one cow, all I had left," she says. "Snipers shot at me when I returned to bury my father." Muslim law requires bodies to be buried within twenty-four hours of death.

Soldiers, who have blocked the entrance to Samashky, talk with Buddhists, led by a Japanese, Junsei Terasawa, whom I know from Moscow. His followers are young Russians, all based in Moscow. "Yeltsin is a fascist," Terasawa says. "On May ninth, all the top world leaders are coming to Moscow to celebrate the fifty-year victory over fascism and yet here the Russians have become fascists. We should boycott Yeltsin's Russia. This is racist, ethnic genocide."

A Chechen World War II veteran listens in the background. He is shell-shocked. He wears the high astrakhan hat of the mountains and a tattered jacket emblazoned with World War II medals. "It's all I took when I left Samashky," he says.

The Buddhists, clad in brilliant yellow flowing robes, are a stark contrast to the army-green soldiers. Yellow Robe and Khaki Uniform sit cross-legged in green grass. The Russians smoke cigarettes. The Buddhists chant, beat on drums, and distribute biscuits.

Zaina Geshaiva, a Chechen member of the Russian committee of soldiers' mothers, walks in the wind, gray hair flying, interviewing every refugee she can. She writes down names of the dead, addresses, statistics. "Every home in Samashky was touched by death," says Geshaiva, who grew up in exile in Kazakhstan.

As she speaks, we hear new explosions. The Russians have moved on to the foothills of Bamut. By April, the war has spread from Grozny into the plains and mountains. Fighters have been pushed into the mountains, from where they vow to fight a partisan war until death. But they are still dependent on the villagers in the plains for food. Villagers also sell animals and whatever they can so the fighters can buy arms—mainly from the Russians.

The first Westerners allowed into Samashky, staffers of the International Committee of the Red Cross, are only let in a full five days after the massacre. Even then they are only permitted into a small section of the village, for two and a half hours. Still, Jean-Paul Corboz, the field coordinator of the ICRC mission in the North Caucasus, says he saw about twenty corpses in the street. The hospital was deserted. "The only doctor left in the village was out burying his father."

Some homes have been burned down and all have been shelled. "The principle to spare as many civilians as possible and to keep the attack under proportion wasn't respected," Corboz tells me that day. "Basic humanitarian law has been violated."

Outside Samashky, Bishlan, eleven, still clutches the white flag he waved while walking out of the village. He is with his grandmother, mother, five sisters and brothers. He wears a brown sheepskin coat and mountain hat. He has a beautiful, seraphic smile.

"Where is your daddy?" I ask him the first day we meet. Bishlan's eyes well up with tears. His daddy is dead. Bishlan has heard the stories about the 1944 deportation. Now he has his own to tell.

"This isn't war, it's fascism," says Bishlan's mother, Zina, whose husband and father were killed in the massacre. When I see Bishlan each day, he runs up and gives me a hug. My heart goes out to him.

Dropping by the central regional hospital in nearby Sleptsovsk, I discover that less than a dozen refugees from Samashky are being treated here. In a cramped room, Zupa Katsuyeva, thirty-seven, rolls up her shirt to show me a bloated stomach with oozing scars from bullet wounds. Only midway through the conversation do I realize that Katsuyeva has been in hospital since January, and is still recovering from wounds inflicted while she was fleeing an attack on her village, Assinovskaya—an attack also noted for its exceptional brutality.

Katsuyeva was trying to escape with fourteen children, aged two to twelve, when the Russians began to shoot. "I picked up my son to show them but they kept shooting," she says. Her eleven-year-old daughter died instantly from a shot to her head.

"If they want blood, they'll get everyone's blood," she says. "The Chechen and Ingush people are everywhere. They won't get away with this. I have four sons [aged two to nine]. They're too young to fight now, but I'm going to teach them to destroy Russia. This war is without end. It will go on for the rest of their lives."

After the killing spree in Samashky, the Russians rounded up village men and took them to what are known as "filtration centers."

When the war began, there was only one prison, in Mozdok, Russian army headquarters. Now there are at least half a dozen regional holding centers. From Samashky, about one hundred men—from young boys to the elderly—were brought in and brutally tortured, says Majip Albakov, a deputy director of the central regional hospital in Sleptsovsk, who treated some of them. "What's happening here is a lot worse than Afghanistan. It's more efficient, cruel, and cleverly controlled."

Michel Kieffeur, a doctor with Médecins du Monde, examined some of the wounded and released prisoners, whose legs, backs, and stomachs had been bitten by dogs and burned. "Human rights were completely violated," Kieffeur says "The prisoners were without food or drink for four days, bitten by dogs, and tortured by electric shock. The army should investigate. This is a scandal. The West cannot allow it."

Sergei Kovalyov, a former political prisoner who is Russia's moral conscience, a post-Soviet Andrei Sakharov, risked his own life in Grozny during the winter and has consistently spoken out against such torture.

Outside Samashky, I meet some of those tortured. One man, with a thick black eye and fresh bruises, is too frightened to talk. Another explains what happened to him.

"Some soldiers asked me where the boyeviki were. I said I didn't know," says Adam Bubursagov, a gaunt, quiet thirty-year-old. Bubursagov was then taken to a field with a group that included a young cripple and an old man. They were told to strip to their underwear, their hands were tied behind their backs, and they were blindfolded. From there, they were taken to a nearby army base.

"I was beaten," Bubursagov says. "Electrodes were placed on my forehead, heart, spine, even inside my mouth. The shocks paralyzed me from my waist down. They threw me into a cage. I was so weak I couldn't even hold on to the bars."

A crowd of men has gathered around Bubursagov, listening to his story. Another man, slumped on the stairs of a bus which is about to take refugees into Samashky, is with his mother. His hands cradle his head.

"I was also taken to the filtration center," he says. "I told them I had already had an operation on my skull, and begged them not to torture me. A soldier asked me to show him where, and that's where he put the electrodes."

After Samashky, many Chechens seem convinced that a new phase of the war has begun: to depopulate Chechnya systematically, village by village.

"They want the Caucasus, but without the Caucasian people," says one man, repeating the Caucasus's most popular mantra. Another widespread belief is that the Russians launch massacres every time the Chechen population reaches one million. "Every time that happens, they try to wipe us out," says Zara Tupayev from her hospital bed.

In some ways, the massacre in Samashky is even worse than the battle for Grozny, which the Russians captured after weeks of air attacks and street-to-street fighting.

"In Grozny, the shelling lasted for weeks. [Samashky] was so quick," says Jean-Paul Corboz, of the Red Cross. "The impression is that the federal troops want to completely take over the villages. We are preparing a report, but reports are just paper. This will continue to happen."

Demoralized Russian troops, so starved for news that they often beg journalists for newspapers at the checkpoints that keep springing up across the occupied area, try to justify the civilian attacks.

"It's sad, but what can you do?" says one weary soldier outside Samashky. "It's the only way you can take a town. If they had listened to us, this wouldn't have happened."

Samashky seems only to have strengthened the fighters' resolve to fight to the death.

"Allah and God will bring justice," says one Chechen woman as she points to a group of young boys around her, Russian attack helicopters hovering in the distance. "When these boys grow up, they will take up arms and fight until we all have freedom."

LIPSTICK AND THE MARKET

From Samashky, we return to nearby Sleptsovsk and head to the market, which sells everything from hard currency to American shampoo with Russian labels; fresh eggs; salty cheese; warm bread; Snickers, Mars, and Twix chocolate bars; Russian and foreign beer; sickly sweet pineapple bubble gum that a Chechen babushka shoves into my hand; spicy carrots sold by a Tatar woman; counterfeit tea supposedly made in India; shaslik.

The wailing, mysterious rhythms of Ingushetia and Chechnya resonate throughout the marketplace. Politics and passion are inextricable as ancient guitar chords blend with the tacky acoustics of Soviet imperialism. The music stand, at the front corner of the market, sells cheap cassettes, in Russian and Chechen, that mourn murdered loved ones and vow to kill the Russian invaders—of the past two centuries.

Chechens have been regularly at war with Russia ever since Sheikh Mansur led the first *ghazawat*, the local version of the jihad, or holy war, in 1783. In the mid-nineteenth century, the tsar's army fought a forty-year rebellion in the Caucasus, led by Imam Shamil.[*]

Shady hard-currency traders, cigarettes dangling, pockets stuffed with one-hundred-dollar bills, lurk outside the market. Inside, babushkas try to sell shoppers plastic bags. The big four-wheel-drives rolling up to the market belong to the fighters: They're the only vehicles, I soon learn, to use when going up hills and mountains while dodging bullets and avoiding Russian checkpoints. The market is also bursting with arms, boyeviki, and a network of KGB informers. As in most villages, the marketplace is information central, where anything (and anyone) can be bought and sold, if the price is right.

"Foreigners!" cries a woman, in ecstatic delight. "Where are you from?" With that, a woman I'll call Lipstick pulls out a Polaroid instant camera and a tattered photo album from beneath her premium front-of-the-market stand, where she sells bubble gum and cigarettes. Neatly captured in the album are foreign correspondents we recognize and aid workers we will soon meet.

Lipstick wears deep dragnet mauve and bloodsucker red lipstick. Her mouth seems to want to devour more than Sleptsovsk has to offer. The fierce battle color cries out against pale, almost sickly white skin, narrow brown eyes, dark, starkly plucked eyebrows, and hair partially bleached the color of burnt straw, which is dark brown underneath. Unlike the women around her, she doesn't wear a head scarf—and only sometimes wears a hairband, as modern Chechen city women do.

---

[*] Shamil Basayev, who spearheads the hostage-taking of Russians in Budyannovsk in June 1995, is named after him. When Basayev storms the village, he says he was on his way to Moscow but he ran out of money to bribe the soldiers. Basayev has lost most of his family in the war. Russians end up killing about 120 of the 1,000 hostages during an attempt to free them. Basayev, protected by "volunteer" hostages from the media, village, and government, makes it back to Chechen rebel headquarters in Vedeno.

Lipstick redoes her thin lips a deep, dark, vamp shade of brown and ties her straw hair into an impromptu chignon. She straightens her long, shapeless print dress and pushes up the collar on her jean jacket with the lace-up leather pockets, imported from Turkey. Even with heels she is small. She pulls out her camera and starts snapping. Although film is hard to get, and expensive, she has a seemingly never-ending supply.

Lipstick takes and poses for dozens of pictures. In one, she stands in the middle, bronzy-metallic lips shining, hands clasped primly in front of her. I stand nearby, with Olivia and our Chechen female friends, in long skirts and head scarves, the market's wooden shacks behind us. Lipstick's eyes are so small you can barely see them. She is the only one not smiling.

"Can I ask you for a lift into the next village?" she says. As we drive through Nesterovskaya, we pass a four-story red brick mansion. "Who owns that house?" I ask. "A thirty-two-year-old millionaire named Ruslan," says Lipstick. "Would you like to meet him?"

We drive through the gates unannounced and are received with gracious Caucasian hospitality. Ruslan is a tall, muscular kick-boxer with a marked-by-battle face.

"Welcome. Please come in," he says, ushering us past pillars, marble, and circular stairways to a large, stark room holding not much more than a dining-room table, some chairs, and a television. The house is so new it still smells of paint. Workers abound. Bodyguards play with a small boy, Ruslan's son, by the TV, which blares Russian techno music and shows women in skimpy costumes trying to imitate a Las Vegas-style dance show.

"Please sit down," Ruslan says. "You must eat." Though they have just finished eating, Ruslan's wife soon serves more food: homemade potato blinis, vegetables, pickled tomatoes, tea. Keeping to tradition, she then disappears, though the bodyguards join us. I ask Ruslan what he does.

"I'm in the import-export business," he says. "My Jewish partners provide the brains. I provide the muscle." This prompts a bodyguard to launch into an unexpected anti-Semitic tirade. It is the usual international Zionist conspiracy stuff.

After lunch, Ruslan gives us a tour. "I flew fifty Georgian craft-workers in to work on the house," he says. It includes an entire gym for his "friends" downstairs, where his son is learning to kick-box.

Ruslan entertains us with some handstands. "You're welcome here anytime," he says. "Just kick the door open, even at three A.M., and make yourself at home. If you come back when the war is over, I'll take you fishing in the mountains."

By now we have found our own driver, or he found us when another driver, from our guest house, ditched us for journalists who pay more. "Magomet" turns out to be our key to the Caucasus. He used to be a parliamentary deputy in President Dudayev's government. "I quit before the war because of all the corruption," he says. At first, Magomet drives me a little crazy. That's because the car barely crawls when he starts telling stories, and once he starts, it's hard for him to stop. But the stories are extraordinary, from almost dying in the Arctic, to doing business in India, Dudayev, and the boyeviki network.

Magomet, his wife, and their children fled Grozny during the winter and now live with Magomet's brother-in-law and his family in Ingushetia. Most Ingush homes now overflow with refugees: an average of ten per home. "There are actually more Chechen refugees—138,000 of them—than the entire population of Ingushetia," says Khamdov Bekov, the Ingush emergency minister. "It's a crisis situation. The regional government lacks the infrastructure and organized aid efforts to help."

Magomet's family houses between ten and fifty refugees at a time the month I am there. They are all part of a close-knit extended family.

The war is so close, I go to sleep sometimes listening to the vibrations from nearby shelling. I wake up to hear a woman crying, sporadic gunfire. Some days I think the war will come here any day. (It does come to Ingush villages, like Sernovodsk, in 1996.)

Magomet gets nervous at Russian checkpoints. He won't drive at night, he doesn't have the proper papers; his brother-in-law drives us into Chechnya. At the Russian checkpoints, soldiers check my accreditation. Sometimes they harass. Sometimes they ask for news, cigarettes, even a smile. Soldiers give a Chechen World War II veteran a hard time, even though his ratty old coat is plastered with Soviet medals. Other Chechens are beaten up, even taken away to prison centers and tortured. A Chechen colleague's car and video footage are confiscated. They've arrested, shot, and killed people at these checkpoints, including journalists.* Sleptsovsk has also been the site of some "border skirmishes": rebel fighters targeting some Russians involved in the massacre at Samashky.

Ingush villages are flooded not only with refugees but also, if you're wise to it, with boyeviki. They're often in town, gathering supplies and information, bribing their way through the checkpoints. You can spot the four-wheel-drive fighting machines. Young boys and men squat in fours and fives on street corners, warily watching who drives by. Welcome to the first post-Cold War war on Russian territory, where Russian tanks wave the red flag and Chechen rebel fighters wear black hammer-and-sickle berets as well as green Allah headbands.

Despite the war, Magomet, our driver, speaks proudly of Russian poets, and writers, like Lermontov and Tolstoy, who loved the Caucasus. This in a region where a neighboring museum, in Makhachkala, Dagestan, proudly displays daggers that Caucasians used to murder Russians for centuries.

In April 1995, media interest in Chechnya is low. I know it will surge the next month, when world leaders will flock to Moscow to celebrate the fiftieth anniversary of the defeat of Nazi Germany. The festivities will be followed by a Clinton-Yeltsin summit. Chechnya will definitely be an issue. I want to start writing before then.

The media's take on the war at this point is best summed up by my Fleet Street editor when I call him from the hundred-dollar-the-first-minute AP satellite phone (reporting from Chechnya is difficult and expensive).

"Where are you calling from?" he asks. "Are you crazy? Okay. We can sell it. 'Chechnya: The Forgotten War.' I like it. Just remember to keep it short."

---

* In June 1995, a Russian journalist is "accidentally" shot to death by Russian troops *after* she drives through a Russian post with her husband, a German journalist.

CHAPTER 20

<--->

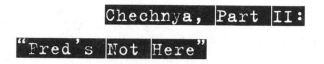

Chechnya, Part II:
"Fred's Not Here"

Mufti, Boyeviki, and Cowboy Boots—
On the Trail through the Mountain
Foothills of Chechnya

When there was trouble, there was Cuny—from Biafra to El
Salvador, from Guatemala to Somalia, from Iraq to Bosnia.
Earthquakes, famine, war were the setting for private citizen
Cuny's bureaucracy-defying good works.

> — KIM MASTERS, "Where is Fred Cuny?"
> *Washington Post*, June 19, 1995

A fifty-year-old, six-foot-three, two-hundred-and-fifty-pound Texan
in cowboy boots disappears in the mountain foothills of Chechnya. Also missing is his translator, an attractive thirty-five-year-old
Belorussian woman who has worked for the Texan in other ex-Soviet
war zones. They were apparently distributing medicine with two
Russian Red Cross doctors, veterans of the Afghan and other wars,
who disappeared with them behind Russian enemy lines. A Western
journalist staying in the missing Texan's room in Nazran discovers
a well-thumbed book left behind on his bed: *Our Game*, by John
Le Carré.

The American is Frederick Cuny. The woman is Galina Oleinik,
whom I was advised to meet as soon as I arrived in Nazran on April
7. By coincidence, Oleinik was staying in the guest house beside

us. Olivia and I begin to informally refer to it as the "Soros house," for reasons I'll explain.

I drop by the house each day. The landlord is increasingly anxious.

"They're still not back yet," he says. "A Russian who worked with the American and a Chechen guide are looking for them."

"I'd like to meet them," I say.

"They leave before eight A.M. and sometimes don't come back till two in the morning, or even a few days later. Then they start again," he says.

Cuny, a veteran of forty-four combat zones, is—or was—president of the Dallas-based Intertect Relief and Reconstruction Corporation, which he founded in 1971. He is on assignment for private foundations funded by the American billionaire George Soros when he disappeared. Soros is an internationalist involved in global politics, and philanthropic and humanitarian projects, where business, politics, and philanthropy tend to overlap.

Soros's foundations grew with the fall of Communism. The way Soros describes their purpose, his foundations sound exactly like U.S. government-sponsored, Cold War-era, anti-Communist "democracy and nation-building" programs, except that his have continued to sprout up in the post-Cold War world. Programs that, as Soros puts it, "help build the infrastructure and institutions necessary for open societies."

By May 1995, everyone—including Yeltsin, Clinton, and Dudayev —will have vowed to help find Cuny. Clinton, who knows Cuny personally, raises the subject of his disappearance with Yeltsin at least three times. The Ingush president, vice president, and emergency minister are also searching. So are the U.S. embassy in Moscow, the Organization for Security and Cooperation in Europe, the Soros Foundations, the American-based Refugees International, Intertect—even the FBI, the Russian secret service, the head mufti of Chechnya—and Cuny's twenty-eight-year-old son, Craig.

I continue to drop by the Soros house, but the search team is never there. I also report on the Samashky massacre, and—what I was sent here to do—profile the rebel fighters for the *Village Voice*.

One reporting day takes me to an international aid agency in a sprawling old home across a bridge and by a mosque. The house has a large courtyard, Muslim-style, complete with free-range roosters. Shiny four-wheel-drives with sleeping drivers in sunglasses are lined up outside the high gate. The visit is unplanned. Olivia and I hitch a ride over: Drivers—even of a crowded public bus—refuse our money and thank us for coming here.

At the agency, a young Ingush woman invites us into the kitchen for coffee. We meet the director, just waking from a late night in the neighboring city of Vladikavkaz, and "Byron," a young Russian, probably in his early thirties.

BYRON, OR THE MAN WITH THE YELLOW HAT

He reminds me of a Polish prince gone to seed, a man who has lost his fortune but not his title. Thinning, long blond hair, blue eyes, slight but solid frame, English thick with an accent more Germanic, or Baltic, than Russian. He grasps my hand, then swoops in for the kill, like a balding eagle, planting his lips on the back of my hand.

Byron, a humanitarian aid worker, dresses like a cross between an Oscar Wilde dandy and modern-day spy. Call it late-twentieth-century romantic adventurist: all black, snazzy vests and colored waistjackets, khaki safari suits that make him look, alternately, like an American photographer, European political adviser, international drug trafficker, double agent, colonialist on an African hunting expedition, or Curious George's Man with the Yellow Hat.

Byron smokes hand-rolled Drum cigarettes and Marlboros. His teeth have the yellowed, marbled look of a heavy smoker, his red-rimmed eyes the swelling of one who likes to drink. His manner is charming, gracious, and ever-so-helpful. But his eyes make notes as we speak.

"The refugee situation is terrible," I say. "Human rights abuses—the number of Russian detention and torture centers keeps increasing."

"What do you expect? This *is* war, you know," Byron chuckles, lacking even a drop of the compassion so ingrained in most members of his profession.

Byron often dismisses human suffering this way. Especially after a few drinks; his pale face pasty red and his words slurred, though his handshake still firm.

"Please excuse my English," he adds. "My Farsi is far better."

Byron is from Belarus, like Galina Oleinik, his friend. "I was working in another division of my agency when a request came to 'borrow' me for the Caucasus," he says, though the move does not seem to please him. "I had a trip to South Africa and Thailand planned. Now I won't be able to keep my appointments and other biznes interests."

Byron spent "some time" in Afghanistan. He studied at a prestigious foreign language institute and well-known KGB training school in Moscow. That was then, this is now, you may say. What would a Russian spy be doing working for a universally acclaimed international aid organization anyway?

I don't know whether Byron is a spy. For the sake of argument, let's say there's a chance. Spooks are of course rampant in the Caucasus, as they are in all war zones.

When I moved to Moscow, I never thought spies would be working under cover as human rights activists and aid workers— endangering the lives of the people they claim to be helping.

"Oh, Jennifer, aid work is the *perfect* cover for espionage. So is journalism—and diplomacy," said a diplomat over lunch back in Moscow. As aid workers, they get to enter villages—even those blocked off, by military checkpoint, to journalists and diplomats —and gain the trust of civilians. Ostensibly, they assess human rights abuses and care for the wounded. They can also be assessing how well armed a village is, and where is the best place to bomb. When international aid agencies allow themselves to be used this way, they also, of course, endanger the lives of legitimate aid workers.[*]

In this context, the disappearance of Fred Cuny, a humanitarian aid expert with close ties to Washington's political elite, takes on a new dimension. The United States has aided groups at war

* On December 17, 1996, six Red Cross workers at a hospital in Chechnya—all of them foreigners and four of them nurses—are shot to death in their sleep. It is the single bloodiest massacre in the 133-year history of the International Committee of the Red Cross. The attack prompts the Red Cross—and all Western aid agencies—to pull out of Chechnya. Earlier in the year, Médecins sans Frontières pulls its staff out of Chechnya after some staff are kidnapped and freed only after ransom payments.

with Russia or her allies. Washington backed Afghanistan's Islamic militants. More recently, Washington trained Shevardnadze's soldiers in the United States and Georgia. Why not help Islamic fighters in oil-rich Chechnya, despite American public fear of Islamic fundamentalism and interest in peace for the sake of stability?

A top Ingush official tells me Cuny gave "military advice" as well as humanitarian assistance to the Chechen rebels. Donald Krum, a State Department humanitarian relief expert, tells the *Washington Post* that Cuny said "he was going to see what he could do to...get at least a cease-fire"* when he disappeared. In Moscow, Strobe Talbot, U.S. undersecretary of state for the CIS, says Cuny briefed him after his earlier trips to Chechnya in the winter of 1995.

Adds Thomas Pickering, the U.S. ambassador in Moscow: "Governments have found that nongovernmental institutions can be useful....What you are starting to see is assistance deliverers playing a mediatory role in resolving problems in a way that governments often can't. The downside for these people is that it puts them at risk...."**

Everyone I interview, from American and Russian government officials to aid workers who knew Cuny, describes him as a brilliant, caring man who helped people around the world. The only area of disagreement: what he was doing when he disappeared.

Soros Foundations officials in New York and Moscow say Cuny disappeared while handing out medicine in Chechnya. However, Soros employees on the ground in the North Caucasus say otherwise.

"I don't know why they went [into Chechnya]," says Vyacheslav ("Slava") Miklayev, coordinator of the Soros-funded Open Society Institute (OSI) in Nazran when Cuny disappears. Miklayev, a close friend of both Cuny and Oleinik, spends weeks searching for the missing group.

"Fred is a very experienced and brave person," he adds. "When he has a goal, he goes for it to the end. I just don't know what his goal here was."

---

* Kim Masters, "Where Is Fred Cuny?" *Washington Post*, June 19, 1995, D1.

** Scott Anderson, "An American Missing in Chechnya," *New York Times Magazine*, February 25, 1996.

The chief doctor of the Soros medical program in the North Caucasus also says that Cuny had "his own agenda," which was separate from the medical program.

Cuny traveled to Chechnya in January and February before setting out again from Nazran on March 31, 1995. "The first time, [Cuny] came here as an inspector of the foundation," says Alexander Samkov, director of the Soros-funded medical project in the North Caucasus. "The second time he came here he had no connection with the medical program. He did his thing and we did ours.... I don't even want to guess what Fred wanted to do. I have no idea.

"We don't know why they went," Samkov adds. "Medicine wasn't their main reason. Fred wanted to go for his own reasons. I never looked for logic with Fred. I never knew what he was doing or why he was here, but we had great relations. He's a great person."

"I'm really worried about Galina," Byron says. "I'm doing some of my own quiet investigating, to see if I can find her."

Although Oleinik is an ethnic Belorussian, she is from South Ossetia. She worked for Cuny's company, Intertect, in ex-Soviet war zones like Abkhazia, South Ossetia, and Karabakh. (Both Abkhazia and South Ossetia were unofficially helped by the Russians in their bid for independence from Georgia.)

Byron has visited the village the Cuny group was last seen in. But the Russian government has forbidden his agency to help refugees in Chechnya—the mandate is for Ingushetia only.

"Still," he says, "I go to border towns to assess the future refugee situation—and hunt for Fred and Galina." One of his visits is to Arshty, a mainly Chechen town, which is bombed shortly after his visit.

SLAVA AND RUSLAN

From the outside, the Soros house looks the same as ours. Inside it's dingier. A television blares from the dimly lit front hall, where men in tracksuits lounge around, looking like somebody's bodyguards. American car chases, Russian techno, and the day's latest bombing news mingle with smells of salami and onions. The landlord, in an undershirt, baggy pants, socks, and slippers, sits by the television. He has a bloated face and small eyes and talks too close to your face. His wife, a hardworking, gray-haired woman, becomes more nervous as the weeks progress.

They try to be helpful. But Olivia has nicknamed the landlord "the Toad" after a previous run-in, when the house was used by journalists and assorted ne'er-do-wells. Her translator shared a room with a drunken, self-confessed KGB provocateur. She was treating her hand, wounded from shrapnel, when the Toad kicked her out. A Moscow official needed her room. (She was offered the kitchen floor.) In a moment of uncharacteristic rage, she threw her flak jacket down the stairs. She missed the Toad, clobbering a perplexed incoming BBC cameraman instead.

Finally, one evening when I knock on the Soros door, the search team is in. It's after 11 P.M. A tall man with a dark beard and black eyes comes to the door. It is the first time I meet Slava Miklayev, of the OSI.

"Please come in," he says.

We walk upstairs to the OSI office, which contains satellite communication equipment. It is also a bedroom. The room contains: two neatly made cots, a table brimming with documents and over-stuffed ashtrays, a computer, satellite phone, and fax. Slava pulls up a chair for me and his Chechen guide, the young Ruslan.

"We've just returned to Nazran for the first time in days," Slava says. They look haggard, utterly exhausted. Slava outlines the basics, and asks if we can continue tomorrow morning.

I return at 8:30 A.M. and catch them just as they are about to leave. We chat over tea.

Slava, forty-three, favors blue workman's overalls and black turtlenecks. He has thick black hair and intelligent eyes that give away nothing. He looks more Chechen than Russian, and seems comfortable in war zones, though he says this is his first.

"I was trained as a geologist. I've only worked in India and Mongolia. I've never been to Afghanistan," he says, adding that he has worked for Soros since 1993.

"What do you think happened to Fred Cuny?" I ask. "Do you think the Russians or Chechens killed him?"

"It wasn't the Chechens. I know that for sure," he says, not ruling out the possibility of the Russians. "Fred was *helping* the Chechens, but a Chechen band not loyal to anyone may have found and then killed him."

Ruslan, twenty-eight, is silent and deferential when Slava is around, though he talks more on his own. Sometimes, when Slava leaves, I stay to chat with Ruslan. He is tall and stocky, wears a burgundy T-shirt, jeans or shiny purple track pants, brown socks, and sandals.

Ruslan was a boyevik until recently. Small burns, water bubbles, and light scars surround his left eye, which never looks directly at you. It's unnerving at first. Ruslan still gets constant headaches from his injury, which he won't talk about.

"Since I can't fight, I'm here to help in a different way," he says. That means risking his life by acting as guide and driver to take Slava behind Chechen lines in the search for Cuny. Ruslan is in constant danger of being picked up and killed at Russian checkpoints. The battered Russian Red Cross ambulance he drives is often fired on, and even followed by helicopter gunships. What Ruslan really needs is treatment—and time to recover. Russian soldiers fly out on leave after injuries. Chechens cannot.

"During the winter, I was fighting beside a sixteen-year-old boy who was fatally wounded," Ruslan said. "He was in agony and knew he was dying.

"He begged me to shoot him. I did, then carried his body, knee-deep in snow, until he could be properly buried."

We talk in the morning or at night, before or after Slava and Ruslan return from their forays into Chechnya. Ruslan comes over to our guest house, unexpectedly, to talk.

A Muslim who says he rarely drinks, Ruslan takes the ambulance to a nearby kiosk and buys chocolate, champagne, and beer. We go back to the Soros house. I invite Olivia and our translator/ fixers. (For one odd moment, we have two.)

We sit in a circle, upstairs in the Soros house. Ruslan uses a dagger to open the champagne. He is so stressed out the knife slips. Blood oozes everywhere. "I'm so sorry I made such a mess," he says, ignoring the pain. We (the women) run cold water on the wound, sterilize it, and fuss. Ruslan is embarrassed. The wound is from champagne, not bullets.

Throughout Slava and Ruslan's Chechen excursions, there is talk of negotiations for Cuny's release: Some hope he—if not the Russians he was traveling with—is still alive. The group could be under cover, hiding until it's safe to resurface. Unfortunately, the chance that Cuny is alive gets slimmer each day.

WHAT SLAVA SAYS

"I'm convinced that Fred and Galina are alive," Slava says. "I think the FSB [the Russian Federal Security Service, the domestic branch of the revamped KGB] might be responsible." He does not discuss the fate of the two missing Russian Red Cross doctors, Sergei Makarov, forty, and Andrei Serada, thirty-two, who were with them.

By April 1995, at least twenty-five thousand civilians and five thousand Russian soldiers have died in the war: Chechens say they see Russians dumping their dead from helicopters and burning corpses to keep the numbers down. Seven journalists—Russian and foreign—are dead and two young St. Petersburg journalists are missing, believed to have been murdered by Russia's secret service.[*]

The Cuny disappearance is different because of the mystery. In a small region as close knit as Chechnya, it's odd that Cuny disappeared without a trace. If he had been killed accidentally, by bombs or soldiers, his body would likely have been discovered by villagers, unless, of course, whoever killed him—Russian soldiers, Chechen fighters, or lawless bandits—tried to cover it up once they realized he was American.

The Soros presence in the North Caucasus also remains a mystery to me even after I talk to government officials in Ingushetia, Soros staff, and George Soros himself. Cuny's disappearance raises questions about what Cuny, Soros, and the American government are actually doing in the Caucasus.

---

[*] Cuny isn't the first American to die or go missing in Chechnya. Cynthia Elbaum of Boston was killed in Grozny on December 22, 1994. In 1994, four journalists died in Russia: Two died in Chechnya; two were murdered while investigating organized crime and corruption in the Russian army. In 1995, thirty-two journalists were murdered in the FSU, fifteen during the first seven months of 1996. More journalists have died in the line of duty in the FSU since 1991 than in all of World War II: One hundred and thirty-five newspeople, including twenty-four reporters killed in Chechnya—eleven of them foreigners.

When I first heard about the disappearance, it immediately reminded me about the fate of that other American Fred, Fred Woodruff, who was murdered in Georgia. Is Cuny's fate another warning from Moscow for Washington to stay out of Russia's old turf?

I meet up with Cigarman again in Samashky. He mentions Cuny. "We were good friends," he says. "We met in Turkey and Iraq."

When I say Cuny's disappearance reminds me of the Woodruff story, Cigarman looks surprised. "Freddie Woodruff was a close friend of mine," he says. "In fact, I was the one who introduced Freddie to Marina."

Later, when we run into each other again, Cigarman stresses Cuny's prowess as an aviator. Cuny began flying at fifteen, and received his pilot's license when he was still in high school.

"Did you know Fred was a champion glider pilot?" Cigarman asks.

I wonder why he finds it so significant. Air power is important in all twentieth-century wars; in Chechnya, it is particularly important to the Russians, because the highly motivated Chechen fighters would most probably be unbeatable on their home ground, but vulnerable to their adversary's superior air power. That's why, for example, the Russians fly a lot of carpet bombing missions. It's also why the Chechens would like to get a good supply of ground-to-air defensive missiles, like the American Stingers that the United States made available to the mujahadeen during the Afghan civil war.

By April 1996, Chechen rebels claim to have shot down about nine Russian helicopters from the ground, and rumors begin to circulate that the Chechens have Stingers. If in fact the United States has been helping the Chechens and need someone in the area to deliver that help, that someone would need to know something about air power.

Cigarman now seems far less sympathetic to Cuny. "Fred was a long-term acquaintance, not really a friend," he says. "This may sound cold, but I don't feel bad for the guy. Fred took a risk. That's what he does. It's the same for me. I hope nobody would shed tears for me if I was bumped off or went missing."

"But even if Fred did know the risks, what about his translator, and the doctors?" I ask.

"They knew what they were doing," he says.

Byron, however, feels differently.

"I have no sympathy for Cuny," Byron says. "If a man takes a risk, it's his business. But I do feel bad for those other people." This from an aid worker talking about colleagues who went into a war zone to deliver medicine and help people.

After our first meeting, Byron starts showing up unexpectedly at our guest house, swooping in with a hand kiss, though sometimes he switches to a peck on each cheek.

One Saturday, Byron promises to take Olivia and me on a picnic in the mountains. When we show up, he delays it. "Why don't you come with us for a traditional Russian Orthodox Easter dinner tonight instead?" Byron says. The dinner, if it's like most international aid agency festivities in the most desolate places on earth, should be relatively lavish and far from tame. We drive to the market to help Byron buy food.

"I'll be back to pick you up in exactly one hour," he says as he drops us off at the guest house.

Just as he's about to leave, Slava and Ruslan drive up in their battered ambulance. Byron takes one look at Slava and exclaims, "I know him. He works for the Russian Emergency Ministry!" Byron jumps out of his car and approaches Slava. They talk for about fifteen minutes. Finally, Byron returns.

"I'm really sorry," he says briskly without explanation. "Look, I'm really late, but I'll be back to pick you both up in an hour." We never see him again.

The next morning, I am sitting on the porch of our guest house. Two men in neatly pressed suits, one in aviator sunglasses, walk out of the fancier guest house on my right. They are Americans. I can tell by their suits. Diplomats from the American embassy in Moscow. We begin to chat, reluctantly on their part.

Suddenly, Slava approaches. "Do you have the money?" he asks in Russian, skipping the formalities. They step aside to continue their conversation.

"*Of course* Slava works for the Russian government. He said he wanted to help the Chechens, but he did nothing," says one top Ingush official. "He had his own agenda."

"I *am not* working for the Russian government," Slava says, "though I used to."

By now, Cuny's brother, Chris, and Cuny's son, Craig, are in the Caucasus with Rick Hill, acting director of Intertect, another Intertect colleague, and American diplomats from Moscow. The Cunys have begun to publicize the disappearances. There is no word from the families of Oleinik—who is married and has children—and the Russian doctors.

The International Red Cross did not even approach the OSI in Nazran until April 23—long after their two Russian Red Cross doctors disappeared.

"I was told there was a dispute within the Russian Red Cross about the two doctors, who had worked for the Russian government in other conflict zones," Aryeh Neier, president of the Soros Foundations, later tells me.

"The local leader strongly disapproved of their crossing into Chechnya and may have told them not to," he says. "There is a war going on. They were treating people who are combatants. Combatants are entitled to be treated, and then they'll become fighters again. It's easy to understand why this would arouse the ire of the Russian military. It's also high risk for the doctors."

Craig Cuny stays in the Caucasus to help search for his father. "The Chechens, who have a real strong sense of family, really respect it," he says.

Soon after Chris and Craig Cuny arrive in Ingushetia, Slava is dismissed from his post, though he continues to work for Soros in Moscow.

The news surprises me. "I understood Fred and Slava were quite close," I say.

"Fred likes to dance with the Devil," Craig says. "He'd take on people with risks. Fred is a great manipulator. He knows how to play that game. He feels that if some people are close to him, he can control them and get information."

Adds Neier: "Slava ran into a conflict with Fred's family, Intertect, and Refugees International. It's very difficult to sort out. There were moments when he was engaged in the search on his own and the others say he wasn't telling them what he was up to. He said he was."

Even after Slava is dismissed, Craig refuses to stay in the Soros house in Nazran. He moves the entire Soros operation to a private house in Sleptsovsk. "That house gave me the creeps," he says.

I know what he means. Each night before going to sleep, Olivia and I look out the window of our room in the guest house. Sometimes I hear sporadic, light gunfire from far away. Often, cars drive up after midnight. People walk around out back, talking in hushed Russian tones.

Our window faces the Soros house. Usually, when I pop my head out the window, I see a face, directly opposite me, duck to the side.

"Quick! Turn off the lights!" Olivia says. We dodge from the window and try to figure out who is watching us. Often we also make out a figure sitting or standing on the stairs below, sometimes talking on a cellular phone.

One morning a helicopter is buzzing particularly close. We poke our heads out the window, then run to our balcony. Three helicopters—two bombers, one reconnaissance—slowly, deliberately, circle over the three guest houses for half an hour. The incident is so unusual that everyone in the neighborhood runs outside to stare. It was definitely a message. But to whom? For what?

By now, Chris, our former translator, is working with Craig Cuny, some American diplomats, and Rick Hill, of Intertect.

Chris answers the door when we drop by the house Craig has rented in Sleptsovsk. Ruslan is also working there. "I think it's best if you concentrate on refugee stories, instead of searching for Fred," our old translator says. "I promise I'll tell you if anything happens."

The search costs about seventy thousand dollars a month. Teams are dispatched to hunt through Chechnya, to negotiate with Chechens, Ingush, and Russians. It's so expensive, the Cuny family is setting up a foundation to help. The MacArthur Foundation also awards Cuny a "genius grant" to help pay for the search. Before Slava leaves, he conducts one last, independent trip into Chechnya—where he disappears for ten days. By chance, I drop by just as he returns: haggard, rushing to the telephone.

The next day, Slava moves into our guest house. He stays up late on the balcony, typing reports into his laptop. I wonder who now lives in the old Soros house. One night, Olivia and I approach.

All the lights are out. The house is pitch-dark. We knock on the door. No answer. We knock again, then push the door open.

"Hello!" we call out. "Is anybody here?" We walk into the hall. Then the kitchen, where the table is set for two. Cold chicken on two plates that has not yet been touched. Two slices of fresh lemon cake. Two cups of tea, just finished. Just after we leave, as we are on our way toward town, I look back toward the house. One upstairs light is turned on.

LIPSTICK RETURNS

Lipstick rushes up to me in the market. "There's a psychic woman I want you to meet—and a village elder. They may be able to help you."

Some elders are KGB informers, Russian collaborators. Others work with the Chechen fighters. Few are neutral. All negotiate on behalf of their villages when Russian commanders issue their ultimatums.

As we are about to leave the market, Lipstick grabs my hand and leads me through the muck to her home by the back of the market, in a dilapidated maze of wooden shack-kiosks.

Lipstick's habitat: a tiny single room with a narrow cot, fridge, and hot plate. She sits on a crate, and motions for me to sit on the cot. It is bitterly cold most of the year but now that it's mid-May, the air is warming. The room is filled with flies. Sacks of humanitarian-aid flour line a wall decorated with a poster of a scantily clad singer, Samantha Fox, who was popular in Europe in the 1980s.

I decline some tea from one of three unwashed, chipped cups that Lipstick dips into some dirty dishwater. I think she has something to tell me. But all she does is change outfits for our visit to the psychic woman.

Preparing for a new role, that of devout Muslin, she takes off her knee-length dress, revealing black lingerie that was not bought in the Caucasus. On goes a long, shapeless dress. She even takes a head scarf with her, which she doesn't put on until we're almost there.

Lipstick takes care to repaint her face, by the light of a single, naked bulb: skinny lips, eyeliner, shadow, blush, and mascara. I decline her offer to try the bloodred shades. The one lipstick I bring to the Caucasus, the only cosmetic, is a pale, almost-not-there shade of apricot that does not impress her. Before I can stop her, Lipstick douses me with cheap, sweet perfume as if it were mosquito spray.

We drive to a small house in a tiny village. Lipstick runs out of the car first and returns, five minutes later, to invite us in. A large elderly woman, her full face lined with wrinkles, sits us down by a kitchen table. She moves some colored, polished stones around on the table.

"Your friend is with a woman who loves him," she says. "But he doesn't love her. He wants to get away, but he can't. He's not that far away. You can talk to him yourself, but the roads are blocked. He is near Urus-Martan." That's a Russian-occupied village near Bamut, where Cuny was last sighted.

Lipstick also takes me to a village elder, an old man in a high mountain astrakhan hat and sheepskin vest, with red-rimmed eyes. "He's famous," Lipstick says. "He's returned from the dead."

The old man lives in a sprawling house teeming with children, women, and well-dressed young men of fighting age, in rooms closed off to us. Men are constantly rushing in and out. Satellite television blares in the background in this backwater village. The man takes us into a small, bare room. He and Lipstick have trouble communicating in Chechen. ("It's a different dialect," she says.)

He speaks in Russian and asks my name, which he has trouble pronouncing. "You must go to Urus-Martan and see the head mufti. He will help you." (Even Chechnya's chief mufti, Magomet Hussein Khajoi, has pledged to help search for Cuny.)

Before we leave, the elder scribbles on notepaper, which he carefully folds and hands me while incanting some sort of prayer.

"It is your talisman," Lipstick says. "You have to sew it into your shirt. Wear it always and you will be protected from harm."

I have already been to Urus-Martan. Though I wanted to return, I never had the time.

By this point, I have my doubts about Lipstick. Why was she so keen to have me meet these people? "There are lots of informers around here," warns my driver. "It's an old Communist tradition that is even more prevalent during war."

Sometimes when I go to the market with my driver's family, Lipstick comes over to say hello. I think she is friends with the other women, but I discover they are just being polite. The suspicions begin in earnest the day my driver's family freezes when I take her into their home.

Early one morning, as Olivia and I we are about to leave to meet Magomet's family and make contact with some fighters, Lipstick appears on the doorstep of a private apartment we have rented. Nazran is far from Sleptsovsk, where she lives. It's 8:30 A.M. We have not given her the address.

"How did you know where we were?" I ask.

"Everyone knows where the journalists stay," she says. Not wanting to be rude, we bring her along. Our driver gives us a look, but says nothing. At the house, Lipstick is treated with icy reserve. Conversations freeze. She is grudgingly served tea and does not eat the meal laid out for us.

"She can't even speak real Chechen," says our host. It's a bad day to bring an unexpected visitor along. An arms dealer-boyevik has also arrived with someone who claims to be looking into Cuny's disappearance on behalf of Dudayev.

Whoever she is, Lipstick's life does not appear to be a happy one. Like many Chechen women I meet, she was kidnapped, she says, at eighteen by a man who became her husband. After a year, Lipstick escaped. "I didn't love him," she says. "My dream is to marry a Frenchman."

Instead of moving back with her family after she left her husband, Lipstick lives in her market shack. She does not seem to be close to her family, whom she describes this way: "My mother works very hard, my father is sick, and my brothers stay home, doing nothing. My mother and I support everyone."

LIONEL

There's a new man in the Soros house. Another humanitarian aid expert, and good friend of Cuny's, who flew in from Washington to help organize the search.

Lionel Rosenblatt is a tall American with a mustache and a passion for Eagle brand vodka. "I'm here to make some recommendations about how to help refugees," he says without mentioning Cuny when we first meet. Rosenblatt, who says he worked in the U.S. State Department for twenty-two years, is now head of the privately funded, Washington-based organization, Refugees International, which gets some money from the Carnegie Endowment for International Peace. The group helps refugees and even makes recommendations to the U.S. government (about what he doesn't say).

Olivia and I have just returned from a trip into Dagestan to write about the refugee problem.

"I'm really interested in hearing about your trip," Rosenblatt says. So interested he takes notes. I wonder if he's really going to write a report about refugees, since he's spending all his time searching for Cuny. If he does write about refugees, I wonder what will be in the report.

With time, Rosenblatt tells us why he's really here: "Fred was a close friend. I came to do what I can."

One night, we sit around drinking vodka (our sips to his gulps). Rosenblatt's eyes are red, though his Oxford button-down and blue-jean combo are perfectly pressed, à la Washington power style.

Finally, after midnight, Pyotr Kosov, President Aushev's chief of staff, and some of his deputies, in combat fatigues, burst into the room.

"Right," Lionel says. "It's time to go." My request to accompany them is denied. "But you're welcome to stay and finish the vodka," he says.

Olivia and I stay for a while. Nothing surprises me in this house anymore.

It is around this time that Rosenblatt sneaks into Chechnya to meet with Dudayev, who again pledges to do what he can to help find Cuny.

PORTRAIT OF A MISSING MAN

Cuny's company has been involved in conflict zones around the world, from the Sudan to Iraq. His interests seemed to coincide with America's interests: Central America in the 1980s, Iraq during the Persian Gulf war, and the FSU today. By all accounts, Cuny *was* Intertect. "The company," says Craig, "is totally dependent on Fred."

When Cuny wasn't traveling in global hot spots, he lived a luxurious lifestyle, complete with his own glider. When asked where Cuny got his money, Craig says, "You know, I've always wondered that myself."

Cuny married young and divorced fast. "He's never been good at settling in," says Craig, who was raised by Fred's parents and grew up like one of their children: There are only six years between Craig and Fred's brother, Chris.

"I saw my dad on school vacations," Craig says. "I got to travel with him to places like Guatemala. The other kids were like, 'You went where? We went to Disneyland.' "

Fred's picture: full, youngish-looking baby face, blondish hair slicked sideways. Pleasant features, straight nose, a full mouth that seems to curve upwards on the right.

Craig: tall, handsome, with an old-school courtesy, trying to make it as the owner of a freelance video company. Gracious and polite even when he doesn't have to be. He offers part of his lunch to unexpected, nosy reporters. He picks wildflowers after meeting with a Chechen boyevik in the woods. Like his father, he has a passion for cowboy boots.

At first, Craig is jealously guarded by two American embassy types from Moscow. Later, Craig and a friend, who traveled with Olivia and me on our search, crisscross Chechnya putting up posters and asking questions. They drive themselves, and meet Shamil Basayev in a mountain hospital shortly after the Budyannovsk hostage-taking incident. Russian guards let them through the posts without too much hassle: The guards fire "accidentally" only once.

Craig talks about his father and "powerful" friends in Washington. Besides Strobe Talbot, Cuny briefed everyone from Joint Chiefs of Staff chair John Shalikashvili to State Department, Pentagon, and UN officials. In Moscow, Craig meets with Clinton, Vice President Al Gore, Strobe Talbot, National Security Adviser Anthony Lake, and Secretary of State Warren Christopher, as well as the American ambassador, Thomas Pickering, senators, and others.

"I thought I'd be coming down here with a knapsack and a photograph, hitchhiking rides and looking for Fred," Craig says. "I was amazed at all the people who are friends of his. Everyone is looking for him. There's so much help."

The way Craig tells it, Cuny was part of an elite but informal Washington-based "think tank" with links to the U.S. State Department, the Soros Foundations, the United Nations High Commission for Refugees, and various other foundations, like the Carnegie Endowment for International Peace.

"[The members of the think tank] crossed paths over the years and recognized that they all thought alike," Craig says. "They've taken it upon themselves to try to steer people in government—and they're effective as hell."

Lionel Rosenblatt is also part of the think tank. "Lionel's a great guy," Craig says. Adds one Western diplomat: "[Lionel] is a brilliant statesman. He's on a first-name basis with top levels of government."

The think tank put Cuny on to Chechnya, according to Craig. "I used to think that he went where he wanted to go, but the think tank sent him to places he never thought about before," he says. "Fred still does stuff in the field. His colleagues really admire him. He's out there pounding bricks, still tapping out volumes of information while they're all now at desk jobs."

In the 1960s, Cuny went to Texas Agricultural and Industrial College in Kingsville, where he studied engineering and led Mexican migrant workers to strike. He then attended the University of Houston, where he received a degree in urban planning. "During the summer," Craig says, "Fred worked on a ship." He kept breezing through ports in countries like Peru. In the early 1970s, he worked on a kibbutz in Israel and began to get involved in helping people around the world who were victims of natural disasters, like earthquakes and floods. The list is long: famine in Ethiopia and Somalia, a Madagascar cyclone, Armenian earthquake, and war in Biafra, Sri Lanka, and Guatemala.

From crisis management, Cuny moved to preventive work, combining his engineering with his planning skills. In Mexico, for example, he found indigenous natural materials to help build better, earthquake-resistant huts.

By the 1980s, Cuny had become a refugee specialist, spotting potential migration movements and carrying out long-term planning. At the time of the Persian Gulf War, Cuny repatriated four hundred thousand Kurdish refugees from the Turkish border region to Iraq, pushing back the Iraqi no-fly zone and avoiding a potential military confrontation that could have threatened the NATO alliance. Craig says this may have been the project Fred

Cuny was most proud of. It is also one of the best examples of how interconnected global politics and international aid have become.

According to the *Washington Post*, Cuny "consulted extensively with U.S. military in Iraq."[*] Craig Cuny describes his father as the chief civilian adviser to the allies. In Sarajevo, while working for Soros, Cuny installed a water system for the city.

"He's a tireless worker," Craig says. "When he focuses on a project, it becomes his life. He'll do whatever it takes to get the job done."

By the end of the Cold War, it seemed that Cuny had succeeded in merging humanitarian relief work with American political and military objectives—even though, in the past, aid workers' neutrality was what was supposed to protect them.

I meet with George Soros in Moscow during a brief and impromptu press conference, in which he admits there was some "financial mismanagement" in his foundations.

Soros's unexpected Moscow visit comes just days before the Yeltsin-Clinton summit, held in conjunction with the celebrations on the fiftieth anniversary of V-E Day. At the time, there is talk that Cuny may be released during the celebrations.

A trim older man who wears European-style plaid jackets, Soros will not say whom he is meeting with in Moscow. His eyes, shielded behind strong-framed glasses, stare straight at you, but through you. He says he is "satisfied" with the Russian government's help in the search for Cuny.

"They're working very closely with us. They're doing all they can, unless they're just acting that way and doing something different," he says, in typical Soros double-talk style.

After the Clinton-Yeltsin summit—when there is still no word about Cuny—the Soros Foundations are more critical. "There was never a good-faith effort from the Russians to help the search," says Neier, the foundations' president. "And there were bizarre comments from some Russian officials that Fred is alive and working with Dudayev. I don't feel kindly about the Russian authorities and their help with the search."

---

[*] Kim Masters "Where Is Fred Cuny?" *Washington Post*, June 19, 1995, D1.

Although Russia's security and intelligence services have pledged to help find Cuny, the Russians do not always provide safe passage for the search parties to get through the increasingly dangerous Russian checkpoints. Worse, members of one search party, including a diplomat from the Organization for Security and Cooperation in Europe and one of Cuny's Intertect colleagues, are even shot at by Russian tanks near the town of Novye Atagi, on May 13. One car in the search party is blown up. The shots come ten minutes after a previously brokered cease-fire has begun so that the group can enter the southeastern town of Shali, which has been under heavy Russian attack. The group is trying to retrieve a dead body believed to be that of Cuny.

Just as in a spy novel, the badly decomposed body, clad in Western clothes, is difficult to identify because—after being shot in the head twice—its face has been dissolved with sulfuric acid. Various reports seek to confirm and then deny that the body is Cuny's, much to the distress of his family. The Russian Federal Security Service then issues a statement through Itar-Tass that the body is definitely not Cuny, although who it is, they won't say.

WHAT HAPPENED

Cuny first visited Chechnya in January 1995, shortly after the war began. Before going, he met with the Ingushetian vice president, Boris Agapov, who tells me he wrote a letter of introduction for Cuny to meet with one of the main Chechen rebel military leaders, General Aslan Maskhadov.

One top Ingush official says the two discussed more than humanitarian aid. "He was also giving Maskhadov military information." Cuny was pleased with the meeting, but still hoped to meet with Dudayev. That's what the March trip may have been about.

Fred wrote about his first trip for the *New York Review of Books*. The much-discussed, highly praised article, which was published around the time he disappeared, highlighted military techniques of Chechen fighters with uncanny—and unusually specific—detail. In part, the article argued that the war could bring down the Yeltsin government and that "the U.S. should now engage in efforts to encourage negotiations and stop the war."

Cuny flew from Moscow to Ingushetia on March 30. The next day, Cuny, Oleinik, and the two Russian doctors left Ingushetia for Chechnya. The trip appears to have been rushed. Slava was on his way, driving from Moscow, and thought Cuny would wait for him. Ingushetian Emergency Ministry officials say they combed the streets of Sleptsovsk looking for Ruslan Muradov, who drove Cuny and Oleinik into Chechnya during the winter. The group was heading toward Bamut, where their guide, Muradov, is from, and then Vedeno, Chechen rebel headquarters.

"If Cuny was trying to meet Dudayev, he didn't take the time to make the proper arrangements," Agapov says. During his earlier trips, it was relatively easy to travel in Chechnya; the war was mainly contained in Grozny. By the end of March, the war had spread. Entering Chechen-controlled territory with a group of unknown Russians could be deadly.

Ten days before the trip, Cuny's translator, Oleinik, had been detained with two other Russian doctors at a particularly dangerous Russian post in Assinovskaya, in western Chechnya. One of the group she was with was badly beaten.

Muradov, the driver, was the last person to see the group alive. He disappeared after preparing a written statement—a copy of which I have obtained—about what happened. When I left the Caucasus, the Ingush authorities were still trying to find and question him.

According to Muradov, the Cuny group was briefly detained as soon as they entered Chechen-controlled territory in Bamut, a center of Chechen resistance, under regular attack from helicopter gunships, tanks, and artillery.

Once released, they picked up a second Chechen guide and traveled on to nearby Stary Achkhoi. They were detained again the next day by the Chechens, tied up, and held at gunpoint. The two Chechen guides were released, taken to the outskirts of Bamut at gunpoint, and told to wait until they were contacted: The boyeviki were checking the Cuny group's documents with regional headquarters in Achkhoi-Martan.

On April 2, the Cuny group was released and instructed to go to Achkhoi-Martan, where, according to Muradov, they were supposed to meet with General Maskhadov. Bad weather and Russian bombs delayed them for two days. Apparently the Russian doctors did not want to go, but the Chechens insisted. On April 4, a tractor pulled the group's ambulance through back roads thick with mud in the direction of Achkhoi-Martan. Before leaving Bamut, Cuny dictated a note written by Oleinik for Muradov to take by foot to the OSI in Nazran, where Muradov arrived later that day.

I have a copy of the note, scrawled hastily in nervous Russian: "All that's been happening has of course thrown us off balance," Oleinik writes, "but very little depends on us at present....As always we have landed in a predicament....If we're not back in three days, get everyone stirred up." Cuny requested that his office cancel meetings in Budapest and Dallas.

Muradov was asked to pick the group up in Bamut on April 7. When he returned, he received a note from a member of the group, it's unclear who, that gave passport information for each member so a search could begin if they didn't return soon. (The Russian doctors may have been using false names.)

The same day, one of the doctors managed to radio Sleptsovsk —the group had two field radios with a range of about twenty miles —to say everyone was fine and they'd be back in a day or two.

By coincidence, I happened to be near Bamut around that time. From the plains, as in Samashky, the Russians were now attacking the hills, particularly Bamut and surrounding villages. Fighters I talk to say Dudayev was in the same place, along with Cuny. According to one Chechen fighter, the house Dudayev stayed in was shelled. In his account to the authorities, Muradov said he heard Dudayev had congratulated fighters for capturing Cuny and the others because they worked for the Russian secret service and Oleinik was a "high official of the KGB" in Kazakhstan. This account has been denied by Dudayev, Chechen fighters, and Ingush officials looking for Cuny.

When I arrived in a small village near Bamut, the local commander told me Dudayev had been there and had given a medal to one fighter. But no foreigners, particularly missing ones, were mentioned in his story or others I heard.

From Bamut, the group appears to have reached Achkhoi-Martan and interviewed a local commander. Then it's difficult to tell. "If they went on to meet Maskhadov, they would have had to pass through territory controlled by Chechen fighters who oppose Dudayev," says Khamzat Bekov, the Ingush emergency minister.

Some search groups believe a breakaway band of Chechen fighters who do not obey Dudayev—and may even be working with the Russians—were holding the group. There are unconfirmed reports that the doctors performed operations in small villages inside rebel-controlled territory.

"Fred Cuny didn't do anything bad to anyone. That's why everyone is looking for him. Maybe he is being held by a group that is not under anyone's control," says Boris Agapov.

Adds one Chechen fighter involved in the search: "If Oleinik is a good woman, she is alive. But if she really did work for the KGB, I don't envy her."

WHAT IS THE OPEN SOCIETY INSTITUTE
AND HOW OPEN IS IT ANYWAY?

In the North Caucasus, the Open Society Institute is about as open as the old Politburo. Nobody can give me a straight answer as to what they do.

Soros Foundations primarily focus on post-Communist Central and Eastern Europe and the FSU, although they have spread to countries like South Africa, Haiti, and Burma. Soros groups have been criticized for being blatantly political, even for shaping policy, creating and promoting policy makers and profiting themselves from such arrangements in some newly independent countries. Aryeh Neier, president of the Soros Foundations, for years headed Human Rights Watch/Helsinki. In the 1980s, the organization was dogged by news reports that it was part of U.S. government-sponsored programs to bring down Communist governments in Central America.

In Russia, a parliamentary commission accused the Russian Soros Foundation of corruption—and of being a front for the CIA. The deputies later retracted their espionage accusations. Russia's secret services did not.

In May 1995, Slava Miklayev says Soros's budget for the North Caucasus is $2 million. In a telephone interview in August 1995, Aryeh Neier says the foundation has spent $1 million in the region, mainly on a hospital in Sleptsovsk, through the Moscow Institute of Traumatology and the Russian Red Cross. Smaller projects, Neier says, have included delivering baby food and working on sanitation projects.

"Fred enlisted Slava and Galina to help with these projects," he says, adding that Soros spent about $100 million in Russia in 1994–95.

"We relied on Fred to make recommendations. His disappearance had a chilling effect on us," he adds. "We would have spent more than one million dollars but because of Fred's disappearance we stopped."

Neier also says he has no idea what medicine Cuny was distributing when he disappeared. "The person who worked on this is Galina. She has disappeared. I don't know where to get the information. I wish I could enlighten you, but I can't."

Belan Barkinkhoyev, deputy head of the Ingush Republican Commission for the Distribution of Foreign Humanitarian Aid, says he has no idea what Soros is doing either.

"How much money did Soros spend? What are they doing here? We have no way of knowing. They didn't give out that information, but I can tell you about all the other agencies," he says as he pulls out a long computer list that outlines exactly what the other international aid groups are doing.

Barkinkhoyev says Soros contacted the commission to say they would be setting up in Nazran. But unlike other aid groups, Soros came in cold and never even asked to see any reports already prepared that assessed the region's humanitarian needs.

"If you're going to help, that's great, but I don't agree with their methods. They said they'd register, but they never did," Barkinkhoyev says. "We have more information on where the needs are and they've never even asked, although every other group has. It's not to control them but to spread the aid around. We need their help. We just wish they'd come in to talk to us. . . . I've never seen anyone [from Soros] ask what the needs are here."

The OSI also kept away from the bimonthly meetings held at the offices of the United Nations High Commission for Refugees (UNHCR), for aid groups to meet and discuss their programs to try to avoid overlap. While the meetings are voluntary, every international aid group in Nazran attends—except the OSI, a UNHCR official says.

Soros officials and Ingush government representatives say that OSI sends medicine to the Sleptsovsk central regional hospital, which then distributes it according to need. But Magomet Nakaskhoyev, the Sleptsovsk hospital doctor who is supposed to be coordinating the aid, says that although the OSI stores medicine on the hospital grounds, it is strictly under OSI control.

"The hospital," Nakaskhoyev says, "receives medicine on a case-by-case basis." They also received one X-ray machine, forty beds, one hundred pillows, and a respirator from Soros. "There were other things we needed, but they said they had no money."

The OSI doctors are first-rate, Nakaskhoyev says. But where they go, who the medicine is for, is all a "fog" to him. What is clear, though, is that most of the Soros aid is not going to Chechen refugees in Ingushetia.

Alexander Samkov, the Moscow doctor in charge of the Soros medical project in Ingushetia, also says he doesn't know why Cuny left for Chechnya.

We speak in a small, stuffy hospital room. Doctors who are well trained in working in conflict zones keep walking in and out, eternally smoking Russian cigarettes. Samkov describes two large convoys that Soros groups have sent from Moscow to Ingushetia since February. The second convoy contained two trucks, one jeep, one Khamaz, and four supertrucks that hold up to twenty tons each.

But Samkov can't adequately explain what was in the convoys, nor can anyone else. I've seen the medicine at Soros storage headquarters in the Sleptsovsk hospital. One small garage-like room on hospital territory filled with boxes, opened and unopened, that looks more like a junk room than an organized, well-categorized humanitarian aid stockroom.

What was in the two large convoys? And where is the stuff now?

"I don't know and I don't know anybody who knows," Neier says.

According to Samkov, Soros has, as of May 1995, so far spent $212,000 on medicine and has given an additional $80,000—with another grant of $80,000 expected soon—to the Russian Red Cross.

Soros does, however, appear to be building a first-rate trauma center on hospital grounds. When I visit, the rooms are filled with expensive new Western equipment—even fancy hospital beds and surgical lights. The hospital looks ready to open immediately, especially with the war on. But the equipment is untouched; some

Ingush women are painting the stairs blue. By July 1995, the hospital still hasn't opened. And Cuny is still missing.

By then, Soros has paid Intertect $170,000 to help pay for the Cuny search, Neier says. "I was very close to Fred personally. His presence looms very large over us."

CHAPTER 21

Chechnya, Part III:
Ode to Grozny

On Helicopters and a City Destroyed:
Fighters, Kidnappers, and Women
with Kalashnikovs You Don't Want to
Mess With

I may go out there. It's God's last good acre, he says. It won't all be fighting. It'll be riding and walks and wonderful people and new music and all sorts of things. The trouble is . . . things are frightfully tense. I'd be a drag on him. Specially with the way they treat women down there. I mean they wouldn't know what to do with me. It isn't that I mind everything being frightfully primitive and basic, but Larry would mind for me. And that would distract him, which is the absolute last thing he needs.

— JOHN LE CARRÉ, *Our Game*

The helicopter gunships hover above us like flies, like a plague. I feel like I'm on the set of a "M*A*S*H" television episode: good atmosphere for a story, too far away to be real.

I go to sleep listening to gunfire, explosions from nearby villages, and the steady helicopter buzz. "I hate helicopters," Olivia says. "I have nightmares about them."

For me, the sound doesn't mean more than what it is. The threat, the killing reality it represents, has not yet been incorporated into my own personal realm of experience. I am not yet afraid.

* * *

Lunchtime at our driver Magomet's. A woman, early thirties, deep bags under her eyes, is there. With Magomet, we not only get fed constantly, we—over time—also get introduced to a network of fighters, including "Rosa," one of the women boyeviki I have so wanted to meet. Rosa has just arrived in Sleptovsk with a new load of refugees, in a car stuffed to capacity. She has been fighting in Bamut and has not slept in days.

Dressed in a bronze metallic sweater, long skirt, and polka-dot head scarf, Rosa looks like just another hardworking Chechen housewife. Dark hair frames a strong face and compassionate eyes.

Rosa tells her story at the dining table. The Muslim culture is so patriarchal that the women, who cook, do not sit down to eat with the men. But Rosa does.

She is from a small mountain village. "When the Russians invaded, I went to find my sister and her family in Grozny," she says. "I felt I had to help. I had this image of my brother lying down, bleeding. Everyone fighting is my brother. I had no training but I knew I could help.

"As soon as I arrived in Grozny, I met an older woman who was organizing female battalions to help care for the wounded. The woman had lived in Afghanistan during the war, with her husband, who was a Soviet officer. She said the fighters really needed women to help. I joined that day."

The women, aged seventeen to fifty-five, soon mastered Grozny's vast underground network of passageways and bunkers. They found injured fighters and transported them for treatment to the bunker of the charred presidential palace. "We never had any men with us," Rosa says. "We acted independently from them. We never even knew each other's last names."

Soon Rosa was on fighting missions. Like most Chechen women, she had learned how to use daggers and guns for hunting at an early age. "Once I got my first machine gun, it was no problem at all," she says. "There were times when the men said they didn't want to take a woman, but I'd go anyway."

Rosa also goes on shopping missions—for weapons. They are bought directly from the Russians. The sales involve such large quantities of weapons, it is difficult to believe the corruption does not reach up to the highest echelons of the Russian army.

"We can make any deal we want with the Russian army and OMON [Interior Ministry] troops, as long as we have the cash," Rosa says. "Sometimes, they even come to us." Rosa's battalion has just bought 36 machine guns at about 1.8 million rubles a gun (at a time when 5,000 rubles equal one dollar), and 2,000 grenades.

"We get a shopping list from our commander and make the deal. It's the Russians who make the contacts. They don't renege. Lots of Russians would sell their own mothers."

Often, the Russians' only request is that the weapons not be used on the troops who sell them. While Rosa negotiates, the actual exchange is between men. The fighters then bribe Russian soldiers at checkpoints to be allowed to pass through.

"Villagers who don't fight also contribute to the war by selling their possessions, even some of their farm animals and cars, so the boyeviki can buy guns," Rosa says. Some weapons are also bought in other countries, like Turkey, while the rest, including APCs, are captured or nabbed from dead Russians.

Rosa also participates in reconnaissance missions, usually working with two men. "Sometimes," she says, "I've seen Russian women doing the same thing." One of the rumors rippling through the war zone is a bizarre tale of Amazon-like, tree-climbing Lithuanian sniper-women. Yet there are very few women boyeviki, perhaps one hundred, just as there are very few female Russian soldiers. (Officially, the Russians say there are none.)

While Rosa says she has no trouble using a gun, she did have a hard time trading her long skirt for a uniform.

"When I first put on a uniform, I was so embarrassed, so ashamed, that I put a skirt on top of the pants," she says. "But the commander said it was ridiculous. 'This is war,' he said. 'You're fighting with us like a man. Now you're our brother, not our sister.' "

The heavy boots were also uncomfortable. "I remember when our battalion was near a shoe store that had just been bombed," she says. "One of the boyeviki brought me back a brand-new pair of women's shoes."

Now Rosa is proud to show me her uniform: neatly folded camouflage pants, a jacket, and a black beret with the Soviet hammer and sickle; the Russian tanks I see wave the red Communist flag. She could be killed if soldiers found the uniform at a checkpoint.

"But they're easy to bribe," she says. "Once they snatched my earrings when I didn't have enough money to give them."

Rosa fights side by side with men, and then spends much of her time for sleeping taking care of the sick. Now she gets the respect she deserves. "When I walk into a room, even the commander will get up," she says proudly.

Magomet is sitting with us. So is another gray-haired man, who has just told us that he is looking for another wife. "When I listen to Rosa, I am ashamed," he says.

Rosa got married just before the war began. Her husband had four children from an earlier marriage. (In Chechnya, if a woman wants to divorce, she must leave her children with her husband.) After the marriage, her husband stuck her with the kids and ran off, apparently to Azerbaijan. According to Chechen law, Rosa is still considered a married woman. Men can divorce their wives by oral declaration in front of witnesses. Women can't.

Delicately, I ask Rosa about love. "Do any relationships develop between the male and female fighters?"

"There is no harassment," she says, embarrassed to speak frankly in front of the men.

"But what about love?" I ask.

I can feel the men prick up their ears. I wish they would leave. "I'm not allowed to fall in love," she says. "Comrades can never have relations with each other. Besides, to be completely honest, there's no time. The smell of fresh blood still lingers with me."

Over time, Rosa's story comes out. Yes, there is a man she is deeply in love with. A soldier who saved her life—three times. "He's a strong man. A very tough fighter."

Over lunch, Rosa agrees to take us to the fighting. She suggests we go by horseback, on a twenty-mile trek, but a car may be safer. We can walk when we have to.

We—Olivia, our translator, our driver, Rosa, and I—are driving near Bamut, which is under Russian attack. The boyeviki are, as usual, stronger than the Russians anticipated. We drive over hills, avoiding main roads and Russian checkpoints, crammed into a broken-down Lada that is painfully slow.

The views: high, green hills overlooking towns, sheep, a lone boy on horseback. Finally, we arrive in a small village of bumpy roads and streams, past barefoot children, old men, shepherds with their flocks, to the gate of a Caucasian mansion in the middle of nowhere. The delicate ironwork above the gate is decked with the Muslim crescent and stars.

We are greeted by a tall young boyevik. He wears jeans, has short, cropped hair and a wide, flat nose, as if he's been in one too many a fight. Later, I discover that I know his mother and grandmother from the network of refugees. His grandmother has often told me I must stay in the Caucasus and marry a Chechen.

Even these matriarchs laugh as they describe him. "He's not exactly beautiful," says his grandmother, though he has a kind disposition, once you get to know him. He greets us with a stiff, tense smile. Rosa introduces us without offering his name.

"He's really an arms buyer," she whispers. "He travels to Moscow and Pakistan—he even kidnapped his wife."

Later, we hear more from Magomet. As usual, there are layers between layers; this man's brother apparently worked for Dudayev and falsified documents to obtain loans from Russia's central bank and now lives in Central Asia. "I don't trust him," Magomet says, displaying, perhaps, the general post-Communist distrust of the nouveaux riches, the belief that the only way to become so rich so fast is through illegal activity.

"He was always an uncultured, uneducated kid, bumming cigarettes when he was seventeen. He got rich too fast," Magomet says.

Invited in for tea, we walk upstairs to the main floor. The large interior has been stripped in case of attack. Bare walls and floor, a few tables. The only sign of former grandeur: a big black leather couch, imported from Moscow.

Our host's wife and child are with relatives in Ingushetia. "It's not safe for them here," he says.

Over tea, we talk about the war, as everyone does. We talk about logistics, where the worst fighting is, about how many tanks we saw on the way, the current fighting in Bamut, the massacre in Samashky. He's trying to get a sense of us. To see if he can trust us.

Finally, we toss on our flak jackets and jump into his four-wheel-drive. Our guide puts on a white Muslim skullcap. As with many boyeviki, religion seems to be new to him. When asked about the elaborate Arabic inscription hanging over his home, he laughs and says he doesn't know exactly what it means.

Loud techno music, the kind heard in Moscow dance clubs, blares. We go slowly through the village, and then fly over bumps and hills. Soon Chechen checkpoints that were invisible suddenly crop up on the hills. Fighters are everywhere, disguised as farmers in tractors, as shepherds with their flocks.

We park our jeep on the plains. A "farmer" jumps out of his tractor, Kalashnikov in hand, and embraces our host. Soon more fighters appear from nowhere (behind trees, from a hill). We climb farther, gasping for breath, till we are perched on a hill overlooking Bamut. We hear explosions; tens of thousands of shells have been pounding Bamut. We see clouds of black smoke, tanks.

Bamut apparently houses a former Soviet nuclear missile base. The boyeviki supposedly survive repeated bombardments because they are holed up in the tunnels and corridors of the complex, which includes four bomb-proof concrete shafts, once used to store medium-range ballistic missiles.

Even more boyeviki join us on the hilltop. Some are in camouflage, machine guns slung over their shoulders and strapped to their waists, daggers tucked into their trousers. A car rolls across the plains and more fighters emerge, one clad in blue jeans, a red T-shirt, and sneakers, another in shiny track pants, his battle gear to change into in hand. They grab a stash of machine guns from a nearby tree and climb up the hill to greet us.

The battalion is from a nearby village. The fighters are young biznesmeni, an architect, farmers. Men with wives and children, homes, dachas, cars. Men who could afford to flee when war began.

A person will forget, over time, the murder of a mother, Machiavelli said—even the Chechen blood feud only lasts one hundred years. But take away someone's land: *That* will never be forgotten.

The commander of the battalion is a forty-five-year-old farmer in a high karakul hat. His nom de guerre is Grandpa. This father of six never fought until the war began. "I signed up the first day," he says, his face etched with deep laugh lines highlighted by the late afternoon sun. "If there wasn't a war on, we'd take you to the mountains to fish and put some sheep on the fire. That's the way we should treat our guests. They call us fighters bandits, but I'm just a farmer who has worked the land all my life."

When war broke out, the Chechen fighters were mainly experienced Spetsnatz (special forces) soldiers who once fought with the Russians in Afghanistan. Doctors and lawyers, fourteen-year-old boys, and even some women joined the battalions in Grozny. But many of them are now dead. The new fighters include villagers drawn into fighting to defend their homes and avenge their loved ones.

The first six months of the war seem to have united Chechens behind Dudayev instead of fragmenting them the way the Russians had tried to do before the war by backing Dudayev's rivals. The war is no longer about independence. It's about survival.

"I'm not for Dudayev or any other politician," says the commander. "I'm for the freedom of my country. Russia is still an empire of evil, as your president used to call it, that has caused a lot of damage around the world. We're a small people, but we're very rich, with oil and mountains. The Russians want to go farther, through us to Turkey."

Adds Lone Wolf, a twenty-something boyevik with dark eyes and a bearded, weathered face: "Religion is a factor in the war but it's also political. Allah is helping us with Russian machine guns." Lone Wolf wears a green beret with the silhouette of a lone wolf sitting under the moon. It is not only his nom de guerre but also Chechnya's national symbol.

While we are talking, Rosa has quietly slipped behind us. She is sitting down, her long red skirt spread around her defiantly. A man's camouflage jacket is wrapped around her, a Kalashnikov at her side. A man in fatigues sits beside her. Their hands almost touch. He is tall, gaunt, exhausted, having just returned from Bamut. "When we last said good-bye, I didn't know if we'd see each other again," Rosa says.

The image that stays with me is of Rosa with her red skirt and Kalashnikov, on a hilltop, her hand close to her fighter's. Two silhouettes leaning into each other as the air grows cold and the sun sets. Explosions and the noise of destruction mix with the chirps of birds.

We head back to the village in twilight, giving Rosa's fighter a lift part of the way. He slips out of the jeep with his machine gun.

Rosa jumps out too. They embrace. "He saved my life," Rosa says again, as she gets back in.

It's dark now. "I think we should leave," Olivia says. She wants to spend the night in Urus-Martan, a safe area because the village is cooperating with the Russians. That means it won't be attacked. For now. But I want to stay with the fighters. The village we are in was shelled recently, but, our fighters say, there is no chance it will be shelled again tonight.

"The elders made a deal with the Russians. There are no fighters in the village, so it won't be shelled," our host says. That should have stopped me right there. Of course there are still fighters in the village. I am with them. Still, I want to stay. Olivia agrees, despite her misgivings.

It is pitch-black outside. We are in a garage, lit by a single dim bulb. (We don't want to be an easier target than we already are.) The garage has been transformed into "fighter central." Machine guns and fatigues are perched at the front.

Rosa is cooking. A broth of mutton with garlic, bread, and pickled tomatoes. Oranges we brought from Nazran. Green onions. About a dozen fighters are in the room. They eat in shifts. Rosa cooks from a small stove. There is no running water.

Around 11 P.M. after dinner, we walk outside, under the stars. Suddenly, the entire sky lights up. Brilliantly. It looks beautiful. I stand with our host and translator. The sky lights up again. They are worried. I don't yet understand what it means.

We go back inside. Then the shelling begins. We hear the first explosion. The walls shake. The room goes silent. "Don't worry," a fighter says. "It's a fluke, a stray. There may be a few more, but that will be all."

The shelling continues, at a steady, frighteningly regular pace. It's a surprise attack. I know it's a bad sign when even the fighters look worried.

We move to the back of the room, the safest place during an attack. There is absolutely nothing we can do. There are no bunkers in the hills to hide in. We just have to wait it out, and hope they miss.

"This can't be happening. They promised," says a bearded architect. He grabs his Kalashnikov and runs out to talk with the local Russian commander.

For me, this is one of the most puzzling and depressing moments. The village elder and Russian commander have an agreement. The Russians promise not to shell the village if the elders promise to give up the fighters and weapons. Of course, the village is filled with fighters. And the Russians are shelling. How this man could expect the Russians to keep an agreement in the midst of war, and then risk his life to negotiate with them, while carrying a weapon he has pledged not to have, is as insane and perplexing as anything I have seen here.

We sit on the floor, our backs against the wall. "You should sleep inside the house," our host says. But Olivia says ground level is safest. Rosa stays with us. The boyeviki are used to shelling; it doesn't seem to bother them. Our host brings some clean sheets, pillows, and mattresses from the house.

He pulls up a chair and offers us whiskey. We decline: Olivia is allergic. Drinking is the last thing I feel like doing.

"You don't have to sit here with us, you know," I say.

"I'm your bodyguard," he answers gallantly. But there's nothing he can do if we're shelled, I assure him. He soon leaves, along with our translator.

I lie down, but can't think of sleeping. Now I understand what Olivia means about helicopters. They buzz over our heads all night long. Rosa is so exhausted from the battle at Bamut that she crashes immediately. My heart is pounding so loud I can hear it. I remember so many stories.

I have never been in this situation before. My fears become irrational. I have just covered the Samashky massacre. I imagine troops, high on some kind of drug, storming this village.

"If the safe house is the target, we could be finished," Olivia says. "If we survive, the worst that could happen is the shelling will go on for days and we'll be trapped. But sometimes it stops at dawn for a few hours before starting again. If that happens, we may be able to leave. It's been their pattern, but they also like changing their patterns."

The helicopters continue to buzz and circle over our heads. Most of the shelling seems to be for Bamut, which is still under siege less than ten miles away. The problem is that we are so close, some of the shells end up here. I know more can drop at any moment.

"What time is it?" I ask. "Eleven twenty," Olivia replies. I ask again, five minutes later. The night continues this way. We hear the door of the main house open and close, fighters moving about. If they try to shoot down planes, we're really in trouble. If the Russians know we're living in fighter central, that's it. If they're just shelling indiscriminately, we have a chance.

We stay up all night, telling stories about stupid things we've done, about responsibilities we have. We talk just to talk. On one level, I am completely calm, save for my pounding heart and my senses, which are on superalert. There is nothing I can do. We both have time to think, analyze, and talk about what's really important. Situations, and relationships, that seemed so complex become surprisingly clear.

Every hour or so, I get up and pace. Briefly, in the middle of the night, I am sick.

We keep talking as we wait for the sun. Olivia talks about the story she is going to write.

"I'm not going to write anything," I say. "It's too close, too personal."

"I think you'll probably change your mind once we get out of here," she says.

By dawn, there is silence. Our driver comes in, soon followed by our translator. "It was very strange," the translator says. "I shared a bed with the host." He doesn't elaborate. I don't ask. We are anxious to leave immediately, before the shelling has a chance to begin again. Rosa wants to go back to Bamut. Our driver wants a cup of tea before anything is decided.

On our way, we stop in Urus-Martan. Rosa's sister and her family, including their sick, dying father and some brothers who have just returned from jobs in other Russian regions, live here. Still, Rosa's sister has buried most of their good stuff, even cutlery, prepared for an attack at any moment. Rosa asks me to take some pictures of the entire family. Her father, lying in bed, suspects, but does not really know how involved Rosa is in the fighting.

After that, we see our host in the most unexpected situations. He is in blue jeans at the market, where he slips some rubles to a grateful, and surprised, Chechen woman who is part of their extended family. He shows up at parliament, in a black suit. We have lunch in a private back room at one of Sleptsovsk's few restaurants.

His village is deserted now. It has been shelled so many times since then, I don't know who, or what, has survived.

A CITY DESTROYED

The hills leading to Grozny are pockmarked by bomb craters, tank encampments, simple white gravestones. On the way, we pick up an old farmer in sheepskin.

"I'm going to Grozny to find my son's body," he says.

The outskirts of Grozny are sprayed with bullets. *Freedom or Death* is scrawled on a wall. A bullet-riddled Soviet mural remains. THE ARMY AND THE PEOPLE ARE ONE.

Nothing, though, prepares me for the city center, which looks like a late-twentieth-century version of Dante's *Inferno* after a nuclear attack. Buildings are blasted beyond recognition, reduced to rubble. Others look like skeletons, Swiss cheese, so bullet-blasted they resemble intricate lacework patterns sewn by Russian babushkas. Naked roofs expose the buildings' guts, entire chunks of interiors that are now heaps of rubble mixed with broken glass, shell fragments, the odd personal possession: a tea kettle, an old helmet.

Striking in its defeat, like the city itself, is the charred corpse of the once-grand presidential palace, where men used to dance religiously each week; where Dudayev displayed the bloody heads of three men who, backed by Moscow, tried to topple his government in the summer of 1994; where fighters like Rosa lived underground during the battle for Grozny last winter.

"I don't speak much English, but welcome to hell," a young man says.

Each person we meet, each phrase uttered in passing, becomes a clue to understanding the incomprehensible: the old man coming to find the body of his son; the young man searching for his brother, who may be prisoner of men he once fought beside; the old woman at the market who grabs my hand—"*I used to have a daughter just like you*," she says, eyes filled with tears.

Grozny is worse than Dresden after World War II. The Russians didn't just capture this city after weeks of bombing and street-to-street battles last February. They destroyed it: vanquished, decimated, obliterated, humiliated it.

The destruction is excessive. Typically Russian. More than forty thousand Russian troops invaded in mid-December. By New Year's Eve, with Yeltsin and his comrades drinking champagne and smoking cigars on Russian television, the bombing of Grozny had begun in earnest. To understand the extent of the destruction, think about this: There were thirty-five hundred detonations a day during the height of the shelling in Sarejevo; in Grozny, there were four thousand detonations *an hour*, wrote Fred Cuny in the *New York Review of Books*.

In the midst of the rubble, the market is again bustling. About two hundred thousand of Grozny's prewar population of four hundred thousand have now returned to this city without water, sewage, electricity. There is nowhere else to go. Many of the returning residents are Russian pensioners who are without family. Often Chechen neighbors take them in. Most residents live in unsafe buildings. Disease is rampant. Packs of wild dogs eat corpses that litter the city. Unexploded mines are everywhere.

Tanks zoom by noisily, blasted buildings in the background. Old ladies sell sun-dried fish, vodka, beer. One bab even sells handfuls of bright yellow daffodils.

The Russian soldiers buy more than the civilians. They come with huge sacks and fill them with vodka, beer, dried fish.

"How can you talk to them?" shouts Heda Susayeva, fifty-two, verging on tears. "They are animals, barbarians. How do you think they can afford to buy things at the market? They buy vodka now because they steal and kill at night."

Masked Russian soldiers perch on tanks that blast through the city, scattering refugees. I snap a picture. A tank screeches to a halt. One soldier, with crazed, glazed eyes, demands my film.

"I didn't get a chance to take any pictures. You were too fast for me," I say. Fortunately, he leaves without the film.

Madness wanders through burned-out streets. One old man, with wide blue eyes, dirty green shirt, and gravity-defying white hair, sings me a mournful Russian ballad. "I play the saxophone," he says. "In 1957 my wife was the most beautiful woman in Moscow." The next time I see him, he has a wreath of leaves around his head. He hugs me and hands me a "Children for Peace" coloring book from the cart he lugs behind him.

Ruslan, a twenty-eight-year-old Afghan vet, handsome, thin, and nerve-wracked, also wanders about aimlessly. It looks like part of his face has been ripped off and sewn on again not exactly quite right, all scarred and twisted. "I was in Afghanistan. The Russians I fought with were my lifetime buddies," he says. "I didn't want to fight in this war. I never wanted to fight again in my life. But now my brother is held by Russians he may once have fought with. If I don't find him, I'm going to go after them. I'm going to find whoever took my brother and kill them."

Ruslan gives us an impromptu tour of his city. We start with the university, reduced to heaps of rubble. Not one room remains standing.

Streets are littered with bullets and shell, rocket, cluster, and needle bomb fragments, little pieces of metal, some as small as the tiniest bullet, others as large as body parts. Ruslan explains which piece of twisted, flat metal does what kind of harm. I reach to pick one up, as I have done many times before. "Don't touch that!" Ruslan shouts. "Some still explode."

We see the decomposing corpse of a man in the primal-soup-like stage, facedown by a flamed kiosk.

In Minutka, a suburb where there was heavy fighting, we meet three teenagers who are now trying to rebuild their family apartments in unsafe buildings that could collapse at any moment. Roman Sadayev, fifteen, takes us up dark stairs to show us his parents' flat. The door is locked. He carefully opens it with a key. Inside is bare. The floors have been freshly swept. The rebuilding is from scratch: Windows, cabinets, carpets, food have all been pilfered.

A terrible smell emanates from the building. "There are still some dead bodies in the basement, but no one will get them because of all the unexploded mines," Roman explains.

As we leave, an old man in an undershirt stares from a bombed building across the way. With true Chechen hospitality, Hassein Bashev invites us in for tea.

"Please excuse the mess. We just moved back two weeks ago. We were living with relatives in Ingushetia," says Bashev, who, at forty-five, looks seventy. The apartment is empty. Windows are taped with plastic. "We just rehinged our front door," adds Tovsari, his wife. "We found our sofa in the rubble outside. The Russians took everything else.

"Our children are with relatives. They'll come back once the house is in order," she says, with more optimism than I think possible. "I also want to wait until it's safer." There's still gunfire, especially at night.

On the outskirts of town, a lone horse nibbles at a glass-flecked rubble heap. Women show me pictures of their families. Fathers, husbands, sons are dead or missing. "I want to know whether anyone I love is still alive," one woman says.

"Where is this democracy we were promised?" she asks, reminding me that 90 percent of all Chechens voted for Boris Yeltsin in the 1991 presidential elections.

Yet despite the appearance of defeat, Grozny is far from conquered; the war for Grozny is far from over. The city is fast becoming a new center for guerrilla war. By day the city is relatively quiet. The soldiers shop in the market, or rip through town in their tanks. At night, gunfire is heard, curfews imposed, tracer bullets light the sky. Rebels raid Russian posts; Russians respond with terror.

"Just the other day, soldiers rushed into my flat and put a gun to my husband's head," one woman says. "Find us flowers, or you're dead." They were so drunk they had killed one of their own and were now going to bury him.

"Russians are animals. They have no respect for human life, women, or children. Only vodka," she adds.

It is a big change from the beginning of the war, when Chechen women felt sorry for the young Russian recruits. Some women— whose own sons were fighting against the Russians—took them in, fed them, and let them wash, for they were often starving and crawling with lice.

Even today, few Chechen women I know blame the young soldiers. Instead, they blame their leaders, and the special OMON and SOBR troops. Boyeviki vow to "get" everyone involved in the decision-making process. Attacks on Russians involved in the Samashky massacre have already begun. Top Russian leaders traveling through Grozny will be attacked soon.

I talk with some young recruits, who try to justify their presence with words that sound like they were brainwashed into their heads. "I want journalists to write the truth," says Dmitri, nineteen, a skinny kid with a gawky smile. "We're not all mercenaries."

"The killing was inevitable," adds Yuri, twenty-one, from Siberia. "People lived badly under Dudayev. Especially the Russians. That's why we're here."

"At least people were alive under Dudayev. Now Russians who live in Chechnya are dying too," I respond.

"My mother thinks the same way," says Yuri. "She came here with the committee of Russian soldiers' mothers. She wanted to bring me home, but I begged her to leave. Some mothers disappear doing that. She could have been arrested for protesting."

Such fear, steeped in decades of Soviet oppression, keeps protest numbers low. There are often no more than a few hundred people; one thousand, at most.

Yuri and Dmitri pose arm in arm, in their fatigues, for my camera. They look like children in soldiers' costumes.

I wander off on my own until I'm in front of the charred presidential palace, where an old man on an even older bicycle—one of the presidential palace's former caretakers—offers me one of several cold potato dumplings from a tattered sack. He has prepared them for some refugees.

Suddenly four soldiers rush up. "Get away!" they shout. "The area is mined!" The soldiers, in their late twenties, early thirties, are part of a special group in charge of disciplining soldiers. They wear earrings, head scarves, and bandannas. They seem to be more liberal, and friendly, than most.

"The soldiers need a lot of disciplining," says Pavel, shouldering his Kalashnikov. "A lot of soldiers lose it. War is war. Lots of innocent people get hurt. With such lawlessness, soldiers could start drinking and killing people, but lots of people who are peaceful during the day shoot at us at night. Even fourteen-year-old boys."

"It's worse than Afghanistan," adds Dmitri. "There is anarchy now. Soon there will be fascism. People voted Hitler into power. If someone like Zhirinovsky gets elected, it will be like 1937 all over again."

The soldiers carry the dog tags of their missing comrades. "We believe they're being held by the Chechens," Dmitri says. We write down the soldiers' names and later pass them on to some boyeviki and Ingush officials we know, along with letters Russian mothers wrote to sons they think are POWs.

At the beginning of the war, the Chechens treated prisoners fairly well. But as the war, and atrocities, have continued, it's gotten ugly on both sides.

"When the mothers of the Russian soldiers came, we helped them with a prisoner exchange," one rebel fighter explains. "But the Russians are killing our people and torturing prisoners in Mozdok. We can't feed the prisoners too well when our own people are starving."

And if the boyeviki know the prisoners were involved in a massacre—or if they capture pilots, whom they consider to be the worst—treatment is as savage as in past centuries.

From the palace, we head to the only hospital that's functioning. It lacks a front door, windows, and lights. The main floor is deserted but there is one floor with a few patients and one doctor, working with electricity from a generator.

"Those who survived the bombing are now dying from cold, hunger, and disease," the doctor says. "Cholera and diphtheria may soon reach epidemic proportions." Disease stems from all the dead bodies lying around, the wild dogs who eat the corpses, and a city-wide lack of water, soap, and sewers.

At one communal water pump, old men in veterans' uniforms, covered with medals, line up with women who carry poles across their shoulders, pails attached to each end. Fred Cuny was working on a water project for Grozny, but he didn't get beyond the talking stage for the project before he disappeared.

To try to cope, the Russians have set up a provisional government in Grozny. Walking into Russian-controlled government headquarters, in an old building that has survived, perhaps for this purpose feels like stepping into Vichy. Swarms of people are lined up outside. Soldiers pose for pictures to send home along with what they've stolen. Russian trucks carry everything from furniture and televisions to carpets and cutlery. We show our passes to OMON troops and make our way inside.

The building is dingy and lacks lights, like the rest of the city. But the people are different. There are more suits with fedoras. Though the combat fatigues of commanders never let you forget the war, the heavily perfumed women are dressed in high heels, short and long skirts. Women with lipstick, hairdos, and jewelry.

Barren offices have vases with fresh-cut roses and tulips. The Russian government says it will spend $1 billion just this year to help rebuild Grozny. (It doesn't happen.)

We are in an office, waiting for an official, when a small woman with badly bleached, Soviet-style hair rushes in. She says she is a Russian journalist, and hugs everyone she sees. "I haven't seen you since Kabul!" she squeals. It's her first time back in Chechnya "in years."

Although she is a journalist, she writes out the valuable press passes we need that no one else will give us. Journalists are issued special passes in Moscow. Once here, they are supposed to be used to get another pass. But "Ivan Ivanov" is always out to lunch or in Moscow, then there's a weekend, and on Monday he's in Mozdok. Come back tomorrow, soldiers say, laughing. In the meantime, other soldiers threaten, and sometimes arrest, some journalists without this pass. Fortunately, the blonde journalist issues them even for our translator, who doesn't have any of the proper documents. This, too, is typically Russian.

We soon meet Ruslan Gaivbekov, the Chechen minister of reconstruction in the provisional administration. Gaivbekov, who has worked in construction for thirty years, says it will take months before water and sewers are restored—and seven or eight years to rebuild the city.

I tell him what we've witnessed: the dead bodies, the unsafe buildings people live in, the wild dogs, the lack of water, the epidemics. "There are so many soldiers cruising around, why don't you give them some reconstruction work to do?" I ask.

"You're mistaken," he says. "Grozny is in fine shape. People living in dangerous flats have already been removed. There are hardly any mines or corpses left."

His state of denial is so outrageous, it seems useless to continue our conversation.

The sun is going down. I go back to the market.

A man who speaks English asks if I can help him get a visa to Canada. We pass the old man in the green shirt, who no longer recognizes me.

Magomet drives us by his old home. *Zdes zhivut lyudi* has been hastily scrawled across the door in white, as it has been on houses across Chechnya. It means "People live here," an appeal to Russian soldiers not to shoot: Civilians, women and children, live here—not fighters.

KIDNAPPED! STEALING THE BRIDE

After Grozny, Olivia, another colleague, and I travel to Dagestan, Chechnya's neighboring Russian republic, to report on the refugee situation. Tens of thousands of refugees are holed up here in inhumane quarters: dozens of people per room, with no water and a single mattress on the floor, on which they take turns sleeping. Some fled their villages in the middle of the night, barefoot. While they can get by in the summer months, they will freeze come winter. There is barely enough humanitarian aid to feed them.

Getting to Dagestan isn't easy. We drive across Chechnya, from embattled Grozny through the destroyed eastern towns of Argun and Gudermes. En route we see shelling, tanks, explosions, a shot-down Russian plane. New graves scattered alongside dusty roads. The bridge to Dagestan has been bombed. We are so close to the shelling that Russian troops, now posted every few miles or so, refuse to let us through. Our route now becomes even more circuitous, by streams and up one hill so steep we have to get out of the car and climb.

We are following the trail of tens of thousands of Chechen refugees who have fled their burned-out villages for the strange and somewhat hostile refuge of Dagestan, home to more than forty nationalities as enmired in ethnic tension as Russia itself. The brightly colored Chechen homes are replaced by Dagestan houses the monochrome color of mud. The roads to Khasavyurt, the capital, which seem to serve as garbage dumps, are even dustier than in Chechnya. Cholera epidemics spread here long before the refugees arrived. By April 1995, more than 110,000 Chechen refugees have flooded into the Khasavyurt region alone, according to the International Committee of the Red Cross.

The first person I meet in the capital is Umar Dzhavtayev, an ethnic Chechen who has transformed his commercial store into an unofficial refugee center. The situation between the Dagestanis and refugees, whom government officials say they don't have enough funds to support, is tense. Dagestanis not only fear the volume of refugees, they also see the war spreading to their own land. The Russians have already bombed inside the borders of Dagestan. Lately bombing and border skirmishes have increased.

Dzhavtayev is already preparing for war in Dagestan. "If that happens," he says, "I'll shoot my wife so the Russians won't get her, then take my boys to fight."

A tall chain-smoker in a burgundy blazer, Dzhavtayev asks where we plan to sleep that night. It is 8 P.M. We have no idea. We have driven straight from Chechnya and there are no hotels in Khasavyurt. We accept his offer of hospitality.

Dzhavtayev drives us to his home, a modest but relatively spacious two-room flat with television and stereo but, like all Chechen homes I know—including millionaires' mansions—lacking basics such as indoor plumbing. Still, it is bigger than the one-room apartments many Russian families are accustomed to. Like most Chechen homes I see, it seems to be connected to a second home, inhabited by relatives.

The home we're in consists of one bedroom and a small sitting room with a coffee table and two chairs, where we eat the delicious soups, pilafs, and pickled tomatoes Medina prepares. The third person sits on a cot. Outside, laundry dries in the dust. By the door are a large pitcher, bowl, and soap for washing.

Dzhavtayev foists us upon his wife, her young girlfriend, and a host of children. "Treat my home as your own," Dzhavtayev says grandly. "Everything I have is yours. My wife is here to serve you." He then disappears until after midnight.

Used to housing refugees, Medina, thirty-two, expertly unfolds three cots complete with extra sheets and blankets. An attractive woman who works too hard, Medina smiles a mouthful of gold teeth, even though she is probably not too pleased to have three strangers invade her home for an indefinite period of time.

"So how did you meet Umar?" I ask.

"He kidnapped me at the market," Medina says matter-of-factly. "I was nineteen. He didn't let me see my family for ten months. I cried every day. But he was used to it. I was his fourth wife."

Umar? The seemingly mild-mannered Chechen who pulled out chairs, held doors, even opened his home to us? It is the first time I have heard such a story first-hand. The fighter near Bamut had also kidnapped his wife. But the incidents I have heard about sounded so, well, romantic, more like eloping than kidnapping: The couple knew each other, it was prearranged, dowry and all. I didn't think women were being taken by force anymore. Not in the 1990s. As I understood it, Chechens, who did not fully convert to Islam until late last century, are moderates—far from fundamentalists. Men drink and smoke, women reject the heavy black chadors of the Iranians for long (but still potentially sexy) skirts and printed head scarves.

Some Chechens do, however, still kidnap their wives and practice polygamy. Only now do I realize that I have only ever heard these stories from a male point of view. I also realize that the farther east I go, the harsher the landscape, the more isolated Chechens are from society around them, and the more harsh, even cruel, the customs become.

In the North Caucasus, Chechen men usually treat me as they would a man. That means I sit at the dinner table with the men while the women serve us and return to the kitchen, despite my request to have them join us. I am treated with respect—by Chechen fighters, commanders, officials, civilians—even though I wear jeans and leave my hair uncovered.

Before this trip, I traveled with a male interpreter and it made a difference. Now I am traveling with two female colleagues. We are still treated with respect, but not with the same camaraderie. This is the first time I have been alone with Chechen women. There are no men, Chechen or Western, to monitor or inhibit the conversation.

Perhaps realizing she has a captive audience, Medina cracks open a bottle of French champagne (never mind that she is Muslim) and offers us the ubiquitous Snickers bars, sliced in quarters like party sandwiches. We settle in for a night of female bonding.

Although men are theoretically (and practically) heads of the family, relations between the sexes are much more complex. Men take on more wives as they age. It is not uncommon for octogenarians to take on "pretty young things." The wife of one man, teased by her family because her fuller figure makes her look more Russian than Chechen, says she is thankful he is looking for a new wife. "It will be great to get him off my hands," she jokes. "It doesn't matter if she has money or not, but she has to be beautiful to get into this family." The first wife may help her husband choose the second wife, who is often wife number one's personal helper, an extra hand to cook, clean, and look after children.

In life-or-death situations, a woman's word, however, rules. If a man insults another man, a cycle of blood revenge can erupt for the next hundred years. But women have the power to stop the feud. "All a woman has to do is take off her head scarf and wave it in the air," Magomet says. "It doesn't matter if it's a fight between two people or two clans, the feud has to stop. Only women have the power to give birth, so only they can stop death."

Yet in all other instances, it is the man who must be obeyed.

"Umar kidnapped his first wife when he was sixteen," Medina says, "But she didn't get pregnant, so a year later he kidnapped his second." By age eighteen he had already married three wives and booted them out when they didn't get pregnant. He decided to wait a few years until, at age twenty-four, he tried again and kidnapped Medina.

Medina has produced four children, the youngest of whom looks uncannily like her husband. Sitting under a large charcoal portrait of Umar, depicted with a fedora angled jauntily on his head, Medina now says she is totally in love with him, and would "kick him out" before letting him take another wife. "What would another wife have that I haven't got?"

Still, her life is tough. Like most Chechen women, Medina spends her days looking after her children, cooking, and cleaning, even as Dzhavtayev places more demands on her. He even makes her polish the gas pedal of his car before driving us into the city center. "Medina is a wonderful woman. I hope you appreciate her," Olivia says. Dzhavtayev laughs. "She has her place—the home. Just as I have mine."

It is even worse for Medina's young girlfriend, also named Medina, who now lives with the family, drinks champagne with us, and, sometimes, when the conversation gets too close, looks ready to burst into tears.

Dark-haired young Medina, twenty, carries herself proudly. She struts into the room, enveloped in heavy perfume that smells like Poison, protected by an armor of makeup, from bright red lips to black-outlined eyes. All this on a girl so slight it looks like a good gust of wind would blow her over.

This Medina was also at the market when she was kidnapped last year. Her abductor was a handsome young doctor of twenty-one. His strategy also seems a little more devious than usual.

"He told me his mother was sick and asked if I would go home with him to help," young Medina says. "He never let me leave." Medina stayed with her husband, trapped, for a year without seeing her parents.

Still, young Medina's husband wasn't a bad guy, she says. "I might even have fallen in love with him." The problem was his family; in particular, his mother. "She treated me like a slave. She made me get up at four thirty every morning to sweep the yard." She even listened outside their bedroom door.

Before the ordeal began, young Medina says, she used to be heavier. The work, combined with stress, shrank her to her current ghost-like state. To prove her point, she pulls out a photo album filled with pictures of her looking pleasantly plump in a white ruffled wedding dress. "He paid five hundred dollars for this," Medina says. The album is filled with pictures of her, and lots of blank spaces. "I ripped him out," she explains, adding that her family wasn't even invited to the wedding, which was held against her will. Finally, Medina escaped, although technically she is still married.

Now young Medina's status in Chechen society has significantly decreased. She can marry again, but she will never be able to be someone's first wife. To be less than that means further subjugation.

"Why don't you pretend it never happened and marry someone from another village?" I ask.

"It's always better to tell the truth," she says, though not for moral reasons. "One woman's husband threw her out of a window, naked, on their wedding night when he discovered she wasn't a virgin."

For now, young Medina smiles bravely through her shield of fierce red lipstick, which she wears even though Dzhatayev, who is effectively her guardian, is opposed to makeup and forbids his own wife to wear any. Although young Medina still wears long skirts, she has replaced her head scarf with the symbolic Chechen hairband. Still, she says she refuses to go to school or to work. "A woman's life is miserable, but it's important to be with the family."

The older Medina, however, dreams of a career. She wants to start trading at the city's bustling, and filthy, marketplace—kidnapper central. Dzhavtayev, as might be expected, has outlawed this plan.

Getting kidnapped, if it's by the right person, may not be so bad, I reason. No more time wasted agonizing over which man to choose. Suddenly, unexpectedly, the decision is made. But the reality, of course, is almost never like this. Most Chechen women end up like my hostess, married and making the best of it, their options limited. Women who try to escape, like young Medina, end up forced to the periphery of Chechen society, strong enough to cut an unhappy bond but too afraid to cut all ties and reach beyond the life they know.

And then there are women like Rosa. Perhaps, through the barbarism of war, the courage of women like Rosa will further the rights of future generations of Chechen women, offering new heroines for this blood-soaked, bullet-and-dagger-ruled country.

By the time I leave Chechnya, the mud-soaked fields are being transformed into meadows of brilliant red poppies in waist-high yellow and green grass. As we fly back to Moscow on Aushev's private presidential plane, courtesy of Ingush vice president Boris Agapov, I wonder how many of the fighters and families I know are still alive.

I can't stop thinking about all this later, at the Kremlin, watching Yeltsin and Clinton in the most ridiculous press conference, following the May 1995 summit. Perhaps it is so outrageous because I'm seeing it up close, the unedited version. Maybe they're all this absurd.

The Washington press pool carted around with Clinton asks questions that have nothing to do with Russia. It is not their fault. The Moscow-based correspondents should be asking the questions.

A Russian woman screeches at Yeltsin about the massacre in Samashky. He says that there has been no massacre, that Russian troops are rebuilding Grozny, and that there is a cease-fire.

Clinton says nothing. It's sickening to see such weakness up close. Three seconds after Yeltsin finishes speaking, a Chechen village is bombed.

The day before, Clinton and other world leaders, except Helmut Kohl, watched a military parade in Red Square, celebrating the fiftieth anniversary of V-E Day. The troops included those fresh with medals from Chechnya, despite a Russian promise to Clinton that troops who fought in Chechnya would not be part of the celebrations.

Russia is now expanding its army's "peacekeeping" roles in ex-Soviet republics, threatening to "defend" ethnic Russians outside Russia's borders and announcing its readiness to break limits on troop use imposed by the 1990 Conventional Forces in Europe Treaty. Russia is also strengthening the power of its newly named Federal Security Service, allowing it to jail Russian citizens independently and to increase its international espionage activities.

How far from the hopes and dreams of 1991. The world was shocked when Gorbachev approved the use of force in the Baltics. Three Soviets died during the August 1991 coup; at least 150 died during the October 1993 parliamentary rebellion. And now, at least 30,000 people have died in Russia's civil war in Chechnya, and world leaders flock to Moscow to celebrate the victory over fascism—and say nothing about the current atrocities.

After the press conference, General Alexander Korzhakov stands outside the Kremlin on a miserable, rainy May day. Journalists from around the world pile out without even noticing this man with the greasy, side-swept hair who looks like a midwestern used-car salesman. He is smiling, pleased, perhaps, that democracy is over.

Over drinks with Cigarman one night, we talk about Chechnya. He, too, is writing a nonfiction book. It's about Central Asian oil, intrigue, and political takeovers.

Like me, he is also working on a novel. "It's about a retired spy and an active spy who make money and launch a revolution, while deposing a democratically elected president in one of the ex-Soviet empire's newly independent republics."

We are in the dungeon-like bar of the Baltschug Kempinski Moskau Hotel. Cigarman walks me across the street to my apartment. The building has no entrance code. Sometimes drunks show up inside. Friends have come home to other flats to find blood and victims of stabbings in their hallways.

"As soon as we open the door," I warn him, "a neighbor's psycho dog will begin to bark." Sure enough, I open the door, and 'Psychadog' begins to bark.

Cigarman, the biker-tough war correspondent, turns pale. "I hate dogs," he says. "You don't know how much I hate dogs."

"Psychadog's bark really is worse than his bite," I explain, though some friends won't even come up the stairs when they hear him. "He really is harmless."

Our flat is still great, but crumbling. The hallway is wretched. Another unpleasant feature besides Psychodog is an evil smell that emanates from the first floor, where a babushka takes care of more than twenty cats. (Even that didn't stop the rat problem when we first moved in.)

We stand at the landing on the second floor. Normally when he sees me, Psychadog stops barking and lets me through. This time, he doesn't stop. He continues his vigil, barking madly, furiously, refusing to let us pass where his master lives. Finally, Cigarman bangs the newspapers he's holding on Psychadog's head. The dog whimpers and scampers away.

"A dog ripped out a chunk of my leg in Sukhumi once," Cigarman says by way of explanation. "I'm off to Alaska to go fishing. It's good to cleanse the soul. I need to disappear for a while—just remember to put me in your book!"

In April 1996, Dudayev is murdered. By the winter of 1997, General Aslan Maskhadov, whom Cuny was believed to have been searching for at the time of his disappearance, is elected president of Chechnya. The status of postwar Chechnya is much like prewar Chechnya—relative independence within the Russian Federation. The main difference: all the murder and carnage that took place in between.

CHAPTER 22

Dress Rehearsal

Election Fever, Part I:
Cappuccino on Hold—An Armed Raid
at the Baltschug Café

> It doesn't matter who people vote for, it's how you count the ballots.
> — attributed to JOSEPH STALIN

I fly back to Moscow to cover the December 1995 parliamentary elections after a six-month absence. It's the longest I've been away since I first arrived almost four years ago. The airport has changed so much since then. While the evolution was gradual, the effect is overwhelming. Food stands and Chanel lipstick, CDs and American news magazines. Even brightly lit signs and a genuine Irish pub. The dismal, ancient duty-free by the baggage carousels, with cheap electronics, cigarettes, and liquor—once an oasis for desperate, last-minute shoppers—is now overlooked by almost everyone.

The customs officer keeps me waiting. (For a time, there were even signs warning travelers that bribing customs officials is a criminal offense.) I just smile at her, knowing there's nothing wrong with my visa. Finally, I'm the last one in line. Anywhere. Soon the other women officials come over to nudge her. "Tanya. *Bystro!* Hurry up! You're making us all late!"

"Is this the only copy of your visa?" she asks. "Yes," I reply. "You should make a photocopy of it. You never know when you could get robbed," she says. Uh-oh. I'm back in the Moscow mind-set. Is she being helpful or is that some kind of message? The paradoxes begin as soon as I disembark. The custom declarations now read "199_." The paper is better quality. But there are no English forms. Only Russian or German.

I head to the rusty baggage carts. When I first arrived, they were one dollar. Now they're ten thousand rubles, or two dollars. But arriving passengers must pay in rubles, even though you're not allowed to take them out of the country, so Russians, and foreigners, often break the law—by paying in rubles they're not supposed to have—before they even leave the airport.

One year ago, a taxi service briefly operated beside the baggage carts. If I used the service, the woman behind the counter would walk me through customs so I, and the driver, wouldn't have to wait in the hours-long line. Now the taxi service is outside customs. They cabs are more expensive than they were, but still safer than the streets. (There are stories of criminals trailing Russians who come off planes with large packages which might contain items like stereo systems. Their homes are often robbed the next day.)

I argue with the taxi service about a price and am soon on my way. I ask Igor, the chain-smoker in the Lada, whom he'll vote for in December's parliamentary elections, which will be followed by two rounds of presidential elections in June and July 1996.

"Yeltsin's a drunkard," he says, flicking his neck the way Russians do to signify drunkenness. "But I don't want to go back to the Communists. Maybe Zhirinovsky. They're all crazy—we're doomed, no matter who we vote for!"

The next morning, I pop into the Duma, the Russian parliament's lower house, for an unscheduled chat with Gennady Zyuganov, the Communist Party leader, who will soon sweep the polls in an unprecedented Communist comeback that would have been unthinkable when I first moved here. Gennady's English, and his suits (banker blue, red ties), are getting better. He no longer publicly hangs out with the anti-Semitic, ultra-nationalist fascists he used to speak with at rallies when he was lower in the polls. "In the past four years, people realize they've lost their jobs, their social security, their education. They yearn to get them back and they're disillusioned with Yeltsin, who is neither a Communist nor a democrat," Zyuganov bellows as we storm through the Duma's halls, trailed by aides and hangers-on. Distinctly unimpressive on television, Zyuganov beams with charisma among small followings.

We head to the Duma's cafeteria. As we stand in line, Zyuga-nov's presence causes a small, whispering buzz. He feasts on two beastly looking boiled hot dogs and lemon tea. My smoked salmon and vegetables cost less than ten thousand rubles, two dollars, ridiculously subsidized in a country where workers haven't been paid in months.

I leave the Duma's seventh floor twenty minutes before a bomb explodes. Typical Moscow: Police believe it's a publicity stunt by a mob-linked member of parliament who has pulled this kind of thing before, in his hometown of Samara. A friend tells me she just turned on TV to see her boyfriend, a Russian photographer, covered in blood, his face cut by flying glass. He has been injured by a car bomb that has killed eleven people in Chechnya.

That's just the beginning. On the way to my old flat, I stop in at the Baltschug hotel, just up the street. Over cappuccino, I read in the *MT* that a dozen plainclothes OMON troops armed with machine guns recently stormed the café looking for mafiya lead-ers who apparently use the hotel as a base. Forcing customers to the ground, the OMON troops arrested every guest carrying a weapon. Fleeing gunmen sprayed bullets on their way out the front door. The hotel has even physically changed. The interior is draped in plastic. There's some sort of remont going on. Soon the lobby looks like any other seedy lounge, with unshaven mobsters smoking on an out-of-place sofa.

Other news I read my first week back: A top Moscow city offi-cial is knifed to death in front of his home; a candidate, his cam-paign adviser, and a business partner are gunned down. Soldiers kill their commander during a drunken rampage in the Far East; three children die when a man holds a kindergarten class hostage in North Ossetia on the border with Chechnya. Back in Moscow, art lovers are evacuated from the Tretyakov Gallery after a bomb threat.

All this in less than one week. Murder is the norm nowadays. I remember when people were shocked in 1993 by stories about mobsters who killed old Muscovites—and then entire families—for their apartments; about corpses uncovered when the snow melted in the forests outside Moscow. Now the number of contract killings has jumped from 102 in 1992 to 562 in 1994, and higher this year. Meanwhile, the papers report how Moscow schools will shut down, and city hospitals, including the elite sanitarium where Yeltsin is recuperating from heart trouble, if not drying out, will be quarantined because of a flu epidemic that has so far hit 338,000 people (myself included). The government is once again threatening to make foreigners submit to AIDS tests, and Moscow police call for army backup to help guard against Chechen terrorism. (Shortly before I arrive, Chechen boyeviki claim they have buried a thirty-pound box of explosives and radioactive material somewhere near Izmailovsky Park. It is a warning from the fighters: They are prepared—and have the capability—to strike in Moscow, if and when they desire.)

These are the scenes that form the backdrop to Russia's supposedly free and fair parliamentary elections. Over the next few weeks, I catch up with old friends. Heidi is still in the flat, taking pictures. Olivia is recovering from a terrible car accident. Georges is still with Katya. They met at one of our parties. I think it was the one with the fist fight. Katya runs an expensive jewelry boutique in a new luxury hotel off Red Square. The hotel also boasts a Maxim's restaurant.

I also catch up with Alexandra, my television journalist friend from Kalmykia. We meet for lunch at El Dorado, an apt name for this trendy restaurant, filled with Russian mobsters and nouveaux, beside a frozen fish supermarket on the Garden Ring. Security types lounge outside. A man with a cell phone decides if, and when, to let you in. (There's often a line, though I've noticed the maître d's propensity to let the broad-shouldered guys in first.) We are the only women in a smoky room full of men in turtlenecks. Alexandra is wearing a bright blue fake fur, looking glamorous as usual. Russian television is finally giving her a decent contract, by Russian standards. The contract includes a spacious new apartment, though Alexandra still takes the metro every day.

Alexandra has also been traveling—India and the United States for business, following Kirsan, the young millionaire president of her republic. She has even met the Dalai Lama, and Richard Gere, who, like Alexandra, is a Buddhist. Alexandra and her sister have also been to Paris.

When she tells me there's now even a Thai restaurant in Moscow, we decide to go. It is 6 P.M. on the night of the parliamentary elections. In the restaurant Alexandra borrows the owner's cell phone and calls Prime Minister Viktor "Cherny" Chernomyrdin's press secretary. He is a former colleague who used to be a Southeast Asia correspondent for Russian television. He joins us from his office in the White House, which is nearby.

We then drive with him to Cherny's campaign headquarters at the Mir Hotel, beside the grandly lit White House. The prime minister is also head of Russia's pro-government new political party, Our Home Is Russia. (Cherny's rivals call it "Their House.") The campaign posters show a bizarre picture of Cherny pressing his thumbs and fingertips together to make a triangular-shaped object which looks like the roof of a house. This is a Russian double entendre, because *krisha*, or 'roof,' also means a mafiya protector —which just about everyone needs in order to survive, and prosper, in the new Russia.

Elections are still a new concept in Russia. The atmosphere at campaign headquarters is far from the sophisticated yet similarly drunken festivities of North America. There are guards at the entrance, special passes to acquire, throngs of drunken officials and yupsters, Russia's golden elite. There is plenty of vodka. Waiters come by with glasses of champagne. Tables are stacked with "party" sandwiches, Russian style: salami on white bread. Two women hand out plastic bags with party favors: Our Home baseball caps and other mementos that I lose by the end of the evening.

Spirits are high, even though Cherny comes in third, behind the Communists and Zhirinovsky. (The pundits play down Zhirinovsky, but his grass-roots organizing has served him well.) The big players in the party watch results in hotel rooms on the upper floors, where more alcohol flows. I interview Sergei Koptev, the young brain behind Our Home's $1.2-million advertising campaign, which was far more visible than those of other political parties. Some critics say the campaign backfired, that people were fed up with so much publicity. (Koptev disagrees: "We tried to create a dominant presence to block our competitors. It was a sophisticated campaign for our country.")

Election night is far more low key than the Hollywood-style fiasco of the 1993 parliamentary elections, when overly confident democrats and outrageous nationalists flirting with fascism, puffed out in stiff suits and black ties, waited eagerly for the election results in the Kremlin Palace of Congresses, a favorite gathering place for Cold War Communists, especially during the Gorbachev era. Yeltsin called those elections by decree instead of law. Many opposition parties were outlawed until the last moment, and even during the elections. Some newspapers were also banned.

In 1993, the democrats, then led by former prime minister Yegor Gaidar, were so confident they televised the election results from the Kremlin. The move backfired. The program was cut off abruptly at around 3 A.M.—hours earlier than expected. By then, it was clear that Zhirinovsky had an unexpected victory. Afterwards, some politicians charged that the election had been monstrously tampered with.

Yeltsin appointed a committee to investigate the 1993 parliamentary election. It concluded that only 16.1 percent of all Russians voted instead of the 52 percent originally reported. The news was particularly damaging because Russian law stipulates that 50 percent of registered voters are required to vote if an election is to be legal. Nevertheless, Russia and the West decided to accept the election as official. The alternative—so close after the October 1993 rebellion—could have been chaos. But a new regime could legally revoke everything Yeltsin has done since 1993, including privatization, on the grounds that it has no legal basis.

This is the background to the 1995 parliamentary elections. The democrats are so split that Gaidar's party doesn't even get enough votes to form a bloc in parliament.

Alexandra leaves Chernomyrdin headquarters after midnight. "I have to be up before dawn to report," she explains. I flag down a gypsy cab with a French colleague I run into, and head to the Slav, where some old colleagues are still filing late-night election stories at the international press center.

There I see one expat, an idealist who moved to Moscow long before the empire's collapse. He and his Russian wife have almost finished building their dream dacha in an elite region outside Moscow, though in the end they may have to sell it: The cost of paying off jealous mobsters and officials may be too high. A Russian student who works at the press center, who says he likes the Communists best, gallantly offers to escort me to election headquarters.

At 2 A.M., election headquarters is a zoo. Young diplomats and mysterious Americans who work with the Russians organizing the election scrupulously observe, while acting as if they are at a cocktail party. Political party leaders drink vodka and cognac and watch election results on TV. Zhirinovsky, sporting his trademark blue worker's hat, is in an especially gleeful mood. "We have more deputies [members of parliament] now than ever—and we're going to do even better," he says. It is the first time we have spoken since the *Playboy* interview. I chastise him for his well-publicized attack on a female member of parliament. "She deserved it," he says.

Nearby is Viktor Anpilov, a former KGB "journalist" at Radio Moscow and current leader of Working Russia. More hard-core than Zyuganov, Anpilov calls for renationalizing property and foreign bank accounts, abolishing the Duma, and rebuilding the Soviet Union. "For five years I've been struggling against the colonization of my country," he says. "There is still no joy."

Later that week I meet my friend Sam, a French journalist. Tired of selling stories to international news agencies who pay the minimum and reap huge profits, Sam and his brother have started their own agency, Mosscoop.

One night, we meet in one of Moscow's trendy new restaurant-bar-cafés. In keeping with the latest fad, the restaurant is dark and spartan: wooden benches, candlelight; simple but hearty food. No decor, no sign out front. It is a reaction to the garishness of the city's new-rich clubs. The new anti-club, you could say. Though the same Jeep Cherokees and Mercedes with drivers line the darkened street outside, inside the crowd is more laid back and unpretentious than the one-hundred-dollar-a-ticket loud-bad-music hang-outs. Its aesthetics seem to typify the very principles of the original Communist Revolution. (It only takes a few months before the charm dies. This, too, is part of a pattern. The restaurant gets "discovered." It becomes an exclusive high-priced club with membership lists, a hang-out for mobsters and molls.)

Another Westerner, "Hunter," soon joins us. "I just came back from visiting the wife of one my best friends. He's a young millionaire who's now in jail. His wife and daughter have nothing. I'm trying to do what I can for them," he says.

I don't know why, but my instincts go into overdrive. "Is your friend Abkhazian?"

"Yes," he says, startled.

"Is his name Volodya?"

"How did you know?" I explain my chance encounter with Volodya, the nineteen-year-old millionaire. "Oh yes," Hunter says. "He told me about you."

Hunter obligingly fills in some of the blanks in Volodya's story. They met in Tbilisi, Georgia, in 1991.

"When I met Volodya, he was a scrawny teenager who was working at the local radio station and lying about his age. He was good, and even won a journalism award for reports he did from the Baltics," Hunter says. "At that time, he was deciding whether to be an artist or a biznesman. Volodya's grandfather was a top apparatchik under Stalin, but his father was a struggling writer."

From journalism, Volodya fast moved into biznes. "I helped him get his start trading hard currency on the black market," Hunter says.

Volodya then began to invest in gasoline stations and oil wells. "I also thought he might have been into arms trading, since the war in Abkhazia was going on, but I don't know and I didn't ask."

Apparently, Volodya's current troubles began when a well-known Russian film industry tycoon with noted mafiya ties approached him—with a lot of money. "He asked Volodya to hold on to it, to invest it for him. He did," Hunter says. "But then he wanted it back, and Volodya couldn't produce it right away, so he had Volodya arrested."

Thugs overpowered his bodyguards and then barged into Volodya's home. "It was real KGB style," Hunter says. "They surrounded him in his bed and dragged him off to Butyrsky prison." The tactics haven't changed since Stalin's time. Volodya has been in jail for a year, but no charges have been laid yet. Just as in Yakubovsky's case.

In the meantime, Volodya's wife and their son are practically penniless. "All their friends deserted them," Hunter says.

After a few drinks, he says good-bye. He's on his way to a nightclub to hear a band. We may join up with him later.

Unlike the nightclubs, there is no gun check/metal detector at the front door of this restaurant. The table facing me is soon occupied by two young toughs. One is in all-black, with a silver-studded belt and brown leather jacket. The other is in sweats, slurping soup. The one in black picks up a video camera. He focuses it on me, and the light goes on. He films me talking to Sam, whose back is to him. It gives me the creeps, but I ignore it, going with my usual "react by not reacting."

Then he pulls out a large knife. He begins to stab it into the table methodically, over and over again. I mention the shenanigans to Sam, who doesn't warm to the idea of a man stabbing a table with a knife behind his back. We decide to leave.

It is just before midnight. We cut across a deserted park, crunching through moonlit snow. We pass an elderly couple out for a stroll. That's it for human contact. More than eleven million people live in this city. We are right in its heart. Yes, Moscow can be ugly and dirty and polluted and smoke- and traffic-plagued and crime-ridden, crowded with beggars and homeless and mobsters and mistresses. A great city filled with the greatest disparity, greed and desperation, the extremes of utter poverty and riches soaked in blood. Yet Moscow still has enough parks, alleys, and hidden streets—an island by the Kremlin and a river running through the center—that it can still sometimes feel like a charming, provincial, backwater town.

I've promised to drop by another club, to hear a friend who plays in a Russian-American band. It's another low-key hangout—with no sign out front—where young Americans, Russians, and a lot of French sit on the floor when the tables are full, listening to old-fashioned folksy rock and blues.

At the bar, which has some of the best chili in town, we run into "Yulia," a twenty-one-year-old Russian student who is friends with some of the band members. I first met Yulia last summer. I was listening to the same friend's band play while I was reading a newspaper. Yulia sat down beside me. "Do you always read newspapers in bars?" she asked.

"Sometimes," I replied. We got to talking. I had just come back from Chechnya.

"Are they really bandits down there, like Yeltsin says?" she asked all wide-eyed, with pixie-short hair. "I don't know anything about the war. I hate politics and I don't want to know anything. I should read the papers more but I don't have time. Besides, what has politics ever done for us?"

I tried to explain what I had seen in Chechnya. "It's in your interests to understand what's happening down there, because it's your age group—your brothers and your friends who are fighting and dying down there," I said.

That summer I tried to give Yulia a brief lesson in American history. I talked about the Vietnam War and how students organized protests against it. "Just imagine what would happen if thousands of students showed up on Red Square protesting the war," I said. The impromptu speech seemed to inspire her, at least temporarily.

"You're right. We *can* do something," she said. "I'm going to organize a meeting with some of my friends. I'll see what we can do."

It has been six months since that conversation. I remind Yulia about her promise. "I tried, Jennifer, but it didn't work," she says. "It was summertime, and I couldn't get anyone interested. But I am doing something for the community—I'm working at a family planning clinic. It's one of the first in Moscow."

At the moment, Yulia has loads of time to work. The dean keeps canceling her classes at Moscow State University, one of the most prestigious colleges in the country. "There have been bomb threats every week since September," she says. Other students tell me the same story.

It has something to do with the mayor and the mob, with MOST-Bank and real estate. "But I'm not exactly sure what," she says. "I go all the way to the university to find my classes have been canceled. Now exams scheduled for December twenty-sixth have been postponed until the end of January. I'll keep studying until then, so I have no holiday time at all. It really sucks."

As for the elections, Yulia doesn't know who she'll vote for. "I like Lebed. Russia needs a strong man," she says, referring to General Alexander Lebed.

There have been rumblings that Lebed would run for president since 1992, when he was commander of the 14th Army based in the separatist, ethnic Russian Trans-Dneistria region of Moldova. Although the army was more like a division, Lebed did end a civil war between ethnic Romanian and Russian residents with effective—but perhaps excessive—force.

Now Lebed is co-leader of an obscure political group, the patriotic Congress of Russian Communities, which purports to defend some twenty-five million ethnic Russians outside Russia's new borders. The group is also led by Yuri Skokov, a Yeltsin ally who created and first filled the top spot in Russia's powerful—and secretive—security council.

But Lebed and Skokov both fought for the number one spot in the congress, and failed miserably. Skokov—a powerful backbencher—looked ill at ease in front of the cameras. And Lebed's bulldog face and gruff, mumbling, grumbling growl, did little to seduce voters. The group did not even get enough votes for representation in parliament. Lebed quit the congress.

Yulia says she also admires the Beer Lovers' Party. Started by a history professor and a human rights activist, the party is made up of young people who are fed up with corruption-as-usual politics.

"We live in a criminal democracy," said Konstantin Kalachyov, the thirty-one-year-old history teacher, and the head of the party, when I interviewed him during the campaign. In December, the Beer Lovers had sixty-five thousand registered members and a five-hundred-thousand-dollar budget, though they did not get enough votes to form a parliamentary bloc. Russia's youth, Kalachyov said, just aren't passionate about politics.

"Protest comes in cycles," he said. "This generation of young people prefers money to anything. Maybe the next generation will be more alternative."

Sitting in the bar, talking with Yulia, I remember when I first moved to Moscow.

I had been living here for a month or so when I was invited to a party thrown by an *MT* freelancer. I was arriving late, from work. A driver dropped me off on the wrong street, in the pitch-dark.

From out of the darkness, I heard voices. I followed them to the inner courtyard of an apartment complex. Leaning against a concrete wall, by a large tree, stood a group of Russians in their early twenties. In 1992 there weren't that many places to go. The group was having a little party in the snow-filled courtyard, as many young people did—and still do. They held plastic cups of champagne and munched Russian chocolates. I approached them and asked, in my dreadful Russian, how to get to where I was going. Before they would help, they were pouring me a glass of champagne and offering me chocolates. They insisted on personally escorting me to where I had to go. I never forgot such gracious gestures. And for all the greed and murder, that warmth of soul and generosity of spirit never disappear.

In December 1995, many of the people I first met in Moscow are gone. Some Russians have either married foreigners or moved to the West on scholarships. Others are jailed, or dead. Some, who were poor students when we first met—one owned two pairs of pants, another charged two dollars an hour to teach Russian—are now in top management jobs and jet-setting around the globe with credit cards and expense budgets many Western executives don't get until after decades of experience.

One of my fixers, who transformed himself from a red-faced, awkward-but-enthusiastic seventeen-year-old into a *GQ*-handsome, skilled, and confident twenty-one-year-old working for top news organizations, has just returned from a scholarship in California. "I'd like to live there for a year. I'd like to live in France for a year— I want to live everywhere!" he says, over Indian food one night.

Now he can.

While many of the Westerners I know working for large companies, embassies, or news agencies have been transferred to new posts, freelancers and free-floating spirits are still around.

Most, though not all, of the women I know over thirty who started off single have found live-in mates. Some marry, some don't. Others are pregnant and plan to keep the baby, regardless of the status of the relationship with the father. The expat women I first knew, however, still in their twenties, have on the whole stayed single. We talk about our single status on an icy Christmas shopping excursion to Izmailovsky Park.

"We found our way to Moscow," one says. "So where are all the cool men?" Many are thinking of leaving Moscow after the 1996 presidential elections. But no one knows where to.

"Since I moved here four years ago, I've traveled to more than fifty countries," one friend says. "I've just returned from Vietnam. But when I was there, all I could say was, 'So what? What's next?' I realized I had lost my sense of wonder, and it frightened me. I found myself in Moscow. But I know I've reached my peak here. I've learned all that I can. It's time to move on. The only problem is that I don't know where to go. How could living anywhere be even remotely as exciting?"

That month, I get a call, out of nowhere, from Olga, one of my first Russian friends. The last time, I had called her, after not having spoken to her for more than a year. "Jennifer!" she then said. "How did you know?"

"Know what?"

"I got married half an hour ago!"

When I met Olga, she had just graduated from university. She spoke fluent English and French. I helped arrange her first job with a foreign company. She was soon buying imported groceries —and even fur coats—for herself and her mother. She then started her own successful translating biznes, though she still lived at home, sharing a tiny room with her grandmother. She then fell in love with one of her (much older) clients and left Russia—for good. ("My mother and her mother waited in lines their whole lives. All I want to do is to get married, have kids, and have someone look after me for a change," she said.)

Now, in the midst of this chapter, Olga calls. We catch up on each other's lives. Olga is still married and living in the American Midwest, though she's not sure for how much longer. "I'm doing a lot of translating work. I'm also going to take a real estate course —there are lots of Russians moving into the area," she says. "And I'm going to get my U.S. citizenship papers soon!"

Olga is now twenty-six. Staying home and having babies is no longer a priority for her, at least not right now. "Oh, I have lots of time for all that," she says. "Marriage hasn't turned out to be exactly what I expected. I don't know how much longer it will last. Living in America has really been eye-opening. Women get married and have children so much later here. My whole mentality has trans- formed. Maybe I truly have become American. I don't want just to raise children. This is a country of possibilities. If you're not lazy, you can really prove to everyone—especially yourself—that you can make anything happen. In Russia, if you're a woman, you can only do that by sleeping with someone or by already having *blat* [connections]. But here, if you know what you want, you can really do anything."

Olga is, however, worried about her parents and siblings, who are still in Moscow.

"We've got to find a way to keep my brother out of the army. He's working as a journalist. His salary is supposed to be good by Russian standards. And although my parents are still young, in their fifties, they don't want to move here. They don't speak English and they don't want to start over. If they did move, they'd have to move in with us, and I don't know if anyone would really be comfortable with that. But my parents have visited. I give them money and clothes to take back.

"They spend their entire salaries on food," she adds. "They're living well. A lot of their friends only eat meat or chicken once a week. We're all terrified about the future. People are scared that the past seventy-four years will return. Everyone just seems to be grabbing whatever they can. It's like they're waiting. The political situation is so insecure. No one knows what tomorrow will bring."

CHAPTER 23

← - →

Elections

The President, the Communist,
the Rock Star—Selling Yeltsin in the
Arctic Circle, Hanging with Zyuganov,
Election Night Dinner with Gorby.
No, This Is Not Good-bye.

> Russia is a whole separate world submissive to the will, caprice,
> and fantasy of a single man. Whether his name is Pyotr or Ivan
> is not important. In all cases the common element is that he is
> the embodiment of arbitrary power.
>
> — PYOTR CHADAYEV, 1854

Victory Day celebrations, May 9, 1996: By chance, Igor, the same cabby I had in December, picks me up at the airport. Another Russian coincidence. "You haven't missed much," he says, though red flags now flutter eerily along the roadside. Yeltsin just signed a decree to bring back the Communist symbol during special occasions. He even bows before a red flag at a military parade commemorating the fifty-first anniversary of the defeat of Nazi Germany.

It feels like a gray cloud is looming over the city. Russia's first post-Communist presidential election is one month away. Almost all eleven candidates say they fear election fraud and even violence. Communist Party leader Gennady Zyuganov is in the midst of an extraordinary comeback, but Moscow is plastered with only one set of posters: Yeltsin and Mayor Yuri Luzhkov. The posters ripple down the length of the bridge by Red Square.

Igor Malashenko, the head of NTV, Russian independent television, has become one of Yeltsin's top campaign managers, running the president's advertising campaign. NTV, backed by MOST-Bank's Vladimir Gusinsky, was once one of Yeltsin's harshest critics, especially over Chechnya. News is now uniformly pro-Yeltsin. Those journalists who are not voluntarily part of the love-in are paid for on a per-story basis.

Behind the Kremlin curtains, Yeltsin's inner circle is in the midst of an intense power struggle. On one side is the party of war, including General Korzhakov, who wants to cancel the election. He makes the tactical error of saying this to a British journalist. He then hopes to make a behind-the-scenes deal with the Communists.

The other side is led by reformers, like Anthony Chubais, the former privatization minister who, for many Russians, personifies their post-Communist hardships. Their access to Yeltsin is aided by the president's daughter, Tatyana, who plays an increasingly prominent role in the campaign. Luzhkov—who once thought of running against Yeltsin—and the mayor's allies, including Gusinsky and MOST-Bank (Yakubovsky's old clients), also play key roles. MOST-Bank has, it seems, come full circle since Korzhakov's daylight raid on it, Yakubovsky's arrest, and Gusinsky's flight to London at the start of the Chechen war.

Gusinsky, a media kingpin who is also behind the liberal newspaper *Segodnya* (*Today*) and the news-radio station *Ekho Moskvy* (*Echo of Moscow*), is also known for his own private army of armed and at least partially KGB-trained security troops numbering more than one thousand men. Brash after his return from self-imposed exile, Gusinsky is now even bold enough to hold a press conference, at the Slav, of course, to announce a new biznes relationship with Gazprom, one of the world's largest companies—with control of one third of the world's gas reserves and interest in an unimaginably diverse range of other businesses. Gazprom was once run by—and is still linked to—Russia's powerful prime minister, Viktor Chernomyrdin. Gazprom has bought into Gusinsky's holdings with —it later turns out—an "interest-free loan" from the government.

But though the fortunes of Gusinsky—a former theater director who introduced the first credit card to Russia—are changing, he is still taking care to distance himself from his former lawyer, the young Yakubovsky. ("He was just one of many lawyers I employed," Gusinsky tells me with a shrug, although their young wives were often seen together, throwing elaborate dining parties at luxury places like the Metropol Hotel.) It makes me wonder how Yakubovsky is doing, now that his old allies' stars are rising again. Yakubovsky's case is up for trial again, so I head to St. Petersburg, an hour away by plane.

The city looks as gray and Soviet as Moscow did four years ago. There's a heatwave in Moscow, but people here still wear wool hats and overcoats as they plow through a chilling rain.

Armed men in combat fatigues block the entrance to a tiny third-floor courtroom. Inside, I feel like I've walked into the dress rehearsal of some weird Soviet play. Yakubovsky, plump and pleasant-faced, wearing a patterned sweater and beige slacks, paces inside a large iron cage. A lone Russian reporter, hunched over his notebook, stands out in a small row of otherwise unoccupied bare wooden benches.

After taking a day and a half to read the one-hundred-and-fifty page prosecution statement out loud, Judge Vyatcheslav Remmer postpones the trial until after the elections. When the court adjourns, the judge—an older man with substantial sideburns who looks like he's stepped out of the pages of Gogol—walks over to Yakubovsky's cage at the side of the courtroom. They chat like colleagues.

Yakubovsky has been forbidden from giving interviews since his 1994 detention. As the guards escort me out, I ask how he's doing. "*Normalno,*" okay, he answers good-naturedly.

Marina, decked out in a serious, smart brown suit, has flown in for the trial. Although she has no legal training, she is on her husband's defense team. (Russian law stipulates that any citizen can be part of a public defense counsel.)

I talk with Marina briefly after the trial, as she waits for her driver. "He looks good," she says.

"Russians are a strong breed. I'm absolutely confident he'll get out. The gods are in our favor," she adds, as she jumps into a dirty cream-colored Lada—far different from the luxury cars she's accustomed to.

Yakubovsky remains in detention, in a cell for common criminals.

By now, other young reformers are also behind bars, like Alexei Illyushenko, Russia's former acting prosecutor general, and a leader of Yeltsin's anti-corruption commission. Illyushenko was charged with bribe-taking in February. Police are also hunting for Sergei Stankevich, a former top Yeltsin advisor, for allegedly accepting a $10,000 bribe in 1992. The charges were delayed because Stankevich had immunity as a parliamentary deputy.

"Yakubovsky, Illyushenko, and the others were all involved in the political machinations of the Yeltsin years together," says one Western diplomat who monitors the case. "Yakubovsky is a key figure if you want to understand Russia from 1991 to 1996, the continuity of the Yeltsin 'democratic' regime with the nondemocratic Soviet regime before it—and even current Israeli politics, the Russian émigrés, and the growth of the extreme right—powerful enough to have assassinated [Yitzhak] Rabin." (Some players in the Yakubovsky case were allegedly planning to smuggle the rare books to Israel, which has become a haven for many arms- and drug-running ex-Soviet gangsters.)

Even if Yakubovsky's fate is tied to how his Communist and democratic krishi, protectors, do in the new government, he may have enough kompromat on all of them to keep him in jail for some time.

"Yakubovsky knows too much about how much the country's top bureaucrats have stolen from the people," says Martin Shakkum, an independent presidential candidate and director of the mysterious-sounding—and until now, unknown—Fund of Economic and Social Reform. (Much to my surprise, I later discover that Yakubovsky's old spokesman, Gulbinsky, now works for Shakkum.)

"Yakubovsky was a member of the team. He helped them and then he started to play his own game. If Yakubovsky began to talk, he'd have a major impact on the elections. But nobody needs him now. He may die behind those walls," he adds.

"Dima made a lot of enemies in Russia," adds the diplomat. "He ruined the careers of powerful people. This is a political trial, but it's very sophisticated. The evidence makes the case appear to have a legitimate basis. Law enforcement here goes way beyond what we know in the West. Yakubovsky walked through the limelight of Russian politics because he understood how to work it.

Maybe Zyuganov hasn't made a big deal out of the Yakubovsky chapters because some of his people are also involved."

Back in Moscow, I plan a series of campaign trail stories. My first trip is with Zyuganov to Bryansk, two hundred and ten miles southwest of Moscow. Fiercely Communist, Bryansk sided with the hard-liners during the October 1993 rebellion. Yeltsin never forgave them.

Zyuganov is a pudgy, bug-eyed bureaucrat and former Party ideologue, who used to saturate his speeches with virulent anti-Semitic ravings before his campaign for presidency. Even now, he will soon equate Yeltsin and Gorbachev with the Antichrist. Lacking large entourages and presidential jets, Zyuganov travels in ordinary train compartments and holds meetings in public squares by old statues of Lenin. He is a fervent atheist, loath to embrace the Russian Orthodox Church, as post-Communist Communists must. (Some Reds now argue that Jesus was not only the son of God but also the world's first Communist.) Zyuganov has just returned from a famous monastery, where he refused to cross himself or beg forgiveness, as the tsars did before him. One voter told him to "repent or die."

Each time the train stops on its way to Bryansk, the people look poorer, the children dirtier and more desperate as they run through the compartments selling warm ice cream, homemade dumplings, talking toy dogs, whatever they have. At one stop, I get off and talk with some young boys. I buy ice cream from one, which infuriates a babushka. (The boy must be encroaching on her turf.) She throws a bucket of cold water on him in anger. A man in his twenties comes by, violently pulls the boy's ear, and begins to wrestle with him. They seem to be friends.

I can tell we're in a Communist region as soon as we arrive. We're kicked out of the first hotel before checking in. "We have no telex confirming your visit," says the hotel manager, referring to a Soviet-era rule for foreigners that we did, in fact, obey. It takes two hours to check into the second hotel. The receptionist rejects the forms we fill out in English, as we do all over the FSU, and makes us fill them out again in Russian. She then rejects my colleague's second form. "You must write it again in proper Russian," she huffs. "Your handwriting isn't neat enough."

Zyuganov smiles stiffly with a babushka for a photo but does not hug a woman who cries. (He does not even hold her hand. His eyes dart around so much it's clear he's not even listening.) Unlike Yeltsin, he does not yell back at angry voters, joke with them, or have any personal interaction. An ancient, lone folk guitarist sings before the rallies—laughable, compared to Yeltsin's big budget rock concerts. The stage is flocked by proud and uncomfortable-looking veterans with World War II medals stiffly holding red flags and, usually, a young boy in shorts, knee-socks, and the ubiquitous red Pioneer scarf.

Zyuganov's message is simple: Communism will restore the Motherland to great nation status *and* make food cheaper. All mobster-pol-biznesmeni will be jailed (if not shot); shelter and education will once again be accessible to everyone. Vote Communist, Zyuganov says, and We will take care of you; your decades of sacrifice have not been in vain. (Other candidates, like Zhirinovsky, seem to have stopped campaigning altogether, further confirmation to some analysts that he has been working for Yeltsin all along.)

At one rally, I sneak backstage, where I am welcomed by a restaurateur who is feeding the local Communists and the boys from Moscow. Zyuganov will hold court here with the locals for about five minutes. For now, some of his bodyguards are wolfing down salmon, whitefish, onions, salami, and vodka. The restaurateur makes up a plate of food for me after I tell her not to, and kindly pours me a cup of tea. Although she is a bizneswoman, she is also pro-Communist. ("It was better before, Yeltsin only made things worse," she says, as she asks why I'm not married, have no children, and am so far from home.)

A press bus chauffeurs us—some North Americans, a German photographer, and a small army of Russians—from village to village. It's pouring rain. The scenery: flat fields thick with mud. I sit beside "Lena," a talented young Russian journalist who lives in London, back to cover the elections.

"Would you like some food?" she asks, her bag stuffed with fruit and pastries. "I came to Bryansk a day early to stay with my aunt and uncle, who live here."

Lena's family is Jewish. She grew up in St. Petersburg, though she and her parents emigrated long ago. During the war, her father and his family moved to Bryansk. Her uncle married a gentile woman and stayed in Bryansk. That side of the family is hard-core, working-class Communist.

"They look alike, but I can't believe this man is my father's brother," Lena says, still shell-shocked. "As soon as I arrived, my aunt told me that Gorbachev and Yeltsin should be shot. They supported the parliament in 1993 and dream of the restoration of Communism and the Soviet Union."

In the meantime, Lena says, they live frugally in cramped quarters. Many of her Bryansk relatives and their friends are unemployed. "I had to talk as little about politics as possible," Lena says. "Both brothers would fight for what they believe in." That's what civil war is about.

We take the night train back to Moscow. Zyuganov is also traveling economy class. The cabins are small. Even with mattresses, the seats are hard and uncomfortable, the sheets and blankets of questionable cleanliness. Four people sleep in each cabin, men and women indiscriminately. Despite the late hour, open cabins reveal old men playing cards, biznesmeni drinking Armenian cognac, young children playing. The ever-present traveling smell of salami and alcohol mixes with cigarette fumes wafting from the alley that links each train car to the next, and cool Russian night air, as darkened fields whiz by.

Zyuganov's two top bodyguards are a few cabins away from me. For Communists, they certainly have expensive tastes: designer suits, though they soon change to shorts and T-shirts. I chat with them in the hall. In their early thirties, these men have been with Zyuganov, they say, since their late teens. No longer standing by their man, shielded by aviators and guns, the tough-guy image dissolves. They are polite, even shy.

A monstrously fat Communist Party photographer waddles over. Sweat streams down his face. He has probably not stopped drinking and eating since I saw him earlier today, backstage at the rally. We did not talk then. Now, he asks my name, which throws him. He can't figure out my ethnicity.

"Who are you working for?" he asks.

"The *Village Voice*," I say.

"Never heard of it. Where is it from?" he asks.

"New York."

"Oh, so it's a Jew paper."

* * *

Next is the Arctic with Yeltsin. The president's schedule is rarely released too far in advance, for security reasons. The Foreign Ministry, which is organizing the trip, charges us far more than if we'd had to pay to make our own arrangements. As usual, getting there is far from easy.

"Tonight's flight to Archangelsk is full, but I'll see what I can do," says Valentina at the Aeroflot office in Moscow near Lubyanka. "My boss is out right now. Can you come back in a few hours?"

I can't miss this flight. My only hope, friends suggest, is a black market option, where mobsters sell sold-out tickets in a suburban train station. I return to Valentina. Miraculously, a ticket is waiting.

At the airport, I'm surprised by a new, small coffee stand. I'm stunned when the woman asks what kind of coffee I want—cappuccino or espresso. The young man seated beside me on the plane is surgically attached to his cell phone. When he takes a break, I borrow it, and offer him some pistachios. Igor, twenty-seven, is the owner of a factory that employs one thousand people. It's in the closed city of Severodvinsk, where nuclear submarines are built, less than an hour's drive from icy Archangelsk.

At twenty-one, Igor graduated from an engineering institute and bought a seat on Moscow's first stock exchange. At twenty-four, he bought the factory, which makes street-cleaning machines. "I paid five million dollars for it. Cash," he says, grinning as he shows me some magic tricks. (They involve a trick coin and a pack of cards.) "I just bought these cards in New York two days ago," he says. "I was there to meet with the owner of an Alabama company who wants to buy into the factory."

"It's quite impressive, Igor. You've accomplished so much at such a young age," I say. Igor looks surprised. "It's not much, really," he says. "One of my best friends is twenty-six and he's head of one of the biggest banks in Russia."

By the time we land, Igor and I have bonded. "My driver will give you a lift to your hotel. Just wait a minute while I get my gun. I had to check it with the captain."

Some military men watch the passengers descend. "You're forbidden from taking photographs," one rushes up to tell me. After a word or two with Igor, he apologizes. Andrei, Igor's fiftyish factory director, walks onto the tarmac to greet us. (Igor phoned him from the plane.) Andrei also sports a pistol, which he displays proudly when asked. He carries an open bottle of vodka in his hand.

"It's the only way to deal with the cold," he says.

A driver is waiting.

Yeltsin landed in Archangelsk half an hour before us. Andrei tape-recorded his airport address. He laughs as he plays it back for us. After two mild heart attacks, Yeltsin's health—and popularity —were so low recently, there was talk the elections may be canceled. Now a reborn, energetic Yeltsin, sixty-five, is fast catching up with Zyuganov. He dives into crowds with a microphone, armed with last-minute cash injections and Red Scare tactics—to combat Zyuganov's rosy nostalgia—that would have made the late senator Joseph McCarthy proud.

Andrei, however, is not impressed.

"Our politicians are all the same—liars and criminals!"

"You have to excuse him," Igor whispers. "Andrei was raised with the Communist system. He still has the old mentality. Yeltsin is a puppet, but he has good commanders. There is no way we can go back now." Besides, Igor adds, many of the people drafting policy for Yeltsin and Zyuganov are the same.

Light, thick, almost artificial-looking clumps of snow fall as the sun shines brilliantly. The subzero Arctic wind is a harsh reminder of how far I am from Moscow and the first heatwave of summer. It is late evening. But the sun doesn't set in Archangelsk. White nights last from May to September. At first, they add a floaty, Chagall-inspired, dream-like quality. The locals love it, but all light, no sleep can torment the soul, like a never-ending interrogation.

Archangelsk is an attractive port town, lined with old wooden houses painted dark Russian blue, green, yellow, and red. It's a town of fishermen and traders, sliced by the Severnaya Dvina River, which runs into the White Sea and a sublime series of islands, with small, wooden churches, called Solovetskiya Ostrova. Its beauty is haunting. So is its history: a former gulag heartland.

Archangelsk also boasts a historic naval academy, where a Moscow friend of mine slit his wrists when he was fourteen. "It was the only way," he says, "to escape the beatings from older recruits."

We drive to the main hotel and hope there will be room. "The main roads have been repaved for Yeltsin's visit," Andrei says. Even the Soviet hotel has undergone a makeover. All this has come from the local government, which is broke. Most workers have not been paid for months.

Prepped for the foreign invasion, the receptionist wears a name tag in Russian and English. Four burly young men sit prominently on the small reception area's couch and chairs, watching a tacky Russian Las Vegas-style show on TV. Our own in-house spy service, they remain there throughout our stay.

Before leaving, Igor hands me his *visitka*, business card. He also writes down the name of someone who runs the region's airport. "If you're ever stuck, give this guy a call," he says.

The next day starts at 7 A.M. With Heidi, my roommate, I head to the port, where Yeltsin meets with navy veterans. Yeltsin strides in as confident as a film star, with superbly thick, coifed white hair, navy blue overcoat, and red paisley scarf. He seems to have more energy than the journalists as he dives, pumped up and wide-eyed, into the crowd, his voice booming, the whites of his eyes shining. Later in the day, he jumps on a swing, and dances with women in folk costume.

In the afternoon, Yeltsin addresses unpaid workers at the Solombala sawmill factory. Along the way, he skillfully handles the grilling he gets on unpaid wages and atrocious living conditions. Shamelessly, he disburses ukazi, presidential decrees worth billions of rubles, like a 1930s Chicago party boss distributing Christmas turkeys.*

The Solombala sawmill warehouse looks empty. Although nobody is working, the machines sometimes whir and clank, providing colorful background for the cameras. The sawmill, which employs two thousand people, was the largest of its kind in Europe when it was privatized in 1992, although it now operates at 28 percent of capacity, as the cost of raw resources rises and government subsidies fade.

---

* In December 1996, a new scandal, complete with secretly recorded Kremlin tapes, will emerge, fueling allegations that Yeltsin has spent between $425 million to $2.5 billion of government money during the campaign—far beyond the $3.6 million allowed under Russian election law. The state's hard-currency reserves fall significantly during the same period.

Yeltsin says privatized factories should operate without Communist-era state-sponsored subsidies. He then announces his approval of a forty-billion-ruble [eight-million-dollar] loan to the sawmill. "I could have come here and said nothing, given nothing. But that's not in my character," he says. "I did not come with empty pockets."

But most of the workers did.

I ask some why they work if they're not getting paid.

"What else can we do?" says fifty-year-old Zhenya Kaladrupskaya, who helps fix machinery when it breaks down, as she stands in an icy, sunless chill for hours, waiting for Yeltsin. "We've got to get the factory out of its rut."

Kaladrupskaya can't even afford to visit her daughter in Ukraine. "When we were all one country, I had money and flights were cheap," she says. "But Yeltsin started the reforms. He should finish them."

Yeltsin's next stop is Vorkuta, where the miners were some of his biggest early supporters. Now they are still threatening to strike, while working reduced hours for less pay. Some haven't been paid for up to nine months. Many unproductive mines may shut down altogether. I have not been back to Vorkuta since 1993. I'm looking forward to the trip.

There are no flights to Vorkuta from Archangelsk, just the Foreign Ministry's charter, which is full. Worse: Flights to Moscow are sold out—for the next two days. We're really stuck. We return to the airport at 5:30 the next morning, and beg the administrator to put us on the morning flight to Moscow. So do a dozen others. Waiting stand-by, with no sleep and no ticket, I feel miserable. The tiny airport is freezing cold. As there are no chairs, anywhere, I sit on my knapsack on the grimy floor, and close my eyes.

Someone taps me on the shoulder. I wake up to discover a handsome young man looking down at me. At first, I think I'm dreaming. I blink, and realize he's a policeman. He has mistaken me for a vagrant.

The crowd thins as the flight takes off. Outside on the street is a Swiss colleague, who was badly beaten the night before. Blue eyes shine from a puffed-out face. There's a thick, sweltering bump on his forehead and dried blood in his hair. "It was all over a girl," he says. The men took his wallet and plane ticket, leaving him in a drunken, blood-spattered heap.

"Do you need anything?" Heidi and I ask.

"I'm fine," he says. "I missed this flight, but I'm on the next one to Moscow."

We make sure he's okay and move on. I've just remembered the number Igor gave me. We head to a VIP lounge in the next building. Luckily, the man we need is in. "Igor who has a factory in Severodvinsk" sent us, we explain.

"What flight do you want to get on?" asks the middle-aged man, as he presses a button that connects to the woman administrator we just left. "Too bad you didn't come five minutes ago. A flight just left."

"Are there any flights to Vorkuta?" I ask, for a joke.

"There's a charter that leaves in an hour," he says. "It's a special military plane for some rock stars who are giving a concert for Yeltsin this evening. I don't see why they wouldn't let you join them. You have my permission. But you have to decide right now —you caught me just as I was about to leave."

"We'll take it, of course."

"Why don't you wait in the VIP lounge?" he adds.

Grateful, we take him up on the offer: warmth, cozy sofas, the promise of tea. The room is empty but for one young, scowling new Russian with a large platter of food in front of him. The older waitress does not serve us. I don't think she likes to see foreigners here. I pull out my laptop and begin to write.

Suddenly the room begins to fill.

"Did you get everything you needed?" smiles a man at the head of a procession of people. "I remember you from the sawmill."

I thought he was another journalist, but it turns out he's a well-known actor and comedian, Leonid Yarmolnik. I explain the situation.

"Stick with us," he says. "You'll be fine."

Guitar cases, dark glasses, young people. No more diplomats, Kremlin guards, and gun-checks. The room fills with artists, actors, and musicians. So much positive energy, I relax. No one treats me with distrust or tries to make me dizzy spinning stories and disinformation. There is talent, even genius—if you listen to some of the songs—in this room.

The woman who runs the lounge now fusses instead of ignoring us. Heaps of food appear. I'm used to spending hours, even days, fighting to get onto overcrowded planes. Now we fly first class —no tickets, no passports, no customs—with Yarmolnik and his best friend, the brilliant Andrei Makarevich, who is like Russia's Bob Dylan. Only in Russia do I experience such extremes—from being mistaken for a vagrant to first-class, customs-free travel— all in the same day.

We sit up front in the plane, where Makarevich and Yarmolnik are in the midst of an intense card game. The attendant constantly comes by with food, from smoked salmon to Belgian truffles. In between vodka toasts, pickles, endless cigarettes, and an onslaught of food too early for this hour in the morning, we talk politics.

"Our people are too used to having the state take care of them," Makarevich says. "People who have lost their jobs have got to learn how to take control of their lives. I'm a musician. If I write songs that people like, fine. But why should the state have to do anything if I write songs that people don't want to buy?"

Snow blankets the airport as the plane lands smoothly. It's ten degrees below zero. A bus takes us into Vorkuta, the driver preferring his own bumpy cross-country route through mud and ice-slicked hills to the roads. We drive by barren shacks and abandoned industrial sites. The musicians' hotel is in the middle of nowhere.

"Why don't you rest? The bus will be back later to bring us into town for rehearsal," Makarevich says.

But Yeltsin is about to meet with some miners. Heidi and I hike to a nearby road. We plan to flag down the first moving object with wheels. A public bus arrives, crammed with people.

I'm about to pay the young ticket collector—two thousand rubles, or forty cents, for two tickets—when an older woman begins to yell at her.

"You can't let her pay. They're *guests* in our country!"

The young woman ignores her.

"Please," says the older woman, digging into her purse. "I'll pay for them myself."

I don't let her pay, but I'm touched. This is what Russia still can be like outside world-weary Moscow, where at least half the people I know have been hit by crime.

The shiny blue presidential limousine, parked outside the mine's entrance, looks absurdly out of place. Some young kids and a stray dog hang out in front, snow piled high on the side of the road. One miner is so angry, his words spill over with hatred. Half a dozen Kremlin guards stand just a few feet away.

"There is no way I'd vote for Yeltsin," says Alexander Zaitsev, thirty-nine, brown eyes shining from beneath his miner's hat.

Following what has become a typical Yeltsin election ploy, Zaitsev and other miners at Vorkutinskaya received 30 percent of their February salary on the eve of the president's visit. "Who knows when we'll ever see the rest?" says Zaitsev. "Almost everyone I know wants to leave, but we just can't afford it. I live with my wife and two children in two tiny rooms. I don't know how our lives will ever get better.

"Still," he adds, "going back to Communism would be worse."

As Zaitsev speaks, Yeltsin is seven hundred feet below ground. On the way down, he chats with the lift operator, who complains that she is stuck in Vorkuta, too poor to leave. Like a tsar, Yeltsin promises her a flat in the south. She then asks for a car. The meeting is sealed with a (rather lengthy) kiss.

Above ground, Yeltsin announces new financial injections—just in time to attract votes. Children of miners in the region will go to state-sponsored summer camp, as they did during Communist days. There will be a new railway, from Archangelsk to Perm, higher salaries, and more funds to build housing in warmer climates for retired workers.

By the end of the day, thousands of people stand in the sub-zero cold, eyes peeking from beneath heavy fur hats, as they wait for a glimpse of Yeltsin, who is about to deliver another speech and launch the evening's concert. But not all who came to see Yeltsin plan to vote for him. Some are even protesting.

Inside, the concert brightens up another miserably cold Arctic day. In between acts, Yarmolnik, the comedian, intersperses new Russian jokes with politics. There are the new Russians in Spain, out to buy a birthday gift for a pal. They stand where they see the longest line. It's for a Salvador Dali art show. Some of the paintings are for sale. They buy a painting for one million dollars. "Okay," the new Russian says to his friend. "We've bought the card, now let's find the present."

Then Yarmolnik gets serious. "Only old people who are alone will be voting for Zyuganov," he tells the crowd. "Those with children and grandchildren will be voting for Yeltsin. They know it may be hard now, but the worst is over."

The cross-country Yeltsin tour culminates in a Red Square concert for half a million Muscovites in early June. The streets are flooded with young people—soldiers and couples, the shirtless and tattooed, hipsters, hippies, impoverished and nouveaux—who drink and dance with an abandonment that makes me wonder, for a moment, how totalitarianism could ever return.

One of my next trips is to Kazan, the capital of Tatarstan, with Mikhail Gorbachev. Perhaps no other single man has made such a difference in our century—without even really meaning to. Gorbachev's reforms, begun without any long-term plan, spun into a revolution, while the superpower he headed shrank almost to banana-republic status. While Gorbachev is still loved, even revered, in the West—where his face graced *Time*'s cover and crowds flocked to see him—the Russians hate him: for bringing down the empire, for caring more about the West than about Russia. And this is the first time the former head of state has ever come to Kazan.

There is another irony. Gorbachev, who introduced democratic reform to all ex-Soviet republics, has never before run for any office. He rejected elections during perestroika, preferring instead to be appointed president of the Soviet Union. Back then, he was so popular, he probably would have won. Instead, when Yeltsin ran for the presidency of Russia—and won—in 1991, he also acquired the moral authority and legitimacy that Gorbachev lost forever. I wonder how Russia would have turned out if Gorbachev had had the courage to subject himself to the will of the people—the consequence of all those freedoms he stirred up in the Soviet soul.

Since the presidential campaign began, Gorbachev, sixty-five, has been slapped in Siberia, and called an agent of the CIA and a traitor to the Motherland. The former superpower leader now gathers the smallest of crowds as he tours a fragment of his old empire, on the cheap.

When Russians aren't shouting, swearing, and trying to physically attack him, they all ask the same question: Why on earth is he running for president?

"It's some kind of psychological catharsis," says Viktor Kuvaldin, one of Gorbachev's political advisers.

"He feels it's his moral duty," explains Raisa Gorbachev.

"The reforms that I started are on the wrong track," explains the great man himself, with dark eyes still famous for their grip. "It's up to me to set them straight."

Gorbachev's visit to Kazan, less than a week before Yeltsin's, is extremely low key. He travels in a blue limousine borrowed from a local millionaire. His entourage includes only one police car. Tatarstan's president, who has already endorsed Yeltsin, does not meet him. As Gorbachev walks down Kazan streets, and steps, impromptu, into a local cafeteria, his presence causes only the smallest of stirs. Some local kids smile, there is a handshake or two.

"Out of all the candidates running for president, only Boris Nikoleivich [Yeltsin] and I have any political experience," Gorbachev tells a few hundred people in the republic's parliament building. "If you want to vote for a man [Yeltsin] who shelled his own parliament and killed fifty thousand people in Chechnya, you can. On June sixteenth, you will hold the rifle in your hand."

Along with Yeltsin and Zyuganov, the other presidential candidates include: liberal economist Grigory Yavlinsky (who calls Yeltsin the "dictator of a bloody, autocratic regime"), Zhirinovsky, a famous weight-lifter named Yuri Vlasov, pioneering eye surgeon Svyatoslav Fyodorov, Shakkum, Lebed, and Vladimir Bryntsalov—a maniacal alcohol and pharmaceutical king who claims to be worth two billion dollars, although no one seems to have heard of him until campaign fever hit.

Bryntsalov tries to take over Zhirinovsky's old role, but without the teeth. While Zhirinovsky genuinely frightened the West for a time, Bryntsalov just tries to be amusing. He launched his career as a smuggler, word has it, and now lives in a huge mansion outside Moscow styled like those in the Caucasus, where he and his second wife are from. Over dinner, he is proud to show off his home and the gun he carries. Cooks barbecue shashlik, while a sniper poses on the roof.

"How old are you?" he asks me. "I'm going to pour you a glass of French wine that is older than you are!"

His wife, who is also around my age, fast changes from a white-and-gold suit and heels to skin-tight patterned pants and black lace. She has shaved the heads of her two young children, giving them rap patterns she says she designed herself, and dyes what is left of their hair pumpkin orange and green.

"I'm like a Siberian tiger," says the four-year-old, as he jumps onto a long dinner table. The chairs are elaborately carved, with plush red, purple, and gold-streaked velvet upholstery; on the wall is a carved wooden depiction of the Last Supper. Portraits of the couple hang like royalty, reminding me of the portraits in Yaku-bovsky's Toronto home.

"Aren't the kids sweet?" says Bryntsalov's mother-in-law, a warm woman who later offers me tea, upstairs, away from the madness.

"Natasha! Come here for a picture!" Bryntsalov yells at his wife.

"No!" she says.

"That's just like a woman," he shouts, as the camera roles.

"I despise you," she answers. "All you're interested in is money and power."

For the first round of elections, I spend the evening at Gorbachev headquarters, a huge complex with a hotel that was given to the former president when he left office, though Gorby says he's been mistreated: Yeltsin even took away his passport when he refused to testify at the Communist Party trial. Gorbachev seems depressed, but not surprised, as the evening's results come in.

It looks as though Yeltsin will scrape up a win with about 35 percent of the June 16 vote, followed by Zyuganov, with about 32 percent. The real winner is Lebed, who is coming in third with 14.5 percent of the vote. His campaign was financed and organized by key Yeltsin campaign organizers. That also explains why he was allowed some state air time at the end of the campaign.

Gorby gets less than 1 percent. After midnight, when the results are in, he holds court over dinner for around thirty people. A huge table is laid out with everything from salmon and caviar to shash-lik. There is plenty of wine, champagne, and vodka. Gorby sits at the top of the table, like Caesar, and launches into a long, rambling toast. Raisa and their daughter are beside him. "It is the start of a new era," Gorbachev says. The extent of the loss has yet to sink in.

I leave around 2 A.M., and head to the Central Elections Commission. Bryntsalov and his wife, swathed in red from head to toe, have just arrived. I sit with two bodyguards as we wait for more results, which are posted on large color screens that are far more sophisticated than last December's setup. On my left is Vladimir Semago, a Communist Party banker, member of parliament, and owner of the Moscow Commercial Club. I used to go there when it first opened, without realizing it was an exclusive club for millionaire biznesmeni—no matter, of course, what their political stripe. We listen to the results together. Around 3 A.M., Semago leaves, and offers to drive me home. He is a small man, in blue jeans and an off-color green blazer, who drives his own car, a Lincoln. We drive by the Duma, on the off chance that Zyuganov will be there. He's not.

"Of course the election is a farce," Semago says. "We're just not prepared to take over now and we realize that. It will all be different next time around."

After the election's first round, Lebed is named head of the powerful security council, once the job of his old December 1995 running mate, Yuri Skokov. Lebed, a son of Don Cossacks, ran on a "law and order" platform. His bulldog face and murky growl, which seems to be set on permanent low speed, have captivated the country. He is also a vociferous critic of the Chechen war, and says the only brigade he'll lead will be made up of politicians' sons and grandsons.

Lebed has made anti-Semitic comments and called Mormons "mold and scum" for trying to convert Russians. He has expressed nostalgia for Stalin-era executions, and threatened to create tougher visa restrictions for foreigners and to increase espionage activity. "He who shoots first laughs last," jokes Lebed.

However, Lebed's appointment doesn't hold much permanent political weight. Lebed says he wants the vice presidency restored —and he wants to fill it and even take over the presidency *before* Yeltsin's term expires in the year 2000. But Yeltsin could toss him, the way he did Rutskoi, once the election is over. (This is, in fact, exactly what Yeltsin does in the fall of 1996. This time around it's far easier, since Lebed was appointed to his post and not democratically elected, like Rutskoi. It is still too early to tell who will back Lebed in the future. Although he comes across as a primitive politician and Russians generally like to keep their military men out of purely political posts like the presidency, he could still become a formidable force—if the right power people choose to back, and shape him.)

Perhaps because he is so conscious of Yeltsin's tsar-like whims, Lebed does what he can—fast.

Within hours of his new appointment, he brags about thwarting yet another coup plot by top generals while conveniently leaving out the details. Yeltsin fires a spate of powerful insiders, including Defense Minister Pavel Grachev—and Korzhakov, as well as his buddies, Mikhail Barsukov, head of the Federal Security Service, and First Deputy Prime Minister Oleg Soskovets.

The men head Yeltsin's so-called party of war. Their unexpected dismissals bring Yeltsin closer to reformers like Chubais. Yakubovsky's old mentor, General Konstantin Kobets, is even suggested as a possible new defense minister, though his nomination is tarred with corruption charges.

Yakubovsky's old spokesman, Gulbinsky, explains his theory about the election to me over drinks at the Baltschug. "The more fringe candidates, the better Yeltsin's chances," Gulbinsky says. "The race between Yeltsin and Zyuganov is close. Yeltsin really could win, but let's say no one wants to take the chance. Pro-Yeltsin officials skim off some of the fringe candidates' support and add it to Yeltsin's—and no one is the wiser."

Shortly after the election, Arizona senator John McCain, chairman of the International Republican Institute (IRI), which helped observe the election, holds a press conference. "We are satisfied with the free and fair nature of the elections," the senator says. Afterward, I mention some of my concerns. All of post-Communist Russia's elections are widely believed—by Western diplomats and analysts and Russian politicians—to have been tampered with. Keep Russian presidential candidates expressed fear that these elections would not be free and fair.

"If it was free and fair, the election would be extraordinary. It just seems like a logical impossibility," I say.

Much to my surprise, the senator agrees.

"Look," he says, "what we're really talking about here is the *extent* of falsification, which, we believe, has not been enough to be contrary to the will of the Russian people."

"Lots of American election results have also been falsified," adds a D.C. lawyer who is part of the IRI team.

While the international community here to monitor the elections is not making a fuss about falsification, Konstantin Borovoi, a millionaire free marketeer, member of parliament, and deputy head of the Economic Freedom Party, who created Russia's first stock exchange, is. "There have been reports of election fraud and I'm going to raise them in the Duma," he tells me.

Russians are so convinced of the crooked nature of their "democracy" that the latest political joke circulating in Moscow goes like this:

"What will happen if Yeltsin is elected?" one Russian asks.

"We'll have a new president," his friend replies.

"And what will happen if Yeltsin loses?"

"Then we'll have the old president."

Following the first round of elections, I go to Makhachkala, the capital of Dagestan, the mountainous Muslim Red republic where Zyuganov won 66 percent of the vote—more than anywhere else in Russia. It's also a long way from 1991, when 63 percent of Dagestan voted for Yeltsin.

Back then, Dagestan was a secret jewel on the Caspian Sea. Now the hidden, fenced-in nomenklatura resort on the way into town is abandoned, though Lenin still towers over the central square. More than 1.3 million of the republic's population of two million live below the fifty-dollar-a-month poverty line, says Eldar Magomedov, a Dagestani historian-turned-biznesman.

"Yeltsin's reforms only benefited a small elite. The vote for Zyuganov was a protest vote," says Makhmoud Makhmoudov, second secretary of the Communist Party of Dagestan, sitting below a towering wallhanging of Lenin. A bronze bust of Lenin and a photograph of youngsters in red Pioneer scarves are to his left.

While the local government is solidly pro-Yeltsin, Dagestanis are less influenced by elected politicians because their authority is bypassed by clan elders. In North Ossetia, which borders Chechnya, Zyuganov received 63 percent of the vote, compared to 19.5 percent for Yeltsin.

Communists are perceived to be more tolerant of the FSU's minorities than Yeltsin, who is now considered to be a war-hungry nationalist, says Rashid Kaplanov, a historian specializing in ex-Soviet minorities at the Moscow Center for University Teaching of Jewish Civilization.

Eldar Magomedov likes to tell an anecdote about the time the Dagestani president visited the village he was born in, trying to drum up support for Yeltsin. "The village elder asked if it was true that Yeltsin gave him a bullet-proof Mercedes," Magomedov said. "'Yes,' the president replied. 'Well, when I get one I will also vote for Yeltsin.'"

Dagestanis are also angered by out-of-control crime and corruption. Makhachkala is so dangerous, people don't go out much after dark. "We sit at home like we're in prison," says Rosa Khalitova, a café worker, who sells a sorry-looking lot of sausages, and hasn't been paid in three months. "I work hard but it's very dangerous. A lot of violent drunks come here. My husband comes and sits with me when he can.

"Of course I voted for Zyuganov," she continues. "It was much more peaceful under the Communists. I'm afraid for my children if Yeltsin is reelected. I'm afraid the war will come to Dagestan."

Her sentiments are echoed by Raisa and Kamil Molakayev, in a tiny village of Muslim Kumyks outside the capital. Raisa, fifty-seven, cries as she shows photographs of her twenty-year-old daughter, who was murdered a few months earlier—just before she was about to leave on a full scholarship for college in the United States.

"There has been so much killing under Yeltsin. It's a regime of bandits. We've got to get rid of them," Raisa tells me, over warm tea, soggy goat cheese, boiled mutton, and homemade dumplings, in this republic ravaged with cholera epidemics. "Five people were killed in Makhachkala on the same night as my daughter. All capitalism has brought us is tragedy."

Every woman I interview in the village says she is voting for Zyuganov. That's why the results of the second round, on July 3, are so surprising. Yeltsin wins the election. In Dagestan, the republic flips from voting mainly for Zyuganov to voting mainly for Yeltsin. Zyuganov says he finds such a switch highly suspect—even though it seems as if he has made a backroom deal not to challenge the election.

Yeltsin disappears during the last week of the campaign—so sick he doesn't even show up to vote in Moscow. Hundreds of photographers wait for him to appear. In the chaos, one Yeltsin in-house photographer sneaks out. Yeltsin is later filmed voting at a hospital-sanitarium outside the capital in Borvikha. Once known as the fourth division of the old Ministry of Health, it has been used by the nomenklatura since Communist days. Yeltsin looks shaky in the footage, which is sent across the country.

After Yeltsin wins, he is still too sick to appear in public. (Rather frightening, if you think about what would happen if he died.) There are some bombs—both before and after the election. Some cynical analysts suggest they are the work of angry security and secret service men. Chernomyrdin's car is almost blown up; some people die in bus bombings in Moscow. Perhaps some hope the bombs can be used as a pretext for imposing a state of emergency. Maybe it's just revenge.

I go to the Izmailovsky market for a Sunday outing, and watch police round up every dark-skinned man. Hundreds of men are marched out, their heads down and their hands behind their backs. Men in combat fatigues and guns take their passports and seat them in buses. I don't know where the buses go. (The men in fatigues don't answer my questions.)

Chechnya heats up. Dudayev was killed last spring. The Russians thought his death would lead to a succession battle that would weaken the Chechen rebel leadership. It didn't. Now Russia's total destruction of Grozny only serves to further politicize the Chechen people.

The Russian government is trying to get all international organizations out of Chechnya. Médecins sans Frontières workers are harassed after the group releases a report stating that "the systematic bombing and killing of civilians" continues in Chechnya, that aid agencies are blocked from helping civilians, and that Chechnya should not be considered an internal Russian issue, as

Clinton and other Western leaders say. Peace attempts begin again during the election. (As do new Russian attacks.)

Shortly after the election, the Chechen rebels finally take Grozny. Lebed flies in and tries to negotiate for peace, though his authority is undermined by Yeltsin, who doesn't seem to have decided whether or not he wants peace. Lebed strongly criticizes Yeltsin, and says that ninety thousand people have died in the war—far higher than the government's estimate of thirty thousand dead, or the fifty-thousand figure cited by government opposition leaders.

For now, even after Yeltsin fires Lebed, a shaky cease-fire remains.

When Andrei Makarevich, the musician and painter, invites Heidi and me to the opening of an exhibit of his work, we take along "Sveta," our Russian friend and a big fan of Andrei's. Sveta works for a Westerner, doing everything from cleaning to clerical work. She is married, in her early thirties, with a daughter. "I'm ready to kill my husband!" she says, explaining that the unemployed snake is in the midst of an affair—and insolent enough to blame it on Sveta. ("He doesn't find me attractive anymore," she says.) Lacking a Moscow propiska and living in *his* flat, Sveta is afraid she'll be kicked out of the capital if she leaves him. We hope the opening will cheer her up. On our way home, we see some soldiers and take some pictures with them, the Kremlin and election posters—Yeltsin and Luzhkov smiling stiffly and maniacally—in the background. "That was so much fun!" Sveta says. "You two just do whatever you want. For a moment I felt like I was also a free woman."

Back at the flat, we're given notice that we must move out soon. Just like our old flat by the Arbat, this one will soon be converted to luxury office space. Our block is becoming even more exclusive. Still, lest we ever forget this is Moscow, "Sally," a temporary summer roommate, returning from a dinner date, has to flee through darkened alleys when she is attacked at our front door by drunken Russians.

It is around this time that I bump into Paul Tatum, part owner of the Slav joint venture, at an American diner, a popular Sunday brunch spot for journalists, biznesmeni, students, and "oil men" in from far-flung regions of the empire. Paul begins to call me, with somewhat alarming regularity. The flamboyant entrepreneur invites me for dinner, to watch a movie, to fly his kite. I opt for a few dinners.

In between taking "urgent" cell-phone calls about the hotel dispute, he talks nonstop. Over Russian Tex-Mex (a surreal Moscow experience of outdoor white-night serenades, guacamole, and margaritas), I hear Paul's life story. Looking back, there is something methodical, well planned, about our talks. It is as if he were trying to record his story, as if he knew the end was coming.

Paul has recently ditched his Mercedes for the subway. He now picks me up on foot, accompanied by two surly-faced thugs. A few doors down from my flat, across the street from the Baltschug, is a new late-night club, restaurant, and designer shopping haven, run by Paul's business rival. We know he is there when a fleet of cars with flashing lights is parked outside, just as in old Communist days. The sight of those cars inflames Paul.

Sometimes we take taxis, as when Paul asks if I'll take him to Canada Day celebrations at the Canadian embassy dacha. Paul sits in the middle, the safest place during a shooting attack. At the festivities, I meet up with Desmond, one of my old YILG friends, whom I haven't seen in some time. "I've just lost millions," he says. "I'm on my way back to London, where it's safer. I can't live with all the threats anymore."*

Over time, Paul tells me how he made his first million, lost it, and became a self-proclaimed follower and friend of Jack Rosenberg, who changed his name to Werner Hans Erhard and founded the fascist-like American cult "EST," which Paul says he introduced to the parliament in Moscow. An Oklahoma Republican Party fundraiser, Paul came to Moscow for the first time with an American wheat board group and fell in love with a Russian woman. He and a business buddy, the late H. R. Haldeman—Nixon's disgraced chief of staff—formed Americom Business Centers and helped create the $50-million Radisson-Slavjayanskaya Hotel. "Now I'm terrified I may lose everything," he says. Paul has become a man obsessed.

---

* By 1996, there are 5 murders a day in Moscow, which has a population of about 10 million, compared with 2.7 murders a day in New York City, with its population of about 7.3 million.

("I'm not leaving until they carry me out in a box," he once tells me.) Still, he remains optimistic, convinced his vindication is imminent. He is determined to surpass all odds and beat the Moscow city government.

"Some American journalists who flew in to Moscow are going to write a story about how corrupt Luzhkov is," Paul says. "They're going to write that the hotel is really a mafiya hangout! Can you believe it?" Paul seems to think that once the West knows "what's really going on," they'll find a way to stop it. I'm amazed by the naïveté.

For now, the hotel is Russifying fast. Before leaving Moscow, I lunch one last time at the Slav's international press club. I remember when the press club first opened. The waiters, smiling stiffly, had only memorized a few English sentences. ("Would you like ice with drink?") There was always the oddest assortment of people. Men from Washington representing benevolent-sounding institutions no one had ever heard of. Shady Europeans working for think tanks, academies, even law firms and publishing houses that often sounded suspect. Sharp, talented young Americans—blazers and chinos, power suits and heels—who seemed to train with Paul or the press club, before moving on to work in various bizneses across the FSU. Over the years, many of the American "democracy-building" groups disappeared. The Caesar salad is now gone from the club's menu, replaced by wilted-lettuce-leaf-in-mayonnaise. The staff stopped receiving their salaries months ago.

Then, suddenly, in the midst of the 1996 presidential election campaign, the press club shuts down—for good. Americans, it seems, are no longer welcome. The press club owes rent, and the joint venture wants to turn the space into a disco. (The hotel now also houses a sleazy Soviet-style casino.) Top mafiya bosses regularly meet in the lobby, which twice hosted Clinton and his entourage of pink-shirted Secret Service bodyguards, barking dogs, and U.S. Marines. "The press center was good while it lasted," a diplomat tells me. "But The Story—the birth and convulsions of the new Russian regime, the euphoria over United States-Russian relations—is all over now."

If the hotel is a symbol of American-Russian relations, the love affair is definitely over. However, Russia: The Story is not—though a new chapter has begun. When I arrived in Moscow, most Russians, and Westerners, were wide-eyed with hope and the belief that capitalism could buy freedom. But the new freedom brought inequality that brought ills (that brought about Communism in the first place): poverty, unemployment, homelessness, falling education and living standards, skyrocketing crime and corruption. How could the West believe in the possibility of Instant Democracy, which took centuries to create in the West? As the past millennium makes perfectly clear, Russia is not part of the West—though some Russians may want it to be.

Maybe something happens to people when they don't see sunlight for months at a time. Something happens when people grow up knowing that their phones are bugged, that they could be followed at any time, that their lovers are spies, that their parents lived in labor camps and their grandparents disappeared in the middle of the night. Half the nation is paralyzed by fear. The other half is captivated by greed.

I've never met so many spies, so many men in shady business. I've never known so many people who moved from destitute to fabulously wealthy to jail—if not the morgue. The madness of Russia even followed me to Toronto. While working on one investigative story in the fall of 1993, my Toronto phone line would click and go dead while I was talking to my editor. (There were never any problems with the line before—or after—that story.)

There is no doubt that Russia is, and has always been, tarred by corruption and greed. At the same time, there is a spirituality, and creativity, that keep pulling me back. Something is always happening in Russia. The canvas is so big, and so old. And yet, I am thankful my grandparents left when they could.

What's so good, and so bad, about being a journalist, is that you can step into someone's life, but then you have to leave. I now know what it's like to be in fear of a Russian attack helicopter, but I don't know what it's like to live in constant fear, year after year, and never know when it will end.

By the fall of 1996, Yeltsin has undergone successful heart surgery, though he remains a gray-haired leader who may die in office, like three Soviet leaders before him. From standing on a tank during the attempted August 1991 coup, Yeltsin has morphed through tyrant, tsar, and clown. In Berlin, he grabbed the baton out of the hands of a startled conductor and led the orchestra himself. In Ireland, he was too drunk to get off the plane. On a riverboat near Krasnoyarsk, he ordered his old spokesman, Vyacheslav Kostikov, to be tossed overboard. After launching the bloody civil Chechen war, Yeltsin went into hospital for a nose operation. During the Budyannovsk hostage crisis, he was in Halifax. No wonder, perhaps, the Communists received 40 percent of the vote in 1996. Big wonder, perhaps, that Yeltsin scraped up enough to win.

In November 1996, Paul Tatum is shot dead, pumped full of eleven bullets by a Kalashnikov-wielding contract killer, while on his way from the Slav hotel into the underground subway passage outside the seedy Kievsky train station. The same month, Henry Kissinger helps introduce Lebed—fired by Yeltsin—to America's political elite in New York. Lebed's freshly manicured wife comes to one of the meetings with her arms full of overflowing designer boutique shopping bags. Lebed then attends Clinton's inauguration and meets with Donald Trump in New York. Despite Lebed's anti-American rhetoric, he and Trump get along well. They talk about building a casino together in Moscow.

Two parallel worlds are growing in Russia. There is a burgeoning middle class, and, of course, some stability. But the murders, the poverty, the corruption keep growing steadily. And war that once ripped through the FSU's borders is now devouring Russia from within. At the same time, I am still drawn to this country, so transparent in its pursuit of the good—and evil. Russia is in my blood. So, no—despite the wishes of my mother and the echo of her mother, whose only nightmare was of returning—no, this is not good-bye.

ACKNOWLEDGMENTS

◀ - ▶

I would like to thank Olivia Ward for her friendship and advice—and for even opening up her home to me when the Moscow madness became too much. Thanks to Marc Cooper, for six degrees of separation; my agent, David Vigliano; Ruth Cavin and Melissa Jacobs at St. Martin's Press; Louise Dennys, Stacey Cameron, and David Kilgour at Knopf Canada; and the Canada Council, which awarded me a twelve-month grant to begin this book in the first place.

Jillian Cohen, Nelrene Dunleavy, and my mother, Marilyn Gould, all read the manuscript and offered invaluable suggestions. My sister, Jillian Gould, was pure wisdom and strength. My father, Michael J. Gould, took the time to edit the entire manuscript. My brother, Jonathan Gould, and my grandfather, C. Lewis Gould, were also strong sources of support.

Guy Lagache helped me through many chapters. Patrick Caddell and Stephen Handelman were expert advisers. Jaime Spitzcovsky read the manuscript with the sharp eye of a Russian specialist. Masha Pavlenko was a treasured help, and friend, as was Shannon Kari.

Thanks also to Derk Sauer, publisher of the *Moscow Times*, for taking a chance; Paul Warnick, then foreign editor of the *Toronto Star*, for buying freelance; Karen Durbin, former editor-in-chief of the *Village Voice*, for her commitment to Russia; Matthew Yeomans, senior editor at the *Voice*, for his humor—and patience—every time the KGB cut off our phone calls in mid-sentence; and Eric Zeldin, in the zero hour, for closure.

And thanks to Mark Abel, Boris Aliabev, Alexandra Bourataeva, Dave Ellis, Aaron Frankel, Jennifer Glasse, Mike Graham, Ken Greenberg, Heidi Hollinger, Natasha Kamchatnaya, Nikolai Katchurin, Natasha Kazina, Mike Kaziner, Tea Khvedelidze, Bruce Kluger, Yulia Mostakova Manton, Nikolai Milchikov, Louis O'Neil, David Richardson, Greg Smith, Will Stewart, and Eduard Topol. All mistakes, of course, remain mine.

Finally, thanks to Don Forst, the new editor-in-chief of the *Village Voice*, for bringing me to New York to start a new chapter.

SELECTED BIBLIOGRAPHY

Bullock, Alan. *Hitler and Stalin: Parallel Lives.* London: HarperCollins, 1991.

Bennigsen Broxup, Marie, ed. *The North Caucasus Barrier.* New York: St. Martin's Press, 1992.

de Custine, the Marquis Astolphe. *Empire of the Czar.* New York: Doubleday, 1989 (first translated into English by Longman in 1843).

Handelman, Stephen. *Comrade Criminals: The Theft of the Second Russian Revolution.* London: Michael Joseph, 1994.

Hiro, Dilip. *Between Marx and Muhammad.* London: HarperCollins, 1994.

Hopkirk, Peter. *The Great Game.* New York: Kodansha America, 1994.

Hopkirk, Kathleen. *Central Asia: A Traveller's Companion.* London: John Murray, 1993.

Kagarlitsky, Boris. *Restoration in Russia: Why Capitalism Failed.* London and New York: Verso, 1995.

Khanga, Yelena. *Soul to Soul: A Black Russian Jewish Woman's Search for Her Roots.* New York: W.W. Norton, 1992.

Maalouf, Amin. *Samarkand.* London: Little, Brown and Company UK, 1989, 1992.

Remnick, David. *Lenin's Tomb: The Last Days of the Soviet Empire.* New York: Random House, 1993.

Riasanovsky, Nicholas V. *A History of Russia.* Oxford: Oxford University Press, 1963.

Steele, Jonathan. *Eternal Russia: Yeltsin, Gorbachev and the Mirage of Democracy.* Cambridge, Mass.: Harvard University Press, 1994.

Troyat, Henri. *Catherine the Great.* New York: Meridian, 1994.

Vaksberg, Arkady. *The Soviet Mafia: A Shocking Exposé of Organized Crime in the USSR.* New York: St. Martin's Press, 1991.

———. *Stalin against the Jews.* New York: Knopf, 1994.

Yeltsin, Boris. *The Struggle for Russia.* New York: Random House, 1994.

INDEX

◀ -- ▶